International Series on Sport Sciences
Volume 19

Series Editor
Chauncey A. Morehouse, PhD
The Pennsylvania State University
University Park, Pennsylvania, USA

Children and Exercise XIII

Edited by
Svein Oseid, MD, DCH
The Norwegian College of Physical Education and Sport and
Children's Asthma and Allergy Institute, Voksentoppen,
Oslo, Norway

and

Kai-Håkon Carlsen, MD
Children's Asthma and Allergy Institute, Voksentoppen,
Oslo, Norway

Human Kinetics Books
Champaign, Illinois

Library of Congress Cataloging-in-Publication Data

International Congress on Pediatric Work Physiology (13th : 1987 : Hurdal, Norway)
Children and exercise XIII / edited by Svein Oseid, Kai-Håkon Carlsen.
p. cm. — (International series on sport sciences ; v. 19)
"Proceedings of the XIIIth International Congress on Pediatric Work Physiology held in Hurdal, Norway, September 1987"—Verso t.p.
Bibliography.
ISBN 0-87322-188-5
1. Chronically ill children—Rehabilitation—Congresses. 2. Exercise for children—Congresses. I. Oseid, S. (Svein) II. Carlsen, Kai-Håkon. III. Title. IV. Title: Children and exercise 13. V. Series.
RJ380.I56 1987
618.92′0062—dc19
88-26665
CIP

ISBN 0-87322-188-5
ISSN 0160-0559

Proceedings of the XIIIth International Congress on Pediatric Work Physiology held in Hurdal, Norway, September 1987

Developmental Editor: Kathy Kane
Production Director: Ernie Noa
Copyeditor: Mary Boylan
Assistant Editors: Holly Gilly, Valerie Hall, Robert King
Typesetters: Brad Colson, Sandra Meier, Yvonne Winsor
Text Design: Keith Blomberg
Text Layout: Denise Mueller, Jayne Clampitt, Jill Wikgren
Cover Design: Jack Davis
Printed by: Braun-Brumfield, Inc.

Printed in the United States of America

10 9 8 7 6 5 4 3 2 1

Human Kinetics Books
A Division of Human Kinetics Publishers, Inc.
Box 5076, Champaign, IL 61825-5076
1-800-DIAL-HKP
1-800-334-3665 (in Illinois)

Contents

Congress Organization

This volume represents the Proceedings of the XIIIth International Congress on Pediatric Work Physiology, held at Hurdalsjøen Conference Hotel, 2090 Hurdal, Norway, on the 14th to 18th of September 1987.

Scientific and Organizing Committee

Svein Oseid, Chairman

Finn Ellingsen

Elisabeth B. Mellbye

Wenche Nystad

Odd E. Reseland

Secretary: Tove Aksøy

Sponsors

ABC Bank, Hurdal
Astra Pharmaceuticals A/S
Astra-Syntex A/S
Boehringer Ingelheim Int. GMBH
Fisons Norway A/S
Gallus Plesner A/S
Lungplus Marknads AB
Meda A/S
Medata Nordic A/S
The Royal Ministry of Cultural and Scientific Affairs—Department of Youth and Sport (STUI)
Public Health Department of the Ministry of Social Affairs
Fred. Olsen A/S

The organizers wish to thank the sponsors who made the symposium financially possible. A special thank you to the Royal Ministry of Cultural and Scientific Affairs—Department of Youth and Sport (STUI), who not only sponsored the symposium but also paid an important contribution to the printing of the proceedings *Children and Exercise XIII*.

Last, but not least, we want to thank everybody at Hurdalsjøen Conference Hotel for their contribution, which created an excellent atmosphere throughout the whole symposium.

Preface

As sufficient daily physical activity often represents an indicator of optimal health, this Symposium, as previous symposia of the European Group for Pediatric Work Physiology, has concentrated upon this and other health indicators. Age-related motor performance and energy delivering processes, body growth, and the effect of training upon muscle strength and development have been discussed. Important topics were health indicators during childhood and adolescence, favorable levels of daily activity for optimal health, training of gifted children and children with chronic diseases, as well as aerobic and anaerobic metabolism in health and illness.

A major problem in pediatric medicine is represented by chronically ill children with functional disabilities. This group of patients has to a large extent been overprotected by their parents and society, particularly in relation to physical activity and training. In addition, medical doctors and exercise physiologists have not until recently contributed to the understanding of the importance of regular physical activity for this subgroup of the pediatric population. Because we now consider that early intervention is important in order to habilitate and rehabilitate children with chronic diseases, physical activity programs have been developed and tested practically and scientifically. Studies have clearly demonstrated that the increase of physical work capacity following training is beneficial not only for physical and neuromuscular development, but also has positive psychological and social implications. This year's conference has demonstrated the clinical value of training programs for children with cardiovascular diseases, asthma, and musculoskeletal disorders. Hopefully, this will increase the interest in and knowledge of the field of exercise physiology in children with various handicaps.

In the tradition of the group, the last section concentrated upon a novel topic that previously had not been discussed. Rating of perceived exertion using the Borg scale has been widely used in adults, but only a few studies concerning the child's ability to understand exercise intensity have been published. This session indicated that rating of perceived exertion using the Borg scale is possible in children when their work loads are selected. However, children have difficulty in determining the appropriate intensity when asked to produce a certain exercise level. Both for obese and asthmatic children it was concluded that the children needed more extensive training before being able to use the Borg RPE scale for the prescription of exercise.

Svein Oseid and Kai-Håkon Carlsen

Part I

Age-Related Motor Performance and Physical Fitness

Exercise Performance in North American Preadolescent Children Residing at 1,600 Meters

Reginald L. Washington
Jeff C. Van Gundy
The Children's Hospital, Denver, Colorado

Several investigators have recorded aerobic (Cooper & Weiler-Ravell, 1984; Cumming, Goodwin, Baggley, & Antel, 1967; Hermansen & Oseid, 1971; Macek et al., 1979; Rutenfranz et al., 1982; Seliger et al., 1971) and anaerobic (Vanden Eynde, Ghesquiere, Van Gerven, Vuylsteke-Wauters, & Vande Perre, 1984; Wasserman & Whipp, 1975) data on male and female adolescents. Most data currently available have been collected in Europe utilizing children who participated in rigorous physical activities and/or organized sports. There are very few data on normal exercise measurements in children living in the urban United States who do not participate in organized sports other than routine physical education classes in their schools. The purpose of this study was to establish normative data for untrained, healthy North American children who reside at an intermediate altitude.

SUBJECTS AND METHODS

All subjects were volunteers, did not participate in any organized physical activity other than routine physical education classes, and resided in Denver, Colorado, U.S.A. (altitude 1,600 m), for a minimum of 2 years. The children (n = 151) with an age range of 7 years 6 months to 12 years 9 months were exercised using the James protocol (James et al., 1980) for bicycle ergometry (Quinton 845). There were 70 females and 81 males in the study population. All subjects were divided by gender and body surface area (BSA).

Heart rates were recorded every minute and at peak maximal effort. Oxygen consumption ($\dot{V}O_2$), CO_2 production ($\dot{V}CO_2$), minute ventilation ($\dot{V}_E$), gas exchange ratio (R), ventilatory equivalent for oxygen ($\dot{V}_E/\dot{V}O_2$), and the ventilatory equivalent for CO_2 ($\dot{V}_E/\dot{V}CO_2$) were recorded every 15 s and at maximum exercise using a Sensormedics Horizon Metabolic Cart.

The noninvasive method for the determination of ventilatory anaerobic threshold (VAT) has been described by Wasserman and Whipp (1975), and the VAT was expressed as a percent total exercise time (%TET), $\dot{V}O_2$max at VAT, work load at VAT, heart rate at VAT, and respiratory exchange ratio at VAT.

Group means with standard deviations were calculated. A two-factor analysis of variance was used to evaluate the effects of gender and BSA, and their interaction. Individual comparisons among BSA groups were conducted by *t* tests. Statistical significance was considered at $p < .05$.

RESULTS

Heart Rate

There were no significant differences in the resting heart rates among the groups (BSA or gender; see Table 1). Maximum heart rates were greater in females ($p = .021$). One-minute recovery heart rates were significantly different in females as compared to males in each BSA group ($p < .001$). The mean difference between maximum and recovery heart rates was also significant by gender ($p = .01$). Finally, the difference in recovery heart rates was also greater in children with smaller BSAs ($p < .001$).

Oxygen Consumption

The $\dot{V}O_2$max expressed in $l \cdot min^{-1}$ increased with increasing BSA and was greater in males in all three groups. This difference was significant only for Groups 2 and 3 ($p < .05$). When $\dot{V}O_2$max was normalized to body size by expressing as $cc \cdot min^{-1} \cdot kg^{-1}$, there were no significant differences among males or females regardless of BSA. The mean $\dot{V}O_2$max was greater in males when compared with females ($p = .004$).

Ventilatory Anaerobic Threshold

When the time of VAT was expressed as a percent of total exercise time (%TET), it did not change significantly when related to gender. When $\dot{V}O_2$ at ventilatory anaerobic threshold was expressed as a percent of maximum oxygen consumption (%$\dot{V}O_2$max at VAT), it did not change regardless of gender or BSA. Absolute $\dot{V}O_2$ ($cc \cdot min^{-1} \cdot kg^{-1}$) at VAT was greater in males but did not change with increasing BSA.

DISCUSSION

Maximum heart rates recorded were consistent with the rates previously reported (James et al., 1980; Pels, Gilliam, Freedson, Geenen, & Macconnie, 1981; Seliger et al., 1971). This study confirmed that females

Table 1 Means, Standard Deviations, and Ranges of Physical and Physiological Characteristics

		Group 1 < 1.0 M²		Group 2 1.0–1.19 M²		Group 3 ≥ 1.2 M²	
		Male	Female	Male	Female	Male	Female
Subjects		22	28	30	18	29	24
Age (months)	Mean ± *SD*	90 ± 10	97 ± 15	112 ± 18	123 ± 18	145 ± 16	153 ± 16
	Range	73–109	73–138	81–159	98–160	109–173	116–182
BSA M²	Mean ± *SD*	0.92 ± .06	0.941 ± .076	1.11 ± .07	1.10 ± .06	1.41 ± .14	1.50 ± .16
	Range	0.82–.99	0.77–.99	1.00–1.19	1.03–1.19	1.22–1.67	1.22–1.74
Total work	Mean ± *SD*	2,601 ± 799	2,645 ± 898	4,156 ± 1,607	3,916 ± 1,327	7,122 ± 3,234	7,259 ± 2,837
	Range	900–5,025	1,050–4,975	2,100–13,800	2,250–6,100	500–14,600	2,900–13,900
Resting heart rate (beats/min)	Mean ± *SD*	106 ± 15	101 ± 17	96 ± 16	101 ± 15	95 ± 14	96 ± 12
	Range	77–160	75–140	35–125	76–128	62–145	80–130
Maximum heart rate (beats/min)	Mean ± *SD*	191 ± 12	196 ± 12	194 ± 11	196 ± 9	193 ± 8	196 ± 9
	Range	165–210	160–210	170–215	180–210	175–210	175–215
Recovery heart rate (beats/min)	Mean ± *SD*	133 ± 16	142 ± 17	138 ± 17	155 ± 15	148 ± 15	160 ± 13
	Range	105–170	90–170	100–175	130–180	115–185	120–180
$\dot{V}O_2$max ($l \cdot min^{-1}$)	Mean ± *SD*	1.10 ± .19	1.04 ± .18	1.48 ± .24	1.37 ± .24	2.13 ± .52	2.09 ± .43
	Range	0.66–1.46	0.63–1.31	1.06–2.10	0.99–2.08	1.31–3.56	0.20–3.04
$\dot{V}O_2$max ($cc \cdot min^{-1} \cdot kg^{-1}$)	Mean ± *SD*	47 ± 6	42 ± 5	46 ± 5	43 ± 7	47 ± 10	41 ± 6
	Range	29–56	29–50	38–62	33–62	29–79	28–54
$\dot{V}O_2$ pulse	Mean ± *SD*	6 ± 1	5 ± 1	8 ± 1	7 ± 1	11 ± 3	11 ± 2
	Range	3–8	4–7	5–12	5–11	6–17	6–17

(Cont.)

Table 1 (Continued)

		Group 1 < 1.0 M^2		Group 2 1.0–1.19 M^2		Group 3 $\geqslant$ 1.2 M^2	
		Male	Female	Male	Female	Male	Female
Percent exercise time at VAT	Mean ± *SD*	73 ± 8	61 ± 13	63 ± 12	60 ± 11	68 ± 10	67 ± 13
	Range	56–87	25–84	43–88	47–88	44–88	39–87
$\dot{V}O_2$ at VAT	Mean ± *SD*	35 ± 7	30 ± 4	33 ± 5	30 ± 5	35 ± 8	30 ± 5
(cc • min^{-1} • kg^{-1})	Range	16–46	21–39	23–42	18–41	23–55	19–40
Percent $\dot{V}O_2max$ at VAT	Mean ± *SD*	75 ± 13	71 ± 9	71 ± 10	68 ± 10	73 ± 10	72 ± 13
(cc • min^{-1} • kg^{-1})	Range	37–97	53–87	52–92	56–95	52–88	42–92
Heart rate at VAT	Mean ± *SD*	169 ± 15	167 ± 16	164 ± 16	166 ± 16	170 ± 15	168 ± 17
(beats/min)	Range	140–190	135–190	130–190	130–190	130–197	130–195
Gas exchange ratio at VAT	Mean ± *SD*	0.98 ± .04	0.99 ± .04	0.99 – .04	0.99 – .04	1.00 – .03	0.97 – .04
	Range	0.89–1.05	0.87–1.09	0.92–1.07	0.91–1.06	0.93–1.07	0.87–1.05

have a higher heart rate than males at maximum exercise (Seliger et al., 1971; Vanden Eynde et al., 1984). It is common practice to predict aerobic fitness by evaluating maximum heart rate during peak exercise (Froelicher, 1984). However, the results of the present study demonstrated that although females had a higher heart rate at maximum exercise, the total amount of work performed by them was less than that performed by males. Males had a significantly more rapid decrease in heart rate (faster recovery) during the initial 1-min postexercise period when compared with females. This phenomenon has been previously recorded (Pels et al., 1981). The heart rate during the immediate recovery period is thought by some to be a good indicator of physical fitness, and the rate of decline from maximum heart rate is thought to be related to overall aerobic fitness. There are few data in the literature to support this belief.

Oxygen consumption is traditionally expressed in $l \cdot min^{-1}$. When $\dot{V}O_2$ was expressed in this manner, the value increased with increasing BSA in both sexes. However, when $\dot{V}O_2$ was expressed in $cc \cdot min^{-1} \cdot kg^{-1}$, $\dot{V}O_2$ was not related to body size. Regardless of how $\dot{V}O_2max$ was expressed, it was always greater in males when compared with females of similar BSA, and this finding was consistent in all three BSA groups. Based on these findings, $\dot{V}O_2max$ in children should be expressed in terms of $cc \cdot kg^{-1} \cdot min^{-1}$ for each sex. This has been suggested by others (Daniels, Oldridge, Nagle, & White, 1978).

The values for maximum oxygen consumption reported here agree with values reported elsewhere (Cunningham & Paterson, 1985; Seliger et al., 1971). Several studies (Andersen, Seliger, Rutenfranz, & Mocellin, 1974; Binkhorst, de Jong-Van de Kar, & Vissers, 1984; Daniels & Oldridge, 1971; Rutenfranz et al., 1984), however, do report $\dot{V}O_2max$ greater than the values found in this study. The majority of these latter studies were performed in Europe and involved preselected children who participated in regular organized sport activities. In addition, the lifestyle in Europe often necessitates the use of a bicycle as the principal mode of transportation. These children may be more efficient with bicycle exercise and in better aerobic condition than their urban American counterparts. In Colorado, mandatory physical education is not required of most students while in school, probably resulting in lower overall physical fitness.

Maximum oxygen consumption obtained during exercise on a treadmill is approximately 10% greater than values obtained with a bicycle ergometer (Smodlaka, 1982), and data obtained in this fashion are not comparable to the data presented here. The term anaerobic threshold (AT) has been used to describe the point at which oxygen supply is thought to no longer meet the oxygen demands of exercising muscle (Wasserman & Whipp, 1975). It is postulated that the AT can be evaluated noninvasively during progressive exercise by determination of the point at which the ventilatory equivalent for O_2 increases in relation to the ventilatory equivalent for CO_2 when both values are plotted against time (Davis, Frank, Whipp, & Wasserman, 1979).

There are very few data on normal children regarding VAT when it is expressed as a percent of VO_2max. The data in this study are in agreement with others (Reybrouck et al., 1985; Vanden Eynde et al., 1984) who studied VAT in unconditioned children.

The VAT remains an extremely useful clinical tool, especially for conditioning and training. Previous work in this laboratory has shown that VAT is very accurate in predicting overall endurance as well as physical fitness (Wolfe, Washington, Daberkow, Murphy, & Brammell, 1986). The data presented in this study should be used in conjunction with maximum heart rate, $\dot{V}O_2$max, and total work to assess overall physical fitness.

REFERENCES

Andersen, K.L., Seliger, V., Rutenfranz, J., & Mocellin, R. (1974). Physical performance capacity of children in Norway: Part I. *European Journal of Applied Physiology*, **33**, 177-195.

Binkhorst, M., de Jong-Van de Kar, M.C., & Vissers, A. (1984). Growth and aerobic power of boys aged 11-19 years. In J. Ilmarinen & I. Valimaki (Eds.), *Children and sport* (pp. 99-105). Berlin: Springer-Verlag.

Cooper, D.M., & Weiler-Ravell, D. (1984). Gas exchange response to exercise in children. *American Review of Respiratory Disease*, **129** (Suppl.), S47-S48.

Cumming, G.R., Goodwin, A., Baggley, G., & Antel, J. (1967). Repeated measurements of aerobic capacity during a week of intensive training at a youth's track camp. *Canadian Journal of Physiology and Pharmacology*, **45**, 805-811.

Cunningham, D.A., & Paterson, D.H. (1985). Age specific prediction of maximal oxygen uptake in boys. *Canadian Journal of Applied Sports Sciences*, **10**, 75-80.

Daniels, J., & Oldridge, N. (1971). Changes in oxygen consumption of young boys during growth and running training. *Medicine and Science in Sports*, **3**, 161-165.

Daniels, J., Oldridge, N., Nagle, F., & White, B. (1978). Differences and changes in $\dot{V}O_2$ among young runners 10-18 years of age. *Medicine and Science in Sports*, **10**, 200-203.

Davis, J.A., Frank, M., Whipp, B., & Wasserman, K. (1979). Anaerobic threshold alterations caused by endurance training in middle aged man. *Journal of Applied Physiology*, **46**, 1039-1046.

Froelicher, V. (1984). *Exercise testing and training*. Chicago: Yearbook.

Hermansen, L., & Oseid, S. (1971). Direct and indirect estimation of maximal oxygen uptake in pre-pubertal boys. *Acta Paediatrica Scandinavica*, **217** (Suppl.), 18-23.

James, F.W., Kaplan, S., Glueck, C., Tsay, J., Knight, M., & Sarwar, C.J. (1980). Response of normal children and young adults to controlled bicycle exercise. *Circulation*, **61**, 902-912.

Macek, M., Seliger, V., Vavra, J., Skranc, O., Horak, J., Piric, M., Handzo, P., Rouse, J., & Jirka, J. (1979). Physical fitness of the Czechoslovak population between the ages of 12 and 55 years. Oxygen consumption and pulse oxygen. *Physiologia Bohemoslovaca*, **28**, 75-82.

Pels, A.E., Gilliam, T.B., Freedson, P.S., Geenen, D.L., & Macconnie, S.E. (1981). Heart rate response to bicycle ergometer exercise in children age 6-7 years. *Medicine and Science in Sports and Exercise*, **13**, 299-302.

Reybrouck, T., Weymans, M., Stijns, H., Knops, J., Van Der Hauwaert, L. (1985). Ventilatory anaerobic threshold in healthy children. *European Journal of Applied Physiology*, **54**, 278-284.

Rutenfranz, J., Anderson, K., Seliger, V., Ilmarinen, J., Klimmer, F., Kylian, H., & Ruppel, M. (1984). Maximal aerobic power expected by maturation and body growth during childhood and adolescence. In J. Ilmarinen & I. Valimaki (Eds.), *Children and sport* (pp. 67-85). Berlin: Springer-Verlag.

Rutenfranz, J., Lange-Andersen, K., Seliger, V., Ilmarinen, J., Klimmer, F., Kylian, H., Rutenfranz, M., & Ruppel, M. (1982). Maximal aerobic power affected by maturation and body growth during childhood and adolescence. *European Journal of Pediatrics*, **139**, 106-112.

Seliger, V., Cermak, V., Handzo, P., Horak, J., Jirka, Z., Macek, M., Pribil, M., Rouse, J., Skranc, O., Ulbrich, J., & Urbanek, J. (1971). Physical fitness in Czechoslovak 12- and 15-year-old population. *Acta Paediatrica Scandinavica*, **217** (Suppl.), 37-41.

Smodlaka, V.N. (1982). Treadmills vs. bicycle ergometers. *The Physician and Sportsmedicine*, **10**, 75-80.

Vanden Eynde, B., Ghesquiere, J., Van Gerven, D., Vuylsteke-Wauters, M., & Vande Perre, H. (1984). Follow-up study of physical fitness in boys aged 10-14 years. In J. Ilmarinen & I. Valimaki (Eds.), *Children and sport* (pp. 111-118). Berlin: Springer-Verlag.

Wasserman, K., & Whipp, B.J. (1975). Exercise physiology in health and disease. *American Review of Respiratory Disease*, **212**, 219-249.

Wolfe, R.R., Washington, R.L., Daberkow, E.D., Murphy, J.R., & Brammell, H.L. (1986). Anaerobic threshold as a predictor of athletic performance in young female runners. *American Journal of Diseases of Children*, **140**, 922-925.

Laboratory and Field Tests in 7-Year-Old Boys

Emmanuel Van Praagh
Guy Falgairette
Laboratoire de Performance Motrice, Aubière, France

Mario Bedu
Nicole Fellmann
Jean Coudert
Laboratoire de Physiologie, Clermont-Ferrand, France

Anaerobic and aerobic metabolisms of young primary school children have not been well researched (Inbar & Bar-Or, 1986; Macek, 1986). The laboratory conditions present a difficult psychological environment for the child, and the ergometric devices are not always adapted for this age group. Moreover, laboratory tests require strong motivation on the part of the subjects (Cumming & Hnatiuk, 1980). Therefore, the purpose of this study was to validate field tests, which are easier to perform by young children, by comparing the results with laboratory test results.

METHODS

A total of 19 boys aged 7 years participated in the study. Table 1 shows their physical characteristics.

Table 1 Anthropometric Data (*n* = 19)

Age (years)	Height (cm)	Weight (kg)	Body fat[a] (%)
7.4	126.3	26.4	15.2
±0.3	±5.5	±4.7	±4.7

[a]In accordance with the Durnin and Ramahan method (1967). Values are means ± *SD*.

Laboratory Tests

Maximal aerobic power, maximal anaerobic power, and anaerobic capacity were measured using a calibrated, mechanically braked cycle ergometer (Brue & Melin, 1983). The ergometer was specially adapted for the young child (cranks of 13 cm). $\dot{V}O_2$max was measured by the triangular method. Expired air was collected in Douglas bags (last 30 s of each work load). Its volume was determined by a Tissot spirometer, and F_EO_2 and F_ECO_2 were analyzed by physical analyzers (Morgan). Heart rate was calculated from the continuous electrocardiogram (ECG). Capillary blood sample [L] was taken from the hyperemized earlobe, 2 min postexercise, for lactate determination (Analox GM7).

Maximal anaerobic power was assessed by determining the relationship between force and velocity (Peres, Vandewalle, & Monod, 1981; Sargeant, Hoinville, & Young, 1981). The subjects performed five to seven sprints with a 3-min recovery after each sprint. The constant braking force for each sprint ranged from 0.5 kp to 2 kp. The inverse linear relationship is illustrated in Figure 1. The optimal load (F_{opt}) corresponded to 50% of maximal force at zero velocity (F_0). For each experimental plot, the peak power output (PP) corresponding to a given force (F) was calculated by the product of F and peak velocity. The relationship of force–peak power was parabolic. The maximal value of peak power output (PPmax) was

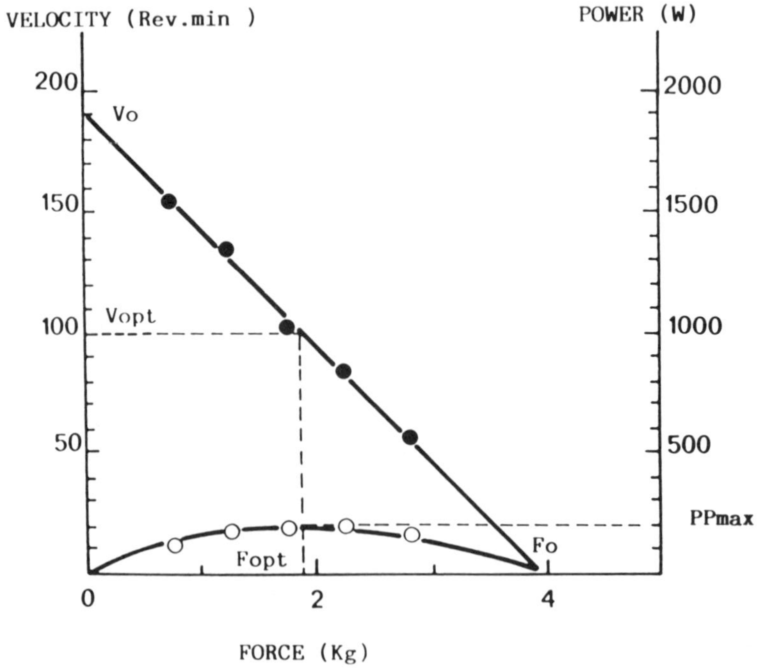

Figure 1. One example of the force (F_0)–Velocity (V_0) relationship in a 7-year-old boy (r = .995); V_{opt} = 0.5 V_0; F_{opt} = 0.5 F_0; PPmax = maximum peak power output.

obtained for a velocity and force corresponding, respectively, to 0.5 maximal velocity at zero force (V_0) and 0.5 F_0.

The anaerobic capacity test (modified Wingate Test) was a 30-s supramaximal cycling exercise against a constant braking force with the maximal velocity sustained from the beginning to the end of the test (Inbar & Bar-Or, 1986). The braking force assigned corresponded to the optimal load (F_{opt}) calculated in the former test. Several capillary blood samples were drawn from the earlobe between the 1st and the 5th min after the test to determine [L] peak value. Total work during 30 s was calculated from the total area of the curve (pedaling rate as a function of time).

Field Tests

All running tests were performed indoors. Anaerobic alactic metabolism was estimated by a 30-m dash with velocity expressed in m • s^{-1}. Anaerobic capacity was assessed in the same session by a 30-s shuttle run (30-m distance). The average speed was calculated from the distance covered in 30 s; [L] was determined from an earlobe blood sample taken 2 min after the exercise bout.

In a second session maximal aerobic power was evaluated from a 20-m shuttle run test (20-MST). Indirect $\dot{V}O_2$max was calculated from the equation established by Léger, Lambert, and Mercier (1983): $\dot{V}O_2$ (ml • min • kg) = 31.025 + 3.238 speed (km • h) −3.248 age (years) + 0.1536 speed • age. During this endurance run, heart rate (HR) was continuously monitored (Sport Tester PE 3000); [L] was measured under the same conditions as the former test.

RESULTS

Maximal Aerobic Power

As shown in Table 2, $\dot{V}O_2$max (ml • min^{-1} • kg^{-1}) and HRmax (b • min^{-1}) were higher in the indoor running tests than during the laboratory tests

Table 2 Maximal Aerobic Results of Laboratory and Field Tests (Mean ± *SD*)

	$\dot{V}O_2$max (ml • min^{-1} • kg^{-1})	HR (beats • min^{-1})	[L] (mmol • l^{-1})
Lab	47.0 ± 5.8	197 ± 4	5.7 ± 2.1
p	*	*	NS
Field	54.2 ± 2.5	202 ± 5	6.5 ± 1.9

*Comparisons made using paired *t* test, $p < .001$.

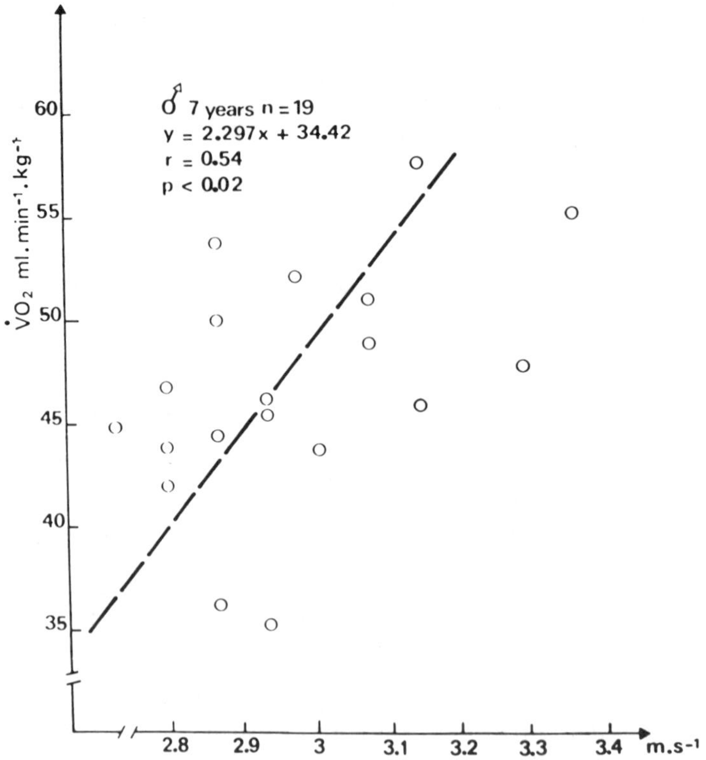

Figure 2. Maximal oxygen uptake ($\dot{V}O_2max$) in relation to running velocity (20-MST).

($p < \times$ .001). [L] was also higher but the values were not statistically significant. There was a significant correlation between direct $\dot{V}O_2max$ and velocity (r = .54, $p < .02$; Figure 2).

Maximal Anaerobic Power

Maximal velocity (V_0), maximal peak power (PPmax), and optimal force (F_{opt}) during the force-velocity test are summarized in Table 3. In the 30-m running test, velocity was 4.63 ± 0.24 m • s^{-1} (mean ± *SD*). A positive correlation was found between PPmax and velocity (r = .45, $p < .05$).

Anaerobic Capacity

Results for the Wingate Test including total work in 30 s (J), mean power (W, W • kg^{-1}), and blood lactate concentration are shown in Table 4. Velocity (mean ± *SD*) calculated during the 30-s indoor running test was 3.70 ± 0.75 m • s^{-1}. A highly significant correlation between power and velocity was found (r = .60, $p < .001$). Blood lactate concentrations were

Table 3 Maximal Anaerobic Power Measured by the Force–Velocity Test in 7-Year-Old Boys (Mean ± *SD*)

V_0 (Rev • min^{-1})	F_0 (kg)	F_{opt} (kg)	PPmax (W)	PPmax (W • kg^{-1})
171.6	3.4	1.7	145.7	5.8
±17.1	±1.0	±0.5	±42.8	±1.3

Note. V_0 = maximal velocity at zero force; F_0 = maximal force at zero velocity; F_{opt} = optimal force; PPmax = maximal peak power output.

Table 4 Anaerobic Capacity Measured by the Wingate Test in 7-Year-Old Boys (Mean ± *SD*)

Work 30 s (J)	Mean power (W)	(W • kg^{-1})	[L][a] (mmol • l^{-1})
3695	123	4.7	7.0
±1138	±38	±1.3	±3.2

[a][L] = peak blood lactate concentration.

not statistically different between laboratory and field tests (7.0 ± 3.2 and 5.5. ± 1.4 mmol • l^{-1}, respectively).

DISCUSSION

$\dot{V}O_2max$ (ml • min^{-1} • kg^{-1}) in 7-year-old children was quite similar to adult values (Bar-Or, 1983; Flandrois, Grandmontagne, Mayet, Favier, & Frutoso, 1982). However, $\dot{V}O_2max$, HRmax, and [L] were higher in maximal indoor running than in laboratory tests. These data suggest that the field test was more suitable for the young child, because the main criteria of maximal exercise were observed: HRmax above 200 b • min^{-1} and [L] at the level of 6 mmol • l^{-1}. These results supported earlier observations that the smaller muscle mass of the legs limited the level of aerobic performance assessed by cycle ergometer (Davies, Barnes, & Godfrey, 1972).

The prediction of $\dot{V}O_2max$ from field test values showed a significant correlation (r = .54). This coefficient was lower than those reported by Mercier, Léger, and Lambert (1983; r = .71) and by Poortmans, Vlaeminck, Collin, and Delmotte (1986; r = .72). These discrepancies could be the result of different experimental conditions. In the previous studies, the age spans were larger—from 6 to 23 years for Poortmans et al. (1986) and from 8 to 19 years for Mercier et al. (1983). Also, the choice of the ergometer (cycle or treadmill) and methods of laboratory $\dot{V}O_2max$ determination could affect the results.

In contrast to maximal aerobic power, the anaerobic power and capacity of young children are lower than in adults, and laboratory tests seemed to give better results than field tests. The present results seemed to be relatively high (PPmax = 146 W; MP = 123 W) as compared with those obtained by Inbar and Bar-Or (1986) in 10-year-old boys (~ PPmax = 160 W and mean power = 149 W). The higher value of blood lactate concentration after the Wingate Test as compared to the 30-s running test suggested that the laboratory test was particularly strenuous. The load assigned to the child that corresponded to 50% of F_0 (i.e., 64 g • kg^{-1} body mass on average), which corresponded closely to that used by Inbar and Bar-Or (1975) in 7- to 9-year-old boys (35 g • kg^{-1} using the Fleisch ergometer). On the other hand, the conditions of the indoor test were probably not sufficiently severe. Running shuttles requires important motor coordination. Klimt, Pannier, and Paufler (1971) obtained higher blood lactate values (9.5 mmol • l^{-1}) after a 200-m track event in 10-year-old boys. However, these subjects were older and the environmental conditions could not be controlled. In conclusion, the significant correlations between laboratory and field tests indicate that field tests seem to be rather good indices of anaerobic and aerobic criteria in young children.

REFERENCES

Bar-Or, O. (1983). *Pediatric sports medicine for the practitioner—from physiological principles to clinical application*. New York: Springer.

Brue, F., & Melin, B. (1983). The direct determination of maximal aerobic and anaerobic power using a new mechanical cycle ergometer. *Proceedings of the 5th meeting of Phys. Fit. Mil. Forces,* NATO Rep., p. 320).

Cumming, G.R., & Hnatiuk, A. (1980). Establishment of normal values for exercise capacity in a hospital clinic. In K. Berg & B.O. Eriksson (Eds.), *Children and exercise IX* (pp. 79-91). Baltimore: University Park Press.

Davies, C.T.M., Barnes, C., & Godfrey, S. (1972). Body composition and maximal exercise performance in children. *Human Biology,* **44**, 195-214.

Durnin, J.V.G.A., & Ramahan, J. (1967). The assessment of the amount of fat in the human body from measurements of skinfold thickness. *British Journal of Nutrition,* **21**, 681-689.

Flandrois, R., Grandmontagne, M., Mayet, M.H., Favier, R., & Frutoso, J. (1982). La consommation maximale d'oxygène chez le jeune français, sa variation avec l'âge, le sexe et l'entraînement [Maximal oxygen uptake of the French teenager, its variation with age, sex, and training]. *Journal de Physiologie* (Paris), **78**, 186-194.

Inbar, O., & Bar-Or, O. (1975). The effects of intermittent warm-up on 7- to 9-year-old boys. *European Journal of Applied Physiology*, **34**, 81-89.

Inbar, O., & Bar-Or, O. (1986). Anaerobic characteristics in male children and adolescents. *Medicine and Science in Sports and Exercise*, **3**, 264-269.

Klimt, F., Pannier, R., & Paufler, D. (1971). Körperliche Belastung neun- bis zehnjähriger Kinder durch einen 200-m Lauf [Biological strain of a 200-m run on 9- to 10-year-old children]. *Schweizerische Zeitung für Sportmedizin*, **19**, 31-39.

Léger, L.A., Lambert, J., & Mercier, D. (1983). Predicted $\dot{V}O_2$max and maximal speed for a multistage 20-m shuttle run in 7,000 Quebec children aged 6-17. *Medicine and Science in Sports and Exercise*, **15**, 142-143.

Macek, M. (1986). Aerobic and anaerobic energy output in children. In J. Rutenfranz, R. Mocellin, & F. Klimt (Eds.), *Children and exercise XII* (pp. 3-9). Champaign, IL: Human Kinetics.

Mercier, D., Léger, L.A., & Lambert, J. (1983). Relative efficiency and predicted $\dot{V}O_2$max in children (Abstract). *Medicine and Science in Sports and Exercise*, **15**, 143.

Pérès, G., Vandewalle, H., & Monod, H. (1981). Aspect particulier de la relation charge-vitesse lors du pédalage sur cyclo-ergomètre [Particular aspect of the force-velocity relationship during pedaling on the cycle ergometer]. *Journal de Physiologie* (Paris), **77**, 10A.

Poortmans, J., Vlaeminck, M., Collin, M., & Delmotte, C. (1986). Estimation indirecte de la puissance aérobie maximale d'un population bruxelloise masculine et féminine âgée de 6 à 23 ans. Comparaison avec une technique directe de la mesure de la consommation maximale d'oxygène [Prediction of maximal aerobic power of a population of Brussels, male and female, aged 6 to 23 years. Comparison with direct measurement of maximal oxygen uptake]. *Journal de Physiologie* (Paris), **81**, 195-201.

Sargeant, A.J., Hoinville, E., & Young, A. (1981). Maximum leg force and power output during short-term dynamic exercise. *Journal of Applied Physiology: Respiratory Environmental, Exercise Physiology*, **51**, 1175-1182.

Endurance Fitness and Peak Height Velocity in Belgian Boys

Bavo Vanden Eynde
Dirk Van Gerven
D. Vienne
M. Vuylsteke-Wauters
J. Ghesquiere
Catholic University of Leuven, Leuven, Belgium

An overview of longitudinal studies on the aerobic capacity at the age of puberty indicates different trends in $\dot{V}O_2max$ (Bailey Ross, Mirwald, & Weese, 1978; Cunningham, Paterson, Blimkie, & Donner, 1984; Kemper et al., 1982; Kobayashi et al., 1978; Rutenfranz, Lange-Andersen, Seliger, Klimmer, Berndt et al., 1981; Sprynarova, 1974). Many factors interact to produce different $\dot{V}O_2max$ values but, with few exceptions (Fahey, Del Valle-Zuris, Oehlsen, Trieb, & Seymour, 1979; Rutenfranz et al., 1982), not much attention has been paid to the sexual maturity status in the test designs. Longitudinal studies on cardiorespiratory response to exertion of teenagers seldom report more than $\dot{V}O_2max$. Daniels, Oldridge, Nagle, and White (1978) stress the importance of tests at submaximal intensities as an indicator of endurance fitness or the training status in youngsters.

The purpose of this study was twofold: first, to establish values for maximal ($\dot{V}O_2max$) and submaximal aerobic power (ventilatory threshold), with special reference to maturity status; second, to evaluate the metabolic conditions at which $\dot{V}O_2max$ and ventilatory threshold are reached.

SUBJECTS, MATERIAL, AND METHODS

Healthy active Flemish boys (N = 30) all from the fifth grade, in 1978 and 1979, were tested once a year over a period of 6 consecutive years. From the yearly height measurements, peak height velocity (PHV) with an accuracy of 1 year was determined for each individual, according to Tanner, Whitehouse, and Takaishi (1966). Anthropometric as well as exercise data were collected annually from 1-1/2 years before to 1-1/2 years after PHV (four consecutive yearly measurements). Anthropometric measurements included stature, body weight, chronological age (Larson, 1974), and sport participation (weekly hours) using a validated checklist (Ostyn, Simons, Beunen, Renson, & Van Gerven, 1980).

Exercise testing consisted of a stepwise increasing cycle ergometer test. The initial load, adjusted to 1 times the body weight in watts (3-min duration), increased every 3 min with the same load (Franz, 1972) up to voluntary exhaustion ($\dot{V}O_2$ peak, according to Rowell, 1974), and ventilatory threshold, according to Wassermann, Whipp, Koyal, and Beaver (1973), was determined during the same test. The following measurements were taken continuously using the Siregnost FD85 (Siemens): heart rate (HR), oxygen uptake ($\dot{V}O_2$), carbon dioxide output ($\dot{V}CO_2$), ventilation ($\dot{V}_E$) and respiratory frequency (f) from which $\dot{V}O_2$ per kilogram body weight ($\dot{V}O_2$ ml • kg^{-1} • min^{-1}), respiratory ratio (R), oxygen pulse ($\dot{V}O_2$/HR), tidal volume (V_T), and ventilatory equivalent for $\dot{V}O_2$ ($\dot{V}_E/\dot{V}O_2$) were calculated. Oxygen uptake at ventilatory threshold was also expressed as a percentage of $\dot{V}O_2$ peak (%$\dot{V}O_2$ peak).

Differences in function of PHV were detected by an analysis of variance for repeated measures (Dixon & Brown, 1979), whereas stability between yearly measurements was calculated by Pearson correlations. The average interyear correlations ($\bar{r}$) for all measurements at the two working loads were calculated by the Fisher Z'technique.

RESULTS

Body weight, stature, and sport participation relative to PHV are given in Table 1. The mean chronological age at PHV was 13.8 years, the average height growth rate was 8.6 cm/year. Weight, as commonly accepted, reached the highest growth rate ± 1 year later. Sport participation (SP) increased significantly from 0.5 year before to 1.5 years after PHV.

Table 1 Analysis of Variance and Mean Stability Coefficients of Stature, Weight, and Sport Participation (SP) Before and After Peak Height Velocity (PHV); N = 30 Healthy, Active Flemish Boys

Age relative to PHV (years)	Weight (kg) $\bar{X} \pm SD$	Stature (cm) $\bar{X} \pm SD$	SP (hours/week) $\bar{X} \pm SD$
−1.5	44.9 ± 8.29	154.6 ± 8.25	3.7 ± 2.07
−0.5	50.5 ± 9.07	161.9 ± 8.77	3.3 ± 2.31
0.5	56.6 ± 9.57	170.5 ± 8.43	4.8 ± 2.59
1.5	62.9 ± 9.21	176.5 ± 8.08	5.4 ± 4.01
Overall variance p of F	***	***	**
Mean stability $\bar{r}$ (p)	.91 ***	.96 ***	.24 (NS)

Note. Significant at ** = .01 and *** = .001 probability levels.

Table 2 Physiological Measurements at $\dot{V}O_2$ Peak as a Function at the Age of PHV (= age 0); N = 30 Healthy, Active Flemish Boys

	Age to peak height velocity (in years)									
	−1.5		−0.5		0.5		1.5			
	$\overline{X}$	± *SD*	$\overline{X}$	± *SD*	$\overline{X}$	± *SD*	$\overline{X}$	± *SD*	*p* of *F*	$\bar{r}(p)$
HR (min)	191	± 10	190	± 10	192	± 7	191	± 9	NS	.74 **
$\dot{V}_E$ ($l \cdot min^{-1}$)	67.0	± 14.2	75.3	± 17.6	90.7	± 18.1	101.4	± 21.7	***	.52 **
F (min)	47	± 9	46	± 9	46	± 7	43	± 7	NS	.36 *
$\dot{V}O_2$ ($l \cdot min^{-1}$)	2.22	± 0.47	2.50	± 0.50	2.90	± 0.52	3.28	± 0.57	***	.61 **
$\dot{V}O_2$ ($ml \cdot min^{-1} \cdot kg^{-1}$)	49.6	± 5.0	50.0	± 5.0	51.6	± 5.2	52.5	± 5.2	NS	.41 *
$\dot{V}_E/\dot{V}O_2$	30	± 3.8	30	± 3.4	31	± 3.5	31	± 4	NS	.25 NS
V_T	1.45	± 0.36	1.64	± 0.30	2.03	± 0.46	2.37	± 0.50	***	.69 **
$\dot{V}O_2$/HR	11.6	± 2.5	13.2	± 2.9	15.1	± 2.9	17.3	± 3.4	***	.68 **
R	0.99	± 0.07	1.01	± 0.07	1.07	± 0.08	1.10	± 0.07	***	.07 NS

Note. Significant at * = .05, ** = .01, and *** = .001 probability levels.

Table 3 Physiological Measurements at Ventilatory Threshold as a Function of the Age at PHV (= age 0); N = 30 Healthy Active Flemish Boys

	Age to PHV (in years)									
	−1.5		−0.5		0.5		1.5			
	$\overline{X}$	± *SD*	$\overline{X}$	± *SD*	$\overline{X}$	± *SD*	$\overline{X}$	± *SD*	*p* of *F*	$\bar{r}(p)$
HR (min)	165	± 16	161	± 17	158	± 16	155	± 15	*	.56 **
$\dot{V}_E$ (l • min^{-1})	37.9	± 8.8	39.0	± 11.1	42.0	± 11	45.8	± 12.3	**	.45 *
F (min)	34	± 9	30	± 6	27	± 5	26	± 5	***	.50 **
$\dot{V}O_2$ (l • min^{-1})	1.52	± 0.31	1.62	± 0.38	1.83	± 0.45	1.95	± 0.39	***	.50 **
$\dot{V}O_2$ (ml • min^{-1} • kg^{-1})	34.5	± 3.5	32.5	± 3.3	32.7	± 3.3	31.5	± 3.1	NS	.42 *
$\dot{V}_E/\dot{V}O_2$	24	± 2.7	24	± 2.7	23	± 2.4	23	± 2.9	NS	.32 NS
V_T	1.16	± 0.29	1.34	± 0.37	1.59	± 0.40	1.79	± 0.46	***	.68 **
$\dot{V}O_2$/HR	9.2	± 1.8	10.1	± 2.3	11.6	± 2.5	12.6	± 2.6	***	.68 **
R	0.85	± 0.06	0.85	± 0.07	0.87	± 0.07	0.89	± 0.08	*	.05 NS

Note. Significant at * = .05, ** = .01, and *** = .001 probability levels.

As can be seen in Table 2, HR, f, $\dot{V}_E/\dot{V}O_2$, and $\dot{V}O_2$ (ml • kg^{-1} • min^{-1}) are unaffected by PHV at peak oxygen uptake. All other measurements, $\dot{V}O_2$ (l • min^{-1}), $\dot{V}_E$, V_T, $\dot{V}O_2$/HR, and R, showed significantly higher values at PHV. The same mean stability patterns calculated at ventilatory threshold were also valid at $\dot{V}O_2$ peak level (Table 2).

As can be seen in Table 3, HR and f decreased significantly in relation to PHV at ventilatory threshold. $\dot{V}O_2$ in ml • kg^{-1} • min^{-1} and $\dot{V}_E/\dot{V}O_2$ remained constant. In contrast, $\dot{V}O_2$ in l min^{-1}, $\dot{V}_E$, V_T, oxygen pulse, and respiratory ratio (R) increased. Except for $\dot{V}_E$, these increases were most pronounced during the period 1/2 year before to 1/2 year after PHV. All direct measurements including HR, $\dot{V}O_2$, $\dot{V}_E$, and f remained stable (Table 3) during the 4-year span of observations.

The average of the intercorrelations among yearly scores ($\bar{r}$) of V_T, oxygen pulse, $\dot{V}_E/\dot{V}O_2$, $\dot{V}O_2$ (ml • kg^{-1} • min^{-1}), and R shows that only V_T and oxygen pulse remained stable (Table 3). The percentage of peak $\dot{V}O_2$ reached at ventilatory threshold decreased from 68.4 at 1-1/2 years before PHV to 59.4 at 1-1/2 years after PHV. The steepest fall was not observed at PHV but was already present 1 year before PHV (see Figure 1).

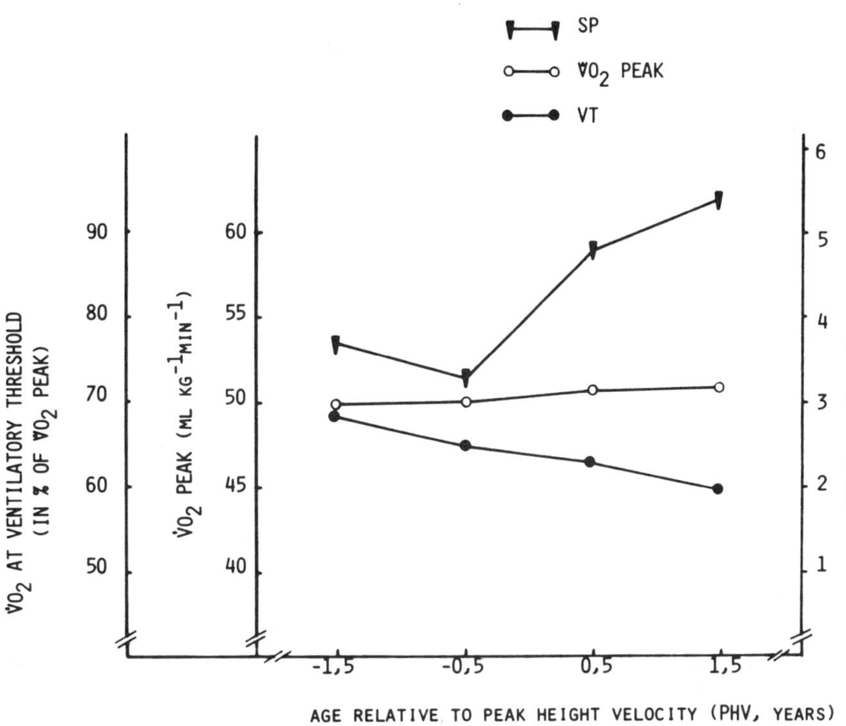

Figure 1. $\dot{V}O_2$ in % of $\dot{V}O_2$ peak at ventilatory threshold (VT), $\dot{V}O_2$ peak (ml • kg^{-1} • min^{-1}), and sport participation (SP in hours/week) of boys (N = 30) in function of peak height velocity (PHV in years).

DISCUSSION

The mean chronological age at which PHV occurred, 13.8 years in these Flemish boys, was slightly lower than in Polish (14 and 13.9 years) (Bielicki, Koniarek, & Malina, 1984) and Norwegian (14.1 years) boys (Rutenfranz et al., 1982). At this age of PHV (13.8 years) stature and weight of the boys were at the 75th %ile of the reference for Belgian school boys (Ostyn et al., 1980) at that age. Comparison with the Fredeborg boys (PHV at 14.8 years), measured by Rutenfranz et al. (1982), is difficult as some of the subjects were rated at the point of greatest height velocity instead of PHV.

Between-years stability for height and weight was high ($\bar{r}$ = .96 for height and .91 for weight). The boys in this study proved to be quite active as can be seen from Figure 1. Their sport participation before PHV was on average 3.3 hr weekly and increased after PHV to 5.4 hr. This increased physical activity was mainly due to the fact that many more commuted from home to school on a bicycle after the age of PHV. However, sport participation did not remain identical over the years of observation as evidenced by the low ($\bar{r}$) = .24) stability coefficient for SP (see Table 1).

The heart rate at maximal load (peak $\dot{V}O_2$) remained very similar over the 4 years of observation (Table 2) and was in agreement with the observations on Norwegian boys (Rutenfranz et al., 1982). The peak oxygen uptake increased linearly with advancing age at PHV, which can be noted in Table 2, but the $\dot{V}O_2$ per kilogram body weight remained quite similar (p = NS).

Simon, Reid, Tanner, Goldstein, and Benjamin (1972) have shown that the age of PHV of heart and lung diameter coincides with PHV-age for stature. Therefore, it seems logical to assume that tidal volume (V_T), which correlates strongly with lung volume (Rutenfranz, Lange-Andersen, Seliger, Klimmer, Ilmarinen et al., 1981), also has its greatest increase at the age of PHV. The respiratory frequency (f) did not change with advancing PHV (see Table 2). The increase in total ventilation was due to an increase in V_T, which followed the increase in lung size.

$\dot{V}_E$, $\dot{V}O_2$, and $\dot{V}CO_2$ all increased with advancing age, whereas the economy of ventilation was not affected as evidenced by the respiratory equivalent ($\dot{V}_E/\dot{V}O_2$) in Table 2. The heart function, however, adapted to changes concomitant to the growth spurt; while the HR at $\dot{V}O_2$ peak remained constant, the O_2 pulse increased significantly. This could be ascribed to a greater (a-$\bar{v}$) 0_2 difference, but most probably is due to an increase in stroke volume of the heart.

The oxygen pulse was still increasing 1-1/2 years after the PHV. According to Israel (1968), the increase of oxygen pulse results from the increase in stroke volume, a function of heart size (Bouchard, Malina, Hollmann, & Leblanc, 1977). It seems logical to conclude that the improved economy of the heart function, witnessed by the greater oxygen pulse, is the result of the increase in the heart size concomitant to the PHV in stature (Simon et al., 1972).

The highest R increases occurred right at the point of PHV and not before. An R above 1 indicates that CO_2 flow is in excess of the oxygen taken up, which can only happen when CO_2 is no longer buffered by the bicarbonates due to lactic acid accumulation in the blood. The conclusion of Ericksson, Karlsson, and Saltin (1971) that the ability to produce lactic acid in growing boys depends on their sexual maturation is confirmed by this finding.

With increasing age, ventilatory threshold was reached at a lower heart rate (Table 3) and a much lower respiratory frequency. Because the $\dot{V}O_2$ peak and $\dot{V}_E$ peak increased markedly (Table 2), the $\dot{V}O_2$ and $\dot{V}_E$ at ventilatory threshold were also higher with advancing age and maturation. By contrast, $\dot{V}O_2$ at ventilatory threshold, expressed as a percentage of the $\dot{V}O_2$ peak, was lower: As maturation increases the ability for lactate accumulation, the ventilatory threshold occurs earlier and at a much lower value than the maximal working capacity expressed as peak $\dot{V}O_2$ (Figure 1).

At the point of the ventilatory threshold, the economy of pulmonary ventilation exposed by the respiratory equivalent remained unchanged as the much higher V_T allowed for a lower respiratory frequency. The increase in oxygen pulse was most pronounced at the time of PHV: This was true for peak O_2 pulse as it was for O_2 pulse at ventilatory threshold. The increase in R was too small to be highly significant, in agreement with the explanation that this point is the threshold where lactacid anaerobic metabolism is solicited.

CONCLUSIONS

In a sample of physically active school boys one can observe that (a) the mean interyear stability of stature and body weight is unaffected by PHV; (b) respiratory equivalent, an indication of ventilatory economy, seems unaffected by the growth spurt as expressed by PHV; and (c) there is an earlier solicitation of anaerobic energy after the PHV as witnessed by the earlier occurrence of ventilatory threshold as a percentage of VO_2 peak and a higher R.

REFERENCES

Bailey, D.A., Ross, W.D., Mirwald, R.L., & Weese, C. (1978). Size dissociation of maximal aerobic power during growth in boys. In J. Borms & M. Hebbelinck (Eds.), *Pediatric work physiology* (pp. 140-152). Basel: Karger.

Bielicki, T., Koniarek, J., & Malina, R.M. (1984). Interrelationships among certain measures of growth and maturation rate in boys during adolescence. *Annals of Human Biology*, **11**, 201-210.

Bouchard, C.C., Malina, R.M., Hollmann, W., & Leblanc, C. (1977). Submaximal working capacity, heart size and body size in boys 8 to 18 years. *European Journal of Applied Physiology*, **36**, 115-126.

Cunningham, D.A., Paterson, D.H., Blimkie, C.J.R., & Donner, A.P. (1984). Development of cardiorespiratory function in circumpubertal boys: A longitudinal study. *Journal of Applied Physiology*, **56**, 302-307.

Daniels, J., Oldridge, N., Nagle, F., & White, B. (1978). Differences and changes in VO_2 among runners 10 to 18 years of age. *Medicine and Science in Sports and Exercise*, **10**, 200-203.

Dixon, W.J., & Brown, M.B. (Eds.) (1979). *BMDP Biomedical Computer Programs, P-Series* (pp. 540-592). Berkeley, CA; University of California Press.

Ericksson, B.O., Karlsson, J., & Saltin, B. (1971). Muscle metabolites during exercise in pubertal boys. *Acta Paediatrica Scandinavica*, **217** (Suppl.), 154-157.

Fahey, T.D., Del Valle-Zuris, A., Oehlsen, G., Trieb, M., & Seymour, J. (1979). Pubertal stage differences in hormonal and hematological responses to maximal exercise in males. *Journal of Applied Physiology*, **46**, 823-827.

Franz, I. (1972). *Vergleichende Untersuchungen zur Messung der PWC170*. 3rd International Seminar Ergometrie Berlin (pp. 136-142).

Israel, S. (1968). *Sport, Herzgrosse und Herz-Kreislauf-Dynamik*. Leipzig: Barth.

Kemper, H.C., van der Bom, C., Dekker, H., Ootjers, G., Post, B., Snel, J., Splinter, P.G., Storm-Van Essen, L., & Verschuur, R. (1982). *Groei en gezondheid van tieners*. Haarlem: De Vrieseborch.

Kobayashi, K., Kitamura, K., Miura, M., Sodeyama, H., Murase, Y., Miyashita, M., & Matsui, H. (1978). Aerobic power as related to body growth and training in Japanese boys: A longitudinal study. *Journal of Applied Physiology*, **44**, 666-672.

Larson, L. (1974). *Fitness, health and work capacity*. New York: MacMillan.

Ostyn, M., Simons, J., Beunen, G., Renson, R., & Van Gerven, D. (1980). *Somatic and motor development of Belgian secondary school boys*. Leuven, Belgium: Leuven University Press.

Rowell, L.B. (1974). Human cardiovascular adjustments to exercise and thermal stress. *Physiological Reviews*, **54**, 75-159.

Rutenfranz, J., Lange-Andersen, K., Seliger, V., Ilmarinen, J., Klimmer, F., Kylian, H., Rutenfranz, M., & Ruppel, M. (1982). Maximal aerobic power affected by maturation and body growth during childhood and adolescence. *European Journal of Pediatrics*, **139**, 106-112.

Rutenfranz, J., Lange-Andersen, K., Seliger, V., Klimmer, F., Berndt, L., & Ruppel, M. (1981). Maximum aerobic power and body composition during the puberty growth period: Similarities and differences between children of two European countries. *European Journal of Pediatrics*, **136**, 123-133.

Rutenfranz, J., Lange-Andersen, K., Seliger, V., Klimmer, F., Ilmarinen, J., Ruppel, M., & Kylian, H. (1981). Exercise ventilation during the growth spurt period: Comparison between two European countries. *European Journal of Pediatrics*, **136**, 135-142.

Simon, G., Reid, L., Tanner, J.M., Goldstein, H., & Benjamin, B. (1972). Growth of radiologically determined heart diameter, lung width, lung length from 5 to 19 years with standards for clinical use. *Archives of Diseases of Childhood*, **47**, 373.

Sprynarova, S. (1974). Longitudinal study of the influence of different physical activity programs on functional capacity of the boys from 11 to 18 years. *Acta Paediatica Belgique*, **28**, 204-213.

Tanner, J.M., Whitehouse, R.H., & Takaishi, M. (1966). Standards from birth to maturity for height, weight, height velocity and weight velocity: British children, 1965: Part 2. *Archives of Diseases of Childhood*, **41**, 613-635.

Wasserman, K., Whipp, B.J., Koyal, S.N., & Beaver, W.L. (1973). Anaerobic threshold and respiratory gas exchange during exercise. *Journal of Applied Physiology*, **35**, 236-243.

Motor Performance of Hungarian School Children

Anikó Barabás
Hungarian University of Physical Education, Budapest, Hungary

The working abilities of future generations are partly determined by their physical fitness as predicted by the biological and physical state of children living today. The decrease in physical performances, the impairment of health in young adults, and the exceptionally high death rate are rather alarming phenomena. These factors require new decisions to be made with regard to both health care and youth policy in Hungary.

The collection of data from a comprehensive, nationwide, cross-sectional sample aimed at assessing the state of biological and physical development, while at the same time recording data concerning the social, cultural, and economic backgrounds of the subjects, has recently been completed.

A number of studies have been published in the past decades dealing with the theoretical and practical aspects of combined longitudinal and cross-sectional analyses of body structure and physical performance in determining biological development. During these investigations physical fitness, national standards, and reference values referring to growth and physical performance have been compiled (AAHPER, 1965; CAHPER, 1966; Clarke, 1971; Hebbelinck & Borms, 1978; Kemper, 1985).

Investigations of body structure in Hungary have a historical tradition. The results of systematic, objective data are available for almost the last hundred years. Based upon these representative investigations, it was possible to obtain information about Hungarian children's physical performance levels and to provide nationwide reference values.

The purpose of the present study was to analyze the differences in the performance scores of groups selected according to their sex and age and the size of their community.

MATERIALS AND METHODS

The subjects in this study were Hungarian schoolchildren from 6 to 18 years of age. The size of the examined sample was 27,430 (Table 1). The random sample was representative of all communities of all sizes in all counties in Hungary and of all types of schools. The sample included 1.5% of the total population.

Table 1 Number of Subjects

Age (years)	Boys			Girls		
	Total	Urban	Rural	Total	Urban	Rural
6	200	89	112	209	95	114
7	1,066	566	500	950	526	424
8	1,168	615	553	1,151	616	535
9	1,262	649	613	1,151	591	560
10	1,160	598	562	1,099	573	526
11	1,176	594	582	1,079	522	557
12	1,107	573	534	1,055	562	493
13	1,165	577	588	1,079	562	517
14	1,164	657	507	1,069	622	447
15	1,551	1,416	135	1,224	1,101	123
16	1,577	1,490	87	1,074	1,009	65
17	1,328	1,253	75	936	879	57
18	737	695	42	537	516	21
over 18	97	96	1	59	58	1
Total	14,758	9,867	4,891	12,672	8,232	4,440

For this investigation, a battery of seven tests was established from internationally accepted and recommended tests (Fleishman, 1964; Haag & Dassel, 1975; Simons & Renson, 1982). These tests were easy to administer at all sites of the investigation, even under the most simple conditions. The tests were selected in order to represent the most important and measurable factors such as general strength (hand grip strength), explosive arm strength (two-hand medicine ball push), explosive leg strength (standing broad jump), muscular endurance of the whole body (Burpee Test), muscular endurance of the trunk (sit-up test), running speed (60-m dash) and aerobic performance (12-min endurance run).

For data processing an IBM 3010 computer was used. The performance scores by age groups of children (boys and girls) living in areas of various sizes were analyzed utilizing variance analysis techniques.

RESULTS

When comparing the performances, I found that boys performed better than girls in all the strength tests. As far as muscular endurance was concerned, the performances of the girls and boys were nearly the same at early ages (i.e., at the ages of 6, 7, and 8). Later, the performances of the various age groups increased gradually in the case of boys. The performances of the age groups of girls gradually decreased and became stable at the age of 13. The greatest difference between the performances of boys and those of the girls occurred in cardiovascular endurance in favor of boys. The performance scores of age groups of boys differed significantly. The differences among the girls' age groups decreased as their age advanced, and they finally stabilized at a relatively low value and at a relatively early age.

Anthropometric characteristics change with age. Asmussen (1973) found that physical performance was influenced by body structure and that strength increased with height. This seemed to be the case for the boys examined in this study because their height continued to increase with age. However, this phenomenon was not observed in the case of girls because, although their height increased up until the age of 16, before they reached their adult height, the strength development had stabilized at around the age of 13, which coincided with age of menarche (Eiben & Pantó, 1985). There was a significant difference between the performance scores of urban and those of rural boys and girls (Tables 2 and 3).

Only in hand grip strength scores did rural children (both girls and boys) perform significantly better than urban ones. Few differences existed between urban and rural children in the standing broad jump test. Only 8- and 9-year-old urban girls did better than rural ones. In the 12-min endurance run significant differences were found in the performances of only a limited number of age groups: 6-, 7-, and 10-year-old urban boys and 7- and 8-year-old urban girls performed better than rural ones. Furthermore, a small difference was recorded in favor of urban girls at 6, 7, 12, and 13 years of age.

In all other tests (medicine ball push, sit-ups, Burpee Test, 60-m dash) urban children performed clearly better than those coming from rural areas. Urbanization is characterized by a more linear body structure. Urban girls and boys surpassed rural ones in longitudinal parameters of body structure, whereas there was no significant difference between urban and rural children in circumferences and widths of the trunks and extremities (Eiben & Pantó, 1985).

One would expect increased levels of performance in tests of strength with greater body sizes, but the shorter rural children surpassed urban children in hand grip strength scores, and, moreover, even the similar results in the standing broad jump underline the superiority of shorter rural children.

DISCUSSION

There were fundamental differences between the performances of boys and those of girls, especially in the strength tests but also in the running speed and endurance tests. The differences between the boys' and girls' performance were primarily the result of sexual dimorphism; girls reach

Table 2 Differences Between the Motor Performances of Urban and Rural School Children

Age (years)	Grip strength (kp)		Ball push (cm)		Broad jump (cm)		Burpee test (N/30 s)		Sit-up test (N/30 s)		60-m dash (s)		12-min run (m)	
	M	*SD*	*M*	*SD*	*M*	*SD*	*M*	*SD*	*M*	*SD*	*M*	*SD*	*M*	*SD*
Urban boys														
6	11,6	3,59	163	30	101	20	12,5	2,60	11,0	3,60	13,6[1]	1,26	1,698[3]	320
7	12,1	3,63	179	34	109	19	13,6[1]	3,86	11,7	3,65	13,0[2]	1,23	1,707[2]	303
8	14,7	4,21	214[3]	41	120	22	14,7[3]	3,10	13,1[3]	3,94	12,4[1]	1,24	1,814	339
9	17,5	4,38	249[3]	43	131	21	15,4[3]	2,95	14,5[3]	3,80	11,8[3]	1,03	1,965	382
10	19,9	5,41	283[3]	50	136	20	15,9[3]	3,17	15,6[3]	3,51	11,3[3]	0,96	2,092[3]	370
11	22,4	4,82	317[3]	54	143	18	16,6[3]	3,48	16,5[3]	4,09	11,0[3]	0,81	2,144	382
12	25,9	5,58	362[3]	70	150	20	17,0[3]	3,67	17,5[2]	3,81	10,6[2]	0,94	2,239	360
13	29,9	6,48	417[3]	82	161	21	17,7[3]	3,82	18,6[3]	3,71	10,2[3]	0,85	2,316	345
14	35,6	7,96	458	87	172	24	17,6[2]	3,21	19,2[3]	3,50	9,8[3]	0,87	2,377	377
15	42,2	8,52	466	81	185	25	17,9[3]	3,14	19,4	3,39	9,3[3]	0,82	2,469	365

Rural boys														
6	10,8	3,09	156	28	100	18	12,9	3,10	11,1	3,70	14,0	1,55	1,523	318
7	12,4[1]	3,53	173	31	107	19	13,3	3,22	11,1	3,71	13,3	1,39	1,655	326
8	14,8	3,94	204	36	118	19	13,9	3,10	12,3	3,79	12,5	1,18	1,778	338
9	18,3[3]	4,13	234	43	128	20	14,7	3,22	13,4	3,57	12,0	1,19	1,950	350
10	20,7[3]	4,82	268	49	136	19	15,3	3,04	14,8	4,00	11,7	1,13	2,019	375
11	23,5[3]	4,87	305	54	143	17	15,5	2,94	15,6	3,62	11,3	1,28	2,158	354
12	27,4[3]	5,42	342	56	151	19	16,3	3,10	16,9	3,42	10,8	0,94	2,275	344
13	31,3[3]	6,41	387	72	160	22	16,7	3,12	17,7	3,63	10,4	1,06	2,294	369
14	36,1	7,85	452	83	172	24	17,0	3,44	18,3	3,34	10,0	1,07	2,400	349
15	41,2	8,63	458	89	184	24	16,8	2,86	18,8	3,17	9,7	0,81	2,473	318

Note. [1] = .05, [2] = .01, and [3] = .001 probability levels.

Table 3 Differences Between the Motor Performances of Urban and Rural School Children

Age (years)	Grip strength (kp)		Ball push (cm)		Broad jump (cm)		Burpee test (*N*/30 s)		Sit-up test (*N*/30 s)		60-m dash (s)		12-min run (m)	
	M	*SD*	*M*	*SD*	*M*	*SD*	*M*	*SD*	*M*	*SD*	*M*	*SD*	*M*	*SD*
Urban girls														
6	9,2	3,56	146	43	97	18	13,0	2,45	11,1[2]	3,00	14,60	1,20	1,508[1]	355
7	10,2	3,26	158[3]	28	102	19	13,7[2]	2,27	11,6[3]	3,23	13,55[3]	1,32	1,546[2]	276
8	12,1	3,79	186[3]	34	116[3]	18	14,4[3]	2,83	13,1[3]	3,68	12,78[3]	1,25	1,678[3]	312
9	14,3	4,25	214[3]	41	127[3]	21	14,8[3]	2,87	14,0[3]	3,62	12,30[3]	1,23	1,757[1]	329
10	16,8	4,45	240[2]	41	131	19	15,2[3]	2,77	14,5[1]	3,67	11,87[3]	1,17	1,835	330
11	20,5	5,06	287[3]	53	137	18	15,2[2]	2,94	15,3[1]	3,38	11,38[3]	1,02	1,941	315
12	23,9	5,77	330[3]	57	145	21	15,8[3]	3,14	16,1[3]	3,29	11,01[3]	0,86	2,007[1]	298
13	27,4	5,33	375[3]	57	149	20	15,7[1]	2,99	16,8[3]	3,27	10,74[3]	0,92	2,003[1]	306
14	29,9	5,55	373	62	153	20	15,4	2,54	16,5	3,17	10,50[3]	0,83	2,001	322
15	32,1	5,01	355	53	154	20	15,6[1]	2,49	16,2[1]	2,88	10,46[3]	0,85	1,980	288

Rural girls														
6	9,1	3,33	139	25	96	18	12,6	2,42	9,9	3,51	14,59	1,35	1,419	272
7	9,9	4,11	149	24	100	20	13,2	2,51	10,5	3,48	14,15	1,29	1,497	288
8	12,4	3,44	176	33	112	19	13,8	2,68	11,8	3,42	13,20	1,19	1,612	293
9	14,8	4,21	201	35	121	18	14,3	2,64	12,8	3,29	12,55	1,11	1,719	300
10	18,1[3]	4,75	233	45	129	20	14,5	2,81	13,9	3,49	12,25	1,34	1,807	312
11	21,1	5,55	276	53	138	18	14,6	2,83	14,9	3,28	11,74	1,19	1,905	305
12	24,9[2]	5,66	313	54	145	20	14,9	2,71	15,4	3,23	11,32	1,10	1,952	318
13	28,2[1]	5,93	349	58	151	20	15,4	2,70	16,1	3,04	10,96	0,93	1,986	315
14	31,3[3]	5,04	374	54	154	21	15,5	3,00	16,6	3,07	10,74	0,93	2,003	325
15	30,9	5,12	356	44	155	22	15,1	2,67	15,6	3,02	10,92	1,27	1,962	283

Note. [1] = .05, [2] = .01, and [3] = .001 probability levels.

their adult height earlier and their maturation finishes earlier as well. (The body size increase of boys continues into later ages).

A certain improvement was experienced in the performance of girls in connection with the growth spurt; however, after maturation their physical performances stabilized at relatively low values. This phenomenon cannot be explained exclusively by the changes in their biological development, that is, the modifications in their hormonal balance and the relative increase in their body weight. It may also have been due to the different way of life of boys and girls. The physical inactivity of girls relative to boys may have caused the lower levels of performance of girls. The comparison of performances of urban and rural children demonstrated the decisive influence of different living conditions. The greater height and weight of urban children was not accompanied by larger circumferential measurements. Rural children performed better in strength tests, especially in hand grip strength. The superiority of the physical fitness of urban children was clearly shown in the performance tests. This may have been due to their having more opportunities for participation in physical activities. People living in cities attach more importance to regular physical training and therefore motivate their children to participate. These results indicate the significance of physical education and sports in schools, and the comprehensive development of this phase of schooling should continue.

Acknowledgments

The Youth Research Project was supported by the Institute of Social Sciences, Budapest, Hungary. The research was carried out at the Department of Anthropology, Eötvös Loránd University (O.G. Eiben) and at the Department of Medical Sciences and the Research Institute, University of Physical Education, Budapest, Hungary.

REFERENCES

AAHPER. (Ed.) (1965). *Youth fitness test manual*. Washington, DC: Author.

Asmussen, E. (1973). Growth in muscular strength and power. In G.L. Rarick (Ed.), *Physical activity, human growth and development* (pp. 60-79). New York: Academic Press.

CAHPER. (Ed.) (1966). *The CAHPER fitness-performance test manual*. Ottawa, Canada: Author.

Clarke, H.H. (1971). *Physical and motor tests in the Medford boys' growth study*. New York: Prentice-Hall.

Eiben, O., & Pantó, E. (1985). Some new data about the biological development of youth in Hungary, in function of socio-demographic factors. *Anthropológiai Közlemények*, **29**, 45-72.

Fleishman, E.A. (1964). *The structure and measurement of physical fitness*. London: Prentice-Hall.

Haag, H., & Dassel, H. (1975). *Fitness-test*. Stuttgart: Verlag Karl Hofmann.

Hebbelinck, M., & Borms, J. (1978). *Körperliche Wachstum und Leistungsfähigkeit bei Schulkindern*. Leipzig: J. Ambrosius Barth.

Kemper, H.C.G. (Ed.). (1985). *Growth, health and fitness of teenagers: Longitudinal research in international perspective*. Basel: Karger.

Simons, J., & Renson, R. (Eds.) (1982). *Evaluation of motor fitness*. Report of the European Research Seminar on the evaluation of motor fitness. Leuven, Belgium: Leuven University Press.

Mechanical Efficiency of Muscular Work and Economy of Walking and Running

Dusan Hamar
Ludovit Komadel
Olga Kuthanova
Research Institute of Sports Sciences, Bratislava, Czechoslovakia

Running and walking economy expressed as oxygen uptake at a given speed or for a covered distance is considered one of the important parameters influencing distance running or race walking performances (Costill, 1979; Conley & Krahenbuhl, 1980; Daniels, 1985; Hagberg & Coyle, 1983).

Interindividual variability of this parameter in an untrained population has been reported to be from about 20% to 50% (Dill, 1965; Mayhew, 1977; Farrell, Wilmore, Coyle, Billings, & Costill, 1979). It is substantially larger than the oxygen uptake at a given work load on the bicycle ergometer. Also, in a relatively homogeneous group of trained runners, the interindividual differences have been observed to be up to 20% (Daniels, 1974; Pollock, Jackson, & Pate, 1980). Age, running technique, weight, and quality of running shoes are considered to be among the most important factors contributing to this variability.

On the other hand, reports about a similar parameter, efficiency of muscular work while running and walking, are rather sporadic (Cavagna & Kaneko, 1977; Ito, Komi, Sjödin, Bosco, & Karlsson, 1983). The reason for this is mainly methodological problems associated with the estimation of mechanical work performed during two basic types of human locomotion. This rather complicated methodology is very probably a reason why there are no available data in the current literature about the relationship between the mechanical efficiency of muscular work and the energy cost of running and walking, respectively. The aim of this study was, therefore, to examine the mechanical efficiency determined on the basis of increased mechanical work and additional energy consumed due to uphill running and walking as a possible determinant of economy (energy cost) of these two types of locomotion.

METHODS

A group of 22 adolescent long- and middle-distance runners (age 15.8 ± 1.3 years; height 171.6 ± 7.6 cm; weight 58.7 ± 6.4 kg) volunteered to participate in the study. They trained regularly on the average of about 50 km a week and their $\dot{V}O_2max$ was 68.2 ± 4.8 ml • kg^{-1} • min^{-1}.

Each subject completed four 6-min submaximal loads on the treadmill followed by 2-min rest periods and a maximal exercise to exhaustion.

Submaximal loads consisted of walking at a velocity of 6 km • h^{-1} on the horizontal level (1st) and 5% grade (2nd) and running at a velocity of 12 km • h^{-1} on the horizontal level (3rd) and 5% grade (4th). During the maximal exercise, slope was increased from 0 by 2.5% every minute while velocity was kept constant at 16 km • h^{-1}. Ventilatory and gas exchange parameters were monitored continually during the entire exercise test by means of open circuit spirometry using computerized equipment (Ergooxyscreen by Jaeger, Höchberg, Federal Republic of Germany).

Differences in energy expenditures per kilogram of body weight while walking or running up an incline were estimated from an increase of steady state oxygen uptake (average of the last 2 min at each exercise load) in comparison with the similar steady state values during horizontal locomotion. Energy equivalent for oxygen according to the steady state respiratory exchange ratio was used for the calculation of energy expenditure at each exercise load (di Prampero, 1976).

Additional mechanical work while walking or running up a 5% incline was calculated from an increase in potential energy resulting from the overall vertical lift of the body during 1 min. This was 5 m at a velocity of 6 km • h^{-1} (walking) and 10 m at a velocity of 12 km • h^{-1} (running). Thus the calculated additional mechanical work during 1 min of walking and running was 49.05 J • kg^{-1} and 98.1 J • kg^{-1}, respectively.

Mechanical efficiency of muscular work while walking and running was estimated as a percent ratio of additional mechanical work and the increase in energy expenditure according to the formula,

$$ME(\%) = \frac{E_m}{E_{ch}} \times 100, \text{ where}$$

ME is mechanical efficiency of muscular work,
E_m is the additional mechanical work while walking or running uphill, and
E_{ch} is the increase in energy expenditure while walking or running uphill.

Economy of walking and running, both horizontal and grade, was expressed as the oxygen uptake per kilogram of body weight for a covered distance (ml • kg^{-1} • km^{-1}). The average steady state values from the last 2 min of each submaximal load were used for the calculation of this parameter. Pearson's product moment correlations and paired *t* tests were used for the statistical analyses of obtained data.

RESULTS

Oxygen cost, or economy of walking and running, as well as calculated energy expenditure for horizontal and grade locomotion (mean ± *SD*), are displayed in Figures 1 and 2. For both horizontal and grade walking, the oxygen cost was significantly lower (164 ± 12 and 224 ± 17 ml • kg^{-1} • km^{-1}, respectively) than in the case of running (188 ± 13 and 236 ± 21 ml • kg^{-1} • km^{-1}, respectively). The same relationship also applied to energy expenditures, which were lower in horizontal and grade walking (3.35 ± 0.24 and 4.49 ± 0.34 kJ • kg^{-1} • km^{-1}) than in running (3.78 ± 0.26 and 4.82 ± 0.42 kJ • kg^{-1} • km^{-1}).

On the other hand, estimated mechanical efficiency of muscular work during running (Figure 3) was 50.7% ± 12.1%, significantly higher than that during walking (41.5% ± 11.2%). Table 1 includes the results of correlation analyses between mechanical efficiency of muscular work and economy of horizontal and grade walking and running. Neither the mechanical efficiency of walking nor that of running was found to be significantly correlated to the economy of either level or grade walking or running, respectively.

DISCUSSION

Mechanical efficiency of muscular work for walking (41.5%) and running (50.7%) estimated by the described method was within the range

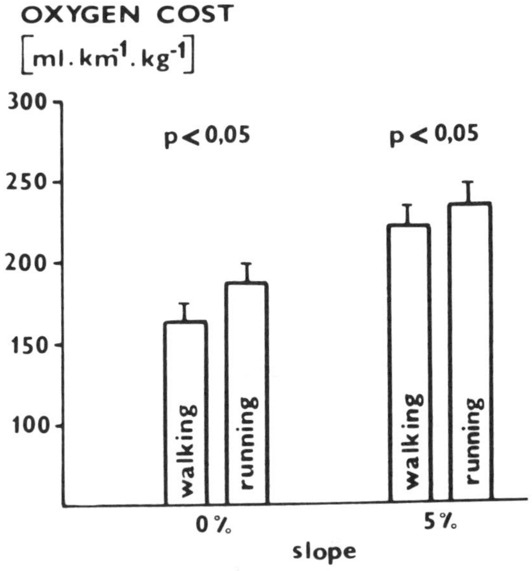

Figure 1. Oxygen cost of horizontal and grade walking and running.

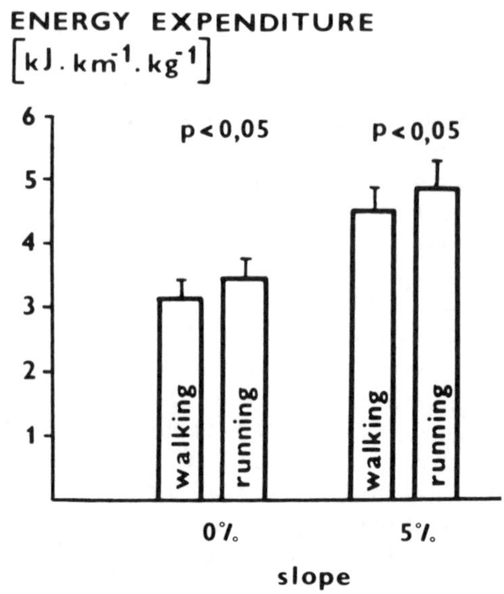

Figure 2. Energy expenditure during horizontal and grade walking and running.

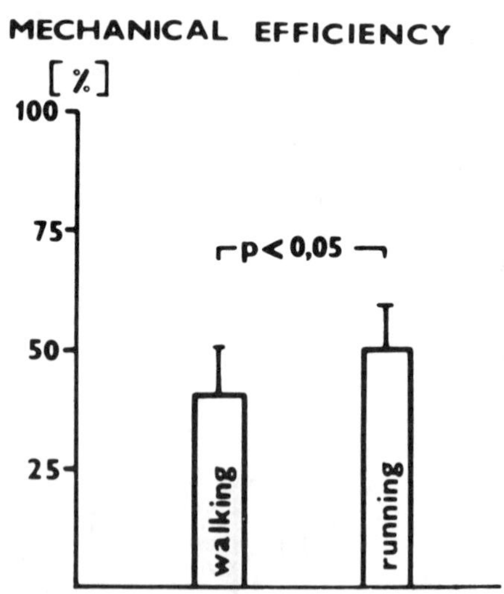

Figure 3. Mechanical efficiency of muscular work during running.

of values calculated on the basis of cinematographic analyses (Cavagna & Kaneko, 1977; Ito et al., 1981). These values for mechanical efficiency were significantly higher than those reported for muscular work of isolated muscle fibers (Whipp & Wasserman, 1969) or for cycling on the bicycle ergometer (Zacks, 1973).

Table 1 Correlations Between Mechanical Efficiency and Oxygen Cost of Horizontal and Grade Walking and Running

	1.	2.	3.	4.	5.
1. Oxygen cost of horizontal walking					
2. Oxygen cost of grade walking	0.86**				
3. Mechanical efficiency during walking	−0.04	−0.41			
4. Oxygen cost of horizontal running	0.58**	0.55**	−0.18		
5. Oxygen cost of grade running	0.37	0.36	−0.14	0.89**	
6. Mechanical efficiency during running	0.34	0.36	−0.09	0.37	0.18

** = $p < .1$.

This was probably due to better use of elastic energy stored in leg extensors during eccentric contraction in an unweighting phase of the movement. Such use of elastic energy can be considered in running and probably also in walking but not in cycling or in the case of isolated muscle fibers. This is because in the latter forms of muscle work there is no eccentric contraction during which elastic energy can be stored.

To accumulate and reuse the elastic energy, immediate and consecutive eccentric and concentric contractions must occur without a marked relaxation phase during muscular work (Asmussen & Bonde-Petersen, 1974). It is very likely, however, that the degree of tension generated in the muscles and elastic tissues at the time of switchover from eccentric to concentric contraction is also of importance for the use of elastic energy. This follows from the results of experiments with hopping kangaroos carried on by Taylor, Heglund, and Maloiy (1982), who reported that the efficiency of muscular work was higher as the frequency of hopping increased. This can be considered a consequence of better use of elastic energy due to higher tension in the muscles at the moment of takeoff.

The same phenomenon may be used to explain the lower mechanical efficiency of muscular work during walking in comparison with running. In walking, slower switchover from eccentric to concentric contraction and lower tension does not allow the use of elastic energy to the same degree as in running. However, the lower mechanical efficiency of walking was not associated with a higher oxygen or energy cost of this kind of locomotion, neither horizontally nor on a slope.

This finding, as well as the lack of a correlation between oxygen cost and mechanical efficiency of muscular work during both types of basic locomotion, suggests that the overall energy cost does not depend on how efficiently chemical energy of substrates is being transferred to mechanical energy during human locomotion. It is probably the entire amount of mechanical work performed, which depends mainly on uneconomical "luxury" movements, that plays a substantially more important role as a determinant of energy expenditure, oxygen cost, or economy of the two basic types of human locomotion. To corroborate or prove this statement, however, the relationship of oxygen cost to total mechanical work performed (which could not be estimated in the present study) should be examined.

REFERENCES

Asmussen, E., & Bonde-Petersen, F. (1974). Apparent efficiency and storage of elastic energy in human muscle during exercise. *Acta Physiologica Scandinavica*, **92**, 537-545.

Cavagna, G.A., & Kaneko, M. (1977). Mechanical work and efficiency in level walking and running. *Journal of Physiology* (London), **268**, 467-481.

Conley, D.L., & Krahenbuhl, G. (1980). Running economy and distance running performance of highly trained athletes. *Medicine and Science in Sports*, **12**, 357-360.

Costill, D.L. (1979). *A scientific approach to distance running*. Los Altos, CA: Tafnews.

Daniels, J. (1974). Physiological characteristics of champion male athletes. *Research Quarterly*, **45**, 342-348.

Daniels, J. (1985). A physiologist's view of running economy. *Medicine and Science in Sports and Exercise*, **17**, 332-338.

Dill, D.B. (1965). Oxygen used in horizontal and grade walking and running. *Journal of Applied Physiology*, **20**, 19-22.

di Prampero, P.E. (1976). Energy stores and supply in exercise. In E. Jokl, R.L. Anand, & H. Stoboy (Eds.), *Advances in exercise physiology* (pp. 132-146). Basel: Karger.

Farrell, P.A., Wilmore, J.H., Coyle, E.F., Billings, J.E., & Costill, D.L. (1979). Plasma lactate accumulation and distance running performance. *Medicine and Science in Sports*, **11**, 338-344.

Hagberg, J.M., & Coyle, E.F. (1983). Physiological determinants of endurance performance as studied in competitive racewalkers. *Medicine and Science in Sports and Exercise*, **15**, 287-289.

Ito, A., Komi, V.P., Sjödin, B., Bosco, C., & Karlsson, J. (1983). Mechanical efficiency of positive work in running at different speeds. *Medicine and Science in Sports and Exercise*, **15**, 299-308.

Mayhew, J.L. (1977). Oxygen cost and energy expenditure of running in trained runners. *British Journal of Sports Medicine,* **11**, 116-121.

Pollock, M.L., Jackson, A.S., & Pate, R.R. (1980). Discriminant analysis of physiological differences between good and elite distance runners. *Research Quarterly in Exercise and Sports,* **51**, 521-532.

Taylor, C.R., Heglund, N., & Maloiy, G.M.O. (1982). Energetics and mechanics of terrestrial locomotion. *Journal of Experimental Biology,* **97**, 1-21.

Whipp, B.J., & Wassermann, K. (1969). Efficiency of muscular work. *Journal of Applied Physiology,* **26**, 644-648.

Zacks, R.M. (1973). The mechanical efficiencies of running and bicycling against a horizontal impeding force. *Internationale Zeitschrift für Angewandte Physiologie,* **31**, 249-258.

Aerobic-Anaerobic Energy Supply and Daily Physical Activity Level in Young Children

Shigehiro Yoshizawa
Utsunomiya University, Japan

Hiroko Honda
Tochogi Kokugakuin Women's Junior College, Japan

Makoto Urushibara
Naka Nakamura
Training Center, Tochigi Prefecture, Japan

Maximal values of young children's lactate concentrations (LA) caused by exercise were detected by sampling blood 5 min (Robinson, 1938) and 1 min (Åstrand, 1952) after cessation of maximal or heavy work load. The values thus obtained were lower than those of older ages; that was assumed to be the result of the children's lack of willpower and quick mobilization of their aerobic work capacity. However, another more probable explanation for such lower values is that their more reduced lactacid anaerobic work capacity, in which a smaller amount of PFK contained in the muscle is involved, necessarily leads to less production of LA even under heavy work loads (Eriksson, 1972).

The first objective of the present study was, in consideration of the above-mentioned suggestions, to find an available clue to identify behaviors of aerobic-anaerobic energy supply during exercise, which are likely to be peculiar to young children, by measuring not only heart rate (HR) and oxygen uptake ($\dot{V}O_2$), but also LA under gradually increasing work loads on the treadmill.

Urbanization, industrialization, and motorization in Japan are now developing; therefore, physical inactivity and overeating, which mean potential risk factors for future adult diseases, often occur in young children as well as in adults. Accordingly, the second objective was (a) to investigate actual conditions of daily physical activity levels of young children obliged to spend most of the daytime in the small areas of nurseries and (b) to obtain concrete materials that are presumably useful for the improvement of the nursery programs. Nurseries now fall under the jurisdiction of the Ministry of Health and Welfare in Japan, and only children whose parents are employed can enter the nurseries. The percentage of mothers of nursery children employed, therefore, is much higher than that of mothers of kindergarteners under the control of the Ministry of Education.

METHOD

Male (N = 6) and female (N = 7) children, aged 5 or 6 years, participated in this study. They spent most of the daytime except Sunday in the nursery. Body heights and weights of the subjects, except one female obese subject, were within 2 *SD* of the mean values of a similar population.

In the preparatory test, they all tried a treadmill run with stepwise increasing speeds until subjective exhaustion. At the first step, they began to run with the initial speed of 80 m • min^{-1} or 100 m • min^{-1} for 2 min. The speed was increased by 20 m • min^{-1} step by step, and rest periods of 30 s were inserted between all adjoining steps. Throughout the single test sessions, HR was continuously monitored and recorded by ECG. By doing so, we were able to confirm the last stages through which each subject could completely run in this protocol in advance.

Two or 3 days later, they underwent the main tests with the same procedure as was used in the preparatory test. Expired air was collected for the last 30 s in Douglas bags, and blood samples of 25 μl were taken from hyperemized earlobe into capillary tubes immediately after the 2-min run at each step. Expired air was analyzed for CO_2 and O_2 by means of the Scholander technique, and LA of the blood was determined by the enzymatic technique (LA-640, Roche).

For the estimations of daily physical activity level, two male and two female children were randomly selected from among the subjects. Their HRs were continuously recorded during their times in the nursery from Monday to Saturday of 1 week. A heart rate memory apparatus (1850a, Takei), with dimensions 10 cm × 6 cm × 2.5 cm and weight of 100 g, was attached to the waist on a belt. HRs were calculated every minute by using a heart rate analyzer (1850b, Takei). Behaviors of the subjects were observed and recorded as precisely as possible.

RESULTS

By applying interpolation, we drew the curves in Figures 1 and 2 as closely as possible to the plotted values of HR, $\dot{V}O_2$, and LA against speeds; the values of HR and $\dot{V}O_2$ equivalent to 3 and 4 mmol • l^{-1} of LA (HR 3 mMLA, HR 4 mMLA, $\dot{V}O_2$ 3 mMLA, and $\dot{V}O_2$ 4 mMLA) were predicted and indicated with their relative values in Table 1. It is important to note that 4 mMLA is the anaerobic threshold (AT). Mean values of $\dot{V}O_2max$ in the present study were almost the same as those obtained in a previous study (Yoshizawa, Ishizaki, & Honda, 1980).

Mean values of peak LA, which were determined immediately after the last treadmill increment, were 5.16 mMLA for males and 4.70 mMLA for

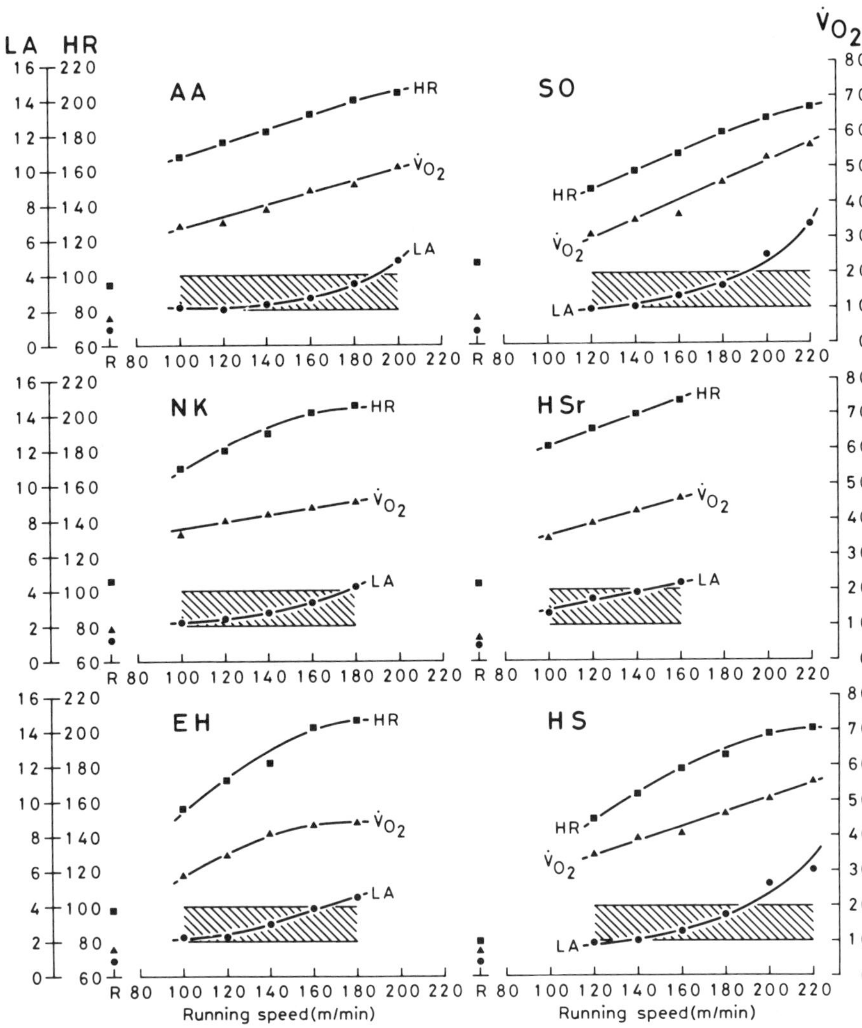

Figure 1. HR (bpm), $\dot{V}O_2$ (ml • kg^{-1} • min^{-1}), and LA (mMLA) of young male children with increasing running speeds on the flat treadmill (shaded areas show ranges of individual running speeds and aerobic-anaerobic transitions).

females. No significant difference due to sex was found. Compared with the results of other authors, it was clear that these values of peak LA were lower than those of older ages—5.94 mMLA for 9-year-old boys (Tanako, Shindo, Shiwa, & Ono, 1981); 6.2 mMLA for 11-year-old boys (Atomi, Iwaoka, Hatta, Miyashita, & Yamamoto, 1986); 8.56 mMLA for 14-year-old boys, and 8.41 mMLA for 14-year-old girls (Yoshizawa, Oka, Munekata, & Hiramatsu, 1987).

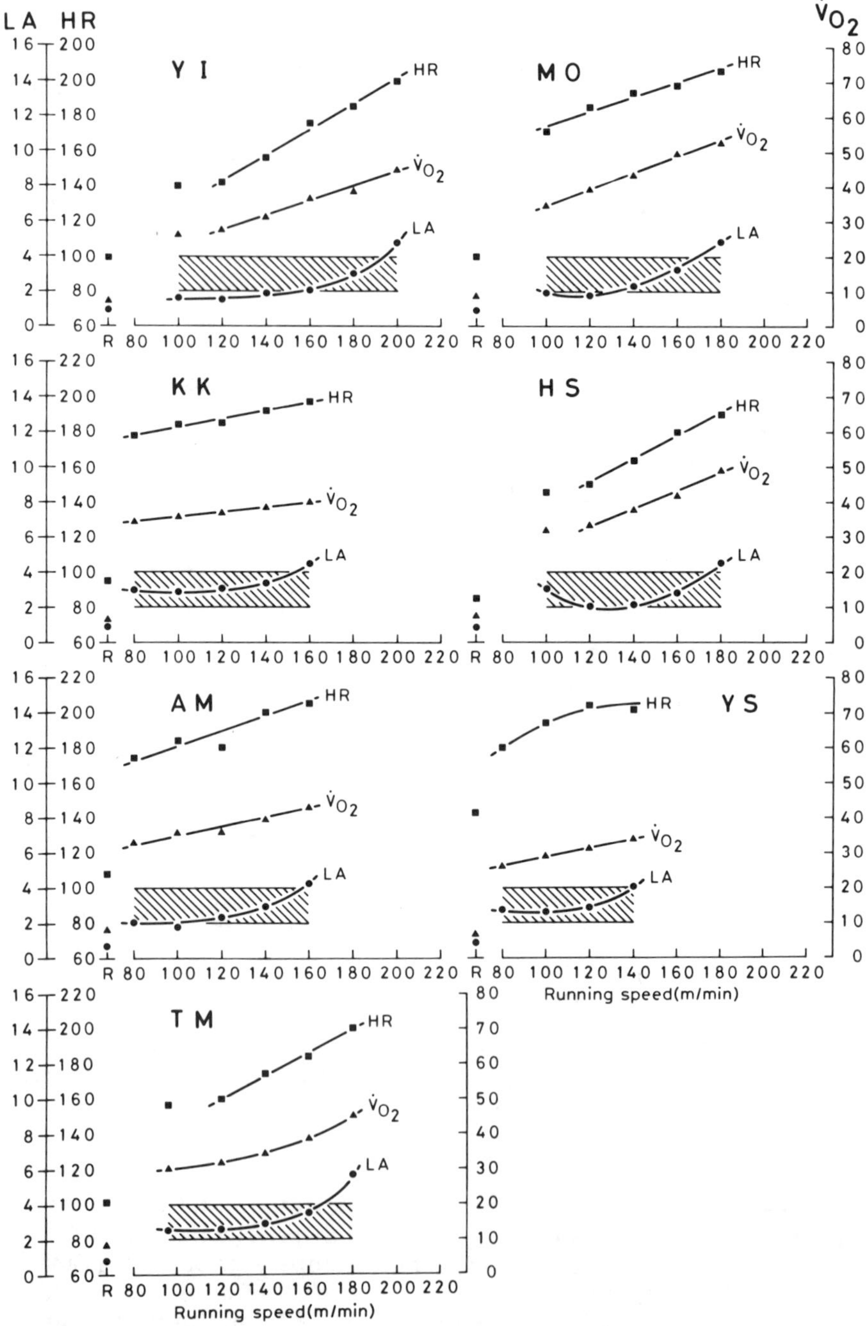

Figure 2. HR (bpm), $\dot{V}O_2$ (ml • kg^{-1} • min^{-1}), and LA (mMLA) of young female children with increasing running speeds on the flat treadmill (shaded areas show ranges of individual running speeds and aerobic-anaerobic transitions).

Table 1 Absolute and Relative Values of Circulorespiratory Variables Equivalent to Maximal Exertion and the Blood Lactate (LA) Concentrations of 3 and 4 mmol/l (mMLA) in Young Children

Subj.	Maximal exertion				3mmol/l, LA					4mmol/l, LA				
	Speed (m/min)	HR max (bpm)	$\dot{V}O_2$ max (ml/kg/min)	LA (mmol/l)	Speed (m/min)	HR (bpm)	% HR max	$\dot{V}O_2$ (ml/kg/min)	% $\dot{V}O_2$ max	Speed (m/min)	HR (bpm)	% HR max	$\dot{V}O_2$ (ml/kg/min)	% $\dot{V}O_2$ max
Male														
AA	200	204	50.8	4.81	169	195	95.6	45.0	88.6	190	202	99.0	48.5	95.5
SO	220	194	55.7	6.78	168	173	89.2	42.5	76.3	191	184	94.8	49.2	88.3
NK	180	206	45.2	4.26	150	198	96.1	42.3	93.6	176	204	99.0	45.0	99.6
HSr	160	208	46.0	4.43	105	184	88.5	36.4	79.1	146	202	97.1	43.3	94.1
EH	180	206	43.6	4.59	146	189	91.7	40.2	92.2	165	203	98.5	43.5	99.8
HS	220	201	55.1	6.10	172	185	92.0	44.8	81.3	190	194	96.5	48.7	88.4
$\bar{x}$	193.3	203.1	49.4	5.16	150.7	187.3	92.2	41.9	85.2	176.3	198.2	97.5	46.4	94.3
sd	26.6	5.1	5.2	1.02	25.7	8.9	3.2	3.2	7.2	18.1	7.5	1.7	2.7	5.1
Female														
YI	200	200	44.5	4.78	182	188	94.0	40.3	90.6	194	192	97.0	42.8	96.2
MO	180	206	52.6	4.89	154	197	95.6	47.2	89.7	161	204	99.0	50.8	96.6
KK	160	197	40.3	4.48	122	188	95.4	37.3	92.6	153	195	99.0	39.4	97.8
HS	180	190	49.0	4.77	162	179	94.2	43.6	89.0	176	188	98.9	47.4	96.7
AM	160	205	43.2	4.25	141	198	96.6	40.3	93.3	157	205	100.0	42.4	98.1
YS	140	202	33.9	4.08	123	202	100.0	31.6	93.2	140	202	100.0	33.8	100.0
TM	180	200	45.1	5.66	146	171	88.5	35.7	79.2	166	191	95.5	40.2	89.1
$\bar{x}$	171.4	200.0	44.1	4.70	147.2	189.0	94.9	39.4	89.7	163.9	196.7	98.2	42.4	96.4
sd	19.5	5.4	6.0	0.52	21.1	11.1	3.5	5.1	4.9	17.3	6.9	1.7	5.5	3.4

Relative values of HR equivalent to 4 mMLA against HRmax (%HRmax:4 mMLA) were 97.5% HRmax:4 mMLA for males and 98.2% HRmax:4 mMLA for females. So these relative values were found to be similar in both sexes. Relative values of %$\dot{V}O_2$max:4 mMLA were 94.3% $\dot{V}O_2$max:4 mMLA for males and 96.4% $\dot{V}O_2$max:4 mMLA for females and were a little lower than those of %HRmax:4 mMLA in both sexes. Furthermore, it was also confirmed that both relative values differed from the inclination of absolute values of peak LA, lower in more advanced ages—97% HRmax:4 mMLA and 90% $\dot{V}O_2$max:4 mMLA for 9-year-old boys and 80% HRmax:4 mMLA and 73% $\dot{V}O_2$max:4 mMLA for 22-year-old male students (Tanaka et al., 1981); 89.9% HRmax:4 mMLA and 85.9% $\dot{V}O_2$max:4 mMLA for 14-year-old boys and 89.6% HRmax:4 mMLA and 84.8% $\dot{V}O_2$max:4 mMLA for 14-year-old girls (Yoshizawa et al., 1987). Accordingly, it is of interest that HR 4 mMLA and $\dot{V}O_2$ 4 mMLA were quite similar to HRmax and $\dot{V}O_2$max, respectively, in young children, but with advancing age the differences between them increased steadily.

Figure 3 includes all the mean values of HR in the nursery with scales of relative values. Net %HRmax depends upon the interval of HR between sleeping and maximal exertion level (Seliger, Trefny, Bartunkova, & Pauer, 1974) and %HR 4 mMLA means the relative level of a given HR against HR 4 mMLA.

Mean values of HR ranged from 102 to 114 beats per minute (bpm), except a comparatively low value on Friday of 89 bpm for Subject EH; 98 to 110 bpm for HS; 123 to 126 bpm for YS, who likely had a touch

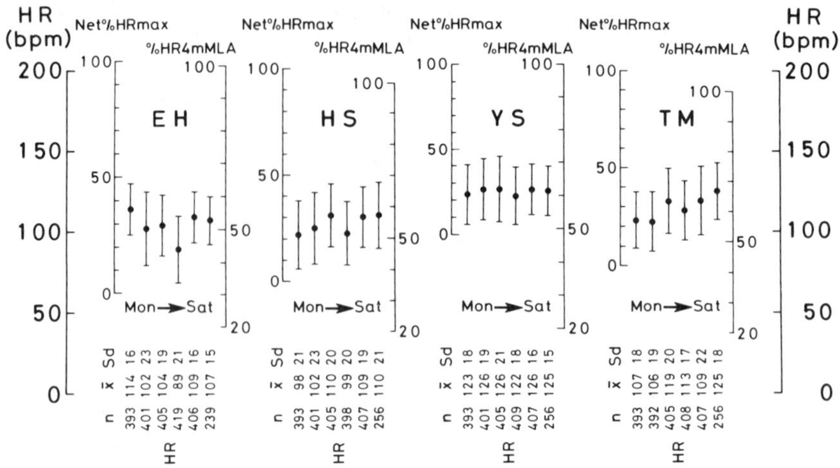

Figure 3. Absolute and relative mean values of HR (bpm) for young children during stays in the nursery on weekdays.

of tachycardia; and 106 to 119 bpm, except a relatively higher value of 125 bpm on Saturday, for TM. Therefore, it was concluded that mean values of HR during stays in the nursery were between 100 and 120 bpm under the usual program.

Ranges of all the mean values of HR, converted into relative values, were net 19% to 36% HRmax for males and net 22% to 38% HRmax for females, and so no difference existed between the sexes. Moreover, if expressed again only in %HRmax, the values corresponded to 43% to 55% HRmax for males and 53% to 62% HRmax for females, respectively. In a third relative value, they were 44% to 57% HR 4 mMLA for males and 57% to 67% HR 4 mMLA for females, and, therefore, females were a little higher than males as in the case of %HRmax.

All the histograms of HR, based on the classification interval of 10 beats, were statistically not good fits to normal distribution curves. Accumulation times, when HR increased above 160 bpm, the intensity of which first becomes effective for the improvement of cardiovascular fitness in children (Gilliam, Freedson, Geenenn, & Shahraray, 1981), were, except during the 800-m endurance run, only 0-4 min for EH, 0-6 min for HS, 4-21 min for YS with a touch of tachycardia, and 0-6 min for TM. The intensities of 160 bpm were equal to 2.2 mMLA and net 68% HRmax for EH, 2.0 mMLA and net 69% HRmax for HS, and 2.7 mMLA and net 67% HRmax for TM. On the contrary, percentages of accumulation times, when HR's were lower than 120 bpm, amounted to 72% to 94% for EH, 77% to 91% for HS, 34% to 70% for YS, and 54% to 78% for TM while in the nursery.

According to the category of behaviors, mean values of HR observed in the 800-m endurance run, which was performed every day as illus-

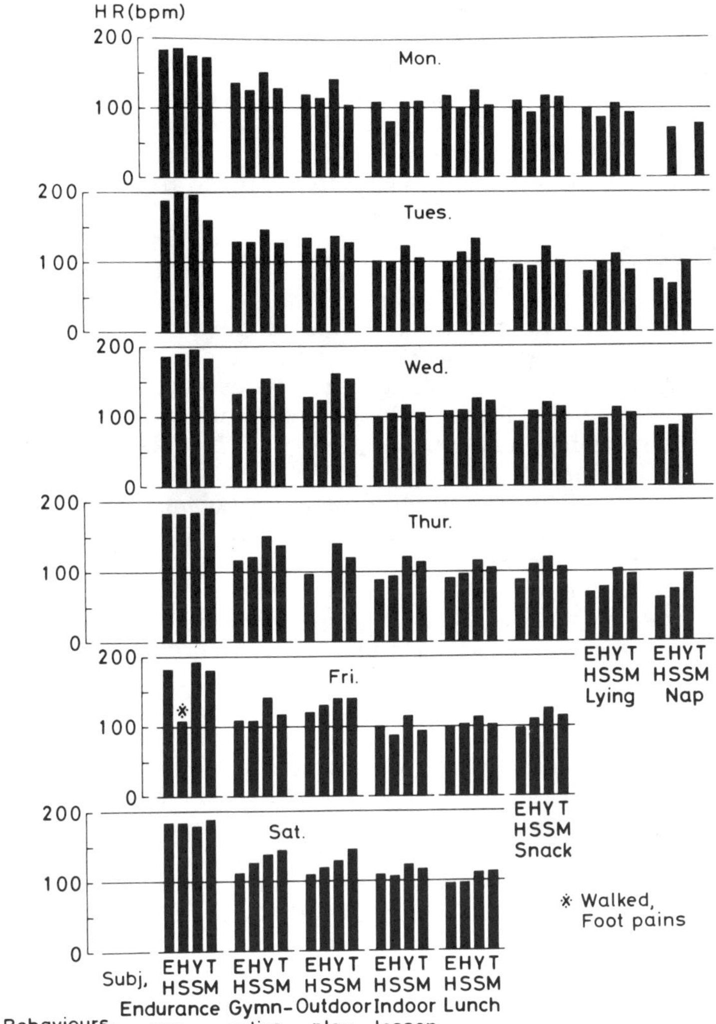

Figure 4. Mean values of HR (bpm) of young children engaged in various kinds of physical activities in the nursery.

trated in Figure 4, ranged from 182 bpm (89% 4 mMLA) to 188 bpm (93% 4 mMLA) for EH, 183 bpm (89% 4 mMLA) to 199 bpm (104% 4 mMLA) for HS, 175 bpm (86% 4 mMLA) to 196 bpm (98% 4 mMLA) for YS, and 160 bpm (86% 4 mMLA) to 191 bpm (101% 4 mMLA) for TM.

During outdoor play, when children are likely to play spontaneously, levels of HR relative to LA were 48% to 67% 4 mMLA for EH, 59% to 72% 4 mMLA for HS, 63% to 79% 4 mMLA for YS, and 56% to 82%

4 mMLA for TM. In gymnastics or calisthenics, which were formally conducted by nurses, the levels of HR were almost the same as those observed in outdoor play. In other behaviors, the levels of HR were, as expected, still less than those of the behaviors already mentioned.

During naptime, TM was able to sleep only on Monday because of her nervousness. Individual mean values of HR varied from day to day. HR of subject YS with a touch of tachycardia ranged from 98 to 107 bpm.

DISCUSSION

The reason the young children had to run for 2 min on the treadmill could be explained by the fact that, owing to their faster acceleration in $\dot{V}O_2$, complete or almost complete steady states were established within 1-1/2 min of beginning the run with gradually increased speeds and that, if the speed was high enough, $\dot{V}O_2$max could be obtained (Yoshizawa, Honda, Urushibara, & Nakamura, 1981).

The question of whether or not $\dot{V}O_2$max was obtained must always be examined. The criteria for adults (Åstrand & Rodahl, 1970; Issekutz, Birdlhead, & Rodahl, 1963) may be inappropriate for young children. It has been proposed that HR must be increased to the level of at least 200 bpm in order to obtain $\dot{V}O_2$max for young children (Cumming, Hastman, & McCort, 1985; Yoshizawa & Honda, 1979). According to this proposal, as shown in Table 1, male SO and females KK and HS should be omitted from the analysis. However, SO and KK reached unity in their respiratory exchange ratios, and HS probably terminated the run one step before exhaustion because of lack of willpower or motivation. Thus it could be recognized that for the most part subjects obtained $\dot{V}O_2$max.

Lower values of peak LA in young children, though to some extent their motivation was of concern, perhaps were largely due to lower or yet underdeveloped lactacid anaerobic work capacities. In addition, %HRmax:4 mMLA and %$\dot{V}O_2$max:4 mMLA were almost equal to 100%. This means that young children mobilize their metabolism more aerobically even during near maximal exertion. Therefore, they can necessarily avoid overstraining themselves and recover more quickly than older children and adolescents. Such relative values that approach 100% also suggest that in young children physical activity levels could be estimated not only on a cardiovascular basis, but also metabolically by using %HRmax.

It has already been confirmed that maximal aerobic power and endurance run performances of young male children were significantly superior to those of young females (Yoshizawa, Ishizaki, & Honda, 1986). Absolute values of $\dot{V}O_2$ 4 mMLA as well as $\dot{V}O_2$max were higher, though not statistically significant, in young male children than in young females (see Table 1). Such a tendency implies that male cardiovascular performance capacities are already higher in young children, probably because there are no gender differences in HRmax (Yoshizawa et al., 1986), $(a\text{-}\bar{v})O_2$ in maximal exertion (Godfrey, 1974), and in heart volume (Nghiem, Schreiber, & Harris, (1967).

The mean values of HR observed in the nursery were slightly lower than those of HR (123 to 135 bpm in the kindergarten; Mimura & Kamibayashi, 1985). This difference was partly due to the lower values found during naptime. However, if three kinds of low relative values of mean HR, as well as very short periods of HR above 160 bpm, are taken into consideration, it is evident that daily physical activity levels under the usual programs were not high enough for young children to develop desirable cardiovascular performance capacities. Accordingly, any special program such as an endurance run must be adapted to the small area that is available for the program of the nursery.

For instance, an 800-m endurance run, the intensity of which lasted only several minutes, mobilized aerobic and lactacid anaerobic metabolism in the muscle to near maximal degrees. Therefore, it must be effective for the improvement of circulorespiratory and metabolic performance capacity in young children. From a practical viewpoint, in the initial stage of endurance training, a speed of 120 m • min^{-1} is safe and optimal (Yoshizawa et al., 1981), and thereafter the speed of 140 m • min^{-1}, which was equivalent to 3 mMLA and hardly yielded any difference between the sexes (Table 1), could be used as an appropriate and effective intensity.

CONCLUSION

Lactacid anaerobic work capacities of young children are lower than those of older children and adolescents, and values of HR and $\dot{V}O_2$ relative to 4 mMLA are very close to HRmax and $\dot{V}O_2max$, respectively. Therefore, physical activity levels can only be estimated by using HR in young children. Daily physical activity levels of young children in the nursery were low; thus any kind of endurance exercise should be planned as a part of the usual program.

REFERENCES

Åstrand, P.O. (1952). *Experimental studies of physical working capacity in relation to sex and age*. Copenhagen: Munksgaard.

Åstrand, P.O., & Rodahl, K. (1970). *Textbook of work physiology*. New York: McGraw-Hill.

Atomi, Y., Iwaoka, K., Hatta, H., Miyashita, M., & Yamamoto, Y. (1986). Daily physical activity levels in preadolescent boys related to $\dot{V}O_2max$ and lactate threshold. *European Journal of Applied Physiology*, **55**, 156-161.

Cumming,. G.R., Hastman, L., & McCort, J. (1985). Treadmill endurance times, blood lactate, and exercise blood pressures in normal children. In R.A. Binkhorst, H.C.G. Kemper, & W.H.M. Saris (Eds.), *Children and exercise XI* (pp. 140-150). Champaign, IL: Human Kinetics.

Eriksson, B.O. (1972). Physical training, oxygen supply and muscle metabolism in 11- to 13-year-old boys. *Acta Physiologica Scandinavica*, (Suppl. 384).

Gilliam, T.B., Freedson, P.S., Geenen, D.L., & Shahraray, B. (1981). Physical activity patterns determined by heart rate monitoring in 6- to 7-year-old children. *Medicine and Science in Sports and Exercise*, **13**, 65-67.

Godfrey, S. (1974). *Exercise testing in children (application health and disease)*. Philadelphia: W.B. Saunders.

Issekutz, B., Birdlhead, N.C., & Rodahl, K. (1962). The use of respiratory quotients in assessment of aerobic work capacity. *Journal of Applied Physiology*, **17**, 47-50.

Mimura, K., & Kamibayashi, H. (1985). A fundamental study of optimum quantity of motion for children in their daily life—A change in heart rate over a period of 24 hours. *Japanese Journal of Physical Fitness*, **34**, 201-210.

Nghiem, Q.X., Schreiber, M.H., & Harris, L.C. (1976). Cardiac volume in normal children and adolescents. *Circulation*, **35**, 509-522.

Robinson, S. (1938). Experimental studies of physical fitness in relation to age. *Arbeitsphysiol*, **10**, 251-323.

Seliger, V., Trefny, Z., Bartunkova, S., & Pauer, M. (1974). The habitual activity and physical fitness of 12-year-old boys. *Acta Pediatrica Belgica*, **28** (Suppl.), 54-59.

Tanaka, H., Shindo, M., Shiwa, K., & Ono, T. (1981). Blood lactate concentration in relation to running velocity in 9-year-aged boys as compared to adults. *Report of Research Center in Physical Education*, **9**, 27-33.

Yoshizawa, S., & Honda, H. (1979). The studies on aerobic work capacities of preparatory school children (II). *Japanese Journal of Physical Fitness*, **28**, 104-111.

Yoshizawa, S., Honda H., Urushibara, M., & Nakamura, N. (1981). The studies on aerobic work capacities of preparatory school children (III). *Japanese Journal of Physical Fitness*, **30**, 73-85.

Yoshizawa, S., Ishizaki, T., & Honda, H. (1980). Maximal oxygen uptakes in young children aged from 3 to 6 years. *Japanase Journal of Physical Education*, **25**, 59-68.

Yoshizawa, S., Ishizaki, T., & Honda, H. (1986). Aerobic power and endurance running in young children. In J. Rutenfranz, R. Mocellin, & F. Klimdt (Eds.), *Children and exercise XII* (pp. 77-90). Champaign, IL: Human Kinetics.

Yoshizawa, S., Oka, S., Munekata, S., & Hiramatsu, K. (1987). Analysis of physical education lesson and extracurricular sport activity on the basis of anaerobic threshold (AT) in junior high school. *Bulletin of the Faculty of Education* (Utsunomiya University, Sect. 2) **37**, 169-209.

Prediction of Performance in Young Competitive Bicyclists

Karsten Froberg
Department of Physical Education, Odense University, Denmark

Endurance training studies typically employ changes in maximal oxygen uptake ($\dot{V}O_2$max) as an indicator of changes in the capacity of endurance exercise. However, it has been suggested that variables measured during submaximal exercise may be more valid indicators of training and performance status (Daniels, Yarbrough, & Foster, 1978; Davis, 1985; Jacobs, 1986; Mader et al., 1976). The blood lactate response to a given exercise is such an indicator and is being increasingly used as a marker of the adaptation to endurance training. Most practical training studies, in which correlations between lactate variables and performance have been discussed, deal with running events. In only one study has there been an attempt to predict cycling performance with physiological variables, despite the popularity of competitive cycling (Krebs, Zinkgraf, & Virgilio, 1986).

The present study investigated effects of long-term endurance training of young competitive cyclists over a 4-year period by measuring, among other things, $\dot{V}O_2$max, lactate threshold using the OBLA concept (LT4 mmol), vital capacity (VC), and percent fat obtained by a skinfold prediction equation. It also attempted to determine if it is possible to predict results in performance using selected physiological variables obtained during ergometer exercise.

The junior bicyclists have now been followed for 2 years. Data from this period are presented and discussed in this article.

MATERIAL AND METHODS

The subjects were 18 elite junior cyclists, 15.1 ± 0.25 years of age at the first test in November 1985. They were the most successful competitive cyclists in their age group in Denmark during the year in which the project started. All of them had been engaged in competitive bicycle training regularly 1 to 2 hr per day, 4 to 5 days per week since the age of 11 or 12 years. Their training schedule in 1986 consisted of an increasing amount of training from 1.5 hr per day, 4 to 5 times per week during the winter period, to 2 to 3 hr per day, 6 to 7 times per week in late spring and in the summer periods, with competitions almost every weekend from late May until mid-September. In a 6-week period from late September until the beginning of November the boys were encouraged not to train regularly. From the beginning of November they again started regular training 1 to 2 hr per day, 4 or 5 times per week.

Different physiological parameters were obtained each year in February, May, July, and November. Mean physical characteristics of the subjects gathered in February 1986 and February 1987 are shown in Table 1. The study was approved by the Ethical Committee for the County of Fyn.

Table 1 Physical Characteristics of Subjects (n = 13) and Maximal Values for Oxygen Uptake and Vital Capacity During a 1-Year Period (Mean ± *SD*)

	February 1986	February 1987	p values
Age (years)	15.6 ± 0.25	16.6 ± 0.25	
Height (cm)	176.2 ± 6.20	178.2 ± 6.61	$p < .01$
Weight (kg)	63.7 ± 6.55	67.0 ± 7.05	$p < .01$
Fat (%)	11.3 ± 2.40	10.6 ± 3.01	NS
$\dot{V}O_2max$ (l • min^{-1})	4.37 ± 0.315	4.57 ± 0.291	$p < .01$
$\dot{V}O_2max$ (ml • kg^{-1} • min^{-1})	68.9 ± 4.30	68.8 ± 4.02	NS
$\dot{V}C_{BTPS}$ (l)	5.4 ± 0.78	6.0 ± 0.71	$p < .001$

At every test session, all subjects underwent a discontinuous incremental exercise test to determine the intensity at which the blood lactate concentration of 4 mmol • l^{-1} appeared (effect at LT4 mmol) by an interpolation between the nearest two values and the maximal oxygen uptake ($\dot{V}O_2max$). The tests were performed on a Monarch bicycle ergometer modified with a racing handlebar, a racing seat, toe clips, and an adjustable stem.

The subjects performed 5-min exercise work loads with 1-min rest after each exercise bout. The initial work load was 135 to 180 W, and load was increased by 45 W until exhaustion. Pedal rate was 90 • min^{-1}. Oxygen uptake ($\dot{V}O_2$), CO_2 output ($\dot{V}CO_2$), minute ventilation ($\dot{V}_E$), and heart rate (HR) were measured during the last minute of each work rate. HLa was measured in each of the 1-min rest periods, as well as 1 and 3 min after completion of the test in order to obtain peak values (HLa max). Based on the information from this test, a second test was initially performed in which a 10-min warm-up was followed by work at supermaximal intensity until exhaustion. After two test rounds it was observed that in no case was the difference between the peak values in the two tests more than 5%. In the following test rounds it was therefore decided to use only the incremental test. Criteria for maximum effect during tests were the attainment of the following test values: HR > 175 beats • min^{-1}, HLa > 7 mmol • l^{-1}, R > 1.05, and ventilatory coefficient for O_2 ($\dot{V}_E$ BTPS • $\dot{V}O_{2STPD}^{-1}$) > 30 l • l^{-1}.

Oxygen uptake and related variables were measured with the conventional Douglas bag technique. From predried air samples, O_2 and CO_2 concentrations were analyzed with Servomex OA 184 and Beckman LB2 analyzers. The analyzers were checked daily by comparisons with results obtained with the Scholander method. The subjects were breathing through a low-resistance Otis-McKerrow valve. Expired gas volume was measured with a 130-l Tissot spirometer. HR was obtained from a Polar Electro Sport Tester PE-3000. Lactate concentration was measured in arterialized blood (Forster, Dempsey, Thompson, Vidruk, & DoPico, 1972) from prewarmed fingertips and analyzed by an enzymatic method (Hohorst, 1970). Skinfold measurements (Harpenden Skinfold Caliper) were performed according to the method of Durnin and Womersley (1974) to provide an estimate of the percentage of body fat. Vital capacity measurements were made using a 7-l Aesculap Spirometer calibrated with a balanced 10-l Krogh Spirometer.

ANALYSIS OF DATA

Mean values and standard deviations were calculated with conventional procedures. The Wilcoxen Signed-Ranks Test was used to test for significant differences in the data between training periods; $p < .05$ was taken to indicate statistical significance.

RESULTS

Between February 1986 and February 1987 the boys increased in height by 2 cm from 176.2 ± 6.20 cm to 178.2 ± 6.21 cm. The corresponding weight gain was 3.3 kg from 63.7 ± 6.55 kg to 67.0 ± 7.05 kg, but there were no significant changes in the fat content (11.3% ± 2.4% to 10.6% ± 3.0%). The average $\dot{V}O_2$max in liters per minute increased 0.20 l from 4.37 ± 0.315 l to 4.57 ± 0.200 l ($p < .01$). This $\dot{V}O_2$max increase corresponded to the height and weight gain in accordance with the theory of Asmussen and Heebøll-Nielsen (1955). Expressed per kilogram of body weight, the values were 68.9 ± 4.3 to 68.8 ± 4.0 ml • kg^{-1} • min^{-1}. There was a 0.6-l increase in vital capacity (5.4 ± 0.78 ± 6.0 ± 0.71) during the year, which was highly significant ($p < .001$; Table 1).

The results from July 1986, when the boys were most fit, and November 1986, just after they had had a 5- to 6-week training break, showed a nonsignificant decrease in $\dot{V}O_2$max (4.52 ± 0.344 to 4.47 ± 0.376 l • min^{-1}), but a significant decrease expressed per kilogram body weight (73.4 ± 3.87 to 70.3 ± 3.88 ml • kg^{-1} • min^{-1}; $p < .01$). Apparently, this was caused by a corresponding significant gain in body fat (9.1% ± 2.09% to 10.2% ± 2.06%; $p < .01$). However, there was a great and highly significant

Table 2 Values for Maximal Oxygen Uptake, Percent Fat Content (%), Effect at LT_{4mmol} and Effect per Kilogram Body Weight at LT_{4mmol} Measured in July 1986 and in November 1986 After a 5- to 6-Week Training Break (Mean ± *SD*, $n = 13$)

	July 1986	November 1986	*p* values
$\dot{V}O_2max$ ($l \cdot min^{-1}$)	4.52 ± 0.344	4.47 ± 0.376	NS
$\dot{V}O_2max$ ($ml \cdot kg^{-1} \cdot min^{-1}$)	73.4 ± 3.87	70.3 ± 3.88	$p < .01$
Fat (%)	9.1 ± 2.09	10.2 ± 2.06	$p < .01$
Effect at LT_{4mmol} (W)	287 ± 33.1	236 ± 46.0	$p < .001$
Effect per kg body weight at LT_{4mmol} ($W\ kg^{-1}$)	4.65 ± 0.486	3.69 ± 0.531	$p < .001$

decrease (21%) in the measured work effect per kilogram of body weight at the lactate threshold (LT4 mmol; Table 2).

Table 3 shows correlations between cycling performance expressed as the mean velocity, calculated from a race performed as a 25-km single start, and physiological measurements obtained during ergometer exercise. The calculations showed that there were no correlations between cycling performance expressed as mean velocity and $\dot{V}O_2max$ expressed as $l \cdot min^{-1}$ or as $ml \cdot kg^{-1} \cdot min^{-1}$. In contrast to that, there was a highly significant ($p < .01$) correlation between $\dot{V}O_2$ in percent of $\dot{V}O_2max$ at LT4 mmol as well as between the work effect per kilogram of body weight at LT4 mmol, with *r* values of .75 and .89, respectively ($p < .001$).

Table 3 Correlations Between Cycling Performance (Mean Velocity in a 25-km Single Start) and Physiological Measurements Obtained During Ergometer Exercise ($n = 15$)

	V_{25km} ($m \cdot s^{-1}$)	*p* values
$\dot{V}O_2max$ ($l \cdot min^{-1}$)	0.15	NS
$\dot{V}O_2max$ ($ml \cdot kg^{-1} \cdot min^{-1}$)	0.42	NS
$\dot{V}O_2max$ at LT_{4mmol} in % of $\dot{V}O_2max$ (%)	0.79	$p < .001$
Effect at LT_{4mmol} (W)	0.54	$p < .05$
Effect per kg body wt at LT_{4mmol} ($W\ kg^{-1}$)	0.89	$p < .001$

DISCUSSION

The results of the present investigation performed on elite junior cyclists showed that they did not differ from ordinary boys of the same age with respect to height or weight, but they were significantly leaner. The vital capacity (VC) was significantly higher compared with both ordinary boys (Rutenfranz et al., 1981) and boys playing soccer at a competitive level using the same amount of time for training but with a slightly lower $\dot{V}O_2max$ (ml • kg^{-1} • min^{-1}; Andersen, Froberg, & Lammert, 1983). From the age of 15.6 to 16.6 years, the VC increased more than expected compared with the height gain. There was an average increase of 0.6 l against an expected calculated increase of 0.12 l using the Asmussen and Heebøll-Nielsen regression (1955). Similar changes in VC in this age group were also found in swimmers (Åstrand et al., 1963; Newman, Smalley, & Thomson, 1961). The increase was attributed to the breath-hold procedures associated with swimming and to the increased hydrostatic pressure, which presumably results in increased strength and endurance capacity of the respiratory muscles. Lange-Andersen et al. (1984) concluded that after the peak height velocity period (PHV), the rate of lung volume increase was relatively greater than the rate of increase in body height, but they also stated that the growth in lung volume was entirely due to growth in body dimensions with no additional effect of changes in the development of physical performance capacity. Based on the present results, which are in agreement with results from Sundberg and Elovainio (1982), the very high increase in VC must be attributed to the strenuous training for this type of competitive event, resulting in a very high degree of ventilatory stress.

The results also indicated that it is necessary even at the early age of 15 years to have a very high maximal oxygen consumption (ml • kg^{-1} • min^{-1}), a value comparable to adult male elite road cyclists (Faria, 1984; Sjøgaard, 1984). During 1 year there were only small variations in $\dot{V}O_2max$ in the group. After a detraining period there was no significant decrease in $\dot{V}O_2max$ expressed in l • min^{-1}. Expressed in ml • kg^{-1} • min^{-1}, the decrease was 4.2% caused by an increase in weight, which was the result of a height and fat gain. These detraining results agreed with results from Sjøgaard (1984), who measured $\dot{V}O_2max$ in elite cyclists four times a year, as well as with results from Henriksson and Reitman (1977). But they conflicted with results from Coyle et al. (1984); Klausen, Andersen, and Pelle (1981); and Houston, Bentzen, and Larsen (1979). Coyle et al. (1984) found a decrease per week of detraining of about 2% in $\dot{V}O_2max$. This should have given a decrease in $\dot{V}O_2max$ of 10% to 12% in the present study. The decrease in $\dot{V}O_2max$ was linked to a decrease in stroke volume (SV) and max $(a\text{-}\bar{v})O_2$ difference. Children do not have the same increase or decrease in max $(a\text{-}\bar{v})O_2$ difference caused by training or detraining as adults (Eriksson, 1972). That is perhaps still the case for 15- to 16-year-old well-trained youngsters. The decrease in

$\dot{V}O_2$max would then mainly be linked to a decrease in SV, and the decrease in SV is slow (Saltin & Rowell, 1980). A disturbing factor could be that the boys were still growing.

Despite the lack of a decrease in $\dot{V}O_2$max, there was a pronounced decrease in the effect at LT4 mmol, measured in both watts and W • kg^{-1}. The decreases were 18% and 21%, respectively. The LT4 mmol is correlated with several important characteristics of the active muscles: the percentage of slow twitch fibers (Farrell, Wilmore, Coyle, Billing, & Costill, 1979; Sjödin & Jacobs, 1981; Tesch, Sharp, & Daniels, 1981), capillary density (Jacobs, Schéle, & Sjödin, 1983; Tesch et al., 1981), respiratory capacity (Ivy, Withers, Van Handel, Elger, & Costill, 1980), and the activities of key oxidative and glycolytic enzymes in skeletal muscles (Sjödin, Jacobs, & Svedenhag, 1982). The only process that changes relatively fast and therefore could account for a great deal of change in a few weeks is the last process—the activities of key oxidative and glycolytic enzymes. Henriksson and Reitman (1977) have found that the half-life of cytochrome oxidase is about 5 days, and the half-life obtained for SDH activity is at least 2 to 3 times longer than that of cytochrome oxidase. Because there was no decrease in the $\dot{V}O_2$max in the detraining period, the results confirm the hypothesis that the oxidative capacity in the local muscles is not the limiting factor determining the subject's maximal capacity to utilize oxygen.

The effect at LT4 mmol, when the junior cyclists were most fit in July, averaged 287 W, or 4.65 W • kg^{-1}. Hess, Hech, Liesen, Olbrecht, and Hollman (1983) and Roth, Pansold, Hasart, Zinner, and Gabriel (1981) measured in male professional cyclists the effects at LT4 mmol of 317 W and 390 W, respectively. The results from the junior cyclists were 90% and 74% of these male professional cyclists despite similar $\dot{V}O_2$max values (ml • kg^{-1} • min^{-1}). In male professional cyclists comparable to those previously mentioned, who were competitors in the Tour de France, Sjøgaard (1984) measured $\dot{V}O_2$max of 71 ml • kg^{-1} • min^{-1}. This was the same as in these junior cyclists. The professionals had a 10- to 15-year training background and rode their bicycles for more than 20,000 km per year, which far exceeded the junior cyclists' experience of specific training for 3 to 4 years with a yearly training amount of 8,000 to 13,000 km.

Jacobs (1986) stated that the lactate-related variables in every case account for a larger proportion of the variation in endurance exercise performances than other variables determined in the exercise laboratory—including the measurements of $\dot{V}O_2$max. Farrell et al. (1979) found a high correlation between performance in various running distances and the running velocity at LT4 mmol. This was later confirmed by many researchers. Because it is difficult to measure cycling velocity in the laboratory with standard ergometer equipment, a similar correlation has not been shown in cycling. Krebs, Zinkgraf, and Virgilio (1986) have tried to predict performance from selected physiological and training parameters in 35 competitive cyclists. Their data indicate that the role of $\dot{V}O_2$max (ml • kg^{-1} • min^{-1}) is less important, whereas experience is more important. They did not use lactate-related variables.

In the present study there was no significant correlation between the $\dot{V}O_2max$ and the performance in the junior cyclists. In contrast, the correlation between the lactate-related variables and the performance in a race over 25 km with single start was significant (effect at LT4 mmol) or highly significant ($\dot{V}O_2$ at LT4 mmol in percent of $\dot{V}O_2max$ and effect at LT4 mmol per kilogram body weight). The missing correlation between the $\dot{V}O_2max$ variables and performance is in contrast to nearly all results mentioned by Jacobs (1986). However, using highly trained runners, Conley and Krahenbuhl (1980) demonstrated that correlation of $\dot{V}O_2max$ with performance in a 10-km race was not statistically significant. The time used for a 10-km race in running is comparable with the time used for a 25-km single start in bicycle road racing. Also, Kumagai et al. (1982) found no correlation between $\dot{V}O_2max$ and average speed in a 5-km and a 10-mi run.

The junior cyclists investigated were very similar in $\dot{V}O_2max$ (ml • kg^{-1} • min^{-1}), training background, cycling economy, and performance. The missing significant correlations between $\dot{V}O_2max$ variables and performance may be because variations in cycling ability and $\dot{V}O_2max$ were comparatively smaller than those in other studies mentioned.

The highly significant correlations between the lactate-related variables and performance are perhaps not very surprising. With nearly equal $\dot{V}O_2max$ and cycling economy, the cyclists with the ability to work at the highest fraction of their $\dot{V}O_2max$ without producing excess lactate in the body will be able to produce the highest mechanical effect over time. The correlations between the two lactate variables were marked (r = .68, $p < .01$) and confirm this hypothesis. Because of the dimensionally determined correlation between muscular force, and, therefore, mechanical effect, and height and weight (Asmussen & Heebøll-Nielsen, 1955), it might be better to use the effect per kilogram body weight. The correlation between performance and effect per kilogram body weight at LT4 mmol was much higher than the correlation between performance and effect at LT4 mmol (r = .89 and r = .54, respectively).

CONCLUSION

In highly trained 15- to 16-year-old competitive cyclists there is a highly significant correlation between the effect per kilogram body weight at the lactate threshold and performance (mean velocity in a 25-km single start). This makes it possible by a simple laboratory cycle-ergometer test to distinguish performance abilities in a competition among elite cyclists with reasonable accuracy.

In young elite cyclists, it seems possible to increase vital capacity more than expected from height gain. This is presumably attributed to the strenuous training for this type of competitive event. Finally, there seems to be no decrease in $\dot{V}O_2max$ after a 6-week break in the training program, although there is a substantial decrease in the power output at the lactate threshold.

REFERENCES

Andersen, B., Froberg, K., & Lammert, O. (1981). A longitudinal study on physical training of boys 10-16 years of age. In P. Russo & G. Gass (Eds.), *Human adaptation* (pp. 47-57). Australia: The Department of Biological Sciences, Cumberland College of Health Sciences.

Asmussen, E., & Heebøll-Nielsen, K. (1955). A dimensional analysis of physical performance and growth in boys. *Journal of Applied Physiology*, **7**, 593-603.

Åstrand, P.O., Engström, L., Eriksson, B.O., Karlberg, P., Nylander, J., Saltin, B., & Thoren, C. (1963). Girl swimmers. *Acta Paediatrica* (Uppsala), 43-63, (Suppl. 147).

Conley, D.L., & Krahenbuhl, G.S. (1980). Running economy and distance running performance of highly trained athletes. *Medicine and Science in Sports*, **12**, 357-360.

Coyle, E.F., Martin, W.H., III, Sinacore, D.R., Joyner, M.J., Hagberg, J.M., & Holloszy, J.O. (1984). Time course of loss of adaptations after stopping prolonged intense endurance training. *Journal of Applied Physiology*, **57**(6), 1857-1864.

Daniels, J.T., Yarbrough, R.A., & Foster, C. (1978). Changes in $\dot{V}O_2max$ and running performance with training. *European Journal of Applied Physiology*, **39**, 249-254.

Davis, J.A. (1985). Anaerobic threshold: Review of the concept and directions for future research. *Medicine and Science in Sports and Exercise*, **17**(1), 6-18.

Durnin, J.V.G.A., & Womersley, J. (1974). Body fat assessed from total body density and its estimation from skinfold thickness: Measurements on 481 men and women aged from 16 to 72 years. *British Journal of Nutrition*, **32**, 77-97.

Eriksson, B.O. (1972). Physical training, oxygen supply and muscle metabolism in 11- to 13-year-old boys. *Acta Physiologica Scandinavica*, 17-19, (Suppl. 384).

Faria, J.E. (1984). Applied physiology of cycling. *Sports Medicine*, **1**, 187-204.

Farrell, P.A., Wilmore, J.H., Coyle, E.F., Billing, J.E., & Costill, D.L. (1979). Plasma lactate accumulation and distance running performance. *Medicine and Science in Sports and Exercise*, **11**, 338-344.

Forster, H.B., Dempsey, J.A., Thomson, J., Vidruk, F., & DoPico, G.A. (1972). Estimation of arterial PO_2, PCO_2, pH and lactate from arterialized venous blood. *Journal of Applied Physiology*, **32**, 134-137.

Henriksson, J., & Reitman, J.S. (1977). Time course of changes in human skeletal muscle succinate dehydrogenase and cytochrome oxidase activities and maximal oxygen uptake with physical activity and inactivity. *Acta Physiologica Scandinavica*, **99**, 91-97.

Hess, G., Hech, H., Liesen, H., Olbrecht, J., & Hollmann, W. (1983). The endurance capacity in well-trained athletes of different disciplines. In H. Hech (Ed.), *Sport, performance and health* (pp. 519-524). Cologne: Deutscher Arzte-Verlag.

Hohorst, J.J. (1970). L - (+) - lactate. Determination with lactatdehydrogenase and NAD. In M.U. Bergmeyer (Ed.), *Methoden der enzymatischen analyse* (2nd ed., pp. 1425-1429). Weinheim: Verlag Chemie.

Houston, M.E., Bentzen, H., & Larsen, H. (1979). Interrelationships between skeletal muscle adaptations and performance as studied by detraining and retraining. *Acta Physiologica Scandinavica*, **105**, 163-170.

Ivy, J.L., Withers, R.T., Van Handel, P.J., Elger, D.H., & Costill, D.L. (1980). Muscle respiratory capacity and fiber types as determinants of the lactate threshold. *Journal of Applied Physiology*, **48**, 523-527.

Jacobs, J. (1986). Blood lactate. Implications for training and sports performance. *Sports Medicine*, **3**, 10-25.

Jacobs, J., Schéle, R., & Sjödin, B. (1983). A single blood lactate determination as an indicator of cycle ergometer endurance capacity. *European Journal of Applied Physiology*, **50**, 355-364.

Klausen, K., Andersen, L.B., & Pelle, J. (1981). Adaptive changes in work capacity, skeletal muscle capillarization and enzyme levels during training and detraining. *Acta Physiologica Scandinavica*, **113**, 9-16.

Krebs, P.S., Zinkgraf, S., & Virgilio, S.J. (1986). Predicting competitive bicycling performance with training and physiological variables. *Journal of Sports Medicine and Physical Fitness*, **26**, 323-330.

Kumagai, S., Tanaka, K., Matsuura, Y., Matsuzaka, A., Hirakoba, K., & Asano, K. (1982). Relationships of the anaerobic threshold with the 5-km, 10-km, and 10-mile races. *European Journal of Applied Physiology*, **49**, 13-23.

Lange-Andersen, K., Rutenfranz, J., Seliger, V., Ilmarinen, J., Berndt, J., Kylian, H., & Ruppel, M. (1984). The growth of lung volumes affected by physical performance capacity in boys and girls during childhood and adolescence. *European Journal of Applied Physiology*, **52**, 380-384.

Mader, A., Liesen, H., Heck, H., Philippi, H., Rost, R., Schürch, R., & Hollman, W. (1976). A judgment of the sport specific endurance capacity in the laboratory. *Sportarzt und Sportmedizin*, **4**, 80-88.

Newman, F., Smalley, B.F., & Thomson, M.L. (1961). A comparison between body size and lung function of swimmers and normal school children. *Journal of Physiology*, **156**, 9.

Roth, V., Pansold, B., Hasart, E., Zinner, J., & Gabriel, B. (1981). The influence of the increase in athletes performance ability on the information from the performance-diagnostic parameters. *Medizin und Sport*, **21**, 326-336.

Rutenfranz, J., Lange-Andersen, K., Seliger, V., Klimmer, F., Berndt, J., & Ruppel, M. (1981). Maximum aerobic power and body composition during the puberty growth period: Similarities and differences between children of two European countries. *European Journal of Pediatrics*, **136**, 123-133.

Saltin, B., & Rowell, L.B. (1980). Functional adaptations to physical activity and inactivity. *Federation Proceedings*, **39**, 1506-1513.

Sjödin, B., & Jacobs, I. (1981). Onset of blood lactate accumulation and marathon running performance. *International Journal of Sports Medicine*, **2**, 23-26.

Sjödin, B., Jacobs, J., & Svedenhag, J. (1982). Changes in onset of blood lactate accumulation (OBLA) and muscle enzymes after training at OBLA. *European Journal of Applied Physiology*, **49**, 45-57.

Sjøgaard, G. (1984). Muscle morphology and metabolic potential in elite road cyclists during a season. *International Journal of Sports Medicine*, **5**, 250-254.

Sundberg, S., & Elovainio, R. (1982). Cardiorespiratory function in competitive endurance runners aged 12-16 years compared with ordinary boys. *Acta Paediatrica Scandinavica*, **71**, 987-992.

Tesch, P.A., Sharp, D.S., & Daniels, W.L. (1981). Influence of fiber type composition and capillary density on onset of blood lactate accumulation. *International Journal of Sports Medicine*, **2**, 252-256.

The Influence of Speed and Strength Characteristics on the Anaerobic Capacity of Adolescent Cyclists

Adalbert Szögy
Institute for Sportsmedicine, Frankfurt, Federal Republic of Germany

Anaerobic capacity, a component of physical work capacity, exerts an important influence on sports performances, especially in track cycling. In road cycling, especially on uphill courses and at the finish of a race, anaerobic capacity can decisively influence the performance of an athlete.

The term *anaerobic capacity*, with its components maximum anaerobic power and anaerobic endurance, is defined as the ability to exert short-term maximum workloads under oxygen deficit conditions. This is influenced by the qualities of speed, strength, and coordination; morphological factors such as muscle mass and percentage of fast twitch fibers; functional factors such as nerve impulse transmission speed, the influence of the biofeedback of proprioceptors, and the utilization of elastic energy; and metabolic factors such as alactacid energy reserves, glycolytic rate, and acidosis tolerance. These factors may be developed to different degrees, from very limited to very high.

Contrary to aerobic capacity, in the assessment of anaerobic capacity there is little tendency for standardization, and therefore a variety of methods for evaluation exist (Bar-Or, Dotan, & Inbar, 1977; Georgescu, 1969; Kindermann, 1984; Margaria, 1966; Simon & Thiesmann, 1985; Szögy & Cherebetiu, 1974).

Using the 1-min anaerobic test introduced in 1974 on a speed-dependent bicycle ergometer at the Institute for Sportsmedicine, Frankfurt, Szögy and Cherebetiu (1974) developed a new test consisting of an alactacid and a lactacid phase based on the following criteria:

1. The subject must be able to adjust the magnitude of the work load.
2. The performance shall be measurable in physical units.
3. It shall permit the assessment of both anaerobic power and anaerobic endurance.
4. In addition to the assessment of anaerobic capacity, it shall also provide for estimation of its potential development.
5. It should be applicable in the laboratory and also in specific field situations (Szögy, 1985).

The aim of this study was to identify the speed and the strength components of anaerobic power to derive supplementary data for an estimate of potential for developing anaerobic power in addition to measuring the current capacity. It is well known that strength may be developed rather easily, but it is quite difficult to develop additional speed.

SUBJECTS AND METHODS

The investigation was performed employing 32 adolescent cyclists, all members of the German Junior National Team. Their mean age was 16.69 ± 0.59 years; the mean body height, 180.66 ± 5.08 cm; and the mean body weight, 73.30 ± 7.71 kg. The anaerobic capacity was determined in the laboratory using a two-phase test. A Universal ergometer produced by Mijnhardt, Odijk, was used as a bicycle ergometer. In the speed-dependent range of this ergometer, the work load increases parabolically with the revolutions per minute (rpm). It is equipped with a switch that permits one to choose work loads of 200, 400, 600, 800, or 1000 W for 100 rpm. For the basic examination a 600-W range was used. This offered a well-balanced relationship between speed and strength demands for these male subjects. The ergometer was equipped with direct-reading instruments of power (W), rpm, and total work performed (J).

The first phase of the test, used to determine maximum anaerobic power, demanded a maximum work load for 15 s produced by a maximum rpm at the 600-W range. During the test, the maximum anaerobic power (W), the maximum rpm, and the total work performed in 15 s (KJ) were noted. The purpose of the 15-s work load was to guarantee a certain lactate production to be used to evaluate alactacid energy reserves. Therefore, blood lactate was determined taking samples from the hyperemized earlobe before the test and 3, 6, and 9 min after the test. A lactate-analyzer-640 produced by Kontron, Eching, was used for these analyses. The resting value was subtracted from the highest lactate value after the test to obtain the Δ-lactate. After recovery periods of 10 min, two additional 5-s maximum tests using the ranges 400 and 800 W for 100 rpm were conducted. The purpose of these supplementary tests was to establish whether the subjects had greater speed or strength qualities. This was evaluated by the percent power and rpm increase or decrease in the 400- and 800-W range compared with the basic 600-W test results.

The highest watt value in these three tests was used as value for the maximum anaerobic power. After a recovery period of 1 hr, the second phase of the test was performed. The purpose of this phase was to assess anaerobic endurance. Therefore, the subject had to reproduce, if possible, the work load of the first phase and continue it for 45 s. In this phase the 600-W range for 100 rpm was used. The total work performed in J was divided by 45 for the calculation of $W \cdot s^{-1}$ for the second phase. This was the value used to assess anaerobic endurance. Before and after the work load, blood lactate was determined. The estimation of the energy involved in anaerobic power and endurance was evaluated by the relationship between the total work performed in the two phases of the test and the energy costs expressed through the Δ-lactate values.

Four different types of relationships may exist between work performed and lactate production:

1. High work, low lactate: characteristic of high energy reserves.
2. Low work, low lactate: characteristic of potential energy reserves, especially in the case of poor motivation during the test.
3. High work, high lactate: characteristic of nearly exhausted energy reserves.
4. Low work, high lactate: characteristic of low energy reserves.

For Phase 1 the alactacid quotient

$$\frac{\text{work 15 s}}{\Delta\text{-La 15 s}}$$

was calculated. A high value is characteristic of high alactacid energy stores and unused lactacid energy reserves.

For Phase 2 of the test the lactacid quotient

$$\frac{\text{work 45 s}}{\Delta\text{-La 45 s}}$$

was determined. A high value is characteristic of high alactacid energy stores or a high aerobic rate during the 45-s work load with lactacid energy reserves still present. The mean values were used as a reference for high or low values of the total work performed and the Δ-lactate in the 32 subjects. Comparisons between groups were made using students' *t* tests for independent samples.

RESULTS AND DISCUSSION

In the supplementary examinations of maximum anaerobic power, the 32 adolescent cyclists were divided into three groups to estimate speed or strength characteristics (Table 1). The first group, consisting of 6 subjects, showed a well-balanced relationship between speed and strength characteristics. This group also showed the highest anaerobic power of 1,141.00 ± 1.52 W and 14.40 ± 1.86 W • kg^{-1}. The second group of 16 subjects showed primarily strength qualities. Their maximum anaerobic power was lower, 1,035.50 ± 111.02 W and 14.12 ± 1.52 W • kg^{-1}. The third group of 10 subjects with greater speed characteristics showed the poorest anaerobic power with 913.20 ± 140.22 W and 13.17 ± 1.91 W • kg^{-1}. The differences among the absolute values of the maximum anaerobic power for the three groups were statistically significant.

Table 1 Mean Values of Age, Body Height (BH), Body Weight (BW), and Anaerobic Capacity in Adolescent Cyclists With Different Speed (Sp) and Strength (St) Characteristics ($N = 32$)

Nr Group	n	Age (y)	BH (cm)	BW (kg)	$Watt_{max}$	$Watt_{max} \cdot kg^{-1}$	$Watt_{45S}$	$Watt_{45S} \cdot kg^{-1}$
	x	16.67	182.33	79.38	1,141.00	14.40	658.17	8.30
1 Sp = St	6							
	s	±0.52	±6.77	±10.64	±104.41	±1.86	±81.22	±0.62
	x	16.75	180.75	73.52	1,035.50	14.12	569.06	7.73
2 Sp < St	16							
	s	±0.68	±4.48	±6.48	±111.02	±1.52	±95.33	±1.02
	x	16.60	179.50	69.28	913.20	13.17	549.40	7.94
3 Sp > St	10							
	s	±0.52	±5.15	±5.43	±140.22	±1.91	±63.28	±0.83
Differences	1-2	NS	NS	NS	*	NS	NS	NS
	1-3 p	NS	NS	*	**	NS	**	NS
	2-3	NS	NS	NS	*	NS	NS	NS

$p > .05$ = NS. *$p < .05$. **$p < .01$.

Table 2 Mean Values of Anaerobic Variables Used for Estimation of Potential in Adolescent Cyclists With Different Speed (Sp) and Strength (St) Characteristics (N = 32)

Nr Group	n	$Work_{15S}$ (KJ)	Δ-La_{15S} (mmol/l)	AlQ	$Type_{1-2}$ (%)	$Work_{45S}$ (KJ)	Δ-La_{45S} (mmol/l)	LaQ	$Type_{1-2}$ (%)
	x	13.60	7.49	1.92		29.62	10.37	2.89	
1 Sp = St	6				33.4				16.7
	s	±1.82	±2.35	±0.47		±3.66	±1.71	±0.37	
	x	10.94	5.29	2.43		25.61	8.49	3.24	
2 Sp < St	16				56.2				68.8
	s	±1.69	±2.29	±1.01		±4.29	±2.72	±0.93	
	x	11.21	5.34	2.25		24.95	8.94	3.08	
3 Sp > St	10				70.0				50.0
	s	±1.59	±1.89	±0.56		±2.42	±2.81	±1.12	
Differences	1-2	**	NS	NS		NS	NS	NS	
in p	1-3	*	*	NS	—	**	NS	NS	—
	2-3	NS	NS	NS		NS	NS	NS	

$p > .05$ = NS. *$p < .05$. **$p < .01$.

Concerning anaerobic endurance, Group 1, with a balanced relationship between speed and strength, also showed the highest values: 658.17 ± 81.22 W and 8.30 ± 0.62 W • kg^{-1}. This group was followed by those with primarily strength characteristics of 569.06 ± 95.33 W and 7.73 ± 1.02 W • kg^{-1}, and the speed group was third with 549.40 ± 63.08 W and 7.94 ± 0.83 W • kg^{-1}.

The influence of the strength and speed characteristics on anaerobic endurance was not as decisive as in the case of anaerobic power. A statistically significant difference among the absolute values was found only between Groups 1 and 3.

Concerning the potential for increasing anaerobic capacity, the best opportunity to improve the measured values existed for the subjects who possessed speed but were deficient in strength. It is well known that speed is difficult to develop, but strength can be increased relatively easily. The subjects with basic speed characteristics already present also have a favorable potential for development of anaerobic power. Their alactacid and lactacid quotients are relatively high, and 70% of them were in Type 1 and 2 categories of the potential for developing anaerobic power. The percentage concerning anaerobic endurance was lower, only 50%.

Although the subjects with primarily strength characteristics presented poorer potential, they still may improve their anaerobic capacity. These subjects present the highest alactacid and lactacid quotients, and high percentages fall into the Type 1 and 2 categories for potential energy development, especially for anaerobic endurance.

The subjects with the well-balanced relationship between speed and strength characteristics have the poorest potential for improving their anaerobic capacity. Their high values of anaerobic power and endurance, low alactacid and lactacid quotients, and small percentages in Type 1 and 2 categories for potential energy development show that they have almost reached the maximum of their anaerobic capacity and nearly exhausted their energetic stores during short-term, high work loads (Table 2).

The value determined for the actual and the potential anaerobic capacity represent, together with the corresponding variables of aerobic capacity, useful selection criteria for scouting talent and at the same time offer efficient data for training guidance in sports medicine.

REFERENCES

Bar-Or, O., Dotan, R., & Inbar, O. (1977). A 30 s all-out ergometric test—its reliability and validity for anaerobic capacity (Abstract). *Israel Journal of Medical Science,* **13**, 326-327.

Georgescu, M. (1969). A method for assessment of physical work capacity and some motorial parameters during hard and short-term workloads. *Sportarzt und Sportmedizin,* **20**, 25-31, 61-67.

Kindermann, W. (1984). Treadmill ergometry and performance diagnostics in top-class sport. In I.-W. Franz, H. Mellerowicz, & W. Noack (Eds.),

Training and sport for prevention and rehabilitation in the technicized environment (pp. 68-80). Berlin-Heidelberg: Springer.

Margaria, R. (1966). Assessment of physical activity in oxidative and anaerobic maximal exercise. *Internationale Zeitschrift für angewandte Physiologie*, **22**, 115-124.

Simon, G., & Thiesmann, M. (1985). Assessment of the aerobic and anaerobic capacity in swimmers. In N. Bachl, P. Baumgartl, G. Huber, & J. Keul (Eds.), *Importance in training physiology and clinical importance of anaerobic capacity* (pp. 308-316). Vienna: Hollinek.

Szögy, A. (1985). Contributions concerning anaerobic power testing in athletes. In N. Bachl, P. Baumgartl, G. Huber, & J. Keul (Eds.), *Importance in training physiology and clinical importance of anaerobic capacity* (pp. 80-91). Vienna: Hollinek.

Szögy, A., & Cherebetiu, G. (1974). A 1-minute test on the bicycle ergometer for assessment of anaerobic capacity. *European Journal of Applied Physiology*, **33**, 171-176.

Body Build and Running Performances of Obese and Lean Adolescent Boys

János Mészáros
János Mohácsi
Anna Farkas
Róbert Frenkl
Hungarian University of Physical Education, Budapest, Hungary

Obesity, when not attributable to endocrine dysfunctions, is basically due to poor dietary habits and inappropriate lifestyles. Hereditary predisposition to obesity, though unquestionable, becomes manifest only when it is associated with the previously mentioned factors. There is a growing public interest in diets and camps advertising weight reduction because there are a great number of overweight adults in Hungary. An even greater concern is that there are too many obese children and adolescents. The relationship between the two factors seems obvious because habits acquired in childhood governing diet and lifestyle generally become somewhat permanent.

Thus the question was not whether there were too many obese children, as this was a fact; rather, the purpose of this study was to compare the body builds and certain motor potentials of adolescents with high, medium, and low percentages of body fat. Though comparisons will not solve this problem, they may arouse attention to the fact that there are a number of endangered children for whom physical education and sports, with their specific goals, may still be vehicles for some protection against obesity.

MATERIAL AND METHODS

The data were collected in 32 general schools in Hungary. Both urban and rural schools were among those selected. The present investigation included 721 adolescents for whom 11 variables were obtained and group means were calculated. The variables were as follows:

1. Chronological age (also used as a grouping criterion).
2. Morphological age as a workable estimate of biological age, estimated by the Mészáros method (Mészáros, Mohácsi, Szabó, & Szmodis,

1985), utilizing measurements of height, body mass, biacromial distance, lower arm girth, and hand circumference).
3. Standing height.
4. Body mass.
5. Body fat expressed as percent of body mass employing Pařízková's (1961) skinfold tables for children (this value was the second criterion of groups).
6. Body fat (for comparative purposes) estimated by Siri's (1956) formula inputting body density obtained by the Durnin and Rahaman (1967) technique.
7. Metric index, which was developed by Strömgren and used by Conrad (1963) to obtain a measure of scaling the leptomorph-pyknomorph axis (more negative values depict leptomorph body build, whereas slightly negative and positive values point to pyknomorph build). In this system of two indices, metric index is the constitutional axis of the growth type. To calculate it the regression formula of Szmodis, Mészáros, and Szabó (1976) was used.
8. Plastic index, which Conrad (1963) defined as a measure of robustness or muscle-bone development calculated by summing biacromial width and lower arm and hand circumferences.
9. A 60-m dash to estimate agility.
10. An 800-m run to estimate medium distance endurance.
11. Cooper's run-walk test to estimate cardiorespiratory endurance.

By using calendar age and percentage of body fat, we formed three groups. Adolescents with a fat content exceeding 25% were Group 1, those under 10% were Group 2, and Group 3 consisted of those with 10% to 25% body fat. Intergroup means were subjected to ANOVA and tested at 5% level of significance by the *F* test.

RESULTS AND DISCUSSION

Group means and *SD*s of the body dimensions and motor test scores, as well as the results of ANOVA, are tabulated in Table 1 for 13-year-olds and in Table 2 for 14-year-olds. As groupings were made according to age (nominal age ± 0.50 years), age means were equal. There were, however, marked differences in morphological age: Lean boys were younger, whereas obese ones were older, than their calendar age. There was a difference of 0.50 to 1.20 years between their morphological ages. This observation did not appear to be sample dependent, because Beunen et al. (1982), analyzing the bone age of Belgian youth, reported similar findings. Additional evidence was found in analyzing age data in adolescent girls (Mészáros, Frenkl, Szmodis, & Farkas, 1986).

The explanation is quite plausible when approaching the problem from the standpoint of diet; the observation that the amount and frequency of food intake influences body development is not new (Király, 1925). An analogous finding was the intergroup difference in stature. Data on

Table 1 Means and Standard Deviations of the Observed Variables in Adolescent Boys, Aged 13 Years

Variable	Under 10% $\bar{x}$	Under 10% s	Over 25% $\bar{x}$	Over 25% s	10%-25% $\bar{x}$	10%-25% s	Overall $\bar{x}$	Overall s	F
CA (yr)	13.10	0.26	13.04	0.22	13.10	0.22	13.09	0.22	0
MA (yr)	12.22	0.91	13.43	0.58	13.01	0.76	12.99	0.80	+
ST (cm)	154.89	5.40	160.10	6.66	156.01	8.29	156.38	8.02	+
BM (kg)	38.23	7.17	60.33	10.00	45.05	8.64	46.23	10.21	+
FP (%)	8.19	1.45	28.98	2.63	16.13	3.87	16.94	6.03	+
FS (%)	9.34	1.71	30.23	2.80	16.75	3.85	17.67	6.11	+
MI	−1.66	0.19	−0.87	0.32	−1.40	0.31	−1.36	0.36	+
PI (cm)	71.70	3.18	77.32	3.99	74.35	3.64	74.47	3.84	+
60 (s)	9.80	0.79	10.87	1.01	9.84	0.75	9.95	0.85	+
800 (s)	147.52	29.35	165.89	37.57	145.28	35.11	156.83	37.28	+
CO (min)	2,585.71	308.77	2,144.40	334.98	2,436.33	343.72	2,415.43	355.02	+
n	26		39		252		317		

Note. CA = chronological age; MA = morphological age; ST = stature; BM = body mass; FP = percentage of body fat calculated by Pařízková's method; FS = percentage of body fat calculated by Siri's method; MI = metric index; PI = plastic index; 60 = 60-m dash; 800 = 800-m run; CO = Cooper's 12-min run-walk test; n = number of subjects in the subgroups.

body mass were included merely for further information as they were closely related to one of the grouping criteria, percent body fat.

In addition to the two techniques of estimating body fat (Pařízková, 1961; Siri, 1956), the number of subjects in the respective groups deserves attention. By using the conditions of grouping already described, we discovered that 10% of the sample belonged to the group of obese children and only 6% belonged to the lean group. This rate of occurrence is obviously too large. When one takes the rate of those who exceeded the plus one standard deviation in percentage of body fat from the overall means, this, too, shows an excessive number of ''well-nourished'' children. It was also stated that the distribution of the sample with respect to percent of body fat was likely to deviate from the normal distribution in that it was slightly skewed toward the fat end as shown by the range test.

The indices of the growth type reflected a pyknomorph and hyperplastic build of the obese children in both age groups and a leptomorph and slightly hypoplastic build in the lean children. Thus, enumerated among the factors predisposing these children to obesity are not only an inactive lifestyle and incorrect dietary habits, but also the pyknic constitution. Fat stores affect, only negligibly if at all, the accuracy of measuring stature,

Table 2 Means and Standard Deviations of the Observed Variables in Adolescent Boys, Aged 14 Years

Variable	Under 10% $\bar{x}$	Under 10% s	Over 25% $\bar{x}$	Over 25% s	10%-25% $\bar{x}$	10%-25% s	Overall $\bar{x}$	Overall s	F
CA (yr)	13.91	0.24	13.95	0.30	14.04	0.29	14.03	0.29	0
MA (yr)	13.78	0.56	14.31	0.84	13.93	0.86	13.96	0.85	+
ST (cm)	160.19	7.43	164.94	7.42	163.41	8.71	163.39	8.57	+
BM (kg)	43.85	5.04	64.92	10.41	51.40	9.74	52.23	10.52	+
FP (%)	8.73	0.95	28.58	2.94	16.08	3.51	16.83	5.24	+
FS (%)	9.97	1.41	30.19	3.06	16.90	3.70	17.66	5.50	+
MI	−1.55	0.24	−0.87	0.35	−1.38	0.38	−1.34	0.40	+
PI (cm)	76.46	3.25	81.47	4.59	78.37	4.01	78.55	4.14	+
60 (s)	9.63	0.73	10.88	1.33	9.85	0.68	9.93	0.82	+
800 (s)	146.88	29.95	166.54	38.11	154.02	31.65	156.94	34.58	+
CO (min)	2,560.00	302.05	2,038.55	486.26	2,499.02	437.13	2,461.01	455.02	+
n	20		41		343		404		

Note. CA = chronological age; MA = morphological age; ST = stature; BM = body mass; FP = percentage of body fat calculated by Pařízková's method; FS = percentage of body fat calculated by Siri's method; MI = metric index; PI = plastic index; 60 = 60-m dash; 800 = 800-m run; CO = Cooper's 12-min run–walk test; n = number of subjects in the subgroups.

chest width, and chest depth used to produce the metric index. That means that the classification of pyknomorphy did not arise from obesity.

This type of physique also offers some explanation concerning some of the demonstrated results. The course of maturation has been reported to be a function of physique (Bodzsár, 1975). Pápai (1985) found significant differences in relative fatness and leanness between early and late maturing girls. The findings of the present study of size differences between lean and fat groups agree with the report of Beunen et al. (1982); that is, the main reasons for the differences should be sought in the differences in maturation levels. For instance, the fat subjects were taller because they were biologically older. Indeed, the stature of the obese children approached the standards corresponding to their morphological age (Mészáros & Mohácsi, 1983).

Scores in the motor tests were consistently poorer for the obese groups. However, this is apparently only a trend and is by no means a necessity; rather, poor performance is an outcome of a lack of practice. This negative effect is then further increased when the developed obesity leads to the subject's drawing back from physical exercise or games. There is evidence, however, that markedly obese adolescents can significantly improve their physical and physiological work capacity with training (Pena, Barta, Regöly-Mérei, Simon, & Gedeon, 1980; Pena, Blanco, & Padrón, 1982). A combination of physical activity and dietary control—not weight loss, because it was suggested (Lángffy, 1984) that during intense development it would be unreasonable to reduce weight—can decrease the amount of stored fat. Such therapy is highly recommended because these children, though not yet ill, are endangered. Prokopec (1980) is of the opinion that obese children will become obese adults, and in a number of instances this is already more than a simple risk factor; it can underlie several forms of organic disease.

In conclusion, it seems essential to emphasize that the sample was classified into subgroups according to the previously mentioned criteria. Even though it was not a representative sample, it was found to be very similar in body dimensions, percent body fat, and indices to other large samples of the country (Mészáros & Mohácsi, 1983; Mészáros, Szmodis, & Mohácsi, 1979; Mohácsi & Mészáros, 1981). In view of this fact it is likely that the overall occurrence of stoutness and obesity is considerably high among Hungarian youth. Reducing this trend is a well-justified goal of society and a precondition of health, which should be created in ways other than through medicine in the coming generations.

REFERENCES

Beunen, G., Malina, R.M., Ostyn, M., Renson, R., Simons, J., & Van Gerven, D. (1982). Fatness and skeletal maturity of Belgian boys 12 through 17 years of age. *American Journal of Physical Anthropology*, **59**, 387-392.

Bodzsár, E.B. (1975). Data to puberty of girls. *Humanbiologia Budapestinensis*, **3**, 13-174.

Conrad, K. (1963). *Der Konstitutionstypus* [Type of physical constitution]. Berlin: Springer.

Durnin, J.V.G.A., & Rahaman, M.A. (1967). The assessment of the amount of body fat in the human body from measurement of the skinfold thickness. *British Journal of Nutrition*, **21**, 681-689.

Király, D. (1925). *Growth relationships in school children of Kispest Deák Ferenc Áll. Reálgimnázium* (in Hungarian). Budapest: Springer.

Lángffy, Gy. (1984). Body weight control. In R. Frenkl (Ed.), *Sportorvostan* [Sportsmedicine] (pp. 189-202). Budapest: Sport.

Mészáros, J., Frenkl, R., Szmodis, I., & Farkas, A. (1986). Physical performance and body fat content of adolescent girls (in Hungarian). *MÉT LI*. Vándorgyülése, Elóadáskivonatok, Keszthely: E 50.

Mészáros, J., & Mohácsi, J. (1983). *Estimation of biological maturity and prognosis of adult stature using the growth curves of urban youth* (in Hungarian). Unpublished doctoral dissertation, Hungarian Academy of Sciences, Budapest.

Mészáros, J., Mohácsi, J., Szabó, T., & Szmodis, I. (1985). Assessment of biological development by anthropometric variables. In R.A. Binkhorst, H.C.G. Kemper, & W.H.M. Saris (Eds.), *Children and exercise XI* (pp. 341-345). Champaign, IL: Human Kinetics.

Mészáros, J., Szmodis, I., & Mohácsi, J. (1979). The constitutional bases of physical education and sports training. *A Sport és Testnevelés Idöszerü Kérdései: 20* [The recent advances of sport and physical education]. Budapest: Sport.

Mohácsi, J., & Mészáros, J. (1981). Changes in total body fat content of school children attending normal and physical education classes (in Hungarian). Budapest: Müvelödésügyi Minisztérium Kiadványa.

Pápai, J. (1985). Body development and physique of early and late maturing girls. *Anthropológiai Közlemények* [Anthropological News], **29**, 89-96.

Pařízková, J. (1961). Total body fat and skinfold thickness in children. *Metabolism*, **10**, 794-807.

Pena, M., Barta, L., Regöly-Mérei, A., Simon, G., & Gedeon, E. (1980). Changes in body composition and physical working capacity after high fiber diet and physical training. *Anthropológiai Közlemények* [Anthropological News], **24**, 179-188.

Pena, M., Blanco, J., & Padrón, P. (1982). Physical fitness in obese, nonobese, and specially trained boys. *Anthropológiai Közlemények* [Anthropological News], **26**, 59-67.

Prokopec, M. (1980). Contribution to the genesis of obesity from the aspect of exercise and nutrition during growth and development. *Anthropológiai Közlemények* [Anthropological News], **24**, 189-194.

Siri, W.E. (1956). The gross composition of the body. In J.H. Lawrence & C.A. Tobias (Eds.), *Advances in biological and medical physics* (pp. 239-280). New York: Academic Press.

Szmodis, I., Mészáros, J., & Szabo, T. (1976). Interrelations of dimensional and functional indices in childhood, adolescence, and young age. *Testnevelés- és Sportegészségügyi Szemle* [Hungarian Review of Sports Medicine], **17**, 255-272.

Part II

Body Growth, Working Performance, and Exercise Physiology in Childhood and Adolescence

Sexual Dimorphism in Somatic and Motor Characteristics

Gaston Beunen
Renée Colla
Jan Simons
Albrecht Claessens
Johan Lefevre
Roland Renson
Dirk Van Gerven
Bart Vanreusel
Rita Wellens
Christiane Schueremans
K.U. Leuven, Leuven, Belgium

The question of the sex differences in human characteristics and the underlying factors that explain these differences has been studied extensively (Ghesquiere, Martin, & Newcombe, 1985; Hall, 1982; Khan & Cataio, 1984). It has been taken for granted that mammalian sexual dimorphism typically develops because of selection pressures between males for breeding access to females and in connection with the defense of the social group against predators (Willner & Martin, 1985). Commonly, the assumption is then made that natural selection has favored an increase in the male's body size relative to some unstated hypothetical ancestral condition. This assumption was challenged by Willner and Martin (1985). They give some evidence from the analysis of relative brain size of simian primates that sexual dimorphism has evolved through body size reduction in females. It thus remains open for further debate what the underlying mechanisms are or have been that caused sexual dimorphism in human beings.

Numerous studies have shown that prior to puberty some differences are already present in somatic and motor characteristics of boys and girls. The differences are, however, rather small and the growth patterns nearly parallel each other (Åstrand, 1985; Bailey, 1982; Branta, Haubenstricker, & Seefeldt, 1984; Espenschade, 1960; Krahenbuhl, Skinner, & Kohrt, 1985; Lieberman, 1982; Malina, 1974; Tanner, 1962). Starting at puberty the sex differences are clearly accentuated. On the average, boys become gradually larger in bone lengths and breadths and in muscle size, but smaller in fat mass. Furthermore, boys exceed girls in most cardiovascular and motor performance characteristics.

In present societies, there is a changing attitude toward females participating in sports and more generally in physical activity that could have an effect on their performance capacities, which in turn could reduce the differences between the sexes. Some evidence indeed suggests that over the last decades girls have improved in some of their performance capacities (Branta et al., 1984; Ross, Dotson, Gilbert, & Katz, 1985). Thus it seems of interest to examine the sex differences at regular intervals in order to evaluate the possible changes taking place. The aim of this study was to investigate sex differences in somatic and motor characteristics in 12- to 18-year-old adolescents in representative samples of the Belgian population studied between 1969 and 1980.

METHODS

The data are from two different studies conducted separately on boys and girls. The boys' data are from a mixed longitudinal study of the physical fitness of a representative sample of Belgian school boys, aged 12 to 19 years (Ostyn, Simons, Beunen, Renson, & Van Gerven, 1980). The test program started in 1969 and ended in 1974. A total of 21,052 examinations were made. The girls' data are from a cross-sectional study of the physical fitness of a representative sample of Flemish school girls aged 6 to 19 years (Beunen, Simons, Ostyn, et al., 1982). The test program started in 1979 and ended in 1980. A total of 9,853 examinations were made.

The tests and measurements used in both studies were the same. They were taken under the supervision of the same principal investigators, thus guaranteeing a similarity in all testing and measurement procedures. Before the data were entered into the computer, several data quality controls were executed as described in Ostyn et al. (1980). In both studies, physical fitness was interpreted in a broad sense, which implies that anthropometric dimensions, somatotype, biological maturation, motor performance capacities, and cardiorespiratory fitness tests were included in the test program together with sport participation and an inquiry about the sociocultural background of the family.

In order to identify the similarities and discrepancies between boys and girls during their adolescent period the median values of the girls for each half-year age group were plotted against the percentile charts of the boys as published by Ostyn et al. (1980).

RESULTS

The large number of subjects observed at each age level (see Table 1) guaranteed the external validity of the differences reported hereafter.

Table 1 Number* of Subjects Examined in Each Age Group

Sex	Age groups (years)												
	12.0	12.5	13.0	13.5	14.0	14.5	15.0	15.5	16.0	16.5	17.0	17.5	18.0
	12.5	13.0	13.5	14.0	14.5	15.0	15.5	16.0	16.5	17.0	17.5	18.0	18.5
Boys	889	1402	1611	1751	1580	1697	1522	1585	1340	1317	1128	1076	609
Girls	320	337	390	341	381	376	320	270	322	353	327	289	145

*Depending on the test or measurement, these numbers can vary somewhat.

Figure 1 gives a summary of the sex differences in somatic characteristics that are observed at 13 to 13.5 years (13^+), 15 to 15.5 years (15^+), and 17 to 17.5 years (17^+). The sex differences seen at these three age levels give a good representation of the differences and the changes in these differences that occurred during the whole adolescent period from 12 through 18.5 years. At 13^+ years girls had larger body dimensions than boys for weight; standing height; sitting height; thigh, calf, and flexed upper arm circumferences; and all subcutaneous skinfolds.

With increasing age the adult sex differences gradually became apparent. At 15^+ years, girls had smaller dimensions for all body measurements except circumferences and skinfolds. At 17^+ years these differences were still more accentuated. For weight, body lengths, and breadths, the medians of the girls were situated at or below the 10th percentile value of the boys. Only for thigh circumference and skinfolds did girls show higher medians than boys. The differences were striking, especially for skinfolds on the limbs, so that the medians of the girls were situated above the 90th percentile value of the boys.

For performance capacities girls exceeded boys at each age level for flexibility (sit and reach). In all other performance tests, the medians of the girls coincided or fell below the medians of the boys. It is also clear that with increasing age the performance capacities of girls became more and more inferior to those of the boys. At 13^+ years girls performed better than boys in flexibility (sit and reach), trunk strength (leg lifts), and running speed (shuttle run). For the other tests the girls' median performances were situated between 10th and 50th percentiles of the boys (see Figure 2). At 15^+ years and 17^+ years, the boys surpassed the girls in all performance capacities except for flexibility (sit and reach). The poorest performance capacities were observed for explosive strength (vertical jump), static strength (arm pull), and functional strength (bent arm hang). For these tests the girls' medians were situated below the 10th percentile of the medians for the boys.

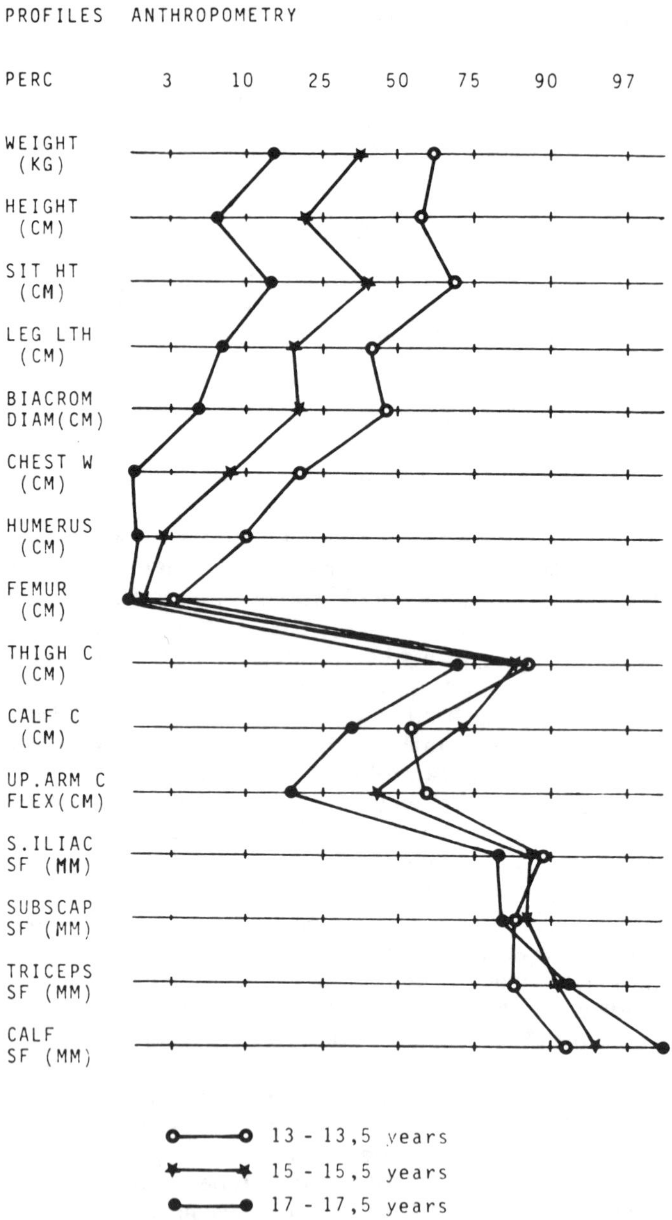

Figure 1. Median anthropometric dimensions of 13⁺-, 15⁺-, 17⁺-year-old girls situated within the percentile charts of boys of the respective age levels.

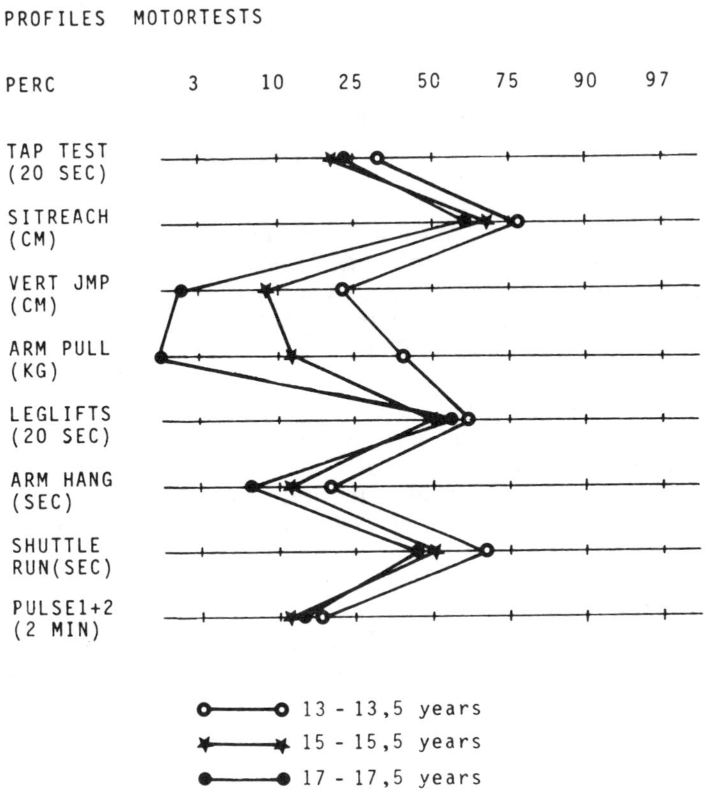

Figure 2. Median motor characteristics of 13^+-, 15^+-, 17^+-year-old girls situated within the percentile charts of boys of the respective age levels.

DISCUSSION

Tanner (1962) has given a detailed description of the size and shape changes that take place during growth and of the sex differences that gradually appear during this process. These differences were further documented and reviewed (Bailey, 1982; Leiberman, 1982; Malina, 1974). The present findings correspond closely with those previously reported. At the beginning of the adolescent growth spurt in boys, the body dimensions of girls were on the average larger than those of boys for lengths, circumferences, and skinfolds. This size advantage is explained mainly by the advanced maturity of the girls. Thereafter, boys grew faster and their body dimensions became larger than those of the girls except for skinfolds and thigh circumferences. For lengths, bone breadths, and trunk widths, the medians of 17^+-year-old girls fell below the 10th percentile value of the boys. For skinfolds, the medians of the girls were situated above the 75th percentile and even above the 90th percentile for limb skinfolds. Circumferences of the upper arm and calf were smaller in girls. These differences reflect not only muscle development but also the larger subcutaneous skinfolds in girls, which is why girls have larger thigh circumferences.

It is also tempting to draw conclusions about the sex differences in body shape based on the relative position of the medians of different body dimensions in the reference values of the boys. However, with increasing age the interrelations of the body dimensions change, and drawing conclusions from the graphs presented here would be premature. A multivariate analysis would be more appropriate.

At the onset of the boys' pubertal spurt, girls performed better than boys in flexibility (sit and reach), trunk strength (leg lifts), and running speed (shuttle run). Except for flexibility (sit and reach), this superiority disappeared, and at 15^{+} years girls performed less well in nearly all motor items. The performance capacity of 17^{+}-year-old girls in three of the four strength measurements fell below the 10th percentile value of boys. This sex difference in strength can be mainly explained by the larger muscle mass of boys (Åstrand, 1985). Again, these findings correspond to what has been reported previously (Branta et al., 1984; Espenschade, 1960; Malina, 1974).

However, as already observed by Branta et al. (1984) and Ross et al. (1985), girls continued to improve in certain performance capacities until the end of the adolescent period. Flemish girls improved their physical performance capacities until 16.0 to 18 years for speed of limb movement (plate tapping), running speed (shuttle run), and the four strength measurements—static strength (arm pull), explosive strength (vertical jump), functional strength (bent arm hang), and trunk strength (leg lifts) (Beunen, Simons, Lefevre, et al.). This observation contradicts Espenschade's (1960) report that after 11 to 12 years of age, girls tend to reach a plateau in motor performance. Whether this changing pattern in motor development reflects changing attitudes toward sports and physical activity for girls or a corresponding change in their physical activities needs to be further investigated and documented.

The improvement in motor performance until late adolescence in girls implies a positive secular trend in their performance capacities. Secular change data for muscular strength and physical performance are largely limited to measures of strength of grip, running, and jumping (Malina, 1984). Furthermore, the period of time over which secular comparisons of strength and performance can be made is generally limited. Finally, the following limitations and assumptions need to be considered: the sampling procedures, reliability of tests, age grouping, testing techniques, and procedures. From his review, Malina (1984) concluded that there is evidence for a secular improvement in strength but that secular changes in running, jumping, and throwing are minimal. When improvement is present, it often parallels secular changes in size. The studies reported by Malina (1984) were conducted before 1970, hence an analysis of the performance capacities over the last decades seems to be needed. The problem is, however, that no such data are available for representative samples of the Belgian population.

Acknowledgments

The Leuven growth study of Belgian boys was conducted with the financial support of the Administrations of Sport, Physical Education, and Open Air Activities (BLOSO and ADEPS) of the Ministry of Nederlandse Kultuur and the Ministry of Culture Française, the administration of Social Medicine of the Ministry of Public Health, and the Foundation of Medical Scientific Research. The Leuven growth study of Flemish girls was conducted with the financial support of the Ministry of Labour, the Belgian Olympic and Interfederal Committee, and Siemens N.V.

REFERENCES

Åstrand, P.O. (1985). Sexual dimorphism in exercise and sport. In J. Ghesquiere, R.D. Martin, & F. Newcombe (Eds.), *Human sexual dimorphism. Symposia of the Society for the Study of Human Biology,* **24** (pp. 247-256). London: Taylor & Francis.

Bailey, S.M. (1982). Absolute and relative sex differences in body composition. In R.L. Hall (Ed.), *Sexual dimorphism in homo sapiens* (pp. 263-316). New York: Praeger.

Beunen, G., Simons, J., Lefevre, J., Claessens, A., Renson, R., Van Gerven, D., Ostyn, M., Vanreusel, B., Wellens, R., Colla, R., & Schueremans, C. *Somatic growth and physical fitness development*. Unpublished manuscript.

Beunen, G., Simons, J., Ostyn, M., Renson, R., Van Gerven, D., Claessens, A., Vanreusel, B., Colla, R., & Schueremans, C. (1982). The Leuven growth study of Flemish girls: Study design and data quality control. In J. Simons & R. Renson (Eds.), *Evaluation of motor fitness* (pp. 59-75). Leuven: Institute of Physical Education.

Branta, C., Haubenstricker, J., & Seefeldt, V. (1984). Age changes in motor skills during childhood and adolescence. *Exercise and Sports Sciences Reviews,* **12**, 467-520.

Espenschade, A. (1960). Motor development. In W.R. Johnson (Ed.), *Science and medicine of exercise and sport* (pp. 419-439). New York: Harper.

Ghesquiere, J., Martin, R.D., & Newcombe, F. (Eds.). (1985). *Human sexual dimorphism. Symposia of the Society for the Study of Human Biology,* **24**, London: Taylor & Francis.

Hall, R.L. (Ed.) (1982). *Sexual dimorphism in homo sapiens*. New York: Praeger.

Khan, A.V., & Cataio, J. (1984). *Men and women in biological perspective*. New York: Praeger.

Krahenbuhl, G.S., Skinner, J.S., & Kohrt, W.M. (1985). Developmental aspects of maximal aerobic power in children. *Exercise and Sport Sciences Reviews*, **13**, 503-538.

Lieberman, L.S. (1982). Normal and abnormal sexual dimorphic patterns of growth and development. In R.L. Hall (Ed.), *Sexual dimorphism in homo sapiens* (pp. 263-316). New York: Praeger.

Malina, R.M. (1974). Adolescent changes in size, build, composition and performance. *Human Biology*, **46**, 117-131.

Malina, R.M. (1984). Secular changes in strength and physical performance. *Studies in Human Ecology*, **6**, 73-91.

Ostyn, M., Simons, J., Beunen, G., Renson, R., & Van Gerven, D. (1980). *Somatic and motor development of Belgian secondary school boys. Norms and standards*. Leuven: Leuven University Press.

Ross, J.G., Dotson, C.O., Gilbert, G.G., & Katz, S.J. (1985). Maturation and fitness test performance. *Journal of Physical Education, Recreation and Dance*, **56**, 67-69.

Tanner, J.M. (1962). *Growth at adolescence*. Oxford: Blackwell.

Willner, L.A., & Martin, R.D. (1985). Some basic principles of mammalian sexual dimorphism. In J. Ghesquiere, R.D. Martin, & F. Newcombe (Eds.), *Human sexual dimorphism. Symposia of the Society for the Study of Human Biology*, **24** (pp. 1-42). London: Taylor & Francis.

A Longitudinal Study of the Growth of Boys From 11 to 16 Years of Age

David A. Brodie
University of Liverpool, Liverpool, England

P.J. Atkinson
J.M.H. Buckler
L. Burkinshaw
A. Laughland
G.W. Reed
University of Leeds, Leeds, England

The initial stimulus for this investigation was an interest in the physical performance and the physiological development of schoolboys during adolescence. In this study as many quantities as possible were measured that seemed relevant to adolescent growth and physical performance and that could be achieved within the available human and physical resources, but this article includes only the measurements of body mass, surface anthropometry, and certain derived measures such as fat-free mass. This article concentrates on the values and interrelationships at the onset of the study (the initial values) and 5 years later (the final values). It also provides the opportunity to establish the viability of the prediction of values over a period of 5 years.

METHODS

Healthy, Caucasian schoolboys (N = 39) entered the study. The consent of the subjects and their parents was previously obtained after full explanation of the procedures involved. The investigation was approved by the Research Ethics Committee of the General Infirmary at Leeds and the Educational Authorities of Leeds City Council. On entry, in 1975, ages ranged from 10.13 to 11.40 years (mean age 10.85 years). All the boys were members of the same form in a middle school in Leeds, England, and were involved in the same pattern of school activities.

The subjects reported three times per year, for 5 years, at intervals of approximately 4 months. At each visit the subjects were weighed in light clothing without shoes. Standing and sitting heights were measured, and subischial leg length was calculated by subtracting the latter from the former. Biacromial and biiliac diameters and the bicondylar widths of the humerus and femur were also measured. The maximum circumferences of the calf and flexed upper arm were measured with a flexible tape, and skinfold measurements were taken at the biceps, triceps, subscapular, and suprailiac sites with a Harpenden caliper. All measurements were carried out as specified by Tanner, Hiernaux, and Jarman (1969). Body density was calculated from the logarithm of the sum of the four skinfold thicknesses by means of an equation derived by Durnin and Rahaman (1967) from measurements made on boys aged 13 to 15 years. The proportion of fat in the body was calculated from body density by a formula given by Siri (1956), and the result was multiplied by body weight to give the mass of fat in the body; fat-free mass was found by subtracting the mass of fat from body weight. Pubertal staging was according to the descriptions of Tanner (1962) and based on pubic hair and genital development.

Means, standard deviations, correlation coefficients, and regression coefficients were computed by the Statistical Package for the Social Sciences (SPSS) on the Amdahl computer of the University of Leeds. To show relative variability, the coefficient of variation (CV) of each measured quantity—that is, the standard deviation expressed as a percentage of the mean—was also calculated.

RESULTS

Initial Values

The means, standard deviations, and coefficients of variation of the initial values are shown in Table 1. Standing height, sitting height, leg length, bone widths, and muscle circumferences conformed approximately to Gaussian distributions. Body weight and fat were more sharply peaked than the Gaussian, and the distribution of body fat was asymmetrical with a preponderance of values above the mode.

The average boy in the sample, on entering the study, weighed 32.5 kg and was found to be made up of 4.7 kg (14.5%) of fat and 27.8 kg of fat-free tissue. Within the sample, both fat and fat-free mass were strongly correlated with body weight ($r = .84$, $p < .001$ and $r = .79$, $p < .001$, respectively). Linear regression analysis showed that, at a given weight, fat and fat-free mass each had a residual standard deviation of 1.05 kg, that is, 24% of mean fat content or 3.8% of mean fat-free mass.

Fat was poorly correlated with skeletal dimensions; only the correlation with the widths of the humerus ($r = .50$, $p < .01$) and femur ($r = .43$, $p < .05$) achieved statistical significance. Fat-free mass, however, was well correlated with all other measures obtained. The correlation coefficients varied from $r = .46$ ($p < .01$) with humeral diameter to $r = .82$ ($p < .001$) with height. At a given height, fat-free mass had a residual standard deviation of 1.3 kg, that is, 4.6% of the mean.

Table 1 Means, Standard Deviations, and Coefficients of Variation of the Initial Values of the Measured Quantities ($N = 34$, Range of Initial Age = 10.13-11.40 Years)

Variable	*M*	*SD*	*CV* (%)
Height (cm)	141.4	4.6	3.3
Sitting height (cm)	75.4	2.2	2.9
Biacromial diameter (cm)	31.6	1.1	3.5
Biiliac diameter (cm)	22.0	0.7	3.2
Humerus width (cm)	5.7	0.3	5.3
Leg length (cm)	66.1	2.9	4.4
Femur width (cm)	8.4	0.4	4.8
Weight (kg)	32.5	3.9	12.0
Fat-free mass (kg)	27.8	2.2	7.9
Arm circumference (cm)	20.7	1.9	9.2
Calf circumference (cm)	27.4	1.8	6.6
Fat (kg)	4.7	2.5	53.2

Table 2 Means, Standard Deviations, and Coefficients of Variation of the Final Values of the Measured Quantities ($N = 34$, Range of Final Age = 14.87-16.09 Years)

Variable	*M*	*SD*	*CV* (%)
Height (cm)	171.9	5.5	3.2
Sitting height (cm)	89.2	3.7	4.1
Biacromial diameter (cm)	38.1	1.7	4.5
Biiliac diameter (cm)	26.3	1.1	4.2
Humerus width (cm)	6.6	0.3	4.5
Leg length (cm)	82.6	3.5	4.2
Femur width (cm)	9.3	0.3	3.2
Weight (kg)	55.7	6.1	11.0
Fat-free mass (kg)	47.7	4.6	9.6
Arm circumference (cm)	26.1	2.0	7.7
Calf circumference (cm)	34.2	2.1	6.1
Fat (kg)	8.0	2.4	30.0

Final Values

The means, standard deviations, and coefficients of variation of the final values at mean age 15.9 years are shown in Table 2. The age range was 14.87 to 16.09 years at this stage of the study.

Changes

The changes in the measured quantities over 5 years are shown in Table 3. The mean changes are given both in the units of measurement and as percentages of the initial mean values together with the standard deviations and coefficients of variation of the changes.

These values compare very favorably with Tanner's standards as calculated from the centile charts in Buckler (1979). The mean percentage increase from age 10.9 to 15.9 years in Tanner's standards differs by only −0.4% in the change in standing height, −0.2% in sitting height, +1.9% in biacromial diameter, +2.3% in biiliac diameter, and −3.2% in leg length. Weight showed the greatest difference between Tanner's standards and the present study, with his boys increasing by 87.6% compared with an increase of only 71.4% in the Leeds group. There was little difference in the values for the initial weights, so it would appear that the present group increased in weight by about 16% less than Tanner's boys, which is corroborated by the skinfold and fat values. Changes in femoral width showed significant negative correlations with initial widths of

Table 3 Means, Standard Deviations, and Coefficients of Variation of the Changes in the Measured Quantities Over 5 Years

Variable	*M*	Mean % increase	*SD*	*CV* (%)
Height (cm)	30.5	21.6	3.8	12.5
Sitting height (cm)	13.9	18.4	3.1	22.3
Biacromial diameter (cm)	6.5	20.6	1.3	20.0
Biiliac diameter (cm)	4.2	19.1	0.9	21.4
Humerus width (cm)	1.0	17.5	0.3	30.0
Leg length (cm)	16.6	25.1	1.9	11.4
Femur width (cm)	1.0	11.9	0.3	30.0
Weight (kg)	23.2	71.4	4.0	17.2
Fat-free mass (kg)	19.9	71.6	3.3	16.6
Arm circumference (cm)	5.4	26.1	1.4	25.9
Calf circumference (cm)	6.8	24.8	1.2	17.6
Fat (kg)	3.3	70.2	1.4	42.4

Table 4 Correlation Coefficients Between Changes in the Measured Quantities Over 5 Years

	Changes										
	Sitting	Biacromial	Biiliac	Humerus	Leg	Femur	Weight	FFM	Arm	Calf	Fat
Height	0.86***	0.71***	0.77***	0.49**	0.54***	0.42*	0.54***	0.62***	0.35*	0.31	0.07
Sitting	—	0.81***	0.71***	0.25	0.03	0.11	0.67***	0.75***	0.48**	0.45**	0.14
Biacromial		—	0.57***	0.40*	0.06	0.18	0.64***	0.68***	0.65***	0.55***	0.23
Biiliac			—	0.27	0.34*	0.22	0.51**	0.57***	0.28	0.33	0.11
Humerus				—	0.53***	0.76***	0.32	0.30	0.35*	0.11	0.19
Leg					—	0.62***	−0.06	−0.03	−0.09	−0.14	−0.09
Femur						—	0.01	0.05	0.09	−0.02	−0.09
Weight							—	0.95***	0.65***	0.64***	0.62***
FFM								—	0.51**	0.55***	0.34
Arm									—	0.68***	0.65***
Calf										—	0.53***
Fat											—

*$.05 \geqslant p > .01$. **$.01 \geqslant p > .001$. ***$.001 \geqslant p$.

humerus ($p < .001$) and femur ($p < .01$). This suggests that the femora of boys whose long bones were initially relatively narrow tended to increase in width more than those of boys whose bones were initially relatively wide. The results for bicondylar femur and humerus must be considered cautiously, however, because the changes were small and therefore the proportional measurement error would be larger.

The gains in weight ($p < .05$) and fat ($p < .05$) were significantly correlated with initial biacromial diameter. Initial biiliac diameter was significantly correlated with changes in weight ($p < .05$) and fat-free mass ($p < .05$). Thus there was some tendency for boys with broader hips to gain weight in the form of fat-free mass, yet boys with broader shoulders tended to increase weight in the form of fat.

An examination of the relationships within the changes (Table 4) revealed that the change in standing height was correlated ($p < .05$) with the change in every other variable except fat and calf circumferences, although the latter nearly achieved the 5% level of significance. This illustrates that fat change is more variable and essentially independent of other measures that seem to change proportionately during growth. The intercorrelations among all the change measures were variable, but the reader's attention is particularly drawn to those measures associated specifically with the total mass of tissue. It can be seen that change in fat correlated only with changes in arm circumference ($p < .001$), calf circumference ($p < .001$), and weight ($p < .001$). Changes in fat-free mass and weight,

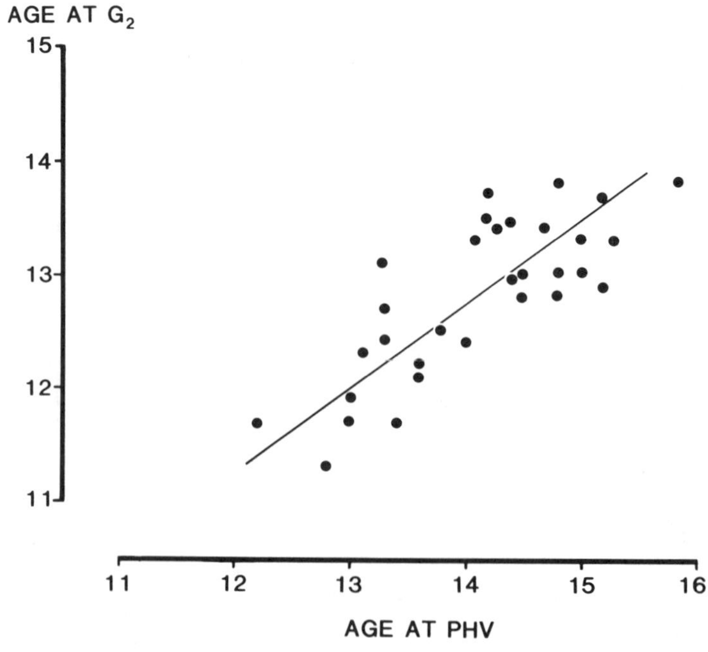

Figure 1. Age at G_2 versus age at peak height velocity.

however, yielded significant correlations with all other measures except the skeletal dimensions of leg length, femur width, and humerus width. This reinforces the above suggestion that fat is more disassociated from weight than fat-free mass, particularly during growth changes. The highly significant correlation between gains in weight and fat-free mass ($r = .95$, $p < .001$) provides further evidence for this suggestion.

Peak Velocities

The age of peak height velocity (PHV) was compared with the age at the onset of the first signs of puberty (G2) as shown on the scatter diagram in Figure 1. Pearson's product-moment correlation coefficient revealed a highly significant relationship ($r = 0.81$; $p < .001$) between the ages of G2 and PHV. This relationship permitted the calculation of a linear regression equation to predict PHV from the age at the first signs of puberty. The regression equation for this group of children was PHV(years) = 0.98G2(years) + 1.49, with a residual standard deviation of 0.52 years.

DISCUSSION

Initial Values

A comparison of weight at the initial age of just under 11 years (32.5 kg) indicates that these children were similar to those of Tanner and Whitehouse (1976), that is, with a mean weight of 33.0 kg, and Haschke (1983) with a mean weight of 33.3 kg, but lighter than those reported by Forbes (1964) at 37.5 kg; Rauh and Schumsky (1968) at 37.7 kg; and Binkhorst, Kar, and Vissars (1984) at 38.5 kg. Such population comparisons are of limited value because of different countries of origin, but of far more epidemiological concern is the percentage of fat within a group of children at that age. The present study produced an initial value of 14.5% fat, which is low compared with those reported by Forbes and Hursh (1963; 21%); Rauh and Schumsky (1968; 17.5%); Cureton, Boileau, and Lohman (1975; 20%); and Haschke (1983; 16%). Fat-free body mass is a proportionately larger fraction of the total body weight in the present group of subjects compared with those reviewed above. Relative values for fat and fat-free components are once again difficult to contrast with other studies, but those already cited were selected because, in addition to the skinfold assessment of body fat, total body potassium values were available.

The low coefficients of variation in standing height, sitting height, biacromial and biiliac diameters, and humerus and femur widths indicated that the boys all had similar skeletal dimensions. These similarities were even more obvious when differences in stature were taken into account. It was then seen that all the skeletal dimensions were practically constant fractions of total standing height over the whole range of heights, and at a given height the residual coefficients of variation of the other dimensions ranged from 1.6% for sitting height to 4.4% for humeral width.

We have accepted the proposition of Asmussen and Heebøll-Neilsen (1955) that weight is proportional to the cube of linear dimensions and thus the coefficient of variation of weight should be about three times that of linear dimensions. It was found to be 12%, which is close to three times the values for the major dimensions of the trunk. However, within the overall variation of body weight, the fat-free component varied relatively less (CV 7.9%) and the fat relatively more (CV 53.2%). Furthermore, fat-free mass was so well correlated with skeletal dimensions that, at a given height, it had a CV of less than 5%, whereas fat was effectively uncorrelated with skeletal size. Thus, at the age of 11 years, these boys were all essentially similar but clothed in variable amounts of fat.

Changes During the 5 Years

Figure 2 plots the distribution of the standing heights of the boys and the ages at which the various stages of puberty were reached on a standard centile chart (Buckler, 1979). The distribution of heights basically corresponded with the normal population with the suggestion that the pubertal acceleration of growth occurs slightly later in life. Figure 2 shows that the earlier stages of puberty also occur later. This may partly be due to a different interpretation of the criteria for the first signs of puberty, although the delay does persist throughout the full course of puberty and is shown by both genitalia and pubic hair assessment procedures.

It is interesting to compare height-weight curves—for example, those reported by Waaler (1983) in his anthropometric studies of Norwegian children. He was able to show that several adolescent boys showed a tendency toward overweight at 150 to 160 cm (10 to 12 years) compared with the normal Norwegian population. The present study, possibly because of smaller numbers, revealed no such tendency even in the higher centiles for any disproportionate increase in weight. In fact, with the generally lower weights of boys in the present study this would have been an unexpected finding. The mean fat content as estimated from the four skinfold thicknesses was initially 14.5% and remained practically constant throughout the study. This is consistent with the findings of Binkhorst et al. (1984), although their fat percentage values were slightly higher at around 16%. Rauh and Schumsky (1968) showed a general decrease in fat percentage from a peak at age 11 years of 17.5% to 12% at age 15 years. This decrease was also noted by Haschke (1983) with a peak of 17.2% at 12 years of age. Johnson, Fulwood, Abraham, and Brynner (1981) have suggested that a decline in fat thickness represents the thinning of the layer of fat in response to pubescent spurt in muscle and skeletal growth. Pařízková's (1977) results most closely resembled those of the present study with mean values between 12.1% and 15.8% from ages 11 to 15 years, but results were more difficult to interpret because they were presented in four activity categories. It is clearly a misconception to assume that adolescent boys must invariably show a dramatic change in fat as a result of the aging process.

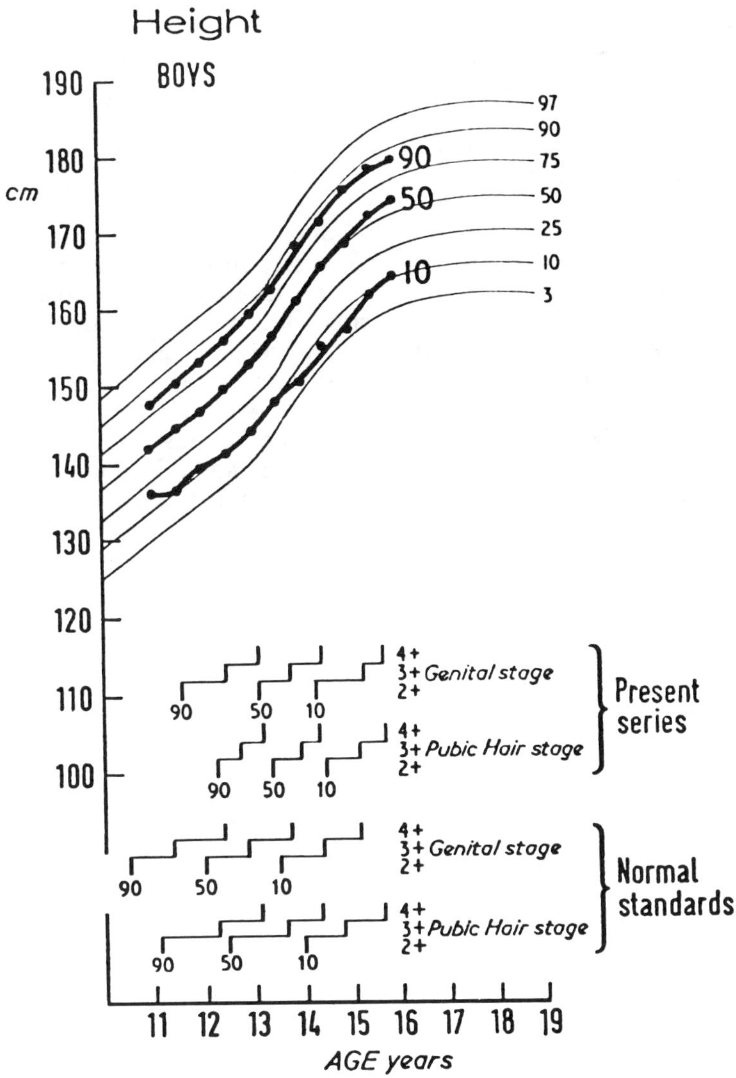

Figure 2. Distribution of the heights of the subjects during the period of observation (heavy lines) compared with a published standard. *Note.* Data from *A Reference Manual of Growth and Development* (p. 104) by J.M.H. Buckler, 1979, Oxford: Blackwell Scientific.

An essential part of the present study was an examination of the growth rates of different parts of the body during adolescence. The changes in body dimensions and mass of tissue were approximately related as would be expected if tissue mass were proportional to the cube of skeletal dimensions. Table 3 shows that, whereas most skeletal dimensions increased by approximately 20%, body weight, fat-free mass, and fat increased by 71.4%, 71.6%, and 70.2%, respectively. Assuming a cubic exponent, we would expect an increase of 73%, and so these results support the anticipated relationship.

Boys who were initially broad in the shoulders and hips tended to gain more weight. This may simply be the geometrical consequence of adding layers of tissue of equal thickness to quasi-cylindrical trunks of different sizes. There is some evidence (from Table 4) that this weight gain can be divided into that caused by fat deposition, which occurs predominantly in the upper body, and that caused by fat-free mass, which occurs predominantly in the hip region. Thus, although large-framed boys at 11 years of age will generally put on more weight than others, they may be more inclined to put on fat if broad shouldered and to put on fat-free mass if broad hipped. The predominant physical activities of British schoolboys are likely to favor development of the musculature surrounding the hip joint over the musculature of the shoulder joint. Thus the musculature required for large hip width is most likely to develop and contribute proportionately to fat-free mass.

Peak Velocities

Figure 1 illustrated the relationship between the age at the onset of the first signs of puberty and the age of peak height velocity. It can be seen that G2 always precedes PHV, usually by over a year. The rapid growth change in height was initiated about 1-1/2 years before PHV. Taranger and Hagg (1980) reported a difference of 2 years between the beginning of the pubertal growth spurt and PHV. Any differences would be a consequence of the methodology used to measure the start of the adolescent growth period. The relationship between PHV and G2 (PHV = 0.98G2 + 1.49) would be expected in any description of growth as exemplified by stature, but it does not take into account the differences in growth of separate parts of the skeleton.

REFERENCES

Asmussen, E., & Heebøll-Nielsen, K. (1955). Physical performance and growth in children. Influence of sex, age and intelligence. *Journal of Applied Physiology*, **8**, 371-380.

Binkhorst, R.A., Kar, M.C., & Vissers, A.C.A. (1984). Growth and aerobic power of boys 11-19 years. In J. Ilmarinen & I. Valimaki (Eds.), *Children and sport* (pp. 99-105). Berlin: Springer-Verlag.

Buckler, J.M.H. (1979). *A reference manual of growth and development*. Oxford: Blackwell Scientific.

Cureton, K.J., Boileau, R.A., & Lohman, T.G. (1975). Relationship between body composition measures and AAHPER test performances in young boys. *Research Quarterly*, **46**, 218-234.

Durnin, J.V.G.A., & Rahaman, M.M. (1967). The assessment of the amount of fat in the human body from measurements of skinfold thicknesses. *British Journal of Nutrition,* **21**, 681-689.

Forbes, G.B. (1964). Growth of the lean body mass during childhood and adolescence. *Journal of Pediatrics,* **64**, 822-827.

Forbes, G.B., & Hursh, J.B. (1963). Age and sex trends in lean body mass calculated from K40 measurements: With a note on the theoretical basis for the procedure. *Annals of the New York Academy of Science,* **110**, 255-263.

Haschke, F. (1983). Body composition in adolescent males. *Acta Paediatrica Scandinavica,* **307**(Suppl.), 23.

Johnson, C.L., Fulwood, R., Abraham, S., & Brynner, J.D. (1981). *Basic data on anthropometric measurements and angular measurements of the hip and knee joints for selected age groups 1-74 years of age: United States, 1971-1975* (DHHS Publication No. PHS 81). Hyattsville, MD: National Center for Health Statistics.

Pařízková, J. (1977). Effect of increased physical activity on body composition during growth in different groups of children. In J. Pařízková (Ed.), *Body fat and physical fitness* (pp. 118-168). The Hague: Nijhoff.

Rauh, J., & Schumsky, D.A. (1968). Human growth—body composition, cell growth, energy and intelligence. In D.B. Cheek (Ed.), *Human growth composition, cell growth, energy and intelligence* (pp. 242-252). Philadelphia: Lea & Febiger.

Siri, W.E. (1956). *Body composition from fluid spaces and density: Analysis of methods* (Rep. No. 3349). University of California, Berkeley: Radiation Laboratory.

Tanner, J.M. (1962). *Growth at adolescence* (2nd ed.). Oxford: Blackwell Scientific.

Tanner, J.M., Hiernaux, J., & Jarman, S. (1969). Growth and physique studies. In J.S. Weiner & J.A. Lourie (Eds.), *Handbook No. 9*. Oxford: Blackwell Scientific.

Tanner, J.M., & Whitehouse, R.H. (1976). Clinical longitudinal standards for height, weight, height velocity, weight velocity and stages of puberty. *Archives of Diseases in Childhood,* **51**, 170.

Taranger, J., & Hagg, V. (1980). The timing and duration of adolescent growth. *Acta Odontology Scandinavica,* **38**, 57-67.

Waaler, P.E. (1983). Anthropometric studies in Norwegian children. *Acta Paediatrica Scandinavica,* **308**(Suppl.), 1-41.

A Longitudinal Study of Development in Growth and Maturation of 10- to 15-Year-Old Girls and Boys

Birger Rasmussen
Klaus Klausen
University of Copenhagen, Copenhagen, Denmark
Birgit Jespersen
Kristen Jensen
Hillerød, Denmark

This investigation was designed to study the influence on behavioral as well as physical parameters caused by increasing the number of physical education (PE) lessons per week from two to five over a period of 3 years. For this purpose, we decided to follow two classes of children. One class was in the fourth grade and the second class in the sixth grade at the start of the study. Because children grow and mature from year to year, we decided also to follow the physical change over the years, and therefore a battery of tests was performed two to three times each year. To be able to see eventual physical changes caused by the increase in number of PE classes, a control group with the normal schedule of two PE classes per week was followed and investigated with the same test battery as used for the experimental group. The control group consisted of girls and boys from a different school but from the same area and community. The children (n = 85) from the experimental and control groups were age matched and consisted of four classes of children with almost equal distribution between boys and girls and almost the same number in the fourth and in the sixth grades.

METHODS

At each test administration in August, December, and June, height and nude weight were measured, and the degree of maturation was evaluated from the development stages (Tanner, 1962) of pubic and axillary hair and size of mammae and testes. The girls were questioned about the time of their first menstruation. Skinfold thicknesses were measured on the left and right sides of the abdomen, one third of the distance from umbilicus to spina iliaca anterior superior, and on left and right knees immediately above the patella. The fat content of the body was calculated from the formula:

$$F = 0.184 \times SF_{abd} + 0.145 \times SF_{knee} - 0.66$$

where F is the fat content of the body in kilograms and SF_{abd} and SF_{knee} are the sum of the skinfold thickness in millimeters from the left and right measurements (Hermansen & von Döbeln, 1971). All the mentioned measurements and evaluations were performed on each child by the same person on all occasions.

Statistical analysis of the growth and maturation data showed no significant differences between the experimental and the control groups. The total group of subjects was divided into four subgroups. Group 1 consisted of 20 girls from fourth to sixth grade, Group 2 of 22 boys from fourth to sixth grade, Group 3 of 22 girls from sixth to eighth grade, and Group 4 of 22 boys from sixth to eighth grade.

RESULTS

The measurements of body height revealed that differences in height between sexes started to develop between 12 and 13 years of age, but statistically significant differences between sexes did not exist except for the last two tests in the sixth to eighth grades. The data obtained for body weight showed no statistically significant differences, probably because the standard deviations for weight measurements were greater than for measurements of height. The fourth- to sixth-grade boys seemed to be relatively light in weight compared with the girls in the same grades. In Figure 1 the height-weight relation is plotted. No significant differences existed between boys and girls, but the figure confirms that the fourth- to sixth-grade boys were relatively light in weight. Figure 2 shows the fat-free weight (FFW) calculated as the difference between the fat content in kilograms (skinfold measurements) and the body weight plotted against mean age. A comparison of the data for the total body weight and the data in Figure 2 reveals a rather constant fat content on all tests of 5 to 7.5 kg.

Based on group height averages, group height standard deviations (*SD*), and number of subjects in each group, the results are plotted as normal distribution curves in relation to height in Figures 3 and 4. These curves illustrate the relatively small variation in the normal distribution that existed within a group of children over a period of 2 years. There seems to be a tendency toward greater variability of height in girls around 12 years and boys around 13 to 14 years. This was expected because it corresponds closely to the time of growth spurt for both sexes.

For each child, the standard score (*SS*) was calculated and defined as

$$SS = \frac{\text{individual height} - \text{mean height (group)}}{\text{standard deviation for group}}$$

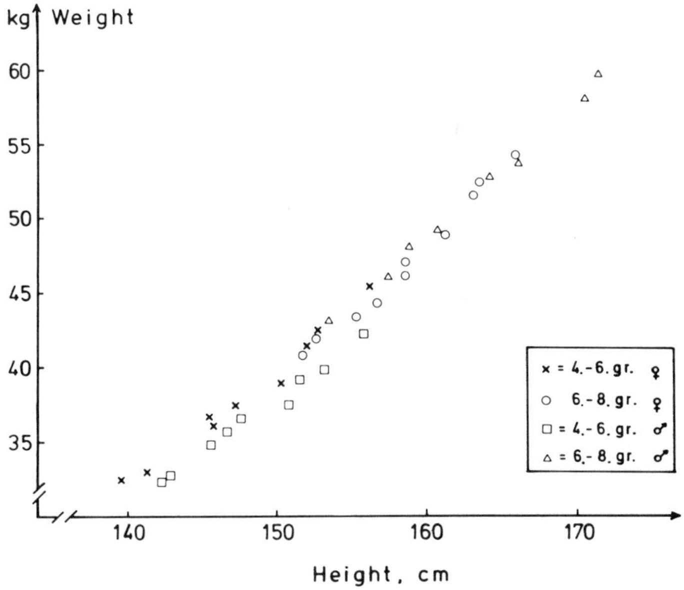

Figure 1. Mean weight (kg) versus mean height (cm). Data from nine different tests on four groups of children over a period of 3 years.

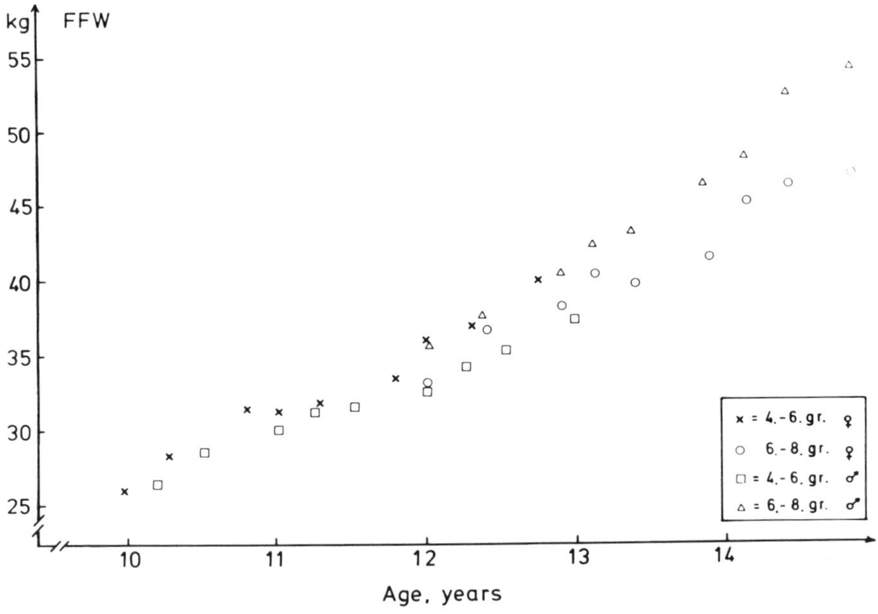

Figure 2. Mean values for fat-free weight (FFW; kg) versus chronological age (years). Groups as in Figure 1. FFW was calculated from skinfold measurements.

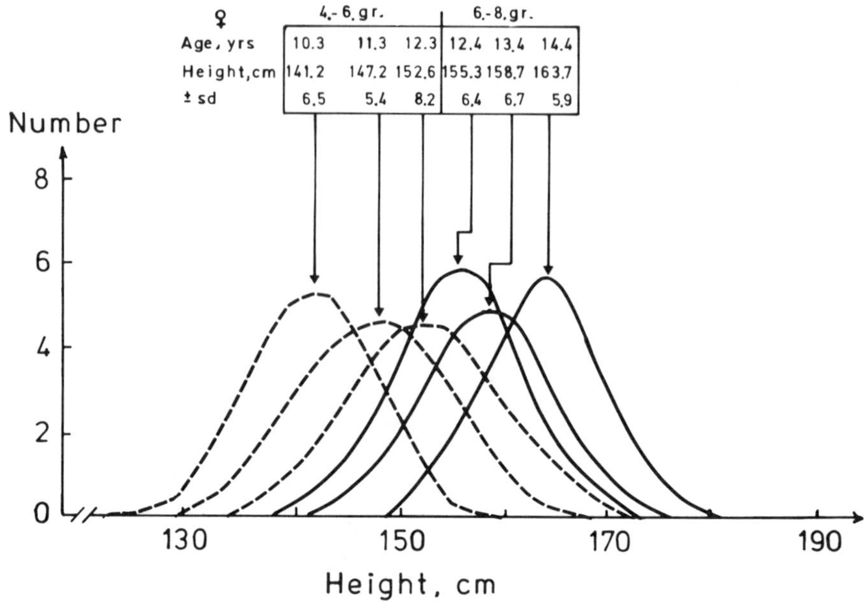

Figure 3. Group development of height (girls). Normal distribution curves from three tests with 1-year interval plotted on the same abscissa (height in centimeters).

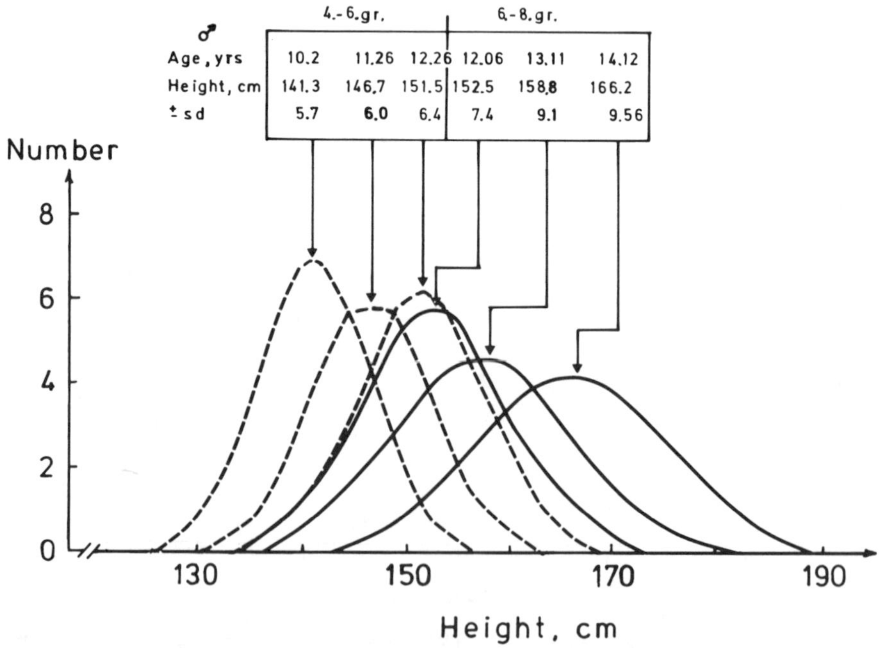

Figure 4. Group development of height (boys). See caption to Figure 3.

This index described the place of a single individual on the normal distribution curve. Examination of all the calculated *SS* values shows that the placement of each individual child in a group was amazingly constant. No child changed the rank position more than two positions within the group when the *SS* values for body height were examined. The weight *SS* values for the girls in sixth to eighth grade showed that five girls changed position within the group, which indicates that weight is a more variable factor than body height.

In Figure 5 the average increase in height per year (cm • year^{-1}) and the average increase in weight (kg • year^{-1}) are plotted for the four groups of children in relation to age. Three of the groups showed pronounced variation in the height growth pattern over the 3-year period, but there were no clear systematic changes in relation to age, sex, or season, and the changes in height and weight were not always in the same direction—that is, a greater increase in height was not necessarily accompanied by a larger increase in weight.

The changes in weight seemed to vary considerably from one test to another among the girls, but over the entire period of investigation the yearly increase in weight was almost constant. In contrast, boys had smaller variations from test to test, but showed a steady increase in weight gain over the 3-year period.

The time of first menstruation was identified by questioning the girls at each clinical investigation. Table 1 gives the mean age for 22 of 41 girls who had their first menstruation either before the study started (3 girls)

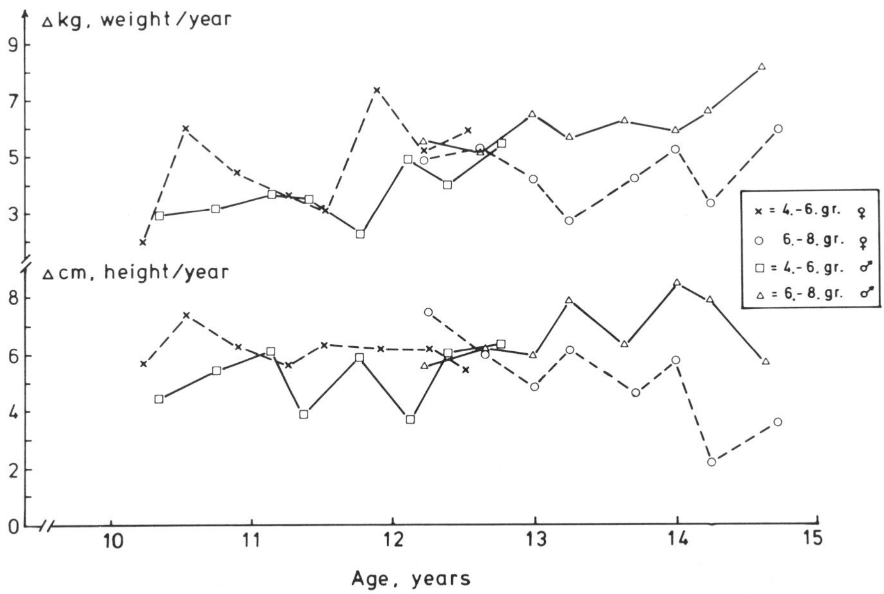

Figure 5. Average increase in weight (kg • year^{-1}) and height (cm • year^{-1}) calculated from differences between each of nine successive tests and mean age for the groups.

or during the period when the study took place (19 girls). From the older group, 5 girls did not have their menstruation before the end of the study and only 4 girls from the youngest group had their first menstruation before the end of the study.

Table 1 also presents the mean age at which 64 children (31 girls, 33 boys) had their growth spurt. The time for the peak of the growth spurt was often difficult to assess. It was done partly by visually inspecting the raw data and partly by calculating the increase in height per year from one measurement to the next and from half-year calculations. In a few cases, it was impossible to determine the time of the growth spurt, but usually there was good agreement between the mathematical calculations and the visual observations. For each individual, the data for height, weight, FFW, pubic hair stage, axillary hair stage, and size of mammae or testes were determined at the time of peak height velocity. No difference was detected in the development of pubic hair, but a significant difference existed for axillary hair development. If one compares the degree of development of mammae and testes in relation to their final development, it seems that both girls and boys reached a development stage of about 50% for these parameters at the age of maximal peak height velocity. The average values of these data are presented in Table 1.

Table 1 Mean Ages of First Menstruation for Girls (n = 22) and Peak Growth Velocity for Girls (n = 31) and Boys (n = 33) and Developmental Stage at Peak Growth Velocity

	Girls (n total = 41)		Boys (n total = 44)
	1st menstr.	PGV	PGV
n	22	32	34
Mean age (yrs)	12.86	12.57	13.17
± *SD*	1.02	0.96	0.84

Developmental stage

	Height (cm)	Weight (kg)	FFW (kg)	Pubic hair	Axillary hair	Mammae	Testis (mm)
Girls	156.0	43.75	37.73	2.766	1.719	2.734	—
± *SD*	6.30	6.29	5.14	0.95	0.729	0.813	—
Boys	158.5	46.0	40.59	2.588	1.182	—	12.59
± *SD*	7.76	6.29	7.82	0.67	0.241	—	4.37

Note. PGV = peak growth velocity. Pubic hair and axillary hair both judged on the Tanner scale 1-5. Tanner scale was also used for mammae development, whereas the size of testis (here left) is given in millimeters.

DISCUSSION AND COMMENTS

As mentioned, no differences were seen between children from the experimental groups and children from the control groups with regard to growth and maturation. This was also the case for most of the tests that measured the children's physical fitness. This may be because the increase in physical education lessons from two to five per week was used not only to obtain more physical training, but also to teach the children how to use exercise as a means to obtain a better life. The data obtained for height and weight showed that the relation between those two parameters was the same as it was for Danish children in 1956, but the height was on the average 3 cm greater in the present study than in the 1956 study (Asmussen & Heebøll-Nielsen, 1956).

Compared with Danish data from 1974 (Andersen et al., 1974), the height-weight relation in the present study was still the same, but both boys and girls were taller than similar children in the 1974 study. Compared with data from the Nijmegen study from the Netherlands (Prahl-Andersen, Kowalski, & Heydendael, 1979), Danish and Dutch children are very much alike. One boy in the sixth- to eighth-grade group was overweight, and his final weight was 105 kg. This single value increased the boy's weight average by about 2 kg, but when this value was excluded, no differences existed between Danish and Dutch children. Compared with a study in Belfast (Boreham, Paliczka, & Nichols, 1987), the Danish children were considerably taller for the same age. At 14.4 years of age, Danish boys were 171 cm in height, and the children from Belfast were only 161.5 cm. At comparable heights and ages Danish boys weighed about 2 kg less and the girls about 4 to 5 kg less than the subjects in the Belfast study. Compared with a study from Turkey (Akgün et al., 1987), Danish and Turkish children were very much alike with regard to the age-weight relationship, but after 12 years of age the Danish children were taller than the Turkish children. Thus, at 14.8 years, Danish boys were about 4 to 5 cm taller and Danish girls about 8 to 9 cm taller than their Turkish counterparts.

The content of fat was rather constant judging from the skinfold calculations, varying from 5.1 kg to 7.5 kg, which meant that percent body fat gradually decreased from about 15% to 20% at 10 years to about 9% to 12% at 15 years. The only difference observed was between the sixth- to eighth-grade girls and the sixth- to eighth-grade boys, where the girls in the very last test had about 11.6% fat and the boys only 8.8%. Compared with data from Boileau, Lohman, and Slaughter (1984), the body fat content and the FFW of the boys in the present study were of the same magnitude as in a well-trained group. This indicated that the subjects in the present study were physically well trained, which also was confirmed by the physical fitness index (ml $O_2 \cdot kg^{-1} \cdot min^{-1}$) for the group (Klausen, Schibye, & Rasmussen, this volume).

In longitudinal studies, one can follow the development of a group or the development of an individual. Figures 3, 4, and 5 illustrate the changes in height over a period of 3 years for each group (a span of 5 years for the children in this investigation). The growth pattern in boys and girls having different ages for peak growth velocity resulted in an increase of the standard deviation for the group around the time for peak growth velocity. Figure 3 shows clearly that at approximately 12.5 years the standard deviations were the greatest for girls. For boys standard deviations increased throughout the study, probably because peak growth velocity takes place later in boys than in girls. On the other hand, the calculation of the *SS* indicates that a single child began with a particular placement in the group, and the chances for change of that position within the group in either height or weight was rather small.

The changes in growth velocity varied from child to child and from time to time. These variations resulted in fluctuations from test to test, and it was difficult to arrive at any firm conclusions about seasonal variations in growth as was also discussed by Tanner (1962). Close inspection of Figure 5 indicates that the boys' increase in weight (kg • $year^{-1}$) accelerated over the years and so did the height spurt (cm • $year^{-1}$), whereas the girls had very little increase (but big fluctations) in weight spurt over the years and a clear tendency for a decrease in the spurt of height. This is in agreement with the fact that girls reach their final height some years before boys. The average changes in height per year and weight per year were of the same magnitude as described by Tanner (1962).

The average age for first menstruation was 12.9 years. Compared with older data from Denmark and Sweden, there has been a decrease in age of about 1 year since 1950, and during the last 100 years the time for the first menstruation has decreased about 3 years. The age for first menstruation is in good agreement with the data from the Nijmegen study (Prahl-Anderson et al., 1979). The spurt of height preceded the first menstruation by about 0.3 year, and the girls spurt of height preceded that of the boys by 0.6 year. This difference was statistically significant. The other variables in Table 1 showed no significant differences between girls and boys at the time for maximal peak height velocity. All data in Table 1 are in agreement with Tanner's diagram for sequences of events at adolescence in boys and girls. Thus this study has confirmed that secular changes take place for some parameters, but on the whole the patterns of development seen in the present study resembled results from earlier investigations.

Acknowledgment

This investigation was supported by grants from the Danish Sports Research Council.

REFERENCES

Akgün, N., Ergen, E., Ertat, A., Islegen, C., Colakoglu, H., & Emlek, Y. (1987). Preliminary results of motor fitness, cardiorespiratory fitness and body measurements in Turkish children. In *5th European Research Seminar on Testing Physical Fitness* (pp. 25-51). Strasbourg: Council of Europe.

Andersen, E., Andersen, H., Hutchings, B., Peitersen, B., Rosen, J., Thamdrup, E., Wichman, R., & Nyholm, M. (1984). Højde og vaegt hos danske skolebørn 1971-1972 [Height and weight in Danish schoolchildren 1971-1972]. *Ugeskrift for Laeger* [Weekly Journal for Medical Doctors], **136**(50), 2796-2802.

Asmussen, E., & Heebøll-Nielsen, K. (1956). Physical performance and growth in children. Influence of sex, age and intelligence. *Journal of Applied Physiology,* **8**, 371-380.

Boileau, R.A., Lohman, T.G., & Slaughter, M.H. (1985). Exercise and body composition of children and youth. *Scandinavian Journal of Sport Sciences,* **7**(1), 17-27.

Boreham, C.A.G., Paliczka, V.J., & Nichols, A.K. (1987). Fitness testing of Belfast schoolchildren. In *5th European Research Seminar on Testing Physical Fitness* (pp. 52-57). Strasbourg: Council of Europe.

Hermansen, L., & von Dobëln, W. (1971). Body fat and skinfold measurements. *Scandinavian Journal of Clinical Laboratory Investigations,* **27**, 315-319.

Prahl-Andersen, B., Kowalski, C.J., & Heydendael, P. (1979). *A mixed-longitudinal interdisciplinary study of growth and development*. New York: Academic Press.

Tanner, J.M. (1962). *Growth at adolescence* (2nd ed.). Oxford: Blackwell Scientific.

A Longitudinal Study of Changes in Physical Performance of 10- to 15-Year-Old Girls and Boys

Klaus Klausen
Bente Schibye
Birger Rasmussen
University of Copenhagen, Copenhagen, Denmark

The low frequency of compulsory physical education lessons (PEL) in Danish public schools (two 45-min lessons per week) has created concern over the state of physical fitness of Danish schoolchildren. Hence the effect of increasing the number of PEL from two to five per week has been followed over a period of 3 years in two classes from fourth to sixth and from sixth to eighth grade. Two comparable classes, with only two PEL per week, served as control classes. It has previously been reported that the physiological training effect of the PEL in all four classes was very small as far as aerobic power was concerned (Klausen, Rasmussen, & Schibye, 1986). However, all classes had a variable exercise program including, for example, various ball games, gymnastics, athletics, orienteering, and so forth. This may imply a training effect on functions other than aerobic power. The aim of the present article is therefore to describe the development of all physiological variables measured in the children in the experimental classes (five PEL per week) and in the control classes (two PEL per week) during the 3-year period.

MATERIAL AND METHODS

The four classes comprised a total of 85 children with an almost even distribution between girls and boys in each class. Each child was tested just before and after the summer holidays in June and August. Also, some of the tests were administered in December.

The maximal aerobic power ($\dot{V}O_2max$, ml • min^{-1} • kg^{-1}) was estimated from the measured maximal heart rate and the heart rate during the 6th min of a submaximal exercise bout on a cycle ergometer. The calculation of $\dot{V}O_2max$ was further based on net efficiencies that were related to work load on the cycle ergometer during each submaximal test (Klausen, Rasmussen, Glensgaard, & Jensen, 1985). The aerobic and anaerobic performance capacities of the children were also evaluated from a 2,000-m run performed on a standard track.

Maximal isometric strength was assessed for the abdominal and back muscles of the trunk; the combined hip and knee extensors (leg extension) of right, left, and both legs; and the finger flexors (handgrip) of right and left hands. The dynamometers and test procedures were the same as described by Asmussen, Heebøll-Nielsen, and Molbech (1959a). The jump and reach test, which is a measure of the functional strength of the extensor muscles in the legs, was carried out as described by Heebøll-Nielsen (1982).

The reaction times for standard white light and standard sound were measured by means of an electrical circuit comprised of an electronic stopwatch and a microswitch. The children used their right index fingers during the reaction tests. All strength tests and aerobic power tests were carried out by the same persons on all occasions. The functional tests (jump and reach, 2,000-m run, and reaction time) were administered by the teacher of physical education in each class.

RESULTS

Age, height, and weight of the children are presented elsewhere in this volume (Rasmussen, Klausen, Jespersen, & Jensen). No significant differences were observed either between the girls or between the boys in the experimental and control classes with regard to mean age, height, and weight.

Average values ($\pm$ *SE*) of all variables were calculated for girls and boys separately in each class. Significant differences between groups were assessed by means of a t test for independent samples. The significance level was set at $p < .05$. No significant differences in performance were observed between the experimental classes and the control classes, except for the 2,000-m running time of the girls in fourth grade. Hence, the experimental and control classes were treated as one group, and mean values ($\pm$ *SE*) were calculated for boys and girls in fourth to sixth and sixth to eighth grades. All mean values, except the reaction times, were plotted against a chronological scale (see Figures 1-7.) In all figures, J, A, and D denote January, August, and December, respectively. Note the overlap of the curves owing to the fact that the average age of the children in the fourth- to sixth-grade classes in August 1982 was the same as the age in the sixth- to eighth-grade classes in 1980 (i.e., 12 years).

Mean values of $\dot{V}O_2max$ are presented in Figure 1. The values vary from 44 to 51 ml • kg^{-1} • min^{-1} for the girls and from 48 to 61 ml • kg^{-1} • min^{-1} for the boys. The mean values of the boys were usually significantly higher than the mean values of the girls (5% to 15%). No systematic change was noted over the 3 years or from 10 to 15 years for either the girls or the boys.

Figure 2 shows the results from the 2,000-m run. Boys ran significantly faster than girls (about 10%). This is only shown for the sixth to eighth grade on the figure, because the measurements in the fourth to sixth grade

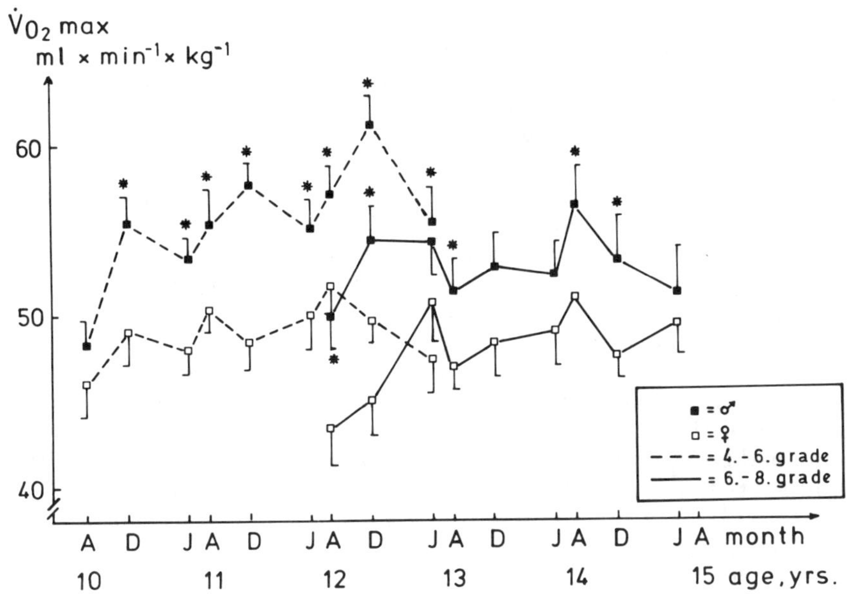

Figure 1. $\dot{V}O_2$max (ml • min^{-1} • kg^{-1}) in relation to age. Mean values ± *SE*. Boys' values are significantly higher than girls' values.

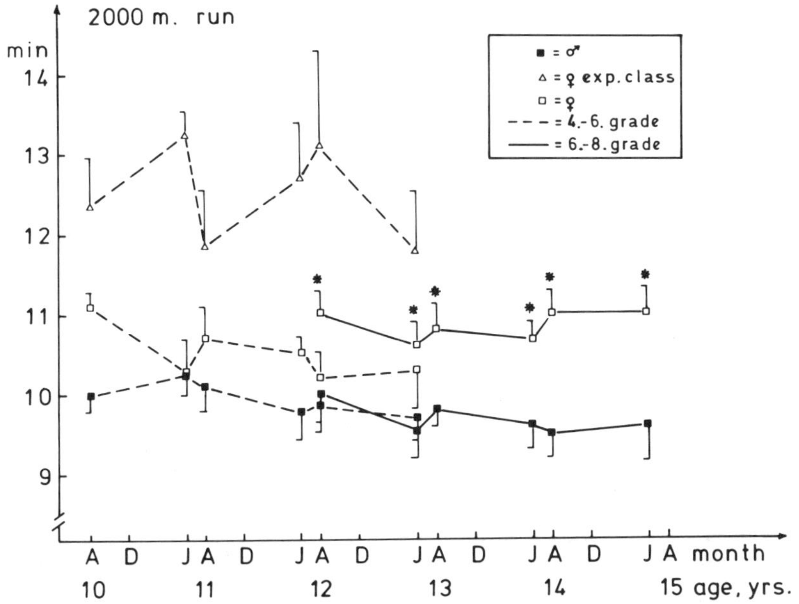

Figure 2. Time (min) for 2,000-m run in relation to age (see caption to Figure 1).

were complicated by the fact that the girls in the experimental class on an average ran much slower than the girls in the control class. There was no significant change in running time from 10 to 15 years.

The results from the strength measurements are presented in Figures 3-6. There was, in general, a significant increase in strength in all muscle groups from fourth to sixth and from sixth to eighth grades. The increase was not continuous over the year, which can be seen from a sharper increase in strength from June to August in most cases. As far as hand grip (Figure 6) and back and abdominal muscles (Figure 5) are concerned, boys were usually significantly stronger than girls (5% to 20%), whereas the strength of the leg muscles was almost the same in girls and boys. Only the strengths of the right hand and leg are presented, and it should be noted that the strength of the left hand and leg on the average was 5% to 10% less than the strength of the right side. The sum of the strength of right and left leg extension was always greater than the combined two-leg extension. This difference decreased from about 35% at 10 years to about 15% at 15 years of age.

The results from the jump and reach test are shown in Figure 7. An increase in performance occurred over the 3-year period in the fourth to sixth grade with no differences between girls and boys. In the sixth to

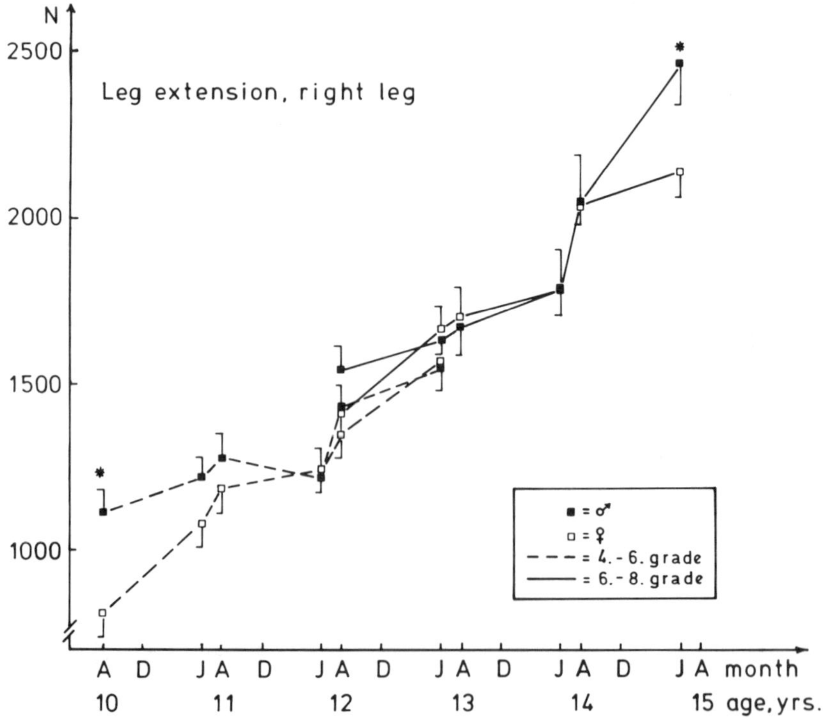

Figure 3. Maximal isometric force (Newton) during leg extension with the right leg in relation to age (see caption to Figure 1).

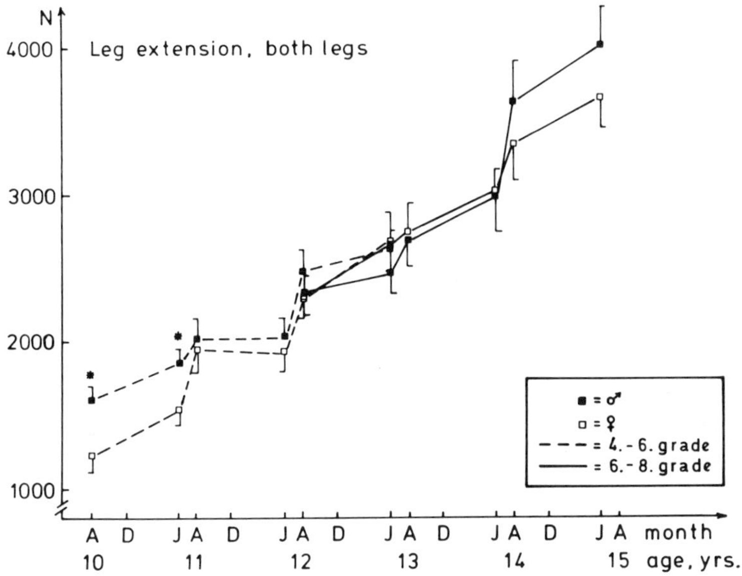

Figure 4. Maximal isometric force (Newton) during leg extension with both legs in relation to age (see caption to Figure 1).

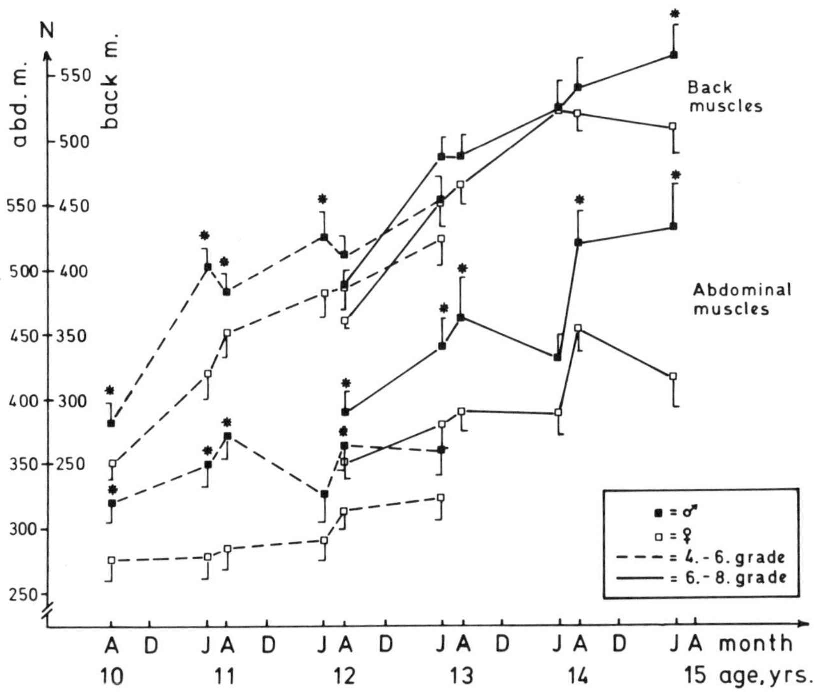

Figure 5. Maximal isometric force (Newton) of the back and abdominal muscles in relation to age (see caption to Figure 1).

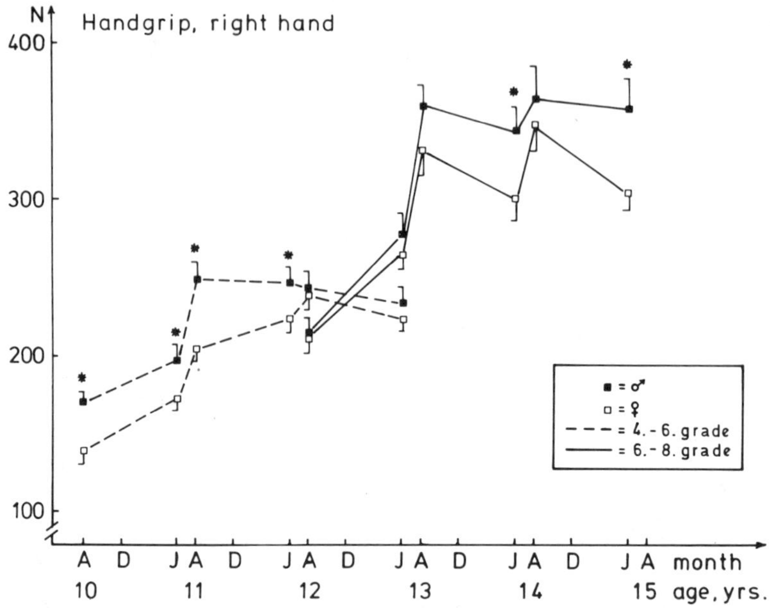

Figure 6. Maximal isometric force (Newton) for hand grip with the right hand in relation to age (see caption to Figure 1).

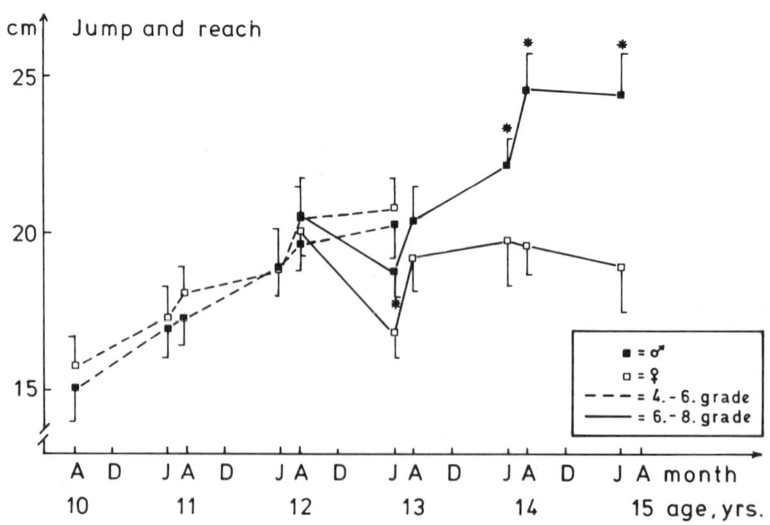

Figure 7. Jumping height (cm) in relation to age (see caption to Figure 1).

eighth grade the girls showed no increase, whereas the boys exhibited a steep increase in jumping height from 13 to 15 years of age.

No systematic change was observed in reaction times from 10 to 15 years. However, a slightly better performance (about 5%) was observed in the sixth to eighth grade than in the fourth to sixth grade. In general, boys showed a better performance than girls, and the difference between the two sexes was significant on several tests. On the average for all tests in all classes, the reaction times to light were about 200 ms and to sound about 160 ms. The reaction time to light was comparable to values obtained from tests of young adults, but the reaction time to sound was 10% to 15% longer than in young adults (Asmussen, 1968; Pedersen & Schomacher, 1981).

DISCUSSION

The $\dot{V}O_2$max values obtained in the present study were high compared with most other studies (Robinson, 1938; Saris, Noordeloos, Ringnalda, Van't Hof, & Binkhorst, 1985; Seliger & Bartinek, 1976) and were even comparable to the very high values reported by Åstrand (1952). The difference between girls and boys also resembled those discovered in previous investigations, except that no tendency of an increase in $\dot{V}O_2$max among the boys and a decrease in $\dot{V}O_2$max among the girls was noted during and after puberty, a phenomenon that was very pronounced in Åstrand's data (1952).

The 2,000-m running times agreed with the $\dot{V}O_2$max values insofar as the better performance of the boys in the 2,000 m coincided with a significantly greater $\dot{V}O_2$max. Otherwise, no correlation was obtained between running times and either $\dot{V}O_2$max or muscle strength (leg extension, jump and reach). The earlier reported improvement in sprint-type running from 11 to 14 years in children (Asmussen, 1973) was almost nonexistent in the 2,000-m run in the present study. Of interest is the marked difference in running times between the fourth- to sixth-grade girls of the experimental and those of the control classes. There were no significant differences between the two groups of girls in the other performance tests, and the reason for the different running times was due to the teacher's constantly encouraging the children in the experimental class to help each other. As a result of this, the more fit girls simply waited for and followed the less fit girls during the 2,000-m run. The teacher's attitude did not influence the performance of the boys, who competed during the 2,000-m run just as the children in the other three classes.

Heebøll-Nielsen (1982) reported from a cross-sectional study that the isometric strength in relation to height decreased on the average by 8% to 10% in Danish girls and boys as compared with values from a cross-sectional study made 25 years earlier in the same locality (Asmussen et al., 1959b). He suggested that the decrease in strength among the children in 1981 was due to decreased physical activity of the children. The present isometric strength measurements were comparable to the results from the two previous investigations, because exactly the same apparatus and procedures were used in the three studies. The results from the 10- to 11-year-old girls and boys in the present longitudinal study supported the opinion that children nowadays are weaker than children of the same age and height 25 years ago, especially in leg extension with both legs and in hand grip. Measurements on the children from about 12 to 15 years do not support this opinion. On the contrary, the children at these ages are stronger than the children in Heebøll-Nielsen's study from 1981 (Heebøll-Nielsen, 1982) and in most cases just as strong or stronger than the children in 1956 (Asmussen et al., 1959b).

From Figures 3-6, it appears that most frequently the increase in muscle strength was greatest from June to August. This phenomenon was not correlated to similar increases in height or weight. One probable explanation is that the children are more motivated to do their best after a long summer holiday than at the end of the school year.

The finding that maximal isometric strength during leg extension with both legs was less than the sum of the strength of right and left legs agreed with measurements on adults (Secher, Rörsgaard, & Secher, 1978; Vandervoort, Sale, & Moroz, 1984). The explanation for the decrease of this difference expressed as percent of the two-leg extension values from 35% at 10 years to 15% at 15 years could be that a maximal activation of the muscles in both legs at the same time is limited by the maximal neural output. If this output is increasing with age (e.g., motor learning or maturation) the degree of activation of the two legs when working together will approach maximal activation of the two legs, one at a time, and hence, the above-mentioned percentage difference will decrease.

The jumping height increased and was the same in girls and boys from 10 to 13 years, but in the older age groups no further performance increase was seen in the girls, whereas the boys' performance continued to increase. From a theoretical point of view, it was expected that jumping height would be independent of physical dimensions. However, Asmussen and Heebøll-Nielsen (1956) found that the jumping height increased with body height to the 1.59 power in girls and the 1.71 power in boys. Thus the more or less continuous increase in jumping height of the boys in the present study agreed with the results of Asmussen and Heebøll-Nielsen. But it is difficult to explain the leveling off noted in the girls, especially because their strength during two-leg extension expressed as Newtons per kilogram body weight increased from 13 to 15 years and, furthermore, was the same as for the boys at the time of leveling off.

The most important findings in the present study were that the general level of physical performance of children nowadays is excellent compared with data from previous reports of cross-sectional studies. Thus it seems that there is no reason to believe that children in 1980 were more sedentary than children in earlier decades. On the contrary, a sociological investigation in the present study has revealed that the children in fourth to sixth and sixth to eighth grades on an average participated in various sports activities for 5 and 8 hr per week, respectively (Klausen et al., 1986).

This was probably the reason why no difference was found in physical performance capacities between the control and the experimental classes. Another explanation is that the main purpose of increasing the number of PEL per week was to educate and motivate the children for physical training when they leave school.

Finally, it should be pointed out that the activities in PEL did not aim specifically at an improvement of the functions that were measured in the present investigation. Maybe future investigations should concentrate on selecting functional measurements that more closely resemble the PEL activities than the test methods used in the present investigation.

Acknowledgment

This investigation was supported by grants from the Danish Sports Research Council.

REFERENCES

Asmussen, E. (1968). Correlations between various physiological test results in handicapped persons. *Communications from the Danish National Association for Infantile Paralysis*, **27**, 3-13.

Asmussen, E. (1973). Growth in muscular strength and power. In G.L. Rarick (Ed.), *Physical activity—human growth and development* (pp. 60-79). New York: Academic Press.

Asmussen, E., & Heebøll-Nielsen, K. (1956). Physical performance and growth in children. Influence of sex, age and intelligence. *Journal of Applied Physiology*, **8**, 371-380.

Asmussen, E., Heebøll-Nielsen, K., & Molbech, S. (1959a). Methods for evaluation of muscle strength. *Communications from the Danish National Association for Infantile Paralysis*, **5**, 3-13.

Asmussen, E., Heebøll-Nielsen, K., & Molbech, S. (1959b). Description of muscle tests and standard values of muscle strength in children. *Communications from the Danish National Association for Infantile Paralysis*, **5**(Suppl.), 3-60.

Åstrand, P.O. (1952). *Experimental studies of physical working capacity in relation to sex and age*. Copenhagen: Munksgaard.

Heebøll-Nielsen, K. (1982). Muscle strength of boys and girls, 1981 compared to 1956. *Scandinavian Journal of Sports Sciences*, **4**, 37-43.

Klausen, K., Rasmussen, B., Glensgaard, L.K., & Jensen, O.V. (1985). Work efficiency of children during submaximal bicycle exercise. In R.A. Binkhorst, H.C.G. Kemper, & W.H.M. Saris (Eds.), *Children and exercise XI* (pp. 210-217). Champaign, IL: Human Kinetics.

Klausen, K., Rasmussen, B., & Schibye, B. (1986). Evaluation of the physical activity of school children during a physical-education lesson. In J. Rutenfranz, R. Mocellin, & F. Klimt (Eds.), *Children and exercise XII* (pp. 93-101). Champaign, IL: Human Kinetics.

Pedersen, S.V., & Schomacher, J.A. (1981). *Influence of age and sex on reaction time during simple and more complicated reaction tests* (in Danish). Unpublished master's thesis, University of Copenhagen, August Krogh Institute.

Robinson, S. (1938). Experimental studies of physical fitness in relation to age. *Arbeitsphysiologie*, **10**, 251-323.

Saris, W.H.M., Noordeloos, A.M., Ringnalda, B.E.M., Van't Hof, M.A., & Binkhorst, R.A. (1985). Reference values for aerobic power of healthy 4- to 18-year-old Dutch children: Preliminary results. In R.A. Binkhorst, H.C.G. Kemper, & W.H.M. Saris (Eds.), *Children and exercise XI*, (pp. 151-160). Champaign, IL: Human Kinetics.

Secher, N.H., Rörsgaard, S., & Secher, O. (1978). Contralateral influence on recruitment of curarized muscle fibres during maximal voluntary extension of the legs. *Acta Physiologica Scandinavica*, **103**, 456-462.

Seliger, V., & Bartinek, Z. (1976). *Mean values of various indices of physical fitness in the investigation of Czechoslovak population ages 12-55 years*. Prague: Czechoslovak Association of Physical Culture.

Vandervoort, A.A., Sale, D.G., & Moroz, J. (1984). Comparison of motor unit activation during unilateral and bilateral leg extension. *Journal of Applied Physiology*, **56**(1), 46-51.

Physical Fitness Aptitudinal Field Tests on Children 6 to 12 Years Old: Experience on 2,000 Cases

Armando Calzolari
Marco Cappa
Fabrizio Drago
Antonella Santilli
Attilio Turchetta
Mario Marino
Ospedale Bambino Gesu', Rome, Italy

Antonio Dal Monte
Luisa Franti
Leonardo M. Leonardi
Mario Sciamanna
CONI Institute of Sports Science, Rome, Italy

Stefano Marzani
Enzo Sammartino
Instituto di Biochimica, Urbino, Italy

Nowadays, the demand for participation in physical activity during childhood in Italy is increasing markedly. The result is that sports physicians not only need to examine physical health in terms of fitness, but they also to be able to assign each child to the most suitable activity for him or her. Taking into account these facts, and because there are not established evaluation methodologies for subject classification, it seemed advisable to have some children undergo a series of tests. These tests were chosen from among those that seemed the most suitable for an evaluation of the individual's physical capabilities as a whole so that reference standards might be establised (Dal Monte, 1978; Leonardi, 1977; Nicoletti, 1982).

MATERIALS AND METHODS

A total of 2,190 children (1,315 males and 875 females), ranging from 6 to 12 years of age, were examined. Some were already participating in sports; others were not. The children were divided into groups according to sex and age and, within the latter, height percentiles (Nicoletti, 1982; Simons & Benson, 1982). Subjects below the 10th percentile and exceeding 20% of their optimal body weight relative to height were excluded. Furthermore, the children were divided into two additional groups depending on whether they were or were not participating in physical activity fairly regularly (at least 2 hr per week). Tables 1 and 2 show the number of subjects in each of the subgroups according to age. Each child, wearing a tracksuit and athletic shoes, performed one test at a time. The tests allowed the following evaluations:

1. Alternate aerobic-anaerobic capability, as determined by the Margaria test, modified by Dal Monte (1978)—five successive sprints (30 m), every minute; measuring the time and heart rate between 45 to 55 s after every sprint.
2. Explosive strength of upper limbs—throwing a medicine ball from behind the head, three trials (meters); reporting the best one.
3. Explosive strength of lower limbs—long jumping, three trials (meters); reporting the best one.
4. Static strength of upper and lower limbs using a dynamometer.
5. Skill: running a slalom through 10 small poles, three trials for time; reporting the best one.

Table 1 Number of Boys Examined in the Study, Divided Into Subgroups According to Age, Height Percentiles (10-25, 25-50, 50-90, > 90), and Physical Activity (if Practiced = *Y*; if Not = *N*)

	10-25		25-50		50-90		> 90	
	N	*Y*	*N*	*Y*	*N*	*Y*	*N*	*Y*
6	6	—	15	—	23	9	17	1
7	7	—	44	5	49	12	21	7
8	14	—	29	15	57	21	24	8
9	38	18	38	18	74	40	21	20
10	19	7	36	17	73	50	27	23
11	16	26	26	35	58	56	32	27
12	1	11	9	19	16	24	10	32

Table 2 Number of Girls Examined in the Study, Divided Into Subgroups According to Age, Height Percentiles (10-25, 25-50, 50-90, > 90), and Physical Activity (if Practiced = *Y*; if Not = *N*)

	10-25		25-50		50-90		> 90	
	N	*Y*	*N*	*Y*	*N*	*Y*	*N*	*Y*
6	3	—	8	3	26	1	12	—
7	8	3	23	3	53	9	18	5
8	4	4	28	13	53	21	14	7
9	12	12	20	13	43	33	16	7
10	9	8	21	11	45	37	28	16
11	9	6	21	11	40	36	20	15
12	2	9	6	13	13	33	4	17

6. Flexibility: forward flexion of the trunk with straight legs; measuring how far the hands extended beyond the feet (in centimeters).
7. Speed of reaction: measuring (in centimeters) the length from the hypothenar eminence to the bottom of a dowel released by the examiner.
8. Endurance: Cooper's test, modified to 6 min of running, measuring the distance covered (meters).

The data were submitted to statistical analysis in order to calculate the means and standard deviations.

RESULTS

The sample of 2,190 subjects was divided into age groups by sex in 1-year intervals and, within the latter, into subgroups according to height percentiles in order to observe, as much as possible, the somatic evolution occurring during this period of life. Obviously, this caused a reduction in the number of the children included in each group with clear implications for statistical analysis. However, this grouping was preferred to large groups that would have been more heterogeneous from the standpoint of growth and development. It should be emphasized that most of the subjects who were examined were classified in the higher percentiles of height. As an example, the results (means and standard deviations) of three tests (long jumping, medicine ball throw, and endurance) in 11-year-old males, divided into percentiles of height and if they practiced (Y) or did not practice (N) physical activity, are shown in Table 3.

Table 3 Means and Standard Deviations of Three Tests on Male 11-Year-Olds. Subgroups: Height Percentiles (10-25, 25-50, 50-90, > 90) and Physical Activity (if Practiced = *Y*; if Not = *N*)

	10-25	25-50	50-90	> 90
Medicine ball throw (meters)				
N				
Mean	5.20	5.62	5.72	7.33
SD	1.63	4.42	0.98	2.81
Y				
Mean	4.35	5.00	6.12	5.53
SD	0.89	0.86	1.30	1.49
Long jump (meters)				
N				
Mean	1.66	1.62	1.78	1.55
SD	0.15	0.09	0.17	0.23
Y				
Mean	1.65	1.62	1.76	1.71
SD	0.22	0.16	0.25	0.10
Endurance test (meters)				
N				
Mean	1127	1229	1103	1037
SD	325	109	199	110
Y				
Mean	1011	1053	1067	1088
SD	225	203	176	74

CONCLUSION

A large population of children was examined and classified according to its growth and development. On the one hand, this decreased the number of children in each group, but, on the other hand, it eliminated many of the factors that might have led to errors by comparing each child with a similar age group but with fairly different physical development. These tests were easy to administer, quick to perform (about 30 min for all), and helpful in determining the level of sports training for each child at the beginning of and throughout the training period (Carbonaro, 1980; Manno, 1981; Tanner, 1982).

REFERENCES

Carbonaro, G. (1980). Aspetti della preparazione dei giovani sportivi [Aspects of physical training in children]. *Scuola dello Sport*, **7**, 27-36.

Dal Monte, A. (1978). I test sul terreno per la valutazione dell'attitudine sportiva nell'età evolutiva [Aptitudinal field test in children]. *Medicina dello Sport*, **31**, 133-150.

Leonardi, L.M., Dal Monte, A., & Gallippi, L. (1977). Su un test pratico per la valutazione degli atleti praticanti attività aerobiche-anaerobiche alternate [Field test for evaluation of aerobic-anaerobic capability in athletes]. *Medicina dello Sport*, **30**, 199-202.

Manno, R. (1981). L'evoluzione delle qualità fisiche: Forza, velocità e resistenza nelle varie età [Strength, speed and endurance by ages]. *Scuola dello Sport*, **7**, 1-19.

Merni, F., & Carbonaro, G. (1981). Test motori [Motor Tests]. *Scuola dello Sport*, **8**, 1-82.

Nicoletti, I. (1982). Avviamento allo Sport: Lo sviluppo fisico del bambino e dell'adolescente [Beginning of sport. Physical development of child and adolescent]. *Scuola dello Sport*, **9**, 1-40.

Simons, J., & Benson, R. (Eds.) (1982). *Evaluation of Motor Fitness*. Paper presented at the Institute of Physical Education of K.U. Leuven, Belgium.

Tanner, J.M. (1982). *Growth and adolescence*. Oxford: Blackwell Scientific.

Four Styles of Swimming Performance and Anthropometry of Child Swimmers

Anna Farkas
János Mohácsi
János Mészáros
Hungarian University of Physical Education, Budapest, Hungary

The intra- and interrelationships of body build, fitness for the event, and performance constitute the major problems when selecting and training young athletes and interpreting their achievements. In his research, Meleski (1979) stated that young swimmers are taller than nonathletes and, furthermore, that functional indices tend to change relative to the intensity of the training.

In Sweden, girl swimmers aged 7 years or older were reported to be taller than the average child (Åstrand et al., 1963), and the difference became more marked in both sexes after 12 years of age. It has been postulated that, other conditions being equal, optimum regular physical training creates favorable predictions for growth.

The purpose of the present study was to answer the question of the nature of the relationship between variables of body build and swimming performances in child swimmers and to determine which variables have the highest relationship to the best and to the average performances in the four styles of swimming.

MATERIAL AND METHODS

Body dimensions, derived indices, and swimming performances were recorded, analyzed, and compared in the child swimmers, ages 9 to 11 years, from a sport club. There were 37 girls and 45 boys. The anthropometric variables obtained were stature, body mass, the metric and plastic indices of Conrad's growth type (1963), the three components of the anthropometric somatotype of Heath and Carter (1971), and the relative lengths of the upper and lower extremities.

Subgroups were formed by expressing age in decimal years. The subjects' grades of development were estimated by the morphological age method (Mészáros, Mohácsi, Szabó, & Szmodis, 1985). In taking body dimensions, we observed the recommendations of the International Biological Program (Weiner & Lourie, 1969). In addition to the swimming times, grip strength was measured and expressed as the mean of the right and left hand scores.

Swimming performances were standardized to allow valid comparisons by relating individual performances to the existing world record, which was taken as the 1,100-point level. Data analysis was performed on both the best and the average scores. The higher the score, the better the performance in a specific style of swimming, and mean performance was the average of the four swimming styles for each subject.

Relationships were estimated by linear correlation coefficients. Where feasible, the data were compared with the representative means of Hungarian schoolchildren (Mészáros & Mohácsi, 1983).

RESULTS

The means and standard deviations of the measured and derived variables were tabulated for the age groups of both sexes. Table 1 contains the data on the anthropometry and grip strength of the swimmers. Swimmers of both sexes were significantly taller than their peers. Except for the 9-year-old boys, where the mean difference was only 1 cm, all the swimmer groups were taller by 5 cm or more than nonswimmers of the same age.

There were no significant differences in body mass between the respective groups. The age curves of the metric index followed the regular trend described by Szmodis, Mészáros, and Szabó (1976) and by Mészáros, Szmodis, and Mohácsi (1979). It was noted that girls of 11 years and boys of 10 years of age were more pyknomorph than their nonswimming peers.

The plastic index, which describes general musculoskeletal robustness, showed that although swimmers and nonswimmers did not differ significantly at the age of 9 years, older swimmers were more robust. Relative lengths of swimmers' extremities showed only random variability; that is, no appreciable change occurred in the relative proportions with increasing age in either sex. There was a significant increase in grip strength between the ages of 9 and 10 years. It might be assumed that certain training effects caused this difference.

Table 2 shows the age group means and variability of the swimming performances. Although the results are only relative to the existing world record, there was appreciable improvement between the groups studied with increasing age; however, it should be noted that this was a cross-sectional study.

In all three age groups, the best scores were significantly higher than the mean scores achieved by the subjects. This difference also increased with advancing age; for example, improvement in the most favored swimming style was already greater than in the other styles of swimming even at this young age. On the other hand, with advancing age, group variability also increased; thus there were increasing differences in efficiency in the respective swimming styles.

Table 1 The Means and Standard Deviations of Body Dimensions and Mean Grip Strength of Two Hands

	Years					
	9 (n = 10)		10 (n = 12)		11 (n = 11)	
	$\overline{X}$	*SD*	$\overline{X}$	*SD*	$\overline{X}$	*SD*
Girls						
DA	8.95	0.31	9.98	0.32	11.09	0.29
MA	9.07	0.40	10.03	0.32	11.45	1.04
ST	138.69	3.79	143.25	6.83	151.04	8.48
BW	29.75	3.34	32.67	4.00	38.95	7.23
MIX	−1.72	0.23	−1.65	0.15	−1.38	0.37
PLX	63.97	2.53	66.52	2.07	70.02	4.55
RLL	58.24	1.23	57.67	0.95	58.11	0.33
RAL	100.86	1.72	100.64	1.77	101.43	0.73
MGS	12.20	1.98	15.86	3.93	16.18	3.40
Boys	9 (n = 16)		10 (n = 15)		11 (n = 13)	
DA	9.05	0.27	10.06	0.31	11.03	0.26
MA	9.06	0.45	10.27	0.61	11.33	0.72
ST	134.69	3.62	144.24	5.66	148.82	5.93
BW	27.63	7.66	34.77	4.20	36.81	4.35
MIX	−1.07	0.19	−1.09	0.17	−1.23	0.23
PLX	64.48	1.35	67.77	3.10	71.42	3.69
RLL	56.89	1.11	56.65	1.32	57.74	1.54
RAL	101.45	2.32	101.74	2.34	103.21	2.07
MGS	13.41	2.44	16.75	5.17	16.97	2.36

Note. DA = chronological age in decimal years; MA = morphological age; ST = stature; BW = body weight; MIX = metric index; PLX = plastic index; RLL, PAL = relative leg and arm length; MGS = mean grip strength of the two hands.

Table 3 shows the correlation coefficients indicating the relationships between selected body dimensions and swimming performance (best and mean scores) for the two sexes. A positive correlation was found between age and performance. Furthermore, positive correlations were found with body mass, which was most likely due to increases in lean body mass; with the plastic index of robustness, which correlated with morphological age; and with grip strength, which was a partial reflection of an overall strength increase.

Table 2 The Best and the Average Swimming Performance Scores of Young Swimmers

	Girls		Boys	
	$\overline{X}$	*SD*	$\overline{X}$	*SD*
9 years				
Best	264.63	39.32	220.31	42.11
Average	227.50	25.61	197.33	36.72
10 years				
Best	384.25	69.30	272.45	30.91
Average	328.00	56.28	247.75	26.80
11 years				
Best	488.17	73.37	373.80	68.34
Average	415.71	67.90	313.30	44.60

Table 3 Correlations Between the Anthropometric Variables and the Swimming Performance Scores

	Girls		Boys	
	Best	Average	Best	Average
ST	.71**	.70**	.81**	.81**
BW	.70**	.70**	.71**	.70**
MIX	.65**	.67**	−.26	−.21
PLX	.71**	.69**	.75**	.75**
I.	−.02	.04	.33*	.33*
II.	.17	.24	−.04	−.06
III.	−.18	−.22	.39*	.40*
RLL	.25	.18	.42*	.31
RAL	.41*	.37*	.28	.25
MGS	.65**	.59**	.60**	.55**

Note. See footnote to Table 1 for abbreviations. (I., II., and III. are somatotype components from "Somatotype Methodology and Kinesiological Research" by B.H. Heath and J.E. Carter, 1971, *Kinesiological Reviews*, **1**, 10-19.)
*p = .05. **p = .01.

The correlations between swimming scores and the metric index were different for the boys and the girls. In the boys it was not related to swimming performance, but in the girls the correlation was positive. This may be an indication that leaner girls performed better. Heath-Carter components of the somatotype were unrelated to performance in the girls, and there were only slight relationships in the boys.

The assumption that relative extremity lengths can affect the performance in swimming was only partially supported in the girls. In them, longer arms and better performance were related. There was a significant relationship between grip strength and swimming performance in both the boys and the girls. As already mentioned, this could not be regarded as a direct cause and effect relationship; instead, both factors progressed with increasing body strength.

DISCUSSION

The purpose of the study was to demonstrate the existence of simple measurable indicators that were possibly related to swimming performance. The finding that swimmers were taller than their peers corresponded to other reports on the differences in stature between athletes and nonathletes (Åstrand et al., 1963; Meleski, 1979). Because the main difference between the sample in the study and the control group was the extent of habitual physical activity, the difference in stature was attributed to the stimulating effect of regular sport training on growth, though selection effects must also be considered as a possible cause.

In the case of the plastic index, the evidence that the difference between swimmers and nonswimmers increased with additional training strongly supported the assumption that greater robustness is the result of regular training. The positive coefficient between age and performance stems from the fact that older age usually means a longer training history. Although body build has an appreciable effect on swimming performance, this cannot be reduced to any single variable studied here; thus several components must interact to bring about better performances.

Based on this observation, it should be emphasized that no single component of body build should be used in the selection of young swimmers. The effect of regular physical training in stimulating body development was indirectly deduced from the faster progress in robustness, for example. This may be an important relationship. Consequently, decisions made by the coach should always rely on more than a single factor of body build and should include an evaluation of the psychological fitness of a child swimmer.

REFERENCES

Åstrand, P.O., Engström, L., Eriksson, B., Nylander, I., Saltin, B., & Thorén, C. (1963). Girl swimmers. *Acta Pediatrica*, **147**(Suppl.), 1-75.

Conrad, K. (1963). *Der Konstitutionstypus: 2. Aufl* [Type of physical constitution]. Berlin: Springer.

Heath, B.H., & Carter, J.E. (1971). Somatotype methodology and kinesiological research. *Kinesiological Reviews*, **1**, 10-19.

Meleski, B. (1979). The physical and physiological development of young swimmers. *Swimming Technique*, **1**, 16-17.

Mészáros, J., & Mohácsi, J. (1983). *Estimation of biological maturity and prognosis of adult stature using the growth curves of urban youth*. Unpublished doctoral dissertation, Hungarian Academy of Sciences, Budapest.

Mészáros, J., Mohácsi, J., Szabó, T., & Szmodis, I. (1985). Assessment of biological development by anthropometric variables. In R.A. Binkhorst, H.C.G. Kemper, & W.H.M. Saris (Eds.), *Children and exercise XI* (pp. 341-345). Champaign, IL: Human Kinetics.

Mészáros, J., Szmodis, I., & Mohácsi, J. (1979). The constitutional bases of physical education and sports training. *A Sport és Testnevelés Időszerű Kérdései* [The Recent Advances of Sport and Physical Education] (Vol. 20, pp. 15-38). Budapest: Sport.

Szmodis, I., Mészáros, J., & Szabó, T. (1976). Growth trend in children under regular sports training. *Proceedings of the Seventh Conference on Pediatric Work Physiology*. Bisham Abbey.

Weiner, J.E.S., & Lourie, J.A. (Eds.) (1969). *Human biology: A guide to field methods* (IBP Handbook No. 9). Oxford: Blackwell Scientific.

Comparison of Heart Rates at the Anaerobic Threshold Determined Invasively and Noninvasively in 11-Year-Old Children

Georgine Gaisl
Gerhard Wiesspeiner
University Graz, Graz, Austria

The determination of the anaerobic threshold (AT) is very interesting and important in sports medicine and in training practice. A noninvasive method of determining AT was introduced by Conconi, Ferrari, Ziglio, Droghetti, and Codeca in 1982. The test person runs continuously for 15 to 20 min. He or she starts with a very low initial speed, which is increased every 200 m by 0.5 km/h until the maximum is reached. From the correlation between heart rate (HR) and running speed, conclusions can be drawn with regard to the change in the linearity of the heart rate curve. The speed at the break point is called *anaerobic threshold velocity*; HR at the break point is known as the *anaerobic threshold heart rate* (Conconi, Ferrari, et al., 1984). Until now, only adult athletes had been examined. Therefore, the purpose of this study was to adapt the Conconi test to allow for the noninvasive determination of AT in children.

When the Conconi test was administered with children on the running track, useful heart rate curves could not be obtained because the children had not checked their pace well enough and thus had not been able to increase running speed gradually as required. Therefore, they did not meet one of the basic requirements of the Conconi test. When the children were tested on a treadmill, the increasing running speed was dictated. However, in practice only a few treadmills were available. On the other hand, bicycle ergometers, on which the same tests can be done, were readily available. Therefore, it was decided that the bicycle ergometer would be the best way to provide a work load for the children.

SUBJECTS AND METHODS

First Investigation (T1)

First, 72 pupils were tested who were in the first grade of a secondary school with an average age of 11.4 years (s = 0.5). There were 27 girls and 45 boys in this investigation.

Experimental Procedures

In the laboratory, tests were started with a treadmill speed of 6 km/h with a 5% upgrade. After each 3-min phase, the speed was increased in increments of 2 km/h with an interruption of 10 s to take blood samples. HR was monitored continuously. Before the test, at the end of each load phase, and in the 3rd min of recovery, blood samples for lactate measurement (Lactate Analyzer Roche 640) were taken from the hyperemized earlobe. Loading was interrupted after the lactate value of 4 mmol/l had been reached. The test results were plotted and running speed, as well as HR at AT with a lactate value of 4 mmol/l, was determined.

After 45 min the loading was done on an electrically braked bicycle ergometer. The children started with a load of 0 W; the load was increased 10 W • min^{-1} until each pupil's maximum was reached. Before the test, during the load application, and in the first 3 min of recovery, HR was measured with a Sport Tester (Polar Electro) and stored every 5 s. The stored HR at the end of each load minute was recorded. The results were determined graphically. For scientific documentation HR was stored with a program of Polar Electro on a computer system Canon X-07/X-710 (Hofer & Rösler, 1985).

Second Investigation (T2)

The second investigation was undertaken 15 weeks later. The anthropometric data of the 59 children who participated in both investigations are presented in Table 1. Experimental procedures were the same in T2 as in T1.

RESULTS

First Investigation

The deflection of the HR curve from linearity could not be found in 8 children. For that reason, Table 2 shows the comparison of HR at AT determined invasively and noninvasively only in 64 children. The methods showed a high correlation (r = .98) between each other (Gaisl & Wiesspeiner, 1987).

Second Investigation

In 52 of the 59 children who participated in both investigations, the break point could be determined. The HRs at AT that were determined invasively and noninvasively in these children are compared in Table 3; T1 and T2 are listed separately. In T2 the difference between the two HR thresholds was even less than it was in T1.

Table 1 Anthropometric Data of Subjects in T1 and T2

		T1			T2		
		Girls $n = 22$	Boys $n = 37$	All $n = 59$	Girls $n = 22$	Boys $n = 37$	All $n = 59$
Age	*M*	11.3	11.5	11.4	11.7	11.8	11.8
(years)	*SD*	0.3	0.7	0.6	0.3	0.7	0.6
Height	*M*	147.5	148.4	148.0	150.0	149.6	149.7
(cm)	*SD*	6.3	6.8	6.6	6.4	6.8	6.7
Weight	*M*	37.9	37.9	37.9	40.9	39.7	40.2
(kg)	*SD*	6.4	5.8	6.1	7.5	6.2	6.7

Table 2 Comparison of Heart Rate at the Anaerobic Threshold Determined Invasively (A) and Noninvasively (B)—First Investigation

		Girls $n = 25$	Boys $n = 39$	All $n = 64$
Heart rate A (b/min)	*M*	188.0	187.6	187.8
	SD	9.4	6.6	7.7
Heart rate B (b/min)	*M*	186.8	186.7	186.8
	SD	9.8	6.3	7.7
	r	.98	.98	.98

Table 3 Comparison of Heart Rate at the Anaerobic Threshold Determined Invasively (A) and Noninvasively (B)—First Investigation (T1) and Second Investigation (T2)

		T1			T2		
		Girls $n = 22$	Boys $n = 30$	All $n = 52$	Girls $n = 22$	Boys $n = 30$	All $n = 52$
Heart rate A (b/min)	*M*	186.8	188.1	187.5	186.9	185.9	186.3
	SD	8.3	6.1	7.1	7.7	7.1	7.4
Heart rate B (b/min)	*M*	185.6	187.1	186.4	187.5	185.8	186.5
	SD	9.2	5.6	7.4	8.0	7.3	7.7
	r	.98	.98	.98	.99	.99	.99

DISCUSSION

The phenomenon of the deflection of the HR curve that has been described by Conconi, Ferrari, Ziglio, Droghetti, and Codeca (1982) could not be found in 8 pupils (2 girls and 6 boys) in T1 and in 2 boys in T2 for the obvious reason that they stopped exercising before they had reached AT. In T1 the break point could be found in all the other children. In T2, however, the HR values of 5 boys were completely linear, that is, no break point could be found although they had all reached AT. Other authors (Aigner & Muss, 1983; Conconi, Borsetto, et al., 1984) also could not find the break point in some athletes. Huber, Stockhausen, and Jakob (in press) could not determine the break point in 10% of the tested athletes, and Vaz and Kruse (1985) reported that another author could not determine a break point in 13% of the athletes tested. None of these authors was able to give any kind of explanation for this lack of a break point in the HR load curve.

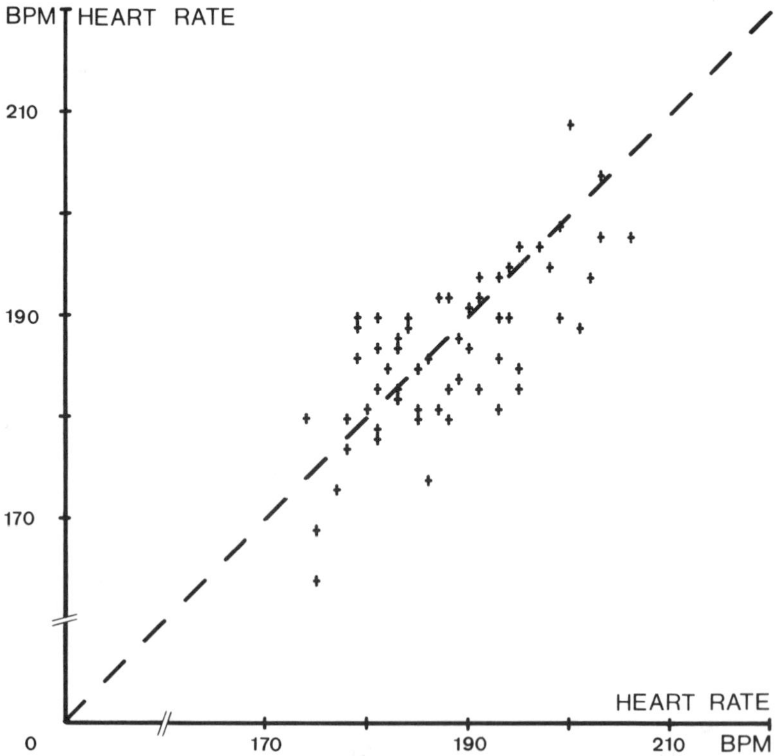

Figure 1. Results of the first investigation: Comparison of heart rate at the anaerobic threshold determined by means of lactate analysis (x-axis) versus heart rate deflection point (y-axis).

From Tables 2 and 3, it can be seen that in T1 the mean values of HR at the lactate threshold and at the threshold according to Conconi, Ferrari, et al. (1984) differed by only 1 beat • min^{-1} (i.e., 0.5%), and in T2 they differed by only 0.2 beats • min^{-1} (i.e., 0.1%). This negligible difference was found in the entire group. The average individual difference was 1.01 beats • min^{-1}. If the measurement error of the digital indicating instrument of 1 beat • min^{-1} is accepted, one can assume with a 99.9% probability ($p < .001$) the equality of the two methods: T1—r = .98 (Figure 1), and T2—r = .99 (Figure 2) for the determination of AT.

Aigner and Muss (1983) did not find a correlation between the invasive and the noninvasive methods of determining AT. They stated that "for investigations in the laboratory the introduced method is obviously not applicable" (p. 289). These authors, however, used 3-min phases instead of 1-min phases, and, furthermore, they started out with a load that was too high. Lacour, Padilla, and Denis (in press) arrived at similar results using 2-min phases. In contrast, Conconi, Borsetto, Casoni, and Ferrari (in press) also carried out the test with cyclists during the winter

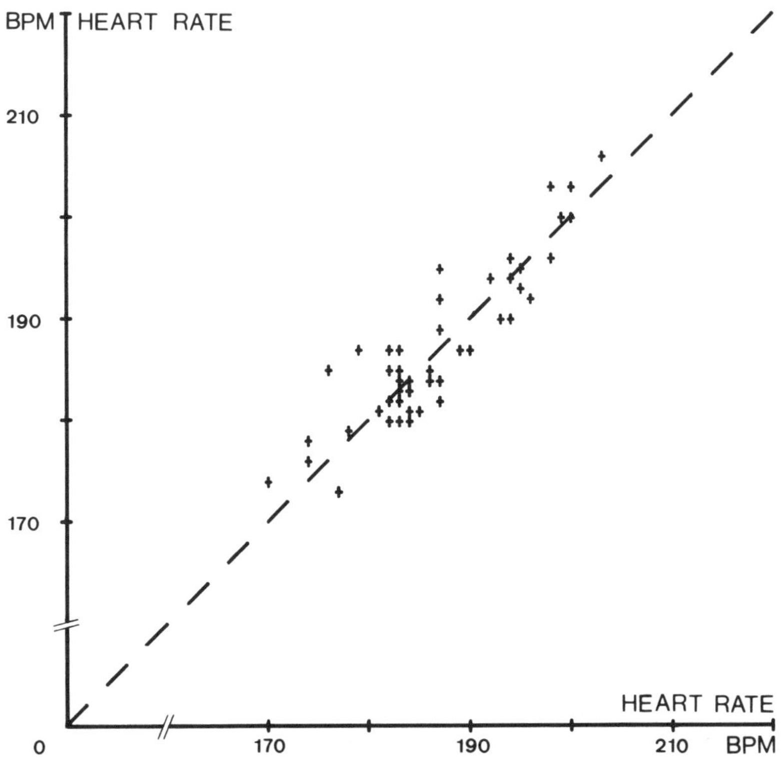

Figure 2. Results of the second investigation: Comparison of heart rate at the anaerobic threshold determined by means of lactate analysis (x-axis) versus heart rate deflection point (y-axis).

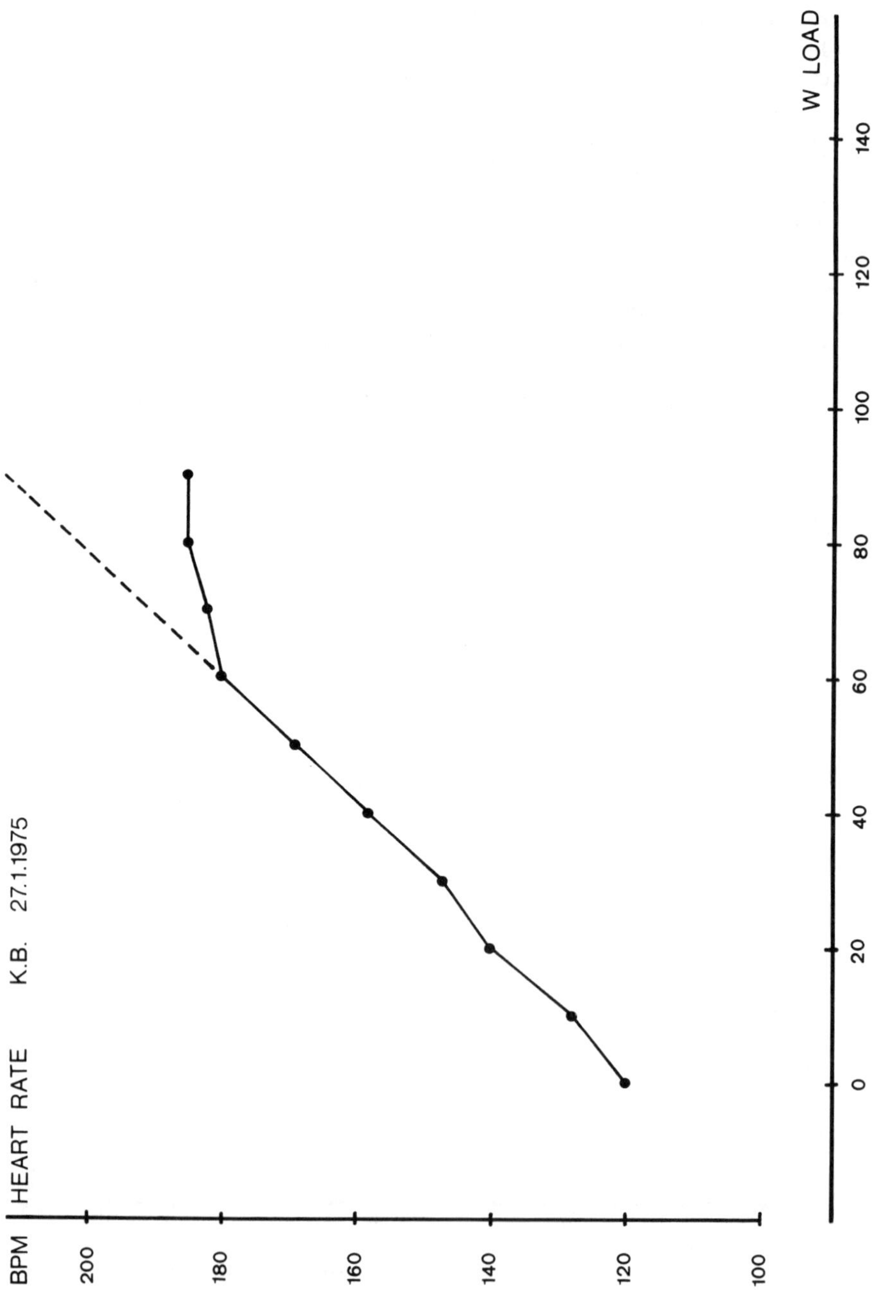

Figure 3. Heart rate curve of a child with below-average physical fitness.

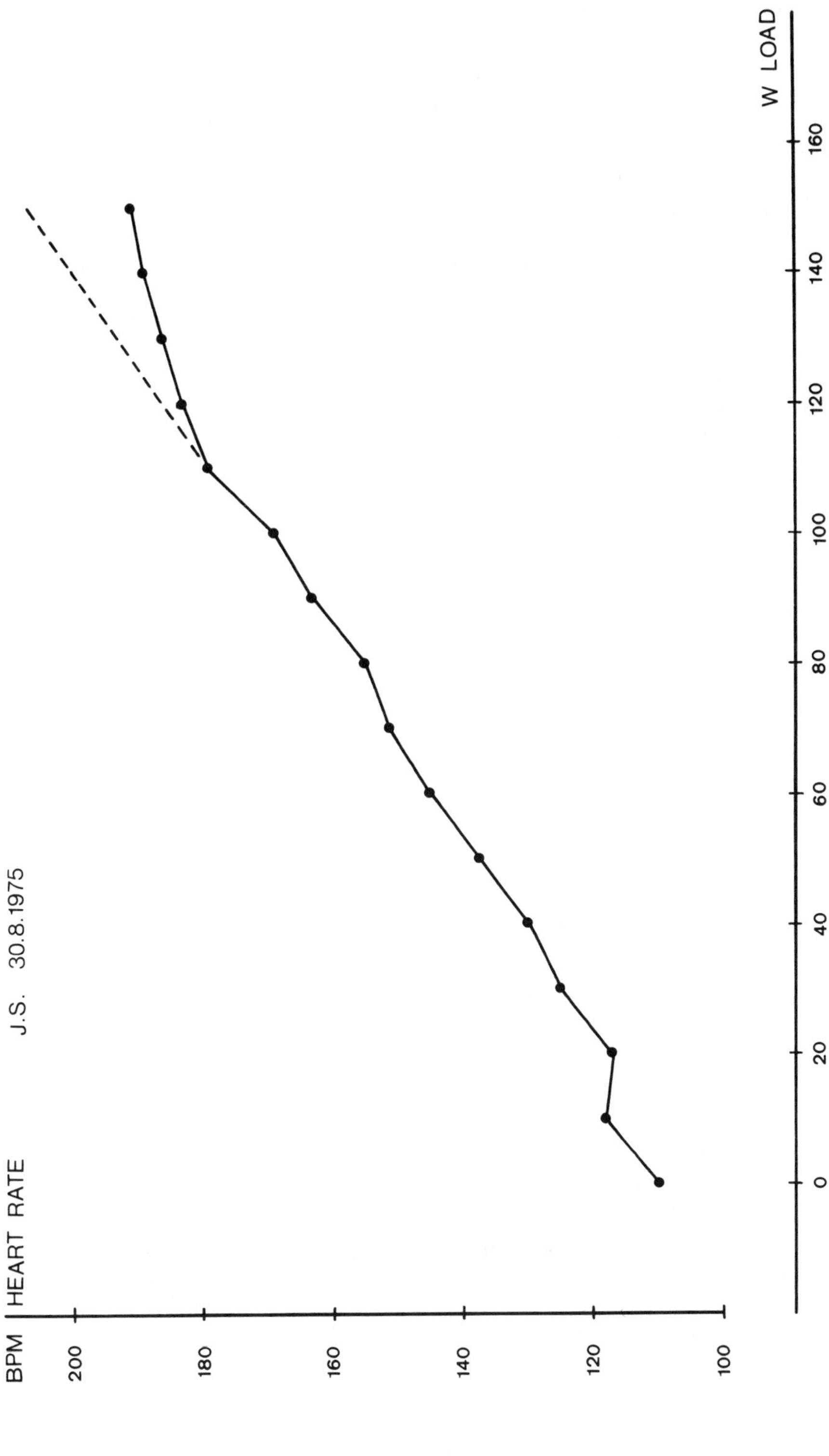

Figure 4. Heart rate curve of a child with above-average physical fitness.

on a bicycle ergometer. They used the incremental test, starting with a load of 50 W and increasing the load by 50 W every minute; therefore, they were successful in finding the break point.

For the present study, different ways were chosen to apply the load using a treadmill for the invasive determination of AT and a bicycle ergometer for the noninvasive method of determining AT. The purpose was to show that the determination of AT does not depend on the kind of load application used.

In order to confirm the correlations between HR values at AT that were determined on a treadmill and those that were determined on a bicycle ergometer, it was possible to use the paired test. Although a larger amount of muscle mass is used when load is applied on a treadmill than when it is applied on a bicycle ergometer, the HR values correlated strongly. This showed that the determination of AT is basically independent of the way the load is applied. The most decisive factors are the initial load, the rate of increments, and the length and number of the various load phases.

The introduced adaptation of the Conconi test in the laboratory can not only be used with children doing sports regularly, but also serve as a method for evaluating the physical fitness of children in general (see Figures 3 and 4). Figure 3 shows the heart rate curve of a child with below-average physical fitness; Figure 4 shows the heart rate curve of a child with above-average physical fitness.

CONCLUSION

It can be concluded from this study that in children the invasive determination of AT can be substituted for by the noninvasive method. With an adapted version of the Conconi test on a bicycle ergometer, it is also possible to evaluate the general physical fitness of children.

Acknowledgments

This study was made possible by the support of the Austrian Ministry of Education, Art, and Sports and by grants (No. 4619 and No. 6011) from the Austrian Research Fund. Thanks are expressed to Evelyn König, who who helped in performing these investigations.

REFERENCES

Aigner, A., & Muss, N. (1983). Wertigkeit einer nicht-invasiven Methode zur Bestimmung der anaeroben Schwelle unter Laborbedingungen und im Feldtest. [Evaluation of a noninvasive method for the determination of the anaerobic threshold in the laboratory and in the field]. *Deutsche Zeitschrift für Sportmedizin*, **34**, 284-289.

Conconi, F., Borsetto, C., Casoni, I., & Ferrari, M. (in press). Noninvasive determination of the anaerobic threshold in cyclists. *Proceedings of the World Congress on the Medical and Scientific Aspects of Cycling*. Colorado Springs, CO.

Conconi, F., Borsetto, C., D'Incal, D., Droghetti, P., Ferrari, M., Paolini, A., & Ziglio, P.G. (1984). Die anaerobe Schwelle beim Skilanglauf [The anaerobic threshold in cross-country skiing]. *Magglingen*, **43**, 11, 13-17.

Conconi, F., Ferrari, M., Ziglio, P.G., Droghetti, P., Borsetto, C., Casoni, I., Cellini, M., & Paolini, A.R. (1984). Determination of the anaerobic threshold by a noninvasive field test in running and other activities. In N. Bachl, L. Prokop, & R. Suckert (Eds.), *Current topics in sport medicine* (pp. 274-281). Wien: Urban & Schwarzenberg.

Conconi, F., Ferrari, M., Ziglio, P.G., Droghetti, P., & Codeca, L. (1982). Determination of the anaerobic threshold by a noninvasive field test in runners. *Journal of Applied Physiology*, **52**, 869-873.

Gaisl, G., & Wiesspeiner, G. (1987). Eine unblutige Methode zur Bestimmung der anaeroben Schwelle bei Kindern [A noninvasive method of the determination of the anaerobic threshold in children]. *Leistungssport*, **17**, 3, 27-29.

Hofer, P., & Rösler, K. (1985). Sport-Tester PE 3000 Trainings-System. *Schweizerische Zeitschrift für Sportmedizin*, **33**, 67-69.

Huber, G., Stockhausen, W., & Jakob, E. (in press). Trainingssteuerung mittels Herzfrequenz und Tretfrequenz bei Radrennfahrern [Training regulation by means of heart rate and pedalling rate in racing cyclists]. In *Proceedings of the International Congress in St. Johann in Tirol*, June, 1987. Wien: Hollinek.

Lacour, J.R., Padilla, S., & Denis, C. (in press). L'inflexion de la courbe frequence cardiaque–puissance n'est pas un temoin du seuil anaerobie [The deflection of the heart rate–power relationship is not an index of the anaerobic threshold]. In *Proceedings of the 23rd FIMS World Congress of Sports Medicine*. Brisbane, Australia.

Vax, K., & Kruse, B. (Eds.). (1985). *The high-performance triathlete*. Chicago: Contemporary Books.

Effect of High-Altitude Chronic Hypoxia on Lactate and Ventilatory Thresholds in Healthy Young Boys

Guy Falgairette
Emmanuel Van Praagh
Université de Clermont-Ferrand II, Aubière, France

Nicole Fellmann
Mario Bedu
Hilde Spielvogel
Jean Coudert
Laboratoire de Physiologie, Clermont-Ferrand, France

At low altitude, lactate and ventilatory thresholds ($mlO_2 \cdot min^{-1} \cdot kg^{-1}$, $\%\dot{V}O_2max$) are higher in children than in adults (Atomi, Fukunaga, Yamamoto, & Hatta, 1986; Becker & Vaccaro, 1983; Medelli, Maingourd, Freville, Nekrouf, & Harichaux, 1985; Reybrouck, Weymans, Stijns, Knops, & Vander Hauwaert, 1985; Vanden Eynde, Ghesquiere, Van Gerven, Vuylsteke, & Vande Perre, 1984). From childhood to adult status a decrease in ventilatory threshold has been observed, in particular between 12 and 16 years of age (Reybrouck et al., 1985; Vanden Eynde et al., 1984), and no training effects have been observed during this pubertal stage (Gaisl & Buchberger, 1984; Reybrouck et al., 1985). Before 12 and after 16 years of age ventilatory or lactate threshold increases with physical training (Atomi et al., 1986; Reybrouck et al., 1985) as in adults. During puberty, the reduction of threshold has been associated with maturation of anaerobic metabolism (Vanden Eynde et al., 1984) and hormonal activity that may neutralize physical training effects (Reybrouck et al., 1985).

Lactate thresholds in high-altitude residents have never been reported. A previous study showed identical ventilatory threshold ($\%\dot{V}O_2max$) and maximal lactate concentrations in low- and high-altitude resident boys who were 11 years old (Fellmann et al., 1986). The aim of this study was to investigate lactate and ventilatory thresholds in high- and low-altitude boys in relation to stages of maturation.

MATERIALS AND METHODS

Subjects

Three groups of healthy boys (N = 51) aged 12 to 14 years participated in the study with their parents' consent. The first group of 12-year-old children (HA12, n = 21) had lived for more than 3 years at high altitude (3,700 m) in La Paz, Bolivia. The other two groups, one of 12-year-olds (LA12, n = 16) and the second of 14-year-olds (LA14, n = 14), lived in France at low altitude (300 m). Both groups had similar socioeconomic status and level of physical activity (5 hr a week). Anthropometric data are given in Table 1.

Experimental Procedures

At HA the environmental parameters (mean ± SD) were 497 ± 2 Torr for barometric pressure (PB) and 20.3 ± 1.1 °C for ambient temperature (Ta). The values at LA were 722 ± 8 Torr for PB and 20.8 ± 1 °C for Ta. All exercise bouts were performed with a Monark cycle ergometer at 70-rpm pedaling frequency. During exercise, heart rate was recorded on an electrocardiogram.

Maximal oxygen consumption ($\dot{V}O_2$max) was determined by the direct method. The subjects increased their work load to exhaustion in three or four successive steps of 2 min duration. Capillary blood samples (50 μl) were taken from the earlobe between the 1st and the 2nd min after exercise. Maximal bioenergetic data are presented in Table 1.

A few days later, the subjects were studied during an incremental exercise test without warm-up. The step incrementation was of 1-1/2 min and of 10% to 12% $\dot{V}O_2$max. During the last 30 s of each step, expired air samples were collected in Douglas bags. The volumes were measured with a Tissot spirometer; the fractions of O_2 and CO_2 in expired air were determined with physical gas analyzers. Pulmonary ventilation ($\dot{V}_E$), CO_2 output ($\dot{V}CO_2$), respiratory ratio (R), and ventilatory equivalents for O_2 ($\dot{V}_E/\dot{V}O_2$) and for CO_2 ($\dot{V}_E/\dot{V}CO_2$) were calculated for each expired air collection. Blood samples (50 μl) were drawn during the last 30 s of each step from a small cannula that had been inserted into an antecubital vein. Blood samples were also drawn during the recovery period at 1, 2, 3, 4, 5, 6, 7, 10, and 15 min. The blood was immediately deproteinized and analyzed for lactate content by the enzymatic method.

Lactate and Ventilatory Threshold Determinations

According to Kindermann, Simon, and Keul (1979), two lactate thresholds can be discriminated. LT_1 (i.e., aerobic threshold) corresponds to the $\dot{V}O_2$ at which a first and definitive increase in lactate concentrations is observed (first break point). LT_2 (i.e., anaerobic threshold) corresponds to the following steep increase in blood lactate concentrations (second break point).

Table 1 Anthropometric and Maximal Bioenergetic Data

	HA_{12yr}	LA_{12yr}	LA_{14yr}	Statistical comparisons between groups		
	$n = 21$	$n = 16$	$n = 14$	HA/LA12	HA/LA14	LA12/LA14
Age (months)	146.2 ± 10.8	147.9 ± 11	170.5 ± 9.8	NS	***	***
Body mass (kg)	39.1 ± 7	42.7 ± 5.9	52 ± 8.4	NS	***	***
Height (cm)	149.3 ± 10	152 ± 8.5	163.1 ± 6.8	NS	***	***
Body surface area (m^2)	1.28 ± 0.15	1.34 ± 0.12	1.54 ± 0.14	NS	***	***
Salivary concentration in testosterone ($mmol \cdot l^{-1}$)	243 ± 71	146 ± 60	238 ± 108	***	NS	**
$\dot{V}O_2max$ ($l \cdot min^{-1}$)	1.59 ± 0.25	1.95 ± 0.31	2.72 ± 0.62	***	***	***
$\dot{V}O_2max$ ($ml \cdot min^{-1} \cdot kg^{-1}$)	41.1 ± 4.9	46.5 ± 6.4	51.9 ± 6.6	***	***	*
HRmax ($b \cdot min^{-1}$)	188 ± 8	202 ± 8	196 ± 6	***	**	*
Rmax	1.12 ± 0.07	1.14 ± 0.06	1.18 ± 0.11	NS	NS	NS
[L]max ($mmol \cdot l^{-1}$)	9.5 ± 2	6.7 ± 1.9	9.4 ± 2.2	***	NS	**

$^*p < .05$. $^{**}p < .01$. $^{***}p < .001$. $M \pm SD$.

Ventilatory threshold was determined as the $\dot{V}O_2$ for which $\dot{V}_E$ and $\dot{V}CO_2$ began to increase nonlinearly with a systematic increase in ventilatory O_2 equivalent without a concomitant increase in ventilatory CO_2 equivalent (Davis, 1985; Wasserman, 1973). Both lactate and ventilatory thresholds were determined visually from individual data by two experimenters. Figure 1 shows an example of determinations.

Statistical analysis

Student tests were used to compare mean measurements between groups. Statistical significance was accepted at the $p < .05$ level.

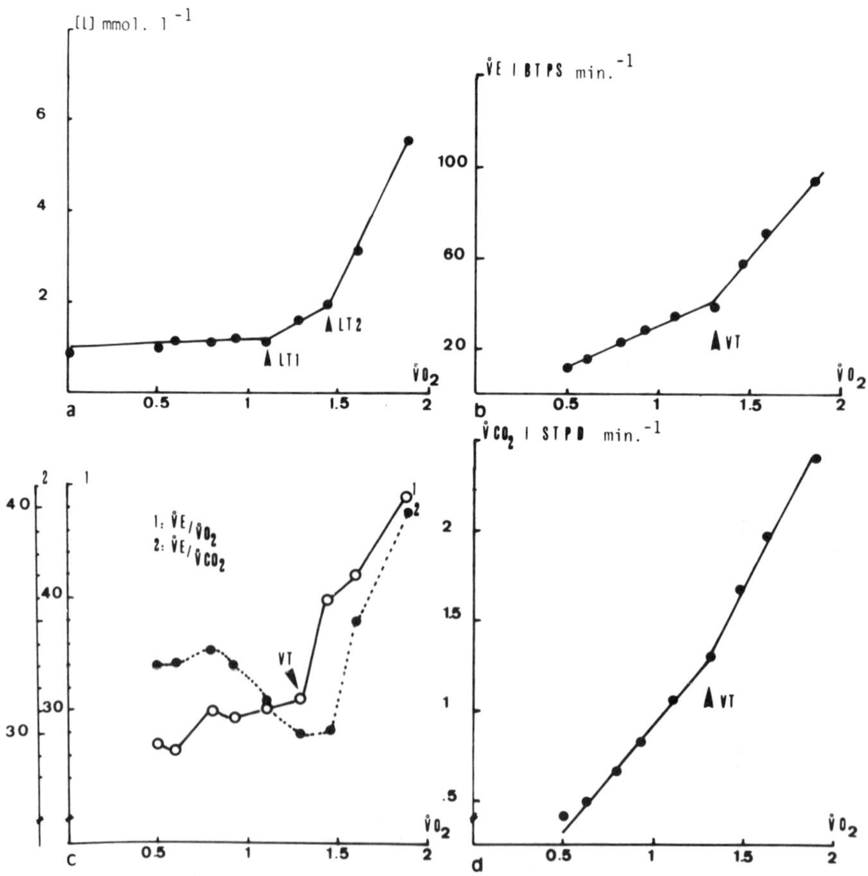

Figure 1. One example of lactate (LT_1 and LT_2) and ventilatory (VT) threshold determinations.

RESULTS

Anthropometric, maturation status, and maximal bioenergetic data are given in Table 1, and lactate and ventilatory threshold data are provided in Table 2. At low altitude, $\dot{V}O_2$ at LT_1, LT_2, and VT increased in boys from 12 to 14 years of age ($p < .05$). In 12-year-old boys, $\dot{V}O_2$ at LT_1, LT_2, and VT were always lower in HA children ($p < .001$), but no differences were observed within the three groups when thresholds were expressed in terms of $\%\dot{V}O_2max$. Blood lactate concentrations at LT_1 did not differ from rest values: An increase in lactatemia was observed from LT_1 to LT_2 and reached similar values in LA groups.

In HA boys, lactate concentrations at rest, LT_1, and LT_2 were higher than in LA groups ($p < .05$). There was a good correlation between $[L]LT_1$ and $[L]LT_2$ ($p < .001$), but there was no significant correlation between salivary testosterone concentrations ([T]) and LT_1, LT_2, and VT ($\%\dot{V}O_2max$), nor between [T] and $[L]LT_1$ and $[L]LT_2$.

The percent of $\dot{V}O_2max$ reached at the last step of incremental exercise did not show significant differences within the three groups (90% to 93% $\dot{V}O_2max$). After incremental exercise, blood lactate concentrations reached peak values during recovery (2nd min). Like maximal lactate concentrations, peak lactate concentrations increased from 12 to 14 years in LA groups ($p < .05$). In 12-year-old boys [L]peak and [L]max were higher in the HA group ($p < .001$), and there were no significant differences between HA12 and LA14. There were significant correlations between [L]peak, [L]max, and [T] ($p < .02$).

DISCUSSION

Methodological Aspects

The 2 and 4 mmol • l^{-1} blood lactate concentrations are usually utilized for aerobic-anaerobic threshold determinations in adults. In the present study, the mean values of lactate concentrations for LT_1 and LT_2 were half those in adults. This was in agreement with lower lactate concentrations after and during submaximal and maximal exercise in children as compared to adults (Eriksson, Gollnick, & Saltin, 1973; Macek, Vavra, & Novosadova, 1976). Use of 2 and 4 mmol • l^{-1} blood lactate concentrations gave a mean overestimation of 20% to 30% for the groups in the present study. It was felt that it is important in studies of children to determine lactate thresholds from the evolution of lactate concentrations with exercise intensity and not from fixed values. Thus a sufficient number of steps is necessary for these determinations; using steps of 10% of $\dot{V}O_2max$, as used in the present study, seemed to be a satisfactory method.

The second methodological aspect concerned correspondence between LT_1 or LT_2 and VT. There have been numerous papers and controversial

Table 2 Incremental Exercise, Ventilatory and Lactate Thresholds

		HA_{12yr}	LA_{12yr}	LA_{14yr}	Statistical comparisons between groups		
		n = 21	n = 16	n = 14	HA/LA12	HA/LA14	LA12/LA14
	$\dot{V}O_2$ (l • min^{-1})	0.92 ± 0.19	1.14 ± 0.13	1.5 ± 0.44	**	***	*
LT_1	$\dot{V}O_2$max (%$\dot{V}O_2$max)	59.7 ± 11.4	55.8 ± 7.4	54.5 ± 8.8	NS	NS	NS
	[L] mmol • l^{-1}	1.7 ± 0.4	1.1 ± 0.3	1.3 ± 0.2	***	**	*
	$\dot{V}O_2$ (l • min^{-1}	1.23 ± 0.21	1.54 ± 0.19	2.03 ± 0.59	***	***	**
LT_2	$\dot{V}O_2$ (%$\dot{V}O_2$max)	75.8 ± 8	73.1 ± 7.3	73.5 ± 5.8	NS	NS	NS
	[L] mmol • l^{-1}	2.7 ± 0.5	1.8 ± 0.5	2.1 ± 0.7	***	*	NS
VT	$\dot{V}O_2$ (l • min^{-1})	1.01 ± 0.17	1.32 ± 0.28	1.75 ± 0.62	***	**	*
	$\dot{V}O_2$ (%$\dot{V}O_2$max)	63.6 ± 7.2	4.66 ± 10.7	63.2 ± 11	NS	NS	NS
Last step intensity (%$\dot{V}O_2$max)		89.4 ± 9.1	94.6 ± 6.9	93.2 ± 5.9	NS	NS	NS
[L] peak during recovery (mmol • l^{-1})		8.5 ± 2.3	6.0 ± 1.7	7.3 ± 1.6	**	NS	*

*$p < .05$. **$p < .01$. ***$p < .001$. M ± SD.

observations on this point. In the present study, VT was not the same as LT_1 or LT_2 ($p < .05$ paired student t test) but in no case (individual values) was VT smaller than LT_1 or higher than LT_2. Thus it seemed reasonable to assume that superposition or dissociation between lactate and ventilatory thresholds depends on determinations, and that VT is localized in aerobic-anaerobic transition in healthy subjects.

Maturation and Altitude Effects

Lactate and ventilatory thresholds ($l \cdot min^{-1}$; $\%\dot{V}O_2max$) and $\dot{V}O_2max$ in LA boys were similar to data reported for children by other authors (Atomi et al., 1986; Becker & Vaccaro, 1983; Medelli et al., 1985; Reybrouck et al., 1985) and greater than values usually observed in sedentary adults. From 12- to 14-years old, salivary testosterone concentrations increased from 146.1 ± 59.7 to 238.4 ± 108.3 mmol $\cdot$ l^{-1} ($p < .01$). This enlargement of free testosterone level gave evidence of a significant pubertal maturation.

An increase of maximal and peak blood lactate concentrations were also observed between 12 and 14 years of age ($p < .05$). In addition, good correlations between [L] peak or [L] max and [T] ($p < .02$) were observed. In spite of this, these children did not show any significant reduction in thresholds ($\%\dot{V}O_2max$) with age. These results were in disagreement with the observations of Reybrouck et al. (1985) and Vanden Eynde et al. (1984). However, these discrepancies may be linked to different levels of physical fitness. Each group of boys in this study participated in physical activities and sports 5 hr a week. At this age, recreational games also play an important part in a child's life.

Endurance training has been shown to increase threshold level in adults (Denis, Fouquet, Poty, Geyssant, & Lacour, 1982; Prud'Homme, Bouchard, Leblanc, Landry, & Fontaine, 1984) and in children (Atomi et al., 1986; Reybrouck et al., 1985). Prud'Homme et al. (1984) showed in monozygotic twins that genetotype dependence of threshold level is not very elevated (less than 50%). It has been established that endurance training increases the fast twitch area, muscle capillaries, and oxidative enzymatic activities, as well as the ability to oxidate pyruvate. Each of these factors is well correlated with threshold levels (Ivy, Withers, Handel, Elger, & Costill, 1980; Tesch et al., 1985).

Lowered values of lactate and ventilatory thresholds ($l \cdot min^{-1}$; $ml \cdot min^{-1} \cdot kg^{-1}$) in high-altitude boys were directly linked to the effect of altitude on $\dot{V}O_2max$. In contrast, LT_1, LT_2, and VT in terms of $\%\dot{V}O_2max$ were similar at both altitudes. Thus high altitude induces an earlier glycolytic maturation but does not alter lactate and ventilatory thresholds ($\%\dot{V}O_2max$). The lack of an altitude effect on thresholds was in agreement with previous observations on ventilatory threshold in prepubertal boys (11-year-olds) living at 3,800 m (Fellmann et al., 1986). The same conclusions have been drawn for adult residents at 2,000 m and during acute hypoxia (Maresh, Noble, Robertson, & Sime, 1983).

The absence of a correlation for both altitudes between thresholds and peak or maximal blood lactate concentrations indicates that active boys' threshold levels are not necessarily linked to glycolytic maturation. Likewise, the absence of a correlation between thresholds and salivary testosterone levels indicates that the decrease in thresholds usually observed from childhood to adulthood is not linked to gonadal maturation.

CONCLUSION

No reduction in ventilatory and lactate thresholds was observed in spite of altitude effects and/or maturation spurt. Glycolytic maturation and gonadal hormonal stimulations during puberty do not always have a determining influence on very active boys' thresholds.

Acknowledgments

The studies in La Paz were supported by the Service de la Coopération Technique. The authors are grateful to Esperanza Caceres and Michel Delaitre for their technical assistance, to Jeffrey Watts for help with the translation, and to Marie Pascual for typing the manuscript.

REFERENCES

Atomi, Y., Fukunaga, T., Yamamoto, Y., & Hatta, H. (1986). Lactate threshold and $\dot{V}O_2$max of trained and untrained boys relative to muscle mass and composition. In J. Rutenfranz, R. Mocellin, & F. Klimt (Eds), *Children and exercise XII* (pp. 53-58). Champaign, IL: Human Kinetics.

Becker, M.D., & Vaccaro, P. (1983). Anaerobic threshold alterations caused by endurance training in young children. *International Journal of Sports Medicine*, **23**, 445-449.

Davis, J.A. (1985). Anaerobic threshold, review of the concept and directions of future research. *Medicine and Science in Sports and Exercise*, **17**(1), 6-18.

Denis, C., Fouquet, R., Poty, P., Geyssant, A., & Lacour, J.R. (1982). Effect of 40 weeks of endurance training on the anaerobic threshold. *International Journal of Sports Medicine*, **3**(4), 208-214.

Eriksson, B.O., Gollnick, P.D., & Saltin, B. (1973). Muscle metabolism and enzyme activities after training in boys 11-13 years old. *Acta Physiologica Scandinavica*, **87**, 485-497.

Fellmann, N., Bedu, M., Spielvogel, H., Falgairette, G., Van Praagh, E., & Coudert, J. (1986). Oxygen debt in submaximal and supramaximal exercise in children at high and low altitude. *Journal of Applied Physiology: Respiratory, Environmental and Exercise Physiology*, **60**, 209-215.

Gaisl, G., & Buchberger, J. (1984). Changes in the aerobic-anaerobic transition in boys after 3 years of special physical education. In J. Ilmarinen & I. Välimäki (Eds.), *Children and sport* (pp. 156-161). Berlin, Heidelberg: Springer-Verlag.

Ivy, J.L., Withers, R.T., Handel, V.P.T., Elger, D.H., & Costill, D.L. (1980). Muscle respiratory capacity and fiber types as determinants of the lactate threshold. *Journal of Applied Physiology, Respiratory, Environmental and Exercise Physiology*, **48**, 523-527.

Kindermann, W., Simon, G., & Keul, J. (1979). The significance of the aerobic-anaerobic transition for the determination of work load intensities during endurance training. *European Journal of Applied Physiology and Occupational Physiology*, **42**, 25-34.

Macek, M., Vavra, J., & Novosadova, J. (1976). Prolonged exercise in prepubertal boys: 2. Changes in plasma volume and in some blood constituents. *European Journal of Applied Physiology and Occupational Physiology*, **35**, 299-303.

Maresh, C.M., Noble, J.B., Robertson, K.L., & Sime, W.E. (1983). Maximal exercise during hypobaric hypoxia (445 Torr) in moderate-altitude natives. *Medicine and Science in Sports and Exercise*, **15**(5), 360-365.

Medelli, J., Maingourd, Y., Freville, M., Nekrouf, A., & Harichaux, P. (1985). Etude de la transition aerobie-anaerobie lors des épreuves d'effort chez l'enfant [Aerobic-anaerobic transition study during exercise in children]. *Cinésiologie*, **104**, 431-436.

Prud'Homme, D., Bouchard, C., Leblanc, C., Landry, F., & Fontaine, E. (1984). Sensitivity of maximal aerobic power to training is genotype dependent. *Medicine and Science in Sports and Exercise*, **16**(5), 489-493.

Reybrouck, T., Weymans, M., Stijns, H., Knops, J., & Vander Hauwaert, L. (1985). Ventilatory anaerobic threshold in healthy children, age and sex differences. *European Journal of Applied Physiology and Occupational Physiology*, **54**, 278-284.

Tesch, P.A., Wright, J.E., Vogel, J.A., Daniels, W.L., Sharp, D.S., & Sjodin, B. (1985). The influence of muscle metabolic characteristics on physical performance. *European Journal of Applied Physiology and Occupational Physiology*, **54**, 237-243.

Vanden Eynde, B., Ghesquiere, J., Van Gerven, D., Vuylsteke Wauters, M., & Vande Perre, H. (1984). Follow-up study of physical fitness in boys aged 10-14 years. In J. Ilmarinen & I. Välimäki (Eds.), *Children and sport* (pp. 111-118). Berlin, Heidelberg: Springer-Verlag.

Wasserman, K. (1973). Anaerobic threshold and respiratory gas exchange during exercise. *Journal of Applied Physiology*, **35**, 236-243.

Effect of High-Altitude Hypoxia on Anaerobic Metabolism in Boys

Nicole Fellmann
Mario Bedu
Jean Coudert
Laboratoire de Physiologie, Clermont-Ferrand, France
Guy Falgairette
Emmanuel Van Praagh
Université de Clermont-Ferrand, Aubière, France
Hilde Spielvogel
Instituto Boliviano de Biologia de Altura, La Paz, Bolivia

Children exhibit a higher level of maximal aerobic power; however, their anaerobic capacity is less than that of adults. Their ability to form lactate is reduced (Eriksson, Karlsson, & Saltin, 1971). During pubertal development, lactate production by muscle increases as glycolytic enzyme activities (aldolase, phosphofructokinase, lactate dehydrogenase) are enhanced (Berg, Kim, & Keul, 1986; Haralambie, 1982). The effects of high altitude on these pubertal changes have never been reported. The aim of this study was to compare the changes in anaerobic metabolism evaluated by blood lactate concentration after maximal exercises throughout the period of 11 to 14 years in boys living at high altitude (3,700 m, HA) and low altitude (330 m, LA).

METHODS

A total of 12 boys, 11 years of age, and 21 boys, 12 years of age, participated in this study of high altitude (La Paz, Bolivia; barometric pressure, P_B = 497 Torr and ambient temperature, θ = 20.5 °C). They either were high altitude natives or had lived for 3 years or more in La Paz. They had good nutritional and socioeconomic status. They were compared with 21 boys, 11 years of age, 16 boys, 12 years old, and 14 boys of 14 years of age living at low altitude (Clermont-Ferrand, France; P_B = 722 Torr; θ = 20.1 °C).

All the children had a similar level of physical fitness (5 to 6 hr a week). All the methods used were exactly the same at both altitudes. The pubertal stages were evaluated by salivary testosterone level. The concentration of the steroid ([T]) was determined by a specific radio-immunoassay for testosterone (Jarrige, André, Grizard, & Boucher, 1982).

The maximal exercise tests were carried out on a cycle ergometer (Monark) at 70-rpm pedaling frequency. Heart rate (HR) was obtained by continuous electrocardiogram recording. Maximal oxygen consumption ($\dot{V}O_2$max) was measured by direct triangular method. Each step duration was of 2 min. The last 30-s samples of expired air were collected in Douglas bags. The fractions of O_2 and CO_2 in the expired air were measured by gas analyzers. Air volumes were determined with a Tissot spirometer. Capillary blood samples (50-100 μl) were drawn from the earlobe between the first and the second minute during the recover period. Blood lactate concentrations ([L]) were measured by the enzymatic method of Gutmann and Wahlfeld (1974). Excluded from the study were cycle bouts for which the criteria of a maximal test were not obtained: actual exhaustion, expiratory gas exchange ratio above unit, and heart rate approximating the maximal theoretical value. Students' *t* test procedures were used to compare mean measurements in the groups. Values were taken to be significantly different for $p < .05$.

RESULTS

Physical characteristics of both HA and LA boys (see Table 1) were statistically the same for the same chronological age of 11 and 12 years, except for height: HA 11-year-old boys were smaller than their counterparts at LA ($p < .01$). $\dot{V}O_2$max ($l \cdot min^{-1}$ or $ml \cdot min^{-1} \cdot kg^{-1}$) and HRmax (see Table 2) were lower at HA for each age group ($p < .001$), that is, a decrease of 24% at 11 years and 18% at 12 years in $\dot{V}O_2$max ($l \cdot min^{-1}$) and of 10 and 14 beats $\cdot$ min^{-1}, respectively, in HRmax.

Saliva testosterone level (Figure 1) in 12-year-old boys at HA indicated a pubertal Stage n °3 according to Sannika, Terho, Suominen, and Santti (1983), but in 12-year-old children at LA, testosterone level corresponded only to Stage n °2. At the age of 14 years, LA boys exhibited the same level of testosterone as 12-year-old boys in La Paz.

[L] values at 11 years were the same at both altitudes (see Figure 1). In contrast, [L] values in 12-year-old boys at HA were higher than at LA ($p < .001$) but were close to LA values at 14 years of age.

DISCUSSION

A similar decrease in $\dot{V}O_2$max was found in high-altitude 11- and 12-year-old boys, as already reported in previous studies: in adolescent swimmers living in La Paz (Greska et al., 1982) and in boys living in the Ethiopian mountains (Andersen, 1973). This decrease resulted primarily in a reduction of maximal heart rate, as already observed in adults at high altitude. However, both at HA and at LA, the maximal aerobic power was as high as the respective adult level. Haralambie (1982) found that at sea level activities of oxidative muscle enzymes (lipoamide dehydro-

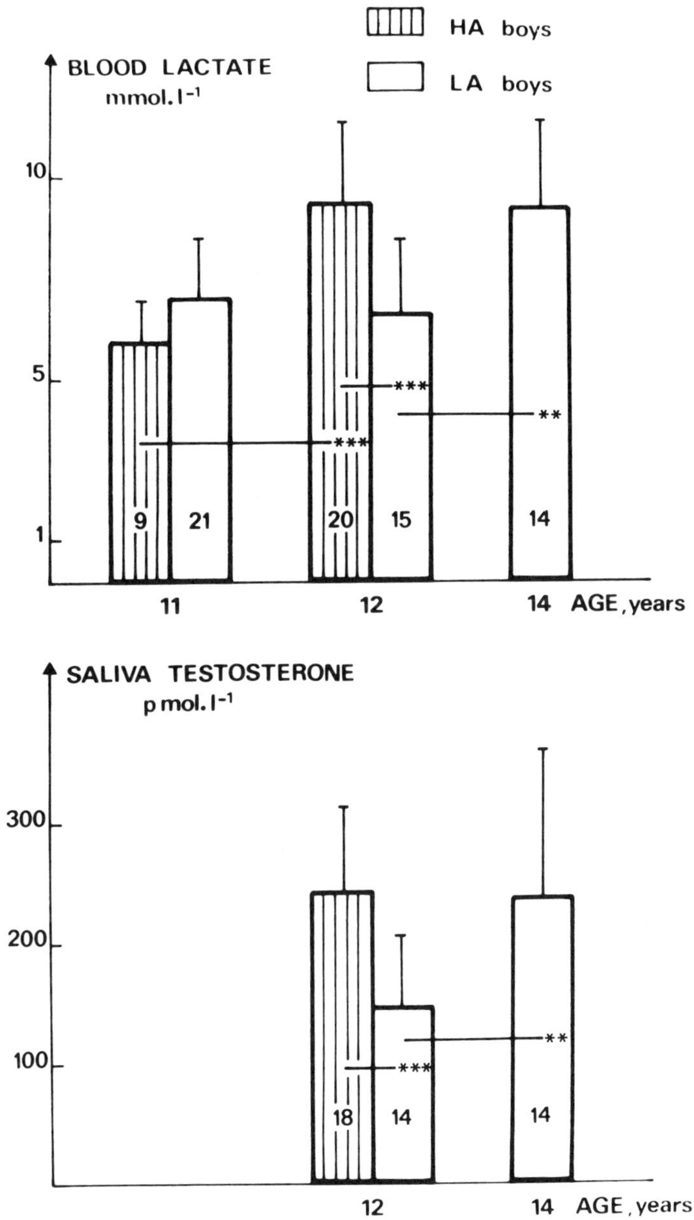

Figure 1. Changes in blood lactate and saliva testosterone concentrations (mean ± *SD*) with age at high and low altitudes (numbers on bars indicate number of determinations).

genase, tricarboxylic acid cycle enzymes) were even higher in young children than in adolescents and adults.

In contrast, anaerobic metabolism in boys of 11 years of age was lower than in adults. It has been demonstrated at low altitude that muscle lactate

Table 1 Anthropometric Data of Boys Studied at High (HA) and Low (LA) Altitudes

	11 years		12 years		14 years
	HA	LA	HA	LA	LA
n	12	21	21	16	14
Age (months)	134 ± 9	135 ± 10	146 ± 11	148 ± 11	171 ± 10
Weight (kg)	36.9 ± 8.7	37.9 ± 4.1	39.1 ± 7.0	42.7 ± 5.9	52.0 ± 8.4
Height (cm)	141.5 ± 6.6	148.3 ± 5.5**	149.3 ± 10.0	152.0 ± 8.5	163.1 ± 6.8

Note. Values are means ± *SD*. At the same chronological ages of 11 and 12 years, all the group means are statistically similar except for mean height, which was greater in LA 11-year-old boys.

**$p < .01$.

Table 2 Comparisons of Maximal Bioenergetic Data Between High- and Low-Altitude Boys

	11 years		12 years		14 years
	HA	LA	HA	LA	LA
$\dot{V}O_2max$ ($l \cdot min^{-1}$)	1.56 ± 0.27	2.06 ± 0.32	1.59 ± 0.25	1.95 ± 0.31	2.72 ± 0.62***
$\dot{V}O_2max$ ($ml \cdot min^{-1} \cdot kg^{-1}$)	43.0 ± 6.7	54.2 ± 7.0	41.1 ± 4.9	46.5 ± 6.4	51.9 ± 6.6*
R	1.20 ± 0.08	1.03 ± 0.07	1.12 ± 0.07	1.14 ± 0.06	1.18 ± 0.11
HR ($beats \cdot min^{-1}$)	193 ± 6	203 ± 7	188 ± 8	202 ± 8	196 ± 6**

Note. Values are means ± *SD*. At the same chronological ages of 11 and 12 years, all the means are statistically different between HA and LA groups ($p < .001$). Comparisons between LA 12-year-old and LA 14-year-old boys are: *$p < .05$, **$p < .01$, ***$p < .001$.

production is reduced as a result of decreased glycolytic enzyme activities (aldolase, phosphofructo-kinase, and lactico-dehydrogenase; Berg et al., 1986; Eriksson, Gollnick, & Saltin, 1973; Haralambie, 1982). Moreover, the present results showed that, first, there was the same pattern in boys at high altitude (blood lactate level after maximal exercise was also lower than in HA adults), and second, there was no difference in blood lactate concentration between HA and LA boys at 11 years of age. In addition, in a previous study (Fellmann et al., 1986) it was reported that oxygen debts and blood lactate concentrations after supramaximal exercise (115% $\dot{V}O_2max$) were also the same.

At the age of 12 years, although there was no alteration in aerobic metabolism at either altitude, blood lactate concentration was increased by 58% at HA but remained unchanged at LA. The same results were observed after submaximal exercise (90% $\dot{V}O_2max$; 8.5 ± 2.3 mmol • l^{-1} at HA and 6.0 ± 1.7 mmol • l^{-1} at LA). These changes at HA seemed to be linked to sexual maturation. When the LA boys between the ages of 12 and 14 years reached the same level of testosterone as the 12-year-old boys at HA, their blood lactate levels also increased and were close to HA values. Eriksson et al. (1973) found an almost significant correlation between muscle lactate following maximal exercise and testicular volume in 12- to 13-year-old boys.

The findings of the present study are in agreement with these results and are more accurate because saliva testosterone, which is related to plasma-free testosterone (Khan-Dawood, Choe, & Dawood, 1984; Smith, Besch, Dill, & Buttram, 1979), is a better indicator of puberty than testicular volume or plasma total testosterone level (Sannika et al., 1983). The effects of testosterone on muscle have been more widely documented in animals. The activities of anaerobic glycolysis enzymes are increased by androgens in the temporal muscle of male guinea pigs and by testosterone injection in young females (Bass, Gutmann, Hanzlíková, & Syrovy, 1971). In contrast, castration of rats induces a decrease in phosphorylase and lactate dehydrogenase activities of the soleus and gastrocnemius muscles (Krotkiemswki, Kral, & Karlsson, 1980). Furthermore, the significant linear relationship between blood lactate and saliva testosterone in all the boys studied ($p < .02$) also confirmed the hypothesis that HA boys produced more lactate than LA boys at the same age of 12 years because they matured earlier. Further investigations would be necessary to determine whether high-altitude environments induce this earlier pubertal development.

Acknowledgments

The studies in La Paz were supported by the Service de la Coopération Technique. The authors are grateful to Esperanza Caceres and Michel Delaitre for their technical assistance, to Jeffrey Watts for help with the translation, and to Marie Pascual for typing the manuscript.

REFERENCES

Andersen, K. (1972). The effect of altitude variation on the physical performance capacity of Ethiopian men. Part II. Development of physical performance capacity during adolescence. In V. Seliger (Ed.), *Physical fitness* (pp. 34-36). Prague: Charles University.

Bass, A., Gutmann, E., Hanzlíková, V., & Syrovy, I. (1971). Sexual differentiation of enzyme pattern and its conversion by testosterone in the temporal muscle of the guinea pig. *Physiological Bohemoslovaca* (Prague), **20**, 423-431.

Berg, A., Kim, S.S., & Keul, J. (1986). Skeletal muscle enzyme activities in healthy young subjects. *International Journal of Sports Medicine*, **7**, 236-239.

Eriksson, B.D., Gollnick, P.D., & Saltin, B. (1973). Muscle metabolism and enzyme activities after training in boys 11-13 years old. *Acta Physiologica Scandinavica*, **87**, 485-497.

Eriksson, B.D., Karlsson, J., & Saltin, B. (1971). Muscle metabolism during exercise in pubertal boys. *Acta Paediatrica Scandinavica*, **217**(Suppl.), 154-157.

Fellmann, N., Bedu, M., Spielvogel, H., Falgairette, G., Van Praagh, E., & Coudert, J. (1986). Oxygen debt in submaximal and supramaximal exercise in children at high and low altitude. *Journal of Applied Physiology*, **60**, 209-215.

Greska, L.P., Haas, J.D., Leatherman, T.L., Spielvogel, H., Paz Zamora, M., Paredes-Fernandez, L., & Moreno-Black, G. (1982). Maximal aerobic power in trained youths at high altitude. *Annals of Human Biology*, **9**, 201-209.

Gutmann, L., & Wahlefeld, A.W. (1974). Determination of lactate dehydrogenase and N.A.D. In H. Bergmeyer (Ed.), *Methods of enzymatic analysis* (pp. 1464-1468). London: Academic.

Haralambie, G. (1982). Enzyme activities in skeletal muscle of 13- to 15-year-old adolescents. *Bulletin Européen de Physiopathologie Respiratoire*, **18**, 65-74.

Jarrige, J.F., André, M., Grizard, G., & Boucher, D. (1982). Freination de la sécrétion de prolactine et fonction androgénique chez le rat mâle adulte [Inhibition of prolactine secretion and androgenic function in adult male rat]. *Comptes-rendus des Séances de la Société de Biologie*, **176**, 517-524.

Khan-Dawood, F., Choe, J., & Dawood, Y. (1984). Salivary and plasma bound and free testosterone in men and women. *American Journal of Obstetrics and Gynecology*, **148**, 441-445.

Krotkiewski, M., Kral, J.G., & Karlsson, J. (1980). Effects of castration and testosterone substitution on body composition and muscle metabolism in rats. *Acta Physiologica Scandinavica,* **109**, 233-237.

Sannika, E., Terho, P., Suominen, J., & Santti, R. (1983). Testosterone concentrations in human seminal plasma and saliva and its correlation with non-protein bound and total testosterone levels in serum. *International Journal of Andrology,* **6**, 319-330.

Smith, R., Besch, P., Dill, B., & Buttram, V. (1979). Saliva as a matrix for measuring free androgens: Comparison with serum androgens in polycystic ovarian disease. *Fertility and Sterility,* **31**, 513-517.

Part III

The Effect of Training Upon Muscle Strength and Development

Strength Training and Muscle Hypertrophy in Children

F. Mersch
Universität Berlin, Berlin, Federal Republic of Germany
Hans Stoboy
Institut für Leistungsmedizin, Berlin, Federal Republic of Germany

Bar-Or (1983) stated that no publications are available concerning the trainability of strength in children. Such a study must include children, adolescents, and adults with comparable muscle strength at the beginning of training. Until such a project is performed, the knowledge concerning the optimal age for strength training will be uncertain and preliminary.

STRENGTH CHANGES DUE TO GROWTH

The possibility of an increase in strength due to training before puberty is controversial. On the one hand, specific strength training is reported to be effective only after puberty (Hebbelinck, 1966; Szabo, 1969). On the other hand, strength training in prepubescent children has been observed to increase muscular strength (Röhmert, 1968). According to Hettinger (1983), the enhancement of strength due to growth is approximately 1.5 kg per year for age 6 to 14 years. According to Asmussen (1973), a rapid increase of strength in males begins when the body height reaches 155 cm, which coincides with the average age of 13 years. This phenomenon is obviously correlated with sexual maturity and due to an increased secretion of testosterone.

According to Bouchard and Thibault (1972), the increase in muscle mass between birth and the onset of puberty occurs when the production of androgens is negligible; thus other mechanisms must be responsible for the hypertrophy of muscles during this time.

In this period of enhanced growth of the muscles of the extremities, fibers are stretched, which stimulates an increase in the number of sarcomeres from 700 to 2,200, as shown in animal experiments (Goldspink, 1980). In addition, the number of fibrils in one fiber is raised from 15 to more than 1,000. Both developments increase muscle strength considerably.

STRENGTH TRAINING

According to Hollmann and Hettinger (1980), strength training in children younger than 8 to 10 years of age does not result in morphological adaptation. An effect of strength training can first be seen in boys 13 to 14 years of age (De Marees, 1981; Hollmann & Hettinger, 1980; Nicu, 1973). Rutenfranz (1983) stated that despite medical objections, strength training with barbell weights and training machines is often begun before the age of 12 years. At this age training should involve only the development of the skills and special coordination required for weight lifting. Goldspink, Howells, and Ward (1976) trained hamsters to lift 60% of their body weight. In the younger animals (8 weeks of age, approximately comparable to puberty in boys) muscle fiber hypertrophy was much more marked (+35.6%) than in adult animals (65 weeks). The normal growth of muscles can be accelerated by training because of the larger biological potential in younger muscles.

STATIC STRENGTH TRAINING

Kirsten (1963) performed static training of the back extensor muscles (pulling a hand grip for several seconds) in girls and boys aged 11 to 14 years. He found no differences between the subjects and the controls, probably because the daily activity of these children was superimposed upon the training stimulus. This investigation confirmed the opinion of many authors that children of this age group cannot be trained in strength (Bührle, 1984).

Fukunaga (1976) investigated the strength of girls 13 years of age, measuring static contractions of the forearm flexors during a 60-day period (Figure 1). Up to the 20th day strength improved without any change in the cross-sectional area of the muscle. Subsequently, the cross-sectional area increased with a further enhancement of strength.

DYNAMIC STRENGTH TRAINING

It is usually stated that for children aged 10 to 14 years the purpose of all-round strength training should be to coordinate strength performance (Berlin, Baumeister, & Apel, 1974; Dworkin, 1976; Jones, 1984). Only a small part of the total training, approximately 30%, should consist of barbell exercises with 60 to 70% of body weight (Berlin, Baumeister, & Apel, 1974; Nicu, 1973). Special strength training with loads of between 70 and 90% of body weight can start at 13 to 16 years of age (Dworkin, 1976; Jones, 1984). According to Bührle (1984), strength training for boys of 8 to 12 years with 50 to 60% of maximum strength is more effective than with students of physical education.

Vrijens (1978) performed a training of 8 weeks with 70.5% of maximum strength. In a prepubescent group with an average age of 10.4 years, only

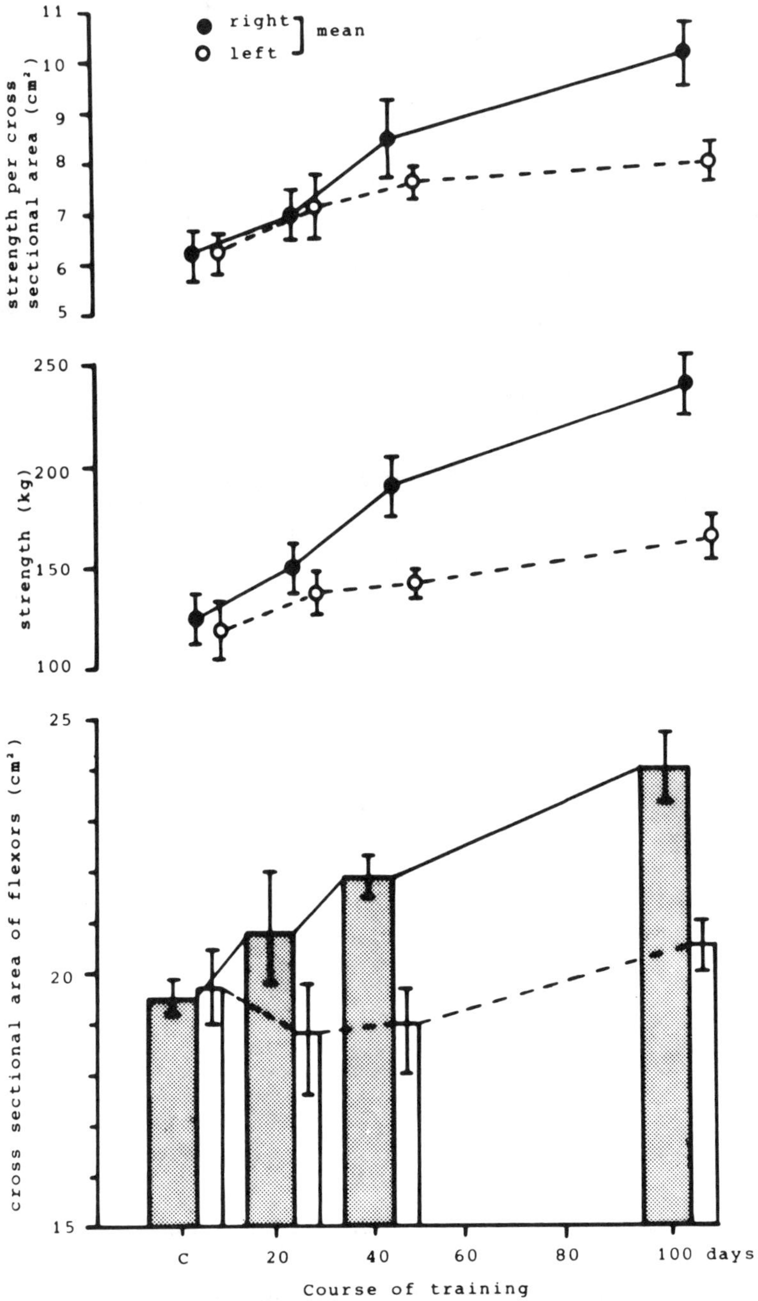

Figure 1. Increases of relative strength/cm², absolute strength, and cross-sectional area of the trained and untrained muscles. *Note.* From "Die Absolute Muskelkraft und das Krafttraining" by T. Fukunaga, 1976, *Sportarzt und Sportmedizin*, **27**, pp. 255-266.

abdominal and back muscle strength increased significantly. In muscles of the extremity, neither a distinct improvement in strength nor an increase in cross-sectional areas, as determined by X-ray examinations, could be observed. In the postpubescent group, with an average age of 16.7 years, strength increased in all investigated muscles, and X-ray investigations showed larger cross-sectional areas in the upper arm and the thigh.

Duffner (1984) and Messmer (1984) measured the training effect during 4 weeks in girls and boys aged 7 to 9 years. Strength increased in the forearm extensors by 24.7% and 27%, respectively. The increased strength of the thigh extensors was 40%. However, in an exercise group emphasizing only the skill of weight lifting, changes in strength were not significant.

MUSCLE HYPERTROPHY

An increase in strength in adults due to training is more or less accompanied by muscle hypertrophy, whereas in children enlargements of cross-sectional area are usually not detected (Bührle, 1984; Hollmann & Hettinger, 1980; Letzelter & Dickmann, 1984). It was suggested that an improved inter- and intramuscular coordination might be responsible for

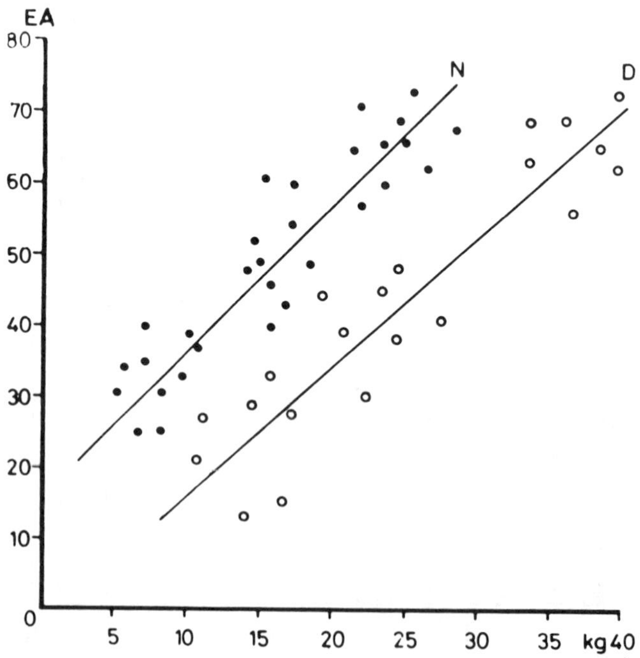

Figure 2. Correlation between static strength (kp) and electrical activity (EA) in untrained subjects (N) and wheelchair drivers (D) (approximately 7 km/day). *Note.* From "Die Beurteilung der Leistungsfähigkeit und die Bestimmung des Energieumsatzes Rollstuhlfahrender Patienten" by H. Stoboy, B.W. Rich, and M. Lee, 1974, *Hefte für Unfallheilkunde*, **117**, pp. 202-207.

strength enhancement due to training (Fukunaga, 1976; Hollmann & Hettinger, 1980; Letzelter & Dickmann, 1984). This was verified by Komi (1986) and Stoboy, Rich, and Lee (1974) (Figure 2). According to Shephard (1972), the dimensions of muscle hypertrophy at different ages are completely obscure. The method of determination of cross-sectional area in children has not been solved satisfactorily. The ultrasound device used by Ikai and Fukunaga (1968) is not available commercially and is difficult to use.

METHODS AND MATERIAL

Three pairs of identical male twins participated in this investigation:

1. Sebastian and Steffen M.: 8.8 years.
2. Matthias and Markus G.: 10.7 years.
3. Thorsten and Michael M.: 11.2 years.

The second pair of twins dropped out after 5 weeks due to chronic infection sustained by Matthias.

One of the twins underwent static training for 10 weeks while the other served as a control. In a fixed and reproducible position, the training twins had to contract the m. quadriceps femoris of the left leg with maximum strength for 10 s 10 times a day, 6 days a week for 2 months. The strength was measured once a week by means of a strain gauge (Hettinger-Isometer) and registered by a Rikadenki-recorder.

Cross-sectional areas of muscles and thigh were evaluated by nuclear magnetic resonance tomography (NMR-T). The central plane of measurement was marked before the experiments by a permanent pen. During one evaluation session, the NMR-signals of four cross-sectional areas could be stored and reproduced. The pen mark represented the central area, proximal and distal to which two shots could be made at distances of 10 mm (Figure 3). Slides were projected and standardized and the areas measured by means of electronic planimetry (Figure 4). To prove the prepubescent condition of the twins before and after training, testosterone (Figure 5) and DHEA-S (dehydroepianteriosteronsulfat) levels in blood plasma were measured by means of RIA (radioimmunassay).

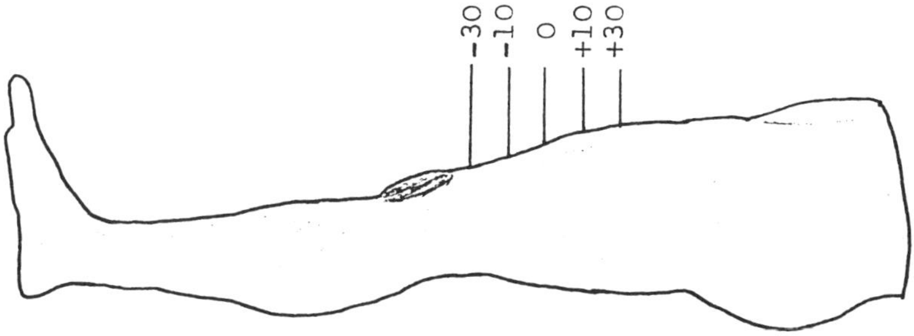

Figure 3. NMR-tomogram localization of four cross-sectional areas.

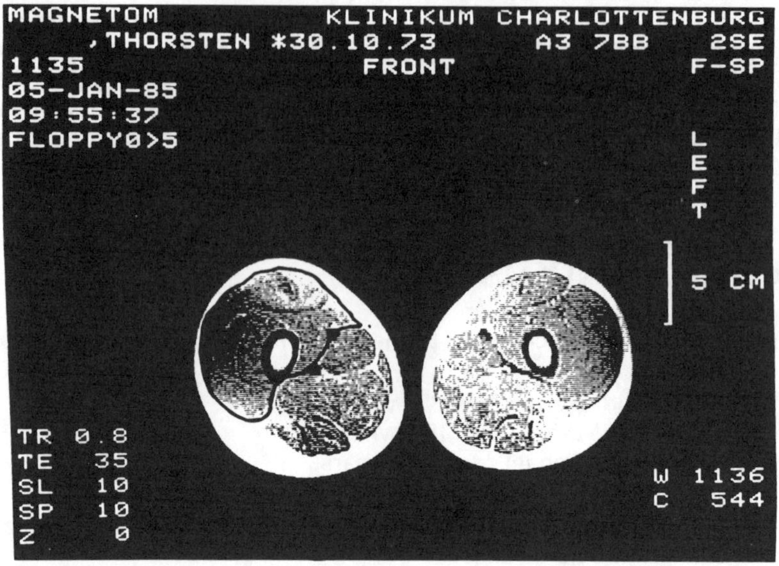

Figure 4. Electronic planimetry of the right m. quadriceps femoris. The extensor muscle group is outlined with a black line.

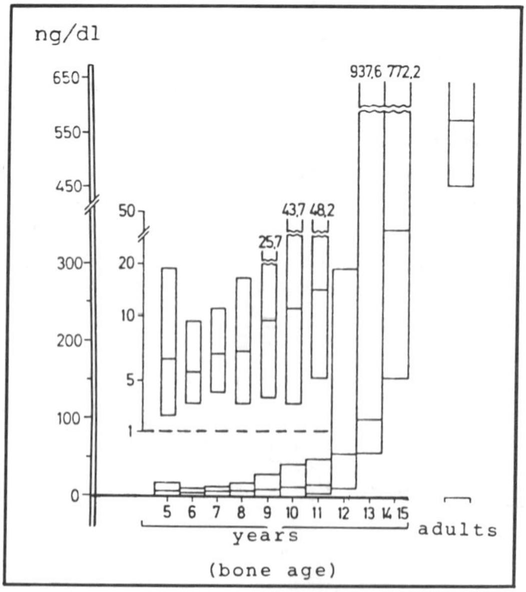

Figure 5. Plasma testosterone from 5 years to adult age. Ordinates: low and high values (ng/dl). *Note.* From "Die Mannlichen Keimdrusen" by J. Girard, 1982, in H. Stolecke (Ed.), *Endokrinologie des Kindes- und Jugendalters* (pp. 163-185), Berlin: Springer.

RESULTS

Development of Maximal Strength

In both the trained and untrained twins, muscle strength increased due to body growth from 0.9 to 12.7% (Table 1). The trained leg extensors

Table 1 Changes of Muscle Strength (N) in Trained and Untrained Muscles During the Course of Training

date	P1t (L)	P1t R	P2 L	P2 R	P3t (L)	P3t R	P4 L	P4 R	P5t (L)	P5t R	P6 L	P6 R
10.1.	230	231	211	221	182	181	183	186	226	240	244	240
14.1.	231	235	221	229	194	183	185	184	248	249	245	246
21.1.	234	233	226	231	201	185	183	191	255	250	245	241
28.1.	245	235	223	226	204	186	190	187	261	246	244	249
4.2.	260	239	231	226	211	190	186	191	274	253	254	250
11.2.	269	234	229	228	222	194	191	192	281	245	251	246
18.2.	284	243	224	223	231	200	192	195	285	256	255	256
25.2.	281	241	226	231	236	196	196	199	-	-	-	-
4.3.	293	249	231	235	235	203	201	196	-	-	-	-
11.3.	303	247	231	231	248	201	201+)	191	-	-	-	-
19.3.	314	255	231	237	255	204	197	203	-	-	-	-

Column heads: maximum strength; subjects.

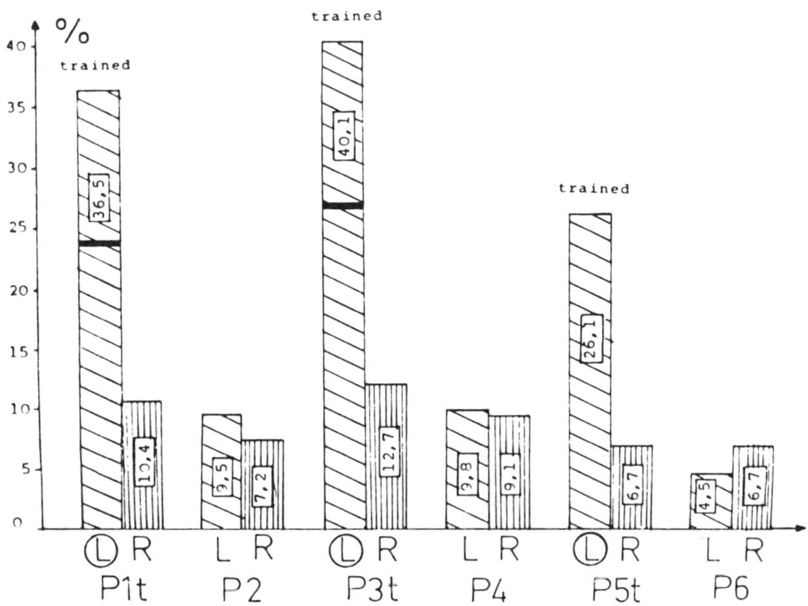

Figure 6. Changes of maximum strength (%) during the course of training; (L) = trained leg.

showed a distinctly greater increase of strength (26 to 40%) than the untrained muscles (Figures 6 and 7). Approximately the same pattern was valid for measurements of relative strength (maximum strength/body weight). All measured muscles increased in weight, but strength training led to a distinctly larger increase.

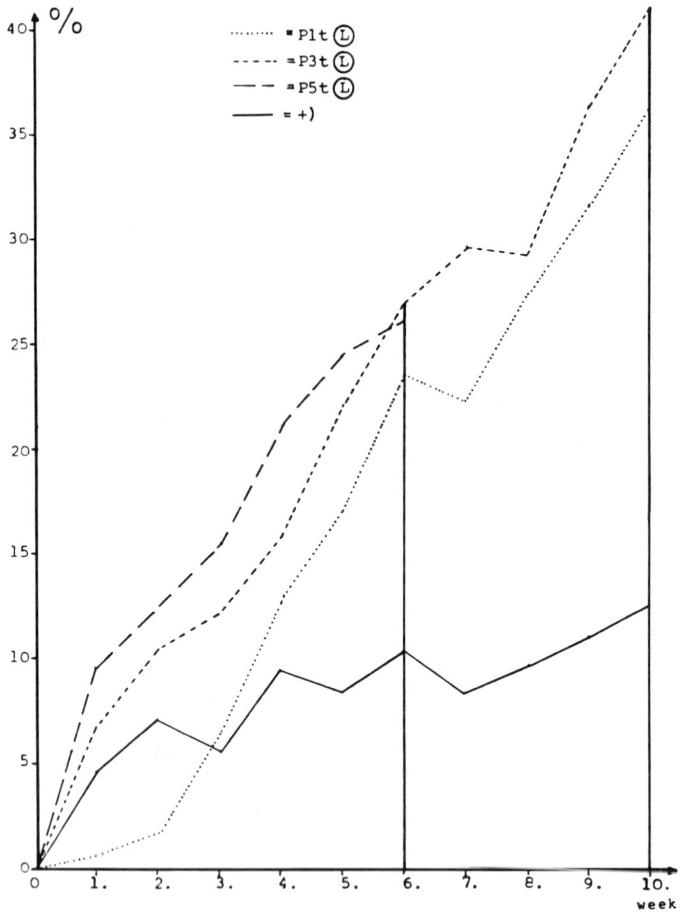

Figure 7. Increase of muscle strength (%) in the trained legs. The change of nontrained muscles is given as mean value (____________); Ⓛ = trained leg.

Evaluation of the Cross-Sectional Areas of the Thigh by Means of NMR-T

The largest areas of muscle were observed at different marks depending on the composition of different tissues at this particular cross section

(Figure 8). The increase in muscle area during the period of training was generally less than that of the total cross-sectional area due to an increase of approximately 10% in the fat content of the extremity and to the proportion of untrained muscles.

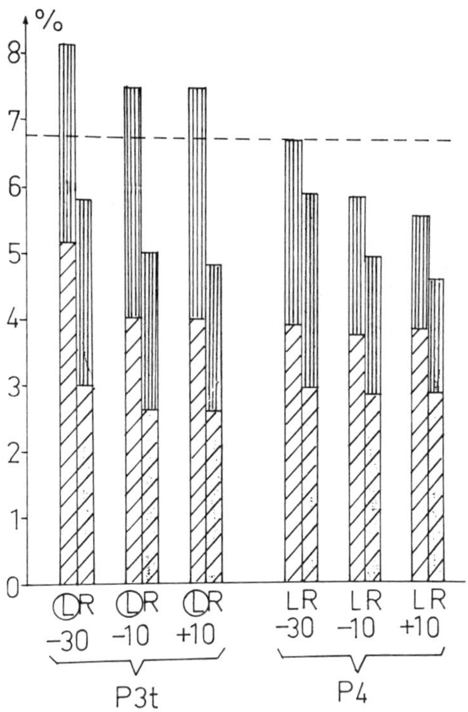

Figure 8. Changes of the total cross-sectional area of the thigh in one trained and one untrained twin (Ⓛ = trained leg) in 3 different planes (NMR).

Changes in the Cross-Sectional Area of the Thigh Extensors

The special interest of this investigation was focused on changes in the extensor muscles during the course of training. An enhanced cross-sectional area of the extensor muscles was observed in all subjects, but the increase was particularly marked in the trained muscles (+4 to 9.2%) (Figure 9). Maximum strength depends without a doubt on the cross-sectional area of the muscle, but also strength increased more than the cross-sectional area, especially in trained muscles (Figure 10). The relative increase in absolute strength (N/cm^2) was considerably larger in the trained muscles (+27 to 28%) than in the untrained (+7 to 10%) (Figure 11). In 10 weeks the increase in strength in all subjects was larger than the growth of the muscles.

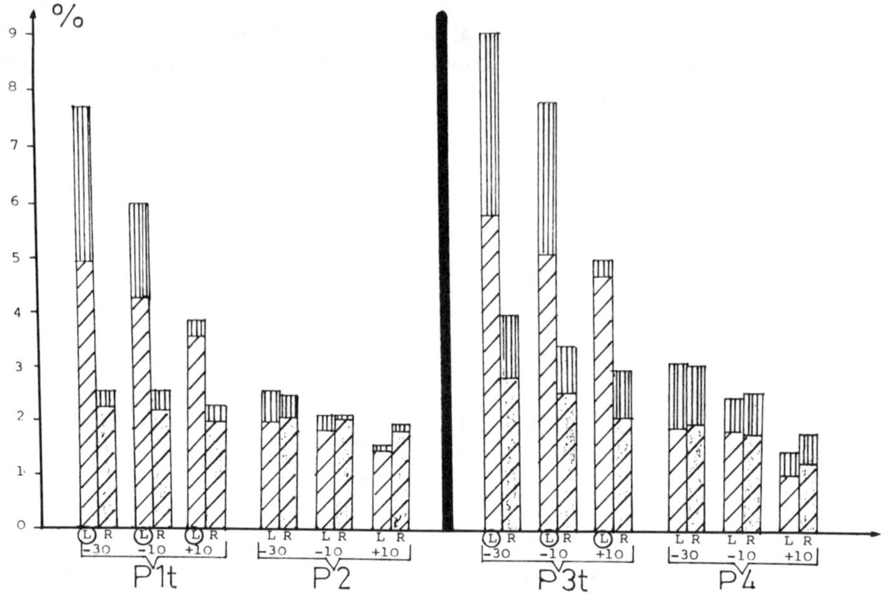

Figure 9. Enhancement of cross-sectional area of extensor (%) in two pairs of twins; Ⓛ = trained leg.

While testosterone levels increased during the period of observation, they remained lower in all subjects than the values characteristic of the beginning of puberty. In this study the individual titer of plasma testosterone (Table 2) and DHEA-S (Table 3) had no correlation to the development of cross-sectional area of trained muscles. DHEA-S is in boys of 10 years approximately 25 to 75 ng/dl (Stolecke, 1982).

DISCUSSION

Increase of Muscle Mass Due to Growth

According to Bouchard and Thibault (1972), muscle mass amounts to 33% of body weight at the beginning of puberty. For the subjects in the present study, the increase in cross-sectional area of muscles was practically identical to that of nontrained subjects. Therefore, it can be concluded that the second pubertal phase of muscle growth was not achieved.

Relationship of Strength to Cross-Sectional Area

Investigations of maximum strength in relation to cross-sectional area per cm^2 yield no uniform results (Davies, White, & Young, 1983; Hettinger, 1983; Ikai & Fukunaga, 1968; Jacobs, Sjödin, & Svane, 1982).

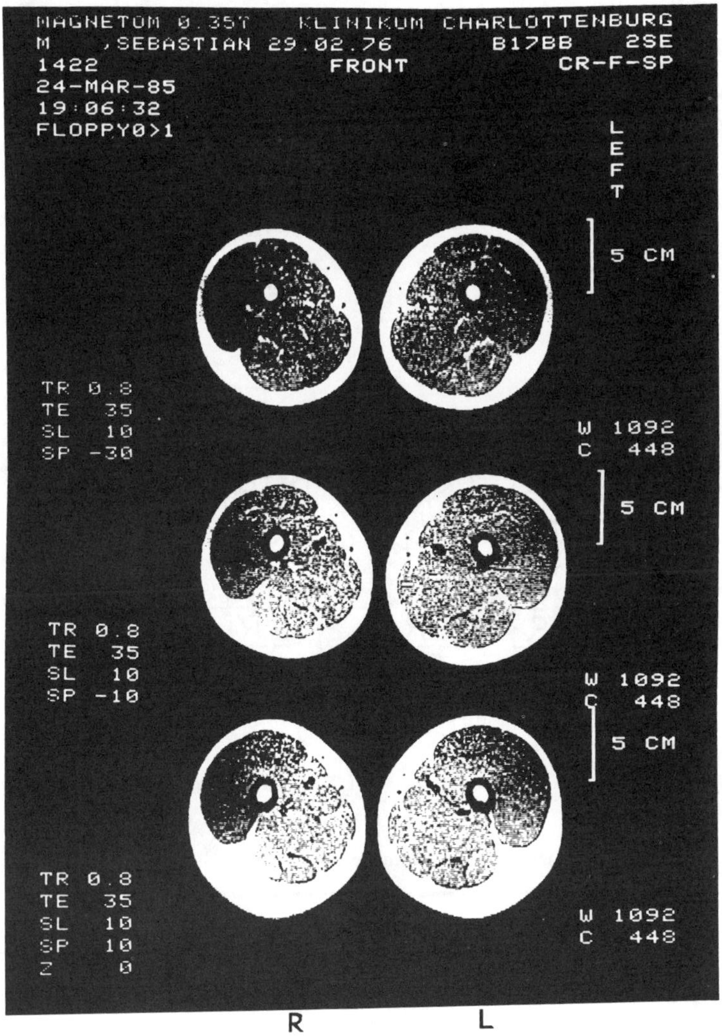

Figure 10. NMR picture of the thigh after training.

The differences in the literature can be explained by the following factors: (a) In a number of muscles the anatomical cross-sectional area is not identical with the physiological value. (b) In voluntary maximum contractions all of the motor units do not contract simultaneously; the number of recruited motor units depends on motivation, danger to life, and condition of strength training. (c) Strength measurements were performed at different joint angles, which prevents accurate comparison of results.

Muscle strength is determined partially by the size of the cross-sectional area (Fukunaga, 1976; Hettinger, 1983; Ikai & Fukunaga, 1968). Immediately

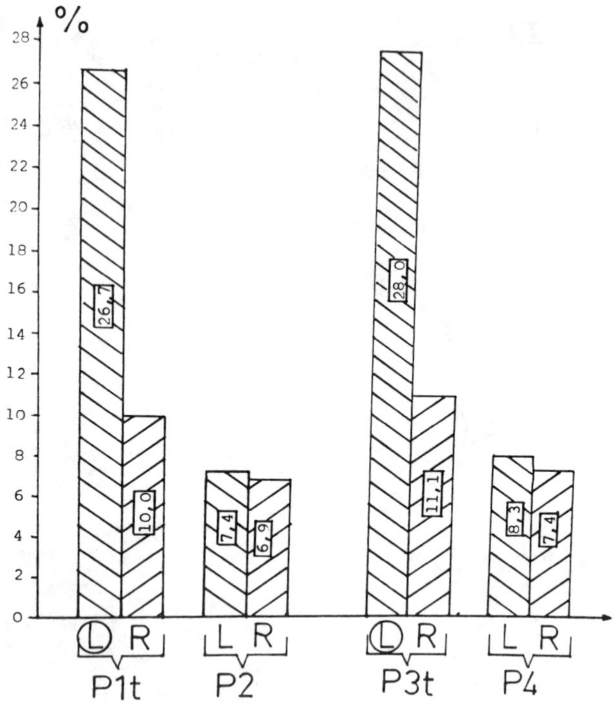

Figure 11. Increase of maximum strength (N/cm²) of thigh extensors in percent; Ⓛ = trained leg.

Table 2 Changes of Plasma Testosterone (ng/dl) During the Course of Training

Testosteron ng/dl				
subject	date of blood sample 10.1.	19.2.	19.3.	changes during the training
P1t	8,5	-	22,0	+ 13,5
P2	12,5	-	20,0	+ 8,5
P3t	<5,0	-	<5,0	± 0
P4	<5,0	-	7,3	+ 2,3
P5t	40,0	55,0	-	+ 15,0
P6	34,0	60,0	-	+ 26,0

Table 3 Changes of DHEA-S (μg/dl) During the Course of Training

DHEA-S (ug/dl)				
subject	date of blood sample			changes during the training
	10.1.	19.2.	19.3.	
P1t	49,5	-	55,0	+ 5,5
P2	50,3	-	38,0	-12,3
P3t	9,6	-	11,8	+ 2,2
P4	14,7	-	20,7	+ 6,0
P5t	56,5	72,0	-	+15,5
P6	61,3	71,5	-	+10,2

after the beginning of training, an increase of strength was observed but not a simultaneous enhancement of cross-sectional area. According to Ikai and Fukunaga (1968) and Hintermann and Hintermann (1983), the increase in cross-sectional area starts after approximately 3 to 4 weeks. On the one hand, the gain in maximum strength can be attributed to the recruitment of motor units (Bührle & Schmidtbleicher, 1981; Ehlenz, Grosser, & Zimmermann, 1983; Fukunaga, 1976). On the other hand, Penman (1970) observed that with increasing strength but constant cross-sectional area, the concentration of contractile filaments per unit of muscle area increased. In the present investigation, hypertrophy due to training was distinctly demonstrable in trained muscles and approximately double that of the untrained muscles.

Dynamic Strength Training

Dynamic strength training has been investigated by a number of authors (Bührle & Schmidtbleicher, 1981; Costill, Coyle, Fink, Lesmes & Witzmann, 1979; Dons, Bollerup, Bonde-Petersen, & Hancke, 1979; MacDonagh & Davies, 1984; Thorstensson, 1976; Tschiene, 1976). However, changes in cross-sectional areas of trained muscles have been reported by only a few investigators.

Walker (1979) established by the aid of ultrasound measurements an increase of 12% following 5 weeks of training of the lower leg extensors. Bührle and Werner (1984) reported an increase in cross-sectional area of the forearm extensors of between 10 and 18% due to different specific types of dynamic strength training in adults (Table 4). The measurements were done by computer tomography.

Table 4 Increase of Maximum Static Strength and Cross-Sectional Area of M. Triceps Before and After Different Kinds of Strength Training

	static maximum strength				cross sectional area of the triceps muscle			
	before	after	difference		before	after	difference	
	kp	kp	kp	%	kp	kp	kp	%
MAX	45,0	53,2	8,3	18,5	27,4	30,1	2,7	9,9
SK	45,1	52,9	7,8	17,3	26,2	29,0	2,8	10,7
MW	43,0	51,9	8,9	20,7	25,2	29,7	4,5	17,8

Note. From "Das Muskelquerschnittstraining der Bodybuilder" by M. Bührle and E. Werner, 1984, *Leistungssport*, **14**, pp. 5-9.

The Effects of Testosterone on the Development of Muscles

The effect of testosterone on the developing muscles is the most efficient factor influencing muscle mass. Before puberty STH is responsible for the increase in muscle mass (Scharschmidt & Pieper, 1982; Shephard, 1972). According to Shephard (1972), thyroid hormones play an important role. At the beginning of puberty, androgens, especially testosterone, cause a pronounced hypertrophy that is combined with an increase of the number of myofibrils, especially during strength training.

The present results point to a connection between the level of testosterone and biological age. The higher testosterone levels were detected in those subjects who had the greater weight, height, and strength. Therefore, it is probable that these twins showed the greater biological age.

During the period between birth and the beginning of puberty, the percentage of muscle mass increases to the same extent as between puberty and maturity. In the prepubescent state the testosterone production is extremely low so that additional mechanisms must be responsible for muscle growth during this period. The results of investigations indicate that the lack of response to strength training in prepubescent children is due to the direct connection between testosterone concentration and muscle hypertrophy.

Causes of Muscle Hypertrophy

Training-induced increases in strength can be influenced by different factors: (a) enhancement of motivation, (b) improvement of intra- and/or intermuscular coordination, (c) increases in the number of contractile proteins per cross-sectional area unit, and (d) hypertrophy of muscle.

A stimulus above the threshold causes hypertrophy of muscle and is an important factor in enhancement of maximum strength. The definitive cause of muscle hypertrophy is obscure. A disturbance in the equilibrium between ATP hydrolysis and resynthesis causes an increase in catabolic processes leading to an amplification of RNA synthesis with the consequence of an enhanced production of proteins in muscle hypertrophy (Keul & Haralambie, 1972). However, an ATP deficiency cannot be observed even in an exhausted muscle fiber (Goldspink, Howells, & Ward, 1976).

This finding diminishes the validity of the theory of Keul and Haralambie. Appell (1983) suggests that muscle training produces microtrauma which leads to a penetration of sarcoplasmatic particles. This is a stimulus for satellite cells to become active and produce new myotubes. Both theories have a common denominator that is an adequate development of tension in the elastic elements of muscle. The importance of strength training in children is related to the poor posture of many prepubescent children (Fomin & Filin, 1975; Hollmann, 1972; Klimt, 1978; Schwerdtner, 1972). According to Möckelmann and Schmidt (1981), approximately 20% of 5-year-old children show poor posture, a condition that increases with increasing age. A well-developed muscle brace enhances the stability of the passive parts of the motor apparatus. However, the ages of 12 and 13 years are critical, especially in boys.

CONCLUSION

This investigation indicates that a hypertrophy of muscle can be caused by training in the prepubescent boys while the testosterone concentration remains at the prepubescent level.

REFERENCES

Appell, H.J. (1983). Mechanismen und Grenzen des Muskelwachstums. In W. Decker & M. Laemmer (Eds.), *Jahrbuch der Deutschen Sporthochschule Köln* (pp. 7-18). St. Augustin: Richarz.

Asmussen, E. (1973). Growth in muscular strength and power. In G.L. Rarick (Ed.), *Physical activity* (pp. 60-79). New York: Academic Press.

Bar-Or, O. (1983). *Pediatric sports medicine for the practitioner*. New York: Springer.

Berlin, K., Baumeister, W., & Apel, J. (1974). Über das Trainings-und Wettkampfsystem bei 10- bis 14jährigen Kindern im Gewichtheben. *Medizin und Sport*, **14**, 211.

Bouchard, C., & Thibault, M. (1972). Jugend und Sport. In W. Hollmann (Ed.), *Zentrale Themen der Sportmedizin* (pp. 324-339). Berlin: Springer.

Bührle, M. (1984). Einmal mehr: Krafttraining im Kindes- und Jugendalter. *Die Lehr der Leichtathletik*, **36**, 1304-1306.

Bührle, M., & Schmidtbleicher, D. (1981). Komponenten der Maximal- und Schnellkraft. *Sportwissenschaft*, **11**, 11-27.

Bührle, M., & Werner, E. (1984). Das Muskelquerschnittstraining der Bodybuilder. *Leistungssport*, **14**, 5-9.

Costill, D.L., Coyle, E.F., Fink, W.F., Lesmes, G.R., & Witzmann, F.A. (1979). Adaptions in skeletal muscle following strength training. *Journal of Applied Physiology*, **46**, 96-99.

Davies, C.T.M., White, M.J., & Young, K. (1983). Muscle function in children. *European Journal of Applied Physiology and Occupational Physiology*, **52**, 111-114.

De Marees, H. (1981). *Sportphysiologie. Medizin von heute*. Bd. 10, Tropon, Köln, BRD.

Dons, B., Bollerup, K., Bonde-Petersen, F., & Hancke, S. (1979). The effect of weight-lifting exercise related to muscle fiber composition and muscle cross-sectional area in humans. *European Journal of Applied Physiology and Occupational Physiology*, **40**, 95-106.

Duffner, B. (1984). *Die Trainierbarkeit der Maximalkraft im Kindesalter. Zulassungsarbeit für das Lehramt*. Sportwissenschaftliches Institut der Universität Freiburg.

Dworkin, L.S. (1976). Das Training 13- bas 16jähriger Gewichtheber. *Leistungssport*, **6**, 3, 190-194.

Ehlenz, H., Grosser, M., & Zimmermann, E. (1983). *Krafttraining*. München: BLV Verlagsgesellschaft.

Fomin, N.A., & Filin, W.P. (1975). *Altersspezifische Grundlagen der körperlichen Erziehung*. Schorndorf: Hofmann.

Fukunaga, T. (1976). Die absolute Muskelkraft und das Krafttraining. *Sportarzt und Sportmedizin*, **27**, 255-266.

Goldspink, G. (1980). Growth of muscle. In *Development and specialization of skeletal muscle* (pp. 19-36). Cambridge: Cambridge University Press.

Goldspink, G., Howells, K.F., & Ward, P.S. (1976). Effect of exercise and muscle fiber size. In E. Jokl, R.L. Anand, & H. Stoboy (Eds.), *Advances in exercise physiology* (pp. 103-113). Basel: Karger.

Hebbelinck, M. (1966). Exercise tolerance of 6 to 10-year-old children and the development of physical performance capacity. *Gymnasion*, **3**, 21-25.

Hettinger, T. (1983). *Isometrisches Muskeltraining*. Stuttgart: Thieme.

Hintermann, B., & Hintermann, M. (1983). *Modifikation der Muskelfasertypen durch Kraft-, Intervall- und Ausdauertraining bei eineiigen Zwillingen*. Dissertation 1981-1983, Forschungsinstitut der Eidgenössischen Turn- und Sporthochschule, Magglingen.

Hollmann, W. (1972). Training und Sport als Mittel der Präventivmedizin in der Kardiologie. In W. Hollmann (Ed.), *Zentrale Themen der Sportmedizin* (pp. 1-22). Berlin: Springer.

Hollmann, W., & Hettinger, T. (1980). Kraft. In W. Hollmann & T. Hettinger (Eds.), *Sportmedizin - Arbeits- und Trainingsgrundlagen* (pp. 176-210). Stuttgart: Schattauer.

Ikai, M., & Fukunaga, T. (1968). Calculation of muscle strength per unit cross-sectional area of human muscle by means of ultrasonic measurement. *Internationale Zeitschrift für angewandte Physiologie einschließlich Arbeitsphysiologie*, **26**, 26-32.

Jacobs, I., Sjödin, B., & Svane, B. (1982). Muscle fiber type, cross-sectional area and strength in boys after 4-years endurance training. *Medicine and Science in Sports and Exercise*, **14**, 123.

Jones, M. (1984). Krafttraining für junge Athleten. *Die Lehre der Leicht athletik*, **35**, 1303-1304.

Keul, J., & Haralambie, G. (1972). Energiestoffwechsel und körperliche Leistung. In W. Hollmann (Ed.), *Zentrale Themen der Sportmedizin* (pp. 80-100). Berlin: Springer.

Kirsten, G. (1963). Der Einfluß isometrischen Muskeltrainings auf die Entwicklung der Muskelkraft Jugendlicher. *Internationale Zeitschrift fur angewandte Physiologie einschließlich Arbeitsphysiologie*, **19**, 387-402.

Klimt, F. (1978). Sportliche Belastbarkeit von Kindern im Primärbereich. In A. Clauss (Ed.), *Sportärztliche und Sportpädogogische Betreuung*. Erlangen: Perimed.

Komi, P.V. (1986). Training of muscle strength and power: Interaction of neuromotoric, hypertrophic, and mechanical factors. *International Journal of Sports Medicine*, **7**(Suppl. 1), 10-15.

Letzelter, M., & Dickmann, W. (1984). Zur Trainierbarkeit der Maximalkraft im Grundschulalter. *Deutsche Zeitschrift für Sportmedizin*, **35**, 62-69.

MacDonagh, M.J.N., & Davies, C.T.M. (1984). Adaptive response of mammalian skeletal muscle to exercise with high loads. *European Journal of Applied Physiology and Occupational Physiology*, **52**, 139-155.

Messmer, A. (1984). *Der Einfluß des motorischen Kraftniveaus auf die Kugelstoßleistung und den Lernfortschritt beim Anfänger. Zulassungsarbeit für das Lehramt*. Sportwissenschaftliches Institut der Universität Freiburg.

Möckelmann, H., & Schmidt, D. (1981). *Leibeserziehung und jugendliche Entwicklung*. Neubearbeitung von D. Schmidt. Schorndorf: Hofmann.

Nicu, A. (1973). Methodische Kriterien der sportlichen Verbreitung von Kindern und Jugendlichen. *Leistungssport*, **3**, 374-380.

Penman, K.A. (1970). Human striated muscle ultrastructural changes accompanying increased strength without hypertrophy. *Research Quarterly American Association for Health and Physical Education*, **31**, 418-424.

Röhmert, W. (1968). Rechts-Links-Vergleich bei isometrischem Arm-muskeltraining mit verschiedenem Trainingsreiz bei acht-jahrigen Kindern. *Internationale Zeitschrift für angewandte Physiologie einschließlich Arbeitsphysiologie*, **26**, 363-393.

Rutenfranz, J. (1983). Die körperliche Belastbarkeit von Kindern und Jugendlichen im Rahmen der sportlichen Erziehung. *Klinische Pädiatrie*, **195**, 4-12.

Scharschmidt, F., & Pieper, K.S. (1982). Adaptabilität an sportliches Training bei Heranwachsenden. *Medizin und Sport*, **22**, 37-40.

Schwertdtner, H.P. (1972). Die Leistungs- und Belastungsfähigkeit des Jugendlichen. III. Der Stutz- und Halteapparat. *Deutsches Turnen*, **117**, 333-334.

Shephard, R.J. (1972). *Alive man*. Springfield, IL: Charles C. Thomas.

Stoboy, H., Rich, B.W., & Lee, M. (1974). Die Beurteilung der Leistungsfähigkeit und die Bestimmung des Energieumsatzes Rollstuhlfahrender Patienten. *Hefte für Unfallheilkunde*, **117**, 202-207.

Stolecke, H. (Ed.) (1982). *Endokrinologie des Kindes- und Jugendalters*. Berlin: Springer.

Szabo, S. (1969). Die Zunahme von Herzvolumen und Leistungsfähigkeit als Folge eines regelmäßigen Trainings beim Schwimmen im Pubertätsalter. *Medizin und Sport*, **IX**, 280-282.

Thorstensson, A. (1976). Muscle strength, fiber types and enzyme activities in man. *Acta Physiologica Scandinavica*, **443**(Suppl.).

Tschiene, P. (1976). Keine Tendenzwende im Krafttraining. *Leistungssport*, **6**, 400-405.

Vrijens, J. (1978). Muscle strength development in the pre- and postpubescent age. In J. Borms & M. Hebbelinck (Eds.), *Pediatric work physiology* (pp. 152-158). Basel: Karger.

Walker, I.C.R. (1979). The effect of unilateral strength training on bilateral measurements related to muscle fibre composition and cross-sectional area in the quadriceps muscle in humans. *Momentum*, **4**, 6-45.

Effects of 10 Weeks of Resistance Training on Strength Development in Prepubertal Boys

Cameron Joe R. Blimkie
Jean Ramsay
Digby Sale
Duncan MacDougall
McMaster University, Ontario, Canada

Karen Smith
Scott Garner
Chedoke-McMaster Hospitals, Ontario, Canada

Numerous studies (e.g., Darcus & Salter, 1955; Ikai & Fukanaga, 1970; Komi, Viitasalo, Rauramaa, & Vihko, 1978; McDonagh, Hayward, & Davies, 1983) have reported significant increases in maximal voluntary strength in the adult population following appropriate strength-training programs. Strength gains during the initial several weeks of training have been attributed primarily to neurological adaptation or improved motor skill performance (Hakkinen & Komi, 1983; Ikai & Fukanaga, 1970; McDonagh et al., 1983; Young, Stokes, Round, & Edwards, 1983), and an increase in muscle size (cross-sectional area) has been associated with, but does not appear to fully account for, longer term (14 weeks) strength gains in the adult population (Ikai & Fukanaga, 1970; Moritani & De Vries, 1979).

Fewer studies have investigated the efficacy of strength training or the underlying factors responsible for, or associated with, strength gains in prepubertal children. Several studies have reported no significant specific effect of resistance training on strength development in prepubertal children (Docherty, Wenger, Collis, & Quinney, 1984; Vrijens, 1978), but others (McGovern, 1984; Nielsen, Nielsen, Hansen, & Asmussen, 1980; Pfeiffer & Francis, 1986; Servedio et al., 1985; Sewall & Micheli, 1986; Weltman et al., 1986) have reported significant gains in muscle strength in response to various types of resistance-training programs. Differences in the nature of the training programs (e.g., mode of training, intensity of the training stimulus, and frequency and duration of training) and the subject population may account for the different conclusions among studies.

Based on limited data, strength gains in prepubertal children following training have been shown to be independent of changes in limb girth

(McGovern, 1984; Weltman et al., 1986) and muscle cross-sectional area (Vrijens, 1978), and have been attributed primarily to neurological adaptation (Weltman et al., 1986). To our knowledge, there have been no studies of either the neurological and electromechanical adaptations of skeletal muscle of children to resistance training, or the relative importance of neurological and morphological adaptations associated with strength gains in this population.

The purposes of this study were (a) to determine the efficacy of 10 weeks of heavy resistance training on voluntary and electrically evoked strength characteristics of the elbow flexor muscles and (b) to differentiate the contribution of neurological adaptation and gross muscle hypertrophy to strength development following training in prepubertal boys. This is an interim report of a 20-week strength training study involving prepubertal boys.

METHODS

Subjects

Boys (n = 27) from 9 to 11 years of age volunteered for the study. The study was approved by a human ethics committee, and informed written consent was obtained from both the subjects and their parents. The experimental (training) group consisted of 14 boys from a local primary school. The control group consisted of 13 boys from three local primary schools. The four schools involved were similar in terms of their academic and extracurricular activity programs and represented similar socioeconomic backgrounds as determined by school administrators. Subjects participated in a variety of organized sports activities, but none was considered to be a sport specialist.

Medical Evaluation

A comprehensive medical history and physical examination, including a detailed musculoskeletal assessment, was conducted by the same physician to document preexisting orthopedic injuries and medical conditions. All subjects were cleared for participation in the study.

Maturational status was determined by a physician, based on Tanner staging of pubic hair development (Tanner, 1962) and by serum concentrations of free testosterone (radioimmunoassay). All subjects were classified as Tanner Stage 1, and all but one had resting testosterone levels less than 50 ng • dl^{-1}, which is considered to be within the normal range for prepubertal boys (Winter, 1978). One control subject had a resting value of 60.6 ng • dl^{-1}, which is considered transitional between Tanner Stages 1 and 2.

Strength Training

Subjects in the experimental group trained three times per week under close adult supervision for 10 weeks. Training consisted of a circuit of six exercises involving two primary (arm curls and double knee extension) and four secondary (bench press, leg press, sit-ups, and pull-downs) exercises. Each session consisted of five and three sets for the primary and secondary exercises, respectively. Sets were performed in a circuit at 75% of the 1 repetition maximum (1 RM) for each exercise, and each session lasted approximately 50 min. With the exception of the first set for both primary and secondary exercises, all other sets were done to failure (10 to 12 repetitions). Subjects performed a warm-up of 10 to 12 repetitions at 60% of the 1 RM for the first set of both groups of exercises. The fifth set of the primary exercises was done to failure at 60% of the 1 RM.

Training was done on a modified Global Gym apparatus (Rubicon, Inc.) requiring both concentric and eccentric muscle contractions. Training loads were increased by 0.45 to 0.68 kg whenever subjects were capable of completing 12 repetitions for the middle three sets of the primary exercises and for the last two sets of the secondary exercises. Subjects were given workbooks with prescribed resistance settings for each exercise (reviewed weekly) and were required to record the number of completed repetitions for each exercise during each training session.

No strength training activities were permitted outside of the supervised training sessions. None of the control subjects weight trained during the 10-week study; however, both groups were permitted to maintain their normal daily activity, including participation in various sports.

Strength Testing

Unless otherwise stated, the following measurements were taken for both the experimental and the control groups before and after 10 weeks of training. All posttraining strength measures were taken following 3 to 5 days of recovery from the last training session for the experimental group. Only those techniques and results related to arm strength testing are reported here.

The 1 RM for bench press was measured on a Global Gym apparatus. Subjects performed a warm-up set of three to seven repetitions at low resistance. Resistance was then gradually increased so that the 1 RM was obtained within six to eight trials. The 1 RM for double arm curl was measured for the experimental group only, on the modified Global Gym apparatus (training device). The same procedure was followed as for the bench press.

For isometric strength testing, subjects sat in a dental chair with the right upper arm resting in a horizontal position on a padded support plate. Subjects were secured to the chair by a strap slung over the right shoulder and attached to the chair. Additionally, a co-investigator placed manual pressure downward against the shoulder to ensure isometric conditions during these testing procedures.

Maximal voluntary isometric strength was measured for elbow flexion at 80°, 100°, 120°, and 150° of flexion at the elbow (180° = full extension) using a custom-made dynamometer. The order of testing at different joint angles was randomized, and subjects performed two trials separated by 15 to 30 s of rest at each joint angle. The average of the two trials was used as the criterion score.

Involuntary electrically evoked twitch torque was measured for the right arm elbow flexors (biceps brachii and brachialis) at the same joint angles and with the same dynamometer as previously described for voluntary isometric strength testing. A series of 100-ms square-wave stimulating pulses was delivered via rubber electrodes placed over the motor point of the biceps brachii (cathode) and on the ventral surface of the forearm just distal to the elbow joint. Maximum twitch torque was determined by delivering progressively higher voltages until supramaximal stimulation was achieved and a plateau was obtained in the torque output, indicating that all the motor units were activated. The order of testing at different joint angles was randomized, and two trials separated by 15- to 30-s rest were obtained at each joint angle. Twitch torque, time to peak torque, and half-relaxation time were recorded for each trial. The average of these trials was used as the criterion score.

Torque was measured with the wrist in the supinated position for both the voluntary and the electrically evoked isometric strength measures. Torque was transmitted via Velcro webbing strapped over the proximal and the distal ends of the forearm to a strain gauge located at the rotational center of the dynamometer. The signal from the strain gauge was amplified and the torque output was displayed on an oscilliscope. The signal was simultaneously analyzed on-line by computer.

The interpolated twitch technique, as described by Belanger and McComas (1981), was used to determine the degree of motor unit activation. With this technique, a single supramaximal stimulus is delivered to the nerve of a muscle engaged in maximal voluntary contraction. Interpolated twitch torque and the percent of motor unit activation for the right arm elbow flexors was determined using this technique and the custom-made dynamometer previously described, at 100° of elbow flexion. Values were calculated from the trial (best of two) that elicited the highest peak torque output.

Performance and isometric strength tests were conducted on separate days. For isometric testing, involuntary electrically evoked twitch torque was measured first, followed by the interpolated twitch technique and then maximal voluntary strength. Testing sessions lasted 20 to 30 min.

Anthropometry and Body Composition

Standing height was measured without shoes, and weight was measured with subjects wearing only their shorts. Skinfolds were measured using a Harpenden skinfold caliper at the following sites (right side): subscapular, suprailiac, triceps, and biceps. Mid-upper right arm circumference (midway between the olecranon and acromion processes) was measured with subjects standing in the anatomical position. Skinfolds were measured at the anterior, posterior, medial, and lateral aspects of the right arm (circumferential skinfolds) at the midpoint level of the upper arm. Percent body fat was calculated using the equation of Lohman,

Slaughter, Boileau, Bunt, and Lussier (1984). Lean cross-sectional area of the mid-upper right arm was calculating using the method described by Moritani and De Vries (1980), based on circumference and four skinfold measurements.

Muscle Morphology

Muscle cross-sectional area was measured at the beginning of the study using computerized axial tomography-CAT scan (fourth generation high resolution Ohio Nuclear 20/20 series scanner). A single CAT scan (radiation exposure of 5 mSv) was taken at the mid-upper right arm level at the same point used for the upper arm circumference measurement. Negative photographic slides were taken of the CAT scan prints, and measurement of total lean area (muscle, bone, and marrow) was made from tracings of the projected slides using manual planimetry.

Statistical Analysis

Two- and three-way factor analyses of variance with repeated measures were used to determine significant effects. Differences were considered significant at the $p < .05$ level. A post hoc Tukey test was used to identify significant differences among the means. A *t* test for dependent measures was used to determine the significance of differences between pretest and posttest double arm curl 1 RM strength measures for the experimental group, and differences between pretest measures of right lean arm area determined from the CAT scan and anthropometric measurements. A Pearson product moment correlation coefficient was computed to determine the degree of association between the anthropometric and the CAT scan measurements for lean arm area (experimental and control groups combined).

RESULTS

The physical and maturational characteristics of subjects are presented in Table 1. There were no differences in age, height, weight, sum of skinfolds, or percent body fat between the experimental and the control groups at the beginning of the study.

Morphological characteristics of the right upper arm are presented in Table 2. There were no differences between groups at the beginning of the study for arm girth, lean area of the arm (anthropometric and CAT scan measurements), or sum of four circumferential skinfolds. There was a significant ($p < .05$) main effect for time (indicative of growth), with posttest values for arm girth and lean area of arm (based on anthropometry) being significantly larger than pretest values. There were no significant treatment-time interaction effects (indicative of the differential effect of training) for any of the morphological parameters of the arm. There were no significant differences between pretest anthropometric and

Table 1 Physical and Anthropometric Characteristics of Subjects at the Beginning of the Study

Group	Age (y)	Height (cm)	Weight (kg)	Σ2 Skinfolds[a] (mm)	Body fat (%)
Experimental (n = 14)	10.4 ±0.8	139.7 ±6.4	36.0 ±9.5	22.9 ±14.8	17.8 ±9.1
Control (n = 13)	10.7 ±0.4	141.0 ±7.8	35.4 ±6.2	21.2 ±10.4	17.6 ±6.6

Note. Values are means ± *SD*.

[a]Sum of the tricep and subscapular skinfolds.

CAT scan measurements for lean area of the arm for either the experimental or the control groups. There was a significant and moderately strong positive correlation (r = .80) between pretest anthropometric and CAT scan measures for lean area of the arm (experimental and control groups combined).

Performance strength measures are presented in Figure 1. Training resulted in significant improvements in the 1 RM bench press and the double arm curl lifts. Isometric strength measures are presented in Table 3. Training significantly increased maximal voluntary isometric strength at all joint angles for both absolute (Nm) and relative ($Nm \cdot cm^{-2}$) torque.

Involuntary electrically evoked strength characteristics and results for the ratio of maximal voluntary isometric to evoked twitch strength are presented in Table 4. Training had no significant effect on either the twitch and interpolated twitch torque measurements or the ratio of maximal voluntary isometric to evoked twitch strength.

Training also had no significant effect on time to peak torque or half-relaxation time for the evoked twitch at any of the joint angles studied. There was a trend, although not a significant one, toward increased motor unit activation in the experimental group during maximal voluntary isometric elbow flexion, following training (Table 5).

DISCUSSION

The results of this study indicated that 10 weeks of traditional circuit weight training involving progressive resistive loading and both concentric and eccentric muscle contractions significantly improved performance strength for the 1 RM bench press and double arm curl, as well as maximal voluntary isometric strength of the elbow flexors, in prepubertal boys.

Results for the 1 RM performance strength measures in the present study appear to agree with McGovern's (1984) findings of increased

Table 2 Morphological Characteristics of the Right Upper Arm

	Groups			
	Experimental (n = 14)		Control (n = 13)	
Variable	Pretest	Posttest	Pretest	Posttest
Anthropometric girth (cm)	20.6 ±3.8	20.8* ±3.8	20.7 ±2.9	21.1* ±2.8
Σ4 Circ. skinfolds (mm)	39.6 ±21.2	38.6 ±21.0	39.2 ±17.2	38.7 ±17.7
Anthropometric lean area (cm^2)	24.8 ±6.4	25.5* ±6.6	24.9 ±5.2	25.6* ±4.9
CAT scan lean area (cm^2)	21.9 ±7.4		23.0 ±3.2	
Correlation between anthropometric and CAT scan lean areas	r = .80, (n = 26)			

Note. Values are means ± *SD*.

*Main effect for time, posttest values > pretest values; $p < .05$.

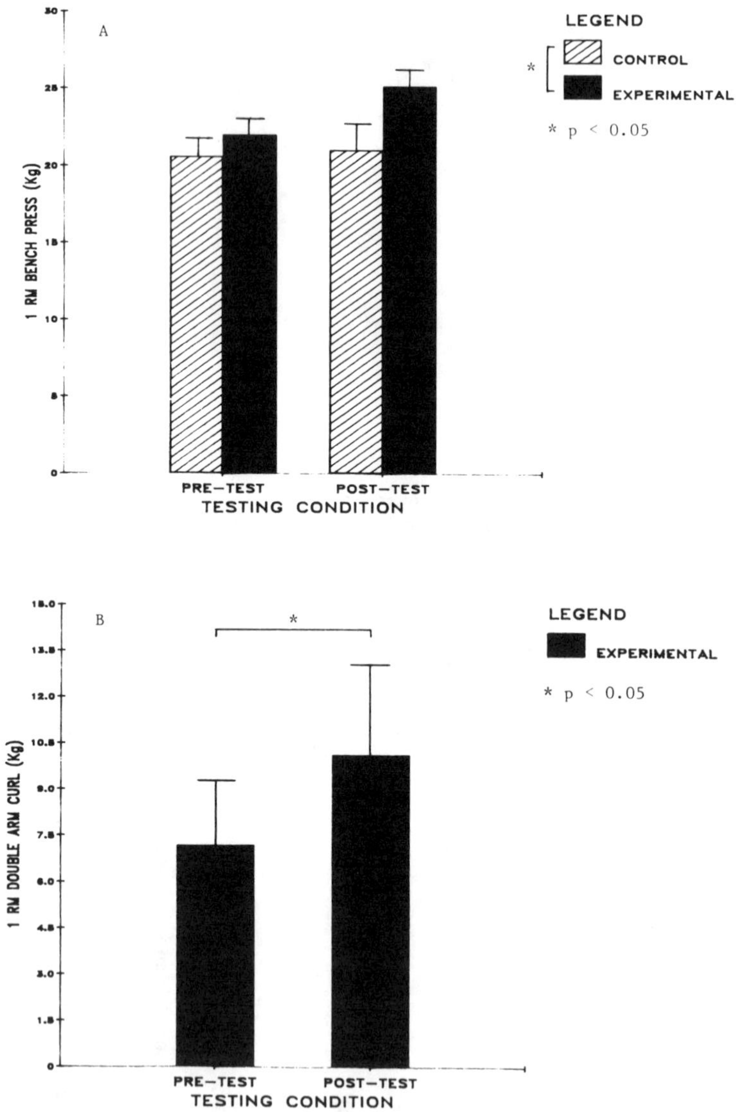

Figure 1. Comparison of performance strength measures for A (the 1-RM bench press) and B (the 1-RM double arm curl), before and after training. Control (N = 13) and experimental (N = 14) groups. Values are means ± SEM.

Table 3 Maximum Voluntary Isometric Strength Measures for Elbow Flexion

Variable	Condition	Elbow joint angle (degrees)							
		Experimental (n = 14)				Control (n = 13)			
		80°	100°	120°	150°	80°	100°	120°	150°
Absolute torque	Pre	16.8 ±8.1	14.7 ±5.3	12.7 ±4.2	8.2 ±3.5	17.2 ±3.6	15.9 ±3.0	13.1 ±2.9	8.8 ±2.9
	Post	19.9* ±5.6	18.0* ±4.8	15.6* ±7.4	11.3* ±4.3	16.2 ±3.3	16.2 ±2.8	13.9 ±2.2	9.1 ±2.5
	% Change	15.6	22.4	22.8	37.8	−5.8	1.9	6.1	3.4
Relative torque ($Nm \cdot cm^{-2}$)	Pre	0.73 ±0.31	0.64 ±0.21	0.55 ±0.17	0.36 ±0.15	0.71 ±0.13	0.65 ±0.14	0.54 ±0.12	0.36 ±0.13
	Post	0.83* ±0.19	0.76* ±0.17	0.64* ±0.16	0.45* ±0.15	0.67 ±0.10	0.64 ±0.12	0.53 ±0.09	0.34 ±0.10
	% Change	13.7	18.8	16.4	25.0	−5.6	−1.5	−1.9	−2.0

Note. Values are means ± *SD*.

Relative torque is derived from absolute torque (Nm) divided by the estimated (anthropometric) lean area (cm^2) of the arm.

*Experimental posttest mean was significantly ($p < .05$) greater than the experimental pretest mean and both the control pre- and posttest means.

Table 4 Electrically Evoked Twitch Strength Measures and the Ratio of Maximal Voluntary Isometric to Evoked Twitch Strength

Variable	Condition	Elbow joint angle (degrees) Experimental 80°	100°	120°	150°	Control 80°	100°	120°	150°
Twitch torque (Nm)	Pre	1.76 +0.62	2.00 ±0.77	1.91 ±0.72	1.68 ±0.74	1.56 ±0.53	1.83 ±0.58	1.78 ±0.56	1.54 ±0.45
	Post	1.64 ±0.66	1.87 ±0.74	1.87 ±0.79	1.84 ±0.90	1.43 ±0.42	1.73 ±0.48	1.67 ±0.43	1.52 ±0.47
	% Change	−6.8	−6.5	−2.1	+9.5	−8.3	−5.5	−6.2	1.2
Ratio: Maximum voluntary torque to twitch torque	Pre	9.0 ±3.1	7.5 ±2.1	6.8 ±1.5	5.1 ±1.7	11.9 ±3.3	9.2 ±2.1	7.9 ±2.6	5.9 ±1.8
	Post	13.0 ±3.7	10.4 ±3.3	8.9 ±3.0	6.3 ±2.0	13.0 ±4.5	9.9 ±3.2	8.3 ±1.9	6.1 ±2.1
	% Change	44.0	38.7	30.9	23.5	9.2	7.6	5.1	3.4
Interpolated twitch torque (Nm)	Pre		16.1 ±6.2				17.5 ±2.7		
	Post		17.7 ±6.7				16.8 ±2.8		
	% Change		+9.9				−0.04		

Note. Values for the evoked twitch and the ratio of maximum voluntary torque to twitch torque are based on 13 boys in each of the experimental and control groups. The interpolated twitch torque values are based on 14 boys in the experimental group and 13 boys in the control group. Values are means ± *SD*.

Table 5 Contractile Properties (Evoked Twitch) and Percent of Motor Unit Activation (Interpolated Twitch) for Elbow Flexors

Variable	Condition	Elbow joint angle (degrees)							
		Experimental (n = 13)				Control (n = 13)			
		80°	100°	120°	150°	80°	100°	120°	150°
Time to peak torque (ms)	Pre	63.1 ±15.1	62.4 ±14.8	63.2 ±10.9	65.4 ± 9.9	75.5 ±13.0	72.8 ±11.4	67.1 ±13.0	66.4 ±14.9
	Post	62.8 ± 7.5	62.1 ±12.4	63.4 ±13.1	53.8 ±10.6	72.0 ± 9.3	68.6 ±11.6	69.1 ±11.2	62.4 ±12.7
Half-relaxation time (ms)	Pre	66.1 ±16.2	75.1 ±11.0	89.7 ±29.6	86.8 ±10.8	66.3 ±11.2	84.5 ±28.3	86.3 ±12.0	90.0 ±15.7
	Post	63.0 ±13.7	73.1 ±10.6	81.1 ±19.6	92.5 ±18.5	69.5 ±23.7	77.5 ±14.6	89.5 ±33.8	92.2 ±24.0
% Motor unit activation	Pre		84.1 ±17.7				94.6 ±11.9		
	Post		93.0 ±13.3				94.8 ±14.5		

Note. Values are means ± *SD*.

strength in the bench press and arm curl for fourth-, fifth-, and sixth-graders following 12 weeks of circuit weight training. Details of the training program and the nature of the criterion strength measures were, however, not reported in McGovern's (1984) study.

The significant increase in maximal voluntary isometric strength for elbow flexion observed in the present study conflicts with Vrijens' (1978) earlier finding of no significant effect of 8 weeks of isotonic strength training on isometric strength of the arm flexors in prepubescent males. The discrepancy in results between studies may be explained by differences in the length of the training programs and, more importantly, by the higher training intensity and volume in the present study.

Results from this study indicate that 10 weeks of resistance training did not significantly change twitch torque, interpolated twitch torque, time to peak torque, or half-relaxation time of the elbow flexors. Because the electrically evoked twitch contraction is a measure of the intrinsic force-producing capacity of muscle (McDonagh et al., 1983) and is believed to be dependent on muscle cross-sectional area (Close, 1972), it appears that the training employed in this study failed to elicit any change in muscle size and, consequently, in the force-producing capacity of the elbow flexors. This conclusion is supported by the lack of a significant training effect in estimated lean cross-sectional area of the arm.

Based on these results, it appears that the training-induced strength increases observed in this study were independent of changes in muscle cross-sectional area. This conclusion appears to be consistent with the observation in adults of a substantial increase in maximal voluntary isometric strength of elbow flexors, largely independent of muscle hypertrophy, following relatively short-term (3 to 14 weeks) resistance-training programs (Ikai & Fukunaga, 1970; McDonagh et al., 1983). Differences in the nature and duration of training, however, make direct comparison of results across studies difficult.

Training-induced strength increases have been related to both hypertrophy of muscle and enhanced motor unit excitation (Coyle et al., 1981; Ikai & Fukunaga, 1970; Komi et al., 1978; Sale, 1987). Results from the present study indicate a tendency toward improved motor unit activation for the elbow flexors following training and suggest that this might, at least in part, account for the training-induced gains in maximal voluntary isometric strength observed in the prepubertal boys in this study. However, since the change in motor unit activation was not significant, the strength gains may also be attributed to other specific neurological adaptations within the prime movers that were not assessed in this study, that is, motor unit recruitment order, synchronization, and firing frequency. Additionally, training may have resulted in more appropriate cocontraction of synergists and increased inhibition of antagonists, both of which may have contributed to the observed increase in isometric force.

It is probable that the training-induced increases in bench press and double arm curl strength could, at least in part, be attributed to specific neuromuscular (motor skill coordination) adaptation to the repetitive motion involved in the execution of these exercises during training. Other specific neurological adaptations already mentioned may also have contributed to these performance strength increases. Although possible, it is unlikely that such specific motor skill adaptation to dynamic training could fully account for the significant increase in maximal voluntary isometric strength observed in this study. It appears, therefore, that the training-induced increase in maximal voluntary isometric strength in this study was due largely to specific neurological adaptation and that both performance and isometric strength increases were independent of changes in muscle size.

CONCLUSION

Ten weeks of circuit resistance training significantly increased performance strength for the 1 RM bench press and double arm curl as well as for maximal voluntary isometric strength of the elbow flexors in prepubertal boys. Strength increases were independent of changes in lean cross-sectional area of the upper arm. Strength increases were attributed instead to improved motor unit activation, and to specific motor skill and other neurological adaptations to training.

Acknowledgments

This study was supported by a grant from the Ministry of Tourism and Recreation, Fitness Services Branch, Ontario, Canada. The authors would also like to thank Joan Martin for her technical assistance and unrelenting commitment to the coordination of the study. Appreciation is extended to the Hamilton Separate Roman Catholic School Board, to Mr. Bill Mattina, and to the principals and students at St Ann's, St. Augustin's, St. Joseph's, and Christ the King's Separate Schools. A special thanks to Gina Loverro for typing the manuscript.

REFERENCES

Belanger, A.Y., & McComas, A.J. (1981). Extent of motor unit activation during effort. *Journal of Applied Physiology*, **51**, 1131-1135.

Close, R.I. (1972). Dynamic properties of mammalian skeletal muscles. *Physiological Reviews*, **52**, 129-197.

Coyle, E.F., Feiring, D.C., Rotkis, T.C., Cote, R.W., III, Robey, F.B., Lee, W., & Wilmore, J.H. (1981). Specificity of power improvements through slow and fast isokinetic training. *Journal of Applied Physiology*, **51**, 1437-1442.

Darcus, H.D., & Salter, N. (1955). Effect of repeated muscular exertion on muscle strength. *Journal of Physiology*, **129**, 325-336.

Docherty, D., Wenger, H.A., Collis, M.L., & Quinney, H.A. (1984). The effects of variable speed resistance training on prepubertal boys. *Canadian Journal of Applied Sport Sciences*, **9**(4), 11P.

Hakkinen, K., & Komi, P.V. (1983). Electromyographic changes during strength training and detraining. *Medicine and Science in Sports and Exercise*, **15**, 455-460.

Ikai, M., & Fukunaga, T. (1970). A study on training effect on strength per unit cross-sectional area of muscle by means of ultra-sonic measurement. *Internationale Zeitschrift für Angewandte Physiologie*, **40**, 45-55.

Komi, P.V., Viitasalo, J., Rauramaa, R., & Vihko, V. (1978). Effect of isometric strength training on mechanical, electrical and metabolic aspects of muscle function. *European Journal of Applied Physiology*, **40**, 45-55.

Lohman, T.G., Slaughter, M.H., Boileau, R.G., Bunt, J., & Lussier, L. (1984). Bone mineral measurements and their relation to body density in children, youth and adults. *Human Biology*, **56**, 667-679.

McDonagh, M.J.N., Hayward, C.M., & Davies, C.T.M. (1983). Isometric training in human elbow flexor muscles. The effects on voluntary and electrically evoked forces. *Journal of Bone and Joint Surgery*, **65-B**, 355-358.

McGovern, M.B. (1984). Effects of circuit weight training on the physical fitness of prepubescent children. *Dissertation Abstracts International*, **45**(2), 452A.

Moritani, T., & De Vries, H.A. (1979). Neural factors versus hypertrophy in the time course of muscle strength gain. *American Journal of Physical Medicine*, **58**, 115-130.

Moritani, T., & De Vries, H.A. (1980). Potential for gross muscle hypertrophy in older men. *Journal of Gerontology*, **35**, 672-682.

Nielsen, B., Nielsen, M., Hansen, M.B., & Asmussen, E. (1980). Training of "functional muscle strength" in girls 7-19 years old. In R.A. Binkhorst, H.C.G. Kemper, & W.H.M. Saris (Eds.), *Children and exercise IX* (pp. 69-78). Champaign, IL: Human Kinetics.

Pfeiffer, R.D., & Francis, R.S. (1986). Effects of strength training on muscle development in prepubescent, pubescent, and postpubescent males. *The Physician and Sportsmedicine*, **14**, 134-143.

Sale, D. (1987). Influence of exercise and training on motor unit activation. *Exercise and Sport Science Reviews*, **15**, 95-151.

Servedio, F.J., Bartels, R.L., Hamlin, R.L., Teske, D., Shaffer, T., & Servedio, A. (1985). The effects of weight training, using Olympic style lifts, on various physiological variables in pre-pubescent boys. *Medicine and Science in Sports and Exercise*, **17**, 288.

Sewall, L., & Micheli, L.J. (1986). Strength training for children. *Journal of Pediatric Orthopedics*, **6**, 143-146.

Tanner, J.M. (1962). *Growth at adolescence* (2nd ed.). London: Blackwell Scientific.

Vrijens, J. (1978). Muscle strength development in the pre- and post-pubescent age. In J. Borms & M. Hebbelinck (Eds.), *Medicine and sport* (Vol 11, pp. 152-158). Basel: Karger.

Weltman, A., Janny, C., Rians, C.B., Strand, K., Berg, B., Tippitt, S., Wise, J., Cahill, B.R., & Katch, F.I. (1986). The effects of hydraulic resistance strength training in pre-pubertal males. *Medicine and Science in Sports and Exercise*, **18**, 629-638.

Winter, J.S.D. (1978). Prepubertal and pubertal endocrinology. In F. Falkner & J.M. Tanner (Eds.), *Human growth: 2. Postnatal growth* (pp. 183-213). New York: Plenum Press.

Young, A., Stokes, M., Round, J.M., & Edwards, R.H. (1983). The effect of high-resistance training on the strength and cross-sectional area of the human quadriceps. *European Journal of Clinical Investigation*, **13**, 411-417.

The Effect of Training on Isokinetic Peak Torque in Knee Extensors of Junior Speed Skaters

Isamu Nemoto
Toho University, Tokyo, Japan

Hiroaki Kanehisa
International Budo University, Chiba, Japan

Mitsumasa Miyashita
University of Tokyo, Tokyo, Japan

It has been well known empirically that a long period of training is necessary for young athletes to achieve high-level performances. For example, most international-caliber speed skaters have undergone training for at least 10 years (Holum, 1984). Such extremely long-term competitive training may affect physical performance capacities such as muscular strength and endurance, even in children (Bar-Or, 1983; Rowland, 1985). The majority of studies conducted on the effect of training in young athletes has mainly focused on aerobic power ($\dot{V}O_2max$).

In contrast, only sparse information is available as to the effect of training on muscular strength in children, and even then the reports are controversial (Funato, Fukunaga, Asami, & Ikeda, 1987; Pfeiffer & Francis 1986; Vrijens, 1978). Furthermore, such information as the age-related changes in muscle fatigability and the effect of training on it is lacking. To investigate the effect of training on isokinetic peak torque (IPT), including muscle fatigability in knee extensors, junior speed skaters were tested in comparison with comparatively sedentary age-matched control subjects.

METHODS

Subjects

Subjects consisted of 132 male and 71 female junior speed skaters (SSs, aged 10 to 18 years) belonging to three different speed skating clubs that were deemed to be representative of the skating clubs in Japan. The subjects trained regularly throughout the year. Training for speed skating usually consists of both aerobic and anaerobic types of exercises at all age levels (Holum, 1984). As a control group (Cs), 236 males and 265 females between the ages of 10 and 18 and living in the same geographic areas were also tested. The majority of the Cs were going through a general educational curriculum. Sample sizes for Cs and SSs at selected ages are summarized in Table 1. Informed consent was obtained from the subjects, their parents, and the school authorities before participation.

Table 1 Number of Control Subjects (Cs) and Speed Skaters (SSs) at Selected Ages

	Male				Female			
		SSs				SSs		
Age (yrs)	Cs	Tsumagoi	Nikko	Nagano	Cs	Tsumagoi	Nikko	Nagano
10	19	11	—	—	16	3	—	—
11	24	—	17	—	21	2	7	—
12	17	4	9	—	25	1	4	—
13	23	7	10	—	20	3	7	—
14	26	5	7	2	25	—	1	4
15	25	5	3	7	28	—	2	5
16	35	4	2	4	35	—	2	8
17	31	1	2	10	46	2	4	9
18	36	3	6	13	49	1	1	5
Total	236	40	56	36	265	12	28	31

Lean Body Mass

Skinfold calipers (Eiyoken-type, Meikosha, Tokyo) were used to measure triceps and subscapular skinfolds. Lean body mass (LBM) was estimated from the equations for Japanese adolescent boys and girls (Nagamine & Suzuki, 1964).

Isokinetic Peak Torque

An isokinetic dynamometer (Cybex II; Lumex, Inc., New York) was used to measure IPT (Nm) produced at angular velocities corresponding to 0° (isometric, at the knee angle of 110°), 30°, 180°, 300° • s^{-1} (the range of motion was between 90° and 180°) during maximal knee extensions. Each subject performed three maximal contractions at the four preset angular velocities in a sitting position. The highest IPT at a given velocity was recorded. Fatigue testing consisted of 50 consecutive maximal voluntary contractions performed at 180° • s^{-1}. One complete examination lasted approximately 70 s (Thorstensson, 1976). In each situation the averaged IPT values for the 46th to 50th contractions were calculated and compared with the corresponding values for the 5 initial contractions. All tests were performed on location at the schools.

Statistical Analysis

The differences between means were determined by the students' *t* tests. In all statistical analyses, the .05 level of significance was used.

RESULTS

The IPT obtained during maximal knee extensions at four angular velocities for males and females are presented in Figures 1 and 2, respectively. As can be seen in these figures, IPT at all angular velocities increased with age from 10 to 18 years in the male Cs and from 10 to 15 years in the female Cs. Male SSs tended to be stronger after age 13 years, and female SSs after age 16 years. However, significant differences between the two groups were obtained only at lower angular velocities from 16 years of age in both sexes. These tendencies were clearly observed in the age-related changes of LBM (Figure 3).

In the fatigue test, fatigue patterns of IPT during 50 consecutive maximal voluntary contractions for males and females are shown in Figures 4 and 5, respectively. As can be seen in these figures, fatigue patterns were almost the same in both groups up to the age of 13 years, regardless of sex. Male Cs showed a gradual increase in the fatigue curves with age; however, in female Cs the fatigue curves increased only up to 15 years of age, and no changes were noted thereafter. On the other hand, SSs showed remarkable increases in fatigue curves with age, particularly in the latter half of contractions, and significant differences between the two groups were noted in the average final values after age 14 years for males and after age 13 years for females.

The fatigue index, that is, the mean decline in IPT with 50 contractions expressed in percent of initial values, increased with age from 13 to 16 years in male Cs and from 12 to 15 years in female Cs (Figure 6). On the other hand, SSs showed similar values regardless of age and sex, and there were significant differences between the two groups from the ages of 14 years in males and 13 years in females (Figure 6).

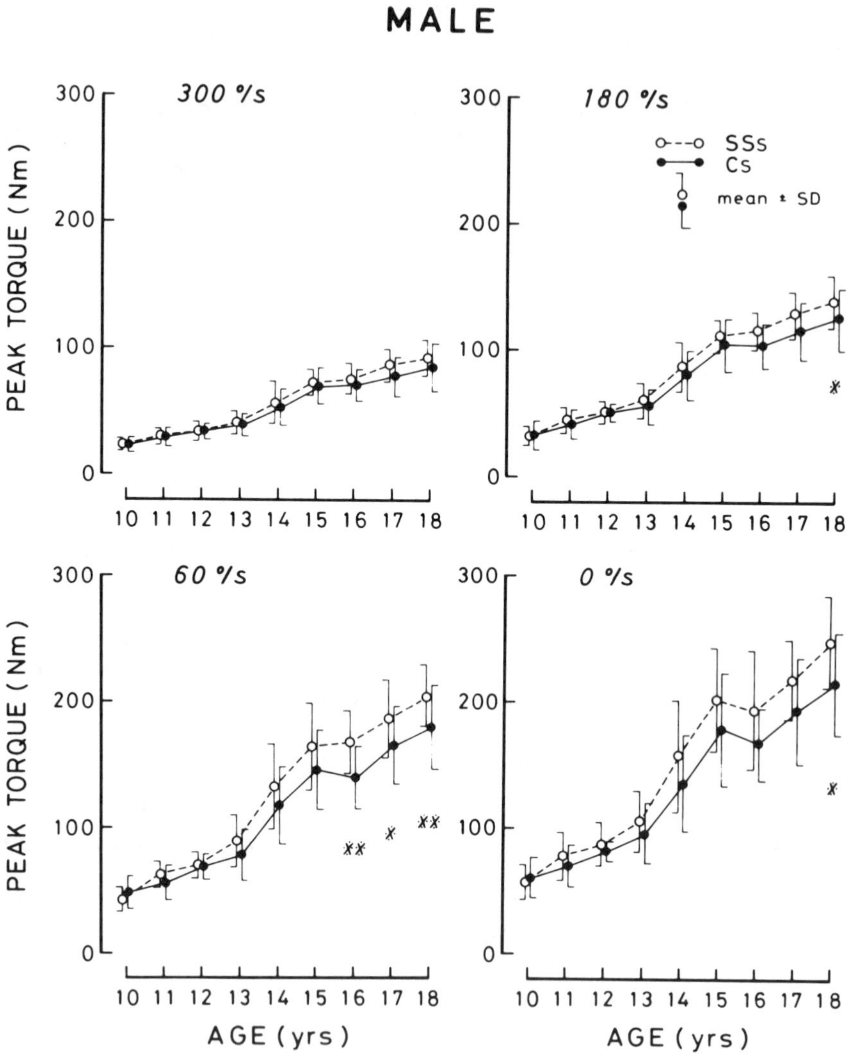

Figure 1. Comparison of age-related changes in isokinetic peak torque (IPT) obtained at four angular velocities in male controls (Cs) and speed skaters (SSs). $^*p < .05$. $^{**}p < .01$.

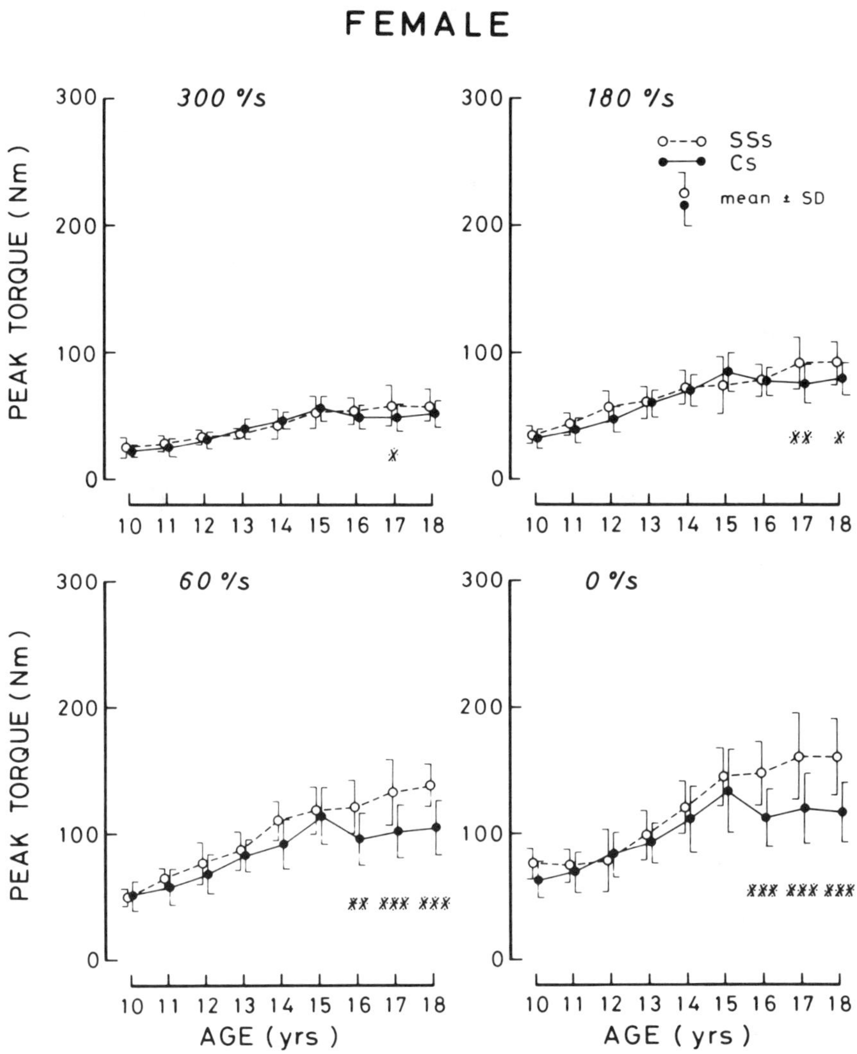

Figure 2. Comparison of age-related changes in isokinetic peak torque (IPT) obtained at four angular velocities in female controls (Cs) and speed skaters (SSs). $^{*}p < .05$. $^{**}p < .01$. $^{***}p < .001$.

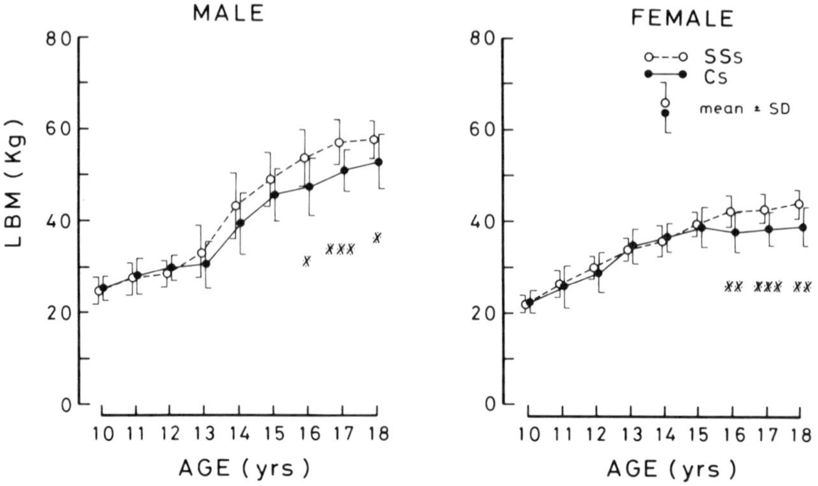

Figure 3. Comparison of age-related changes in estimated lean body mass (LBM) in control subjects (Cs) and speed skaters (SSs). $^*p < .05$. $^{**}p < .01$. $^{***}p < .001$.

DISCUSSION

The Effects of Training on IPT

The major finding of the present study was that SSs showed similar development patterns in IPT to those of Cs up to the age of 13 years, and significant differences between the two groups were obtained after 16 years of age in both sexes, particularly at lower angular velocities. There is considerable debate (American Academy of Pediatrics, 1983; Duda, 1986) as to the safety and effectiveness of strength training in children. Vrijens (1978) reported no consistent strength gains in the prepubescent groups he studied. It has been reported that insufficient quantities of circulating androgens might be the rationale for limiting strength training in children (American Academy of Pediatrics, 1983). On the contrary, Pfeiffer and Francis (1986) and Weltman et al. (1986) demonstrated significant increases in isokinetic strength in response to appropriate resistive exercise programs, even before puberty, and pointed out that neural rather than hypertrophic factors were responsible for the improvement in neuromuscular power. Furthermore, Funato et al. (1987) showed that the effect of strength training on cross-sectional area and muscle strength for prepubescents was similar in direction but different in magnitude from that found in adults.

The results of the present study were in accordance with those of Vrijens (1978), but somewhat different from those of Pfeiffer and Francis (1986), Weltman et al. (1986), and Funato et al. (1987). One possible explanation for this discrepancy might be that training for SSs under 13 years of age

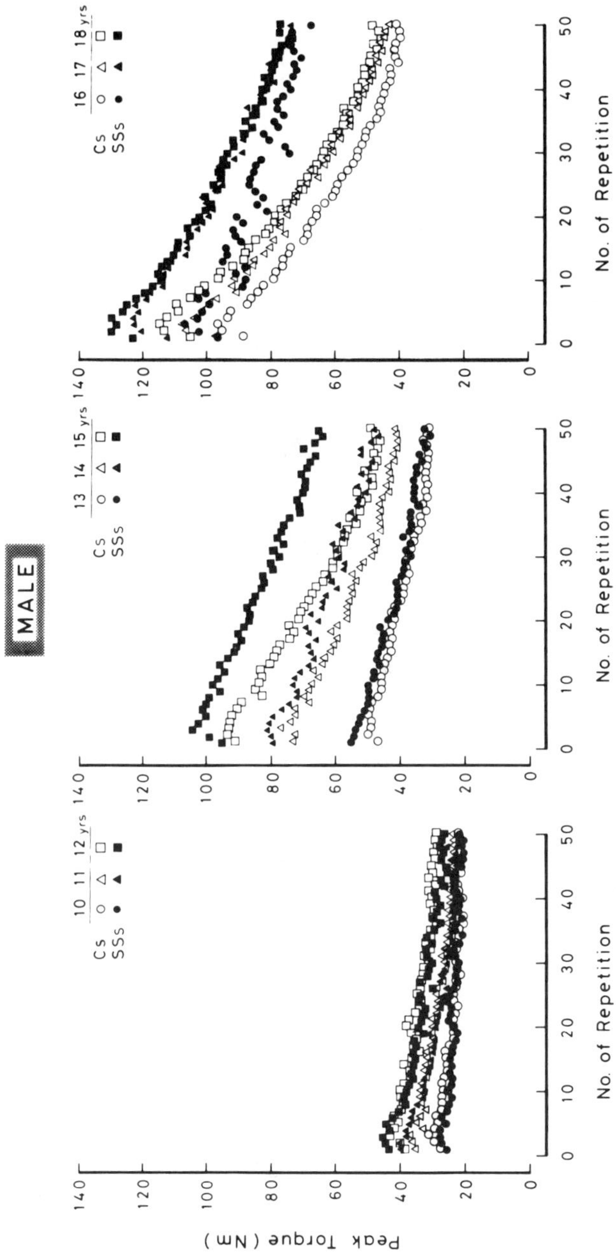

Figure 4. Comparison of fatigue patterns of isokinetic peak torque (IPT) during 50 consecutive maximal voluntary contractions in male control subjects (Cs) and speed skaters (SSs).

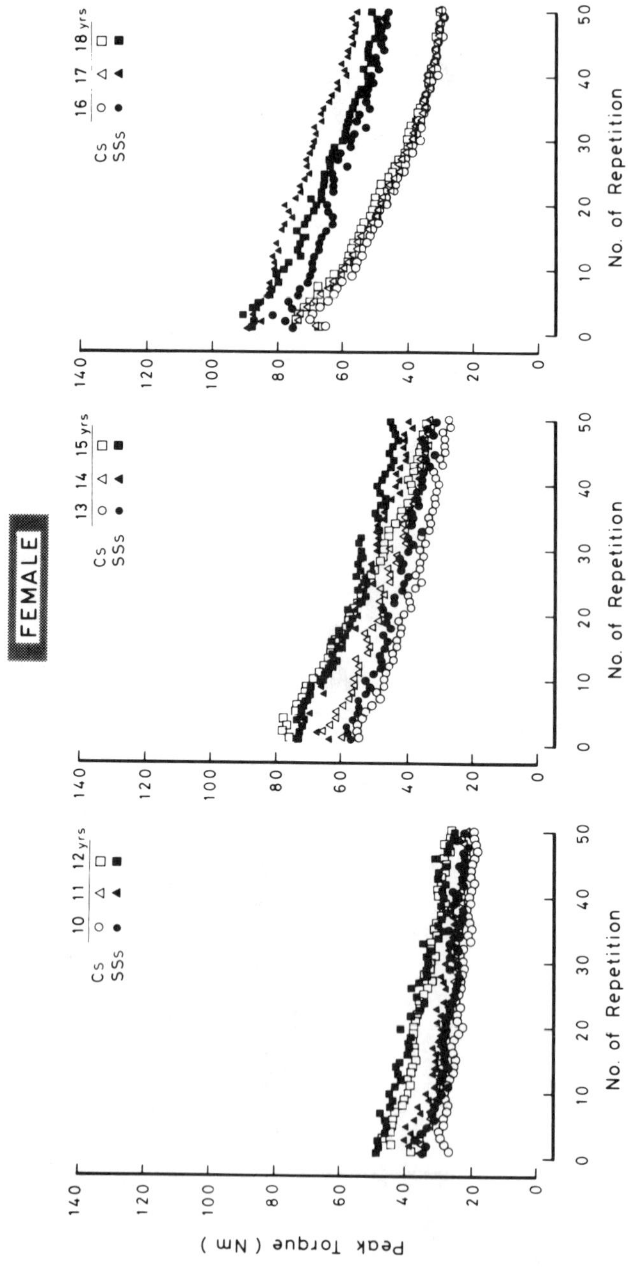

Figure 5. Comparison of fatigue patterns of isokinetic peak torque (IPT) during 50 consecutive maximal voluntary contractions in female control subjects (Cs) and speed skaters (SSs).

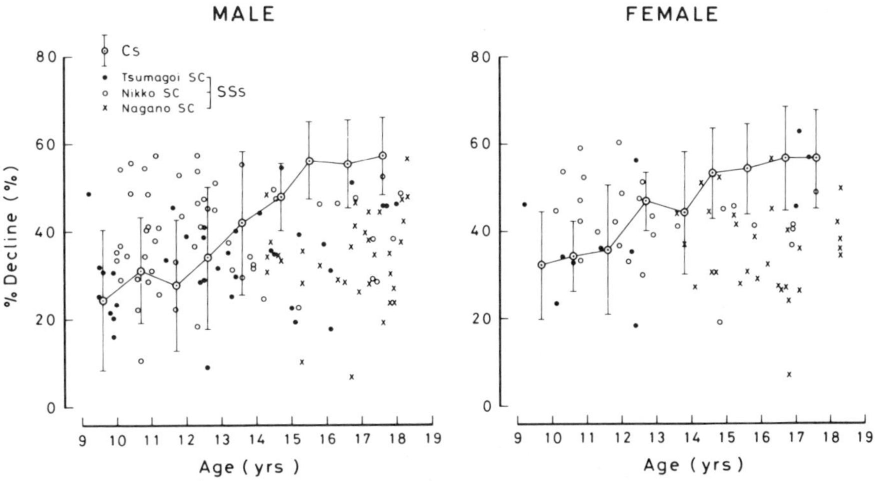

Figure 6. The fatigue index, that is, the mean decline in isokinetic peak torque (IPT) with 50 contractions, expressed in initial values for control subjects (Cs) and for speed skaters (SSs). SC = skating club.

was characterized by increased aerobic capacity rather than strength increases. Other authors have reported mainly strength increases as a result of training during late adolescence of both sexes. Moreover, the same tendency as IPT was demonstrated in the age-related changes in LBM (Figure 3). Therefore, this finding also conforms with earlier results that indicated that muscle hypertrophy might be primarily responsible for training-induced improvements in muscular performances (Funato et al., 1987; Ikai & Fukunaga, 1968; Wilmore, 1983).

In this study, the specificity of velocity training for speed skating has also been demonstrated, inasmuch as significant differences between the two groups were observed only at lower angular velocities from 16 years in both sexes (Figures 1 and 2). Kanehisa and Miyashita (1983) suggested that the existence of velocity-specific training effects derived from slow and fast contractions and that low-velocity training brought about power improvement mainly at slow muscular contractions. Furthermore, study of the changes of speed in the skating stroke clearly demonstrated that acceleration occurs in the late gliding phase where the knee is fixed and/or extended gradually at a relatively slow velocity and not during the push-off phase (Yoshioka, 1981). Taking all these reports into consideration, we might assume that the velocity that is the focus of training for speed skating mainly consists of and stresses the importance of isometrics and/or slow rather than fast physical movements (Holum, 1984).

The Effects of Training on Muscle Fatigability

Study of SSs showed significantly less fatigability than Cs from the age of 14 years for males and from 13 years for females, indicating the effectiveness of training for speed skating on muscle fatigability after puberty. Factors affecting the development of muscular fatigue during exercise have been amply reported. The causes are still not clearly established; accumulation of lactate and/or associated decreases in muscle tissue pH have been regarded as the most likely factors responsible for the impairment of muscular output (Sahlin, 1986). It has been speculated that increases in intracellar H^+ that accompany lactate production interfere with Ca^{2+} binding to troponin during excitation-contraction coupling (Fuchs, Reddy, & Briggs, 1970; Nakamura & Schwartz, 1972).

Under the same experimental setup, Tesch, Sjödin, Thorstensson, and Karlsson (1978) observed that muscle lactate accumulation was maximal after 50 contractions, and that after 25 contractions lactate had already reached such levels that increased H^+ probably resulted in force loss by interfering with muscle cross-bridge formation. On the other hand, it has been demonstrated that muscle performances are closely related to the muscle's capacity to utilize oxygen, which can be significantly affected by alterations in endogenously produced lactate and H^+ (Hogan & Welch, 1984). Ivy, Sherman, Miller, Maxwell, and Costill (1982), using a similar protocol to our own, were able to demonstrate a negative relationship ($r = -.63$) between the muscle tissue's capacity for aerobic metabolism and the rate of fatigue development. Furthermore, Eiken and Tesch (1984) found that hyperoxia and hypoxia might improve and impair dynamic muscle performance of the quadriceps during repeated isokinetic contractions.

Based upon these reports, it can be speculated that improved fatigability, expressed as the mean decline in IPT with 50 contractions in SSs, particularly after the age of 14 years for males and 13 years for females, resulted from an increase in oxidative capacities in the leg extensors in response to the effects of training regimens for speed skating.

Although quantifications of training for different ages and gender are not know, it appears that after pubescence, speed skating training programs that consist of both aerobic and anaerobic modes of exercise first alter the endurance capacities (Figure 6) and then increase muscle mass (Figure 3) and muscular strength (Figures 1 and 2) of leg extensors during late adolescence in both sexes.

CONCLUSION

These results indicate that after pubescence, speed skating training programs facilitate the morphological and functional development of the knee extensors. Moreover, it is speculated that training for speed skating mainly results in the improvement of endurance capacities during the lower teens, followed by increases in muscle mass and muscle strength.

Acknowledgments

The authors gratefully acknowledge Jeffrey D. Winchester for his skillful advice concerning English usage. This study was supported by the Project Research Grant of the Japan Amateur Sports Association and a grant from the Japan Skating Federation.

REFERENCES

American Academy of Pediatrics (1983). Weight training and weight lifting: Information for the pediatrician. *The Physician and Sportsmedicine,* **11**, 157-161.

Bar-Or, O. (1983). *Pediatric sports medicine for the practitioner.* New York: Springer-Verlag.

Duda, M. (1986). Prepubescent strength training gains support. *The Physician and Sportsmedicine,* **14**, 157-161.

Eiken, O., & Tesch, P.A. (1984). Effects of hyperoxia and hypoxia on dynamic and sustained static performance of the human quadriceps muscle. *Acta Physiologica Scandinavica,* **122**, 629-633.

Fuchs, F., Reddy, V., & Briggs, F.N. (1970). The interaction of cation with the calcium-binding site of troponin. *Biochimica et Biophysica Acta,* **221**, 407-409.

Funato, K., Fukunaga, T., Asami, T., & Ikeda, S. (1987). Strength training for prepubescent boys and girls. *Proceedings of the Department of Sports Sciences, College of Arts and Sciences, University of Tokyo,* **21**, 9-19.

Hogan, M.C., & Welch, H.G. (1984). Effect of varied lactate levels on bicycle ergometer performance. *Journal of Applied Physiology,* **57**, 507-513.

Holum, D. (1984). *The complete handbook of speed skating.* Hillside, NJ: Enslow.

Ikai, M., & Fukunaga, T. (1968). Calculation of muscle strength per unit cross-sectional area of human muscle by means of ultrasonic measurement. *International Zeitschrift für Agewandte Physiologie,* **26**, 26-32.

Ivy, J.L., Sherman, W.M., Miller, J.M., Maxwell, B.D., & Costill, D.L. (1982). Relationship between muscle $\dot{Q}O_2$ and fatigue during repeated isokinetic contractions. *Journal of Applied Physiology,* **53**, 470-474.

Kanehisa, H., & Miyashita, M. (1983). Specificity of velocity in strength training. *European Journal of Applied Physiology,* **52**, 104-106.

Nagamine, S., & Suzuki, S. (1964). Anthropometry and body composition of Japanese young men and women. *Human Biology,* **36**, 8-15.

Nakamura, Y., & Schwartz, A. (1972). The influence of hydrogen ion concentration on calcium binding and release by skeletal muscle sarcoplasmic reticulum. *Journal of General Physiology,* **59**, 22-32.

Pfeiffer, R.D., & Francis, R.S. (1986). Effects of strength training on muscle development in prepubescent, pubescent, and postpubescent males. *The Physician and Sportsmedicine*, **14**, 134-143.

Rowland, T.W. (1985). Aerobic response to endurance training in prepubescent children: A critical analysis. *Medicine and Science in Sports and Exercise*, **17**, 493-497.

Sahlin, K. (1986). Muscle fatigue and lactic acid accumulation. *Acta Physiologica Scandinavica*, **128**(Suppl. 556), 83-91.

Tesch, P., Sjödin, B., Thorstensson, A., & Karlsson, J. (1978). Muscle fatigue and its relation to accumulation and LDH activity in man. *Acta Physiologica Scandinavica*, **103**, 413-420.

Thorstensson, A. (1976). Muscle fatigue, fiber types and enzyme activities in man. *Acta Physiologica Scandinavica*, **98**(Suppl. 443), 1-45.

Vrijens, J. (1978). Muscle strength development in the pre- and postpubescent age. In J. Borms & M. Hebbelinck (Eds.), *Pediatric work physiology* (pp. 152-158). Basel: Karger.

Weltman, A., Janney, C., Rians, C.B., Strand, K., Berg, B., Tippitt, S., Wise, J., Cahill, B.R., & Katch, F.I. (1986). The effects of hydraulic resistance strength training in pre-pubertal males. *Medicine and Science in Sports and Exercise*, **18**, 629-638.

Wilmore, J.H. (1983). Body composition in sport and exercise: Directions for future research. *Medicine and Science in Sports and Exercise*, **15**, 21-31.

Yoshioka, N. (1981). *A kinematic analysis of speed skating*. Unpublished master's thesis, University of Tokyo, Japan.

Longitudinal Effects of Participating in a 3-Year Sports Class on Selected Physiological and Anthropometric Variables of Pubescent Children

Amos Grodjinovsky
Raffy Dotan
Wingate Institute for Physical Education and Sports, Netanya, Israel

The time of growth and development in children is a period during which physical and physiological changes take place (Anderson et al., 1984; Asmussen, 1974; Bar-Or, 1983; Malina, 1980). During this period, the child's body increases in size and the organs develop and mature until they function on the level required to meet the demands of daily life and the physical activities of a typical adult. The time span from early childhood to maturity brings about a great increase in physical performance capacity. This increase is due to the biological changes occurring during the process of maturation regardless of physical training.

As late as 1973, Klissouras and Weber indicated that "we are still largely ignorant regarding the question of whether physical activity at an earlier stage of maturation is more effective in altering functional adaptability than at a later one" (p. 209). There is a lack of longitudinal studies in which the effects of training on physical performance of the growing child are evaluated (Kemper, 1983; Rutenfranz, 1986). Furthermore, a limited number of studies examine the effects of training on fitness components of the exercising child (Bar-Or & Zwiren, 1973; Grodjinovsky & Bar-Or, 1984; Rowland, 1985; Rotstein et al., 1986).

It is clearly necessary to separate the effects of training from the effects of maturation in order to ascertain whether the increase in performance is a consequence of training or of heredity and maturation only. It was the purpose of this study to investigate the longitudinal effects of a 3-year program of additional physical education and physical training on selected physiological and anthropometric parameters of children enrolled in a sports class.

METHODS

Subjects

A total of 65 boys and girls (aged 12 to 13 years at the beginning of the study) were tested over a period of 3 years. The subjects were selected from a large student population (over 1,000 students) of a junior high school in Herzelia, Israel. Two intact school classes constituted the subject population: a sports class (S) and a randomly chosen regular class serving as a control group (C).

The experimental class (S) consisted initially of 14 boys and 18 girls. The boys practiced European handball and had been selected according to their level of performance in simple handball skills such as dribbling and scoring goals. The girls, on the other hand, practiced track-and-field, having been selected because of their performance levels in specific events.

The control class (C) consisted initially of 18 boys and 15 girls. They were of similar age and comparable socioeconomic background to those of the S class. Data were analyzed using three-way ANOVA (treatment × sex × time) with repeated measures on the last factor. The statistical analysis was performed on an IBM-PC microcomputer using the SPSS PC statistical package.

Training

The S group had 6 hr of physical education (PE), 1 hr a day, as compared with only 2 hr a week of PE for the C subjects. A typical PE hour started with a warm-up and some calisthenics followed by a game or additional running and strengthening exercises. The same methods were used for both classes because they were taught by the same instructor. The morning PE was given by an accredited physical education teacher, and the afternoon training session was conducted by a professional coach. In addition, the S group had three 2-hr sessions per week of handball training in the afternoons. For the boys, a typical training session included 30 to 45 min of conditioning followed by tactical, technical, and skill training. For the girls, the training included 30 to 45 min of conditioning followed by various drills and specific training: sprints, middle- and long-distance running, various jumps, and so forth. In all, the S subjects had 12 hr of different types of physical activities per week as compared with 2 hr for C subjects. No attempt was made to control or account for the physical activities that children of either group engaged in during their leisure time.

Tests

The tests were of four categories as follows: (a) anthropmetric measurements of height, weight, and skinfolds; (b) static strength and grip strength of both hands; (c) aerobic fitness represented by heart rate (HR) response to a standard cycle ergometer load; and (d) anaerobic performance as determined by the 30 s Wingate Anaerobic Test (WAnT).

Protocol

All subjects were tested at the beginning (September) and at the end (June) of each school year of the 3-year study period. In this study, data are presented only from subjects ($n = 49$) who completed all six tests. All tests were conducted at school. On a test day, the children reported to the nurse's office for height, weight, skinfold, and left and right grip strength measurements. The skinfolds (triceps, subscapular, and abdomen) and grip strength were measured by the same person throughout the 3-year period using the same skinfold caliper (Lange) and the same dynamometer. This was followed by a 4-min submaximal cycle ergometer (Bodyguard) test. In order to assess aerobic fitness, a fixed standard test load of 75 W (450 kg • min^{-1}) was used. Heart rate was recorded during the last 20 s of the 4-min work period on an ECG recorder (M.G. Electronics, Israel).

The WAnT was administered on a separate day. For this test, a modified Monark cycle ergometer was used in which the breaking force was applied by weights. Resistance was determined relative to the subject's body weight (45 g • kg^{-1} bw) with an accuracy of $\pm$ 100 g. The number of revolutions was recorded for each 5-s interval for a total of 30 s. Two indices were calculated: peak power output (PP; the highest 5-s output) and mean power output (MP) throughout the entire test duration of 30 s. A more detailed description of the test is given elsewhere (Dotan & Bar-Or, 1983; Grodjinovsky, Inbar, Dotan, & Bar-Or, 1980; Inbar & Bar-Or, 1986).

RESULTS

In general, no distinguishing trends were observed between the two groups throughout the 3-year study period (except possibly height and weight gains; Figures 1 and 2). Therefore, only results of the last (post-) and initial (pre-) tests are compared and presented in this report.

The results of the height, weight, sum of three skinfolds, and grip-strength measurements are presented in Table 1. The S boys, although initially heavier, gained more weight than the C boys (2.5 kg). There were no significant differences in initial height or subsequent height gain between the S and C groups (Grodjinovsky & Bar-Or, 1984). Both S and C boys showed a tendency toward a decrease in the sum of three skinfolds, whereas the girls tended toward an increase in this variable. As expected by growth, all subjects improved in their grip strength. S boys and girls were initially stronger and gained somewhat more in strength than the C boys and girls. However, when corrected for body weight, grip strength was no longer greater in either of the groups of females.

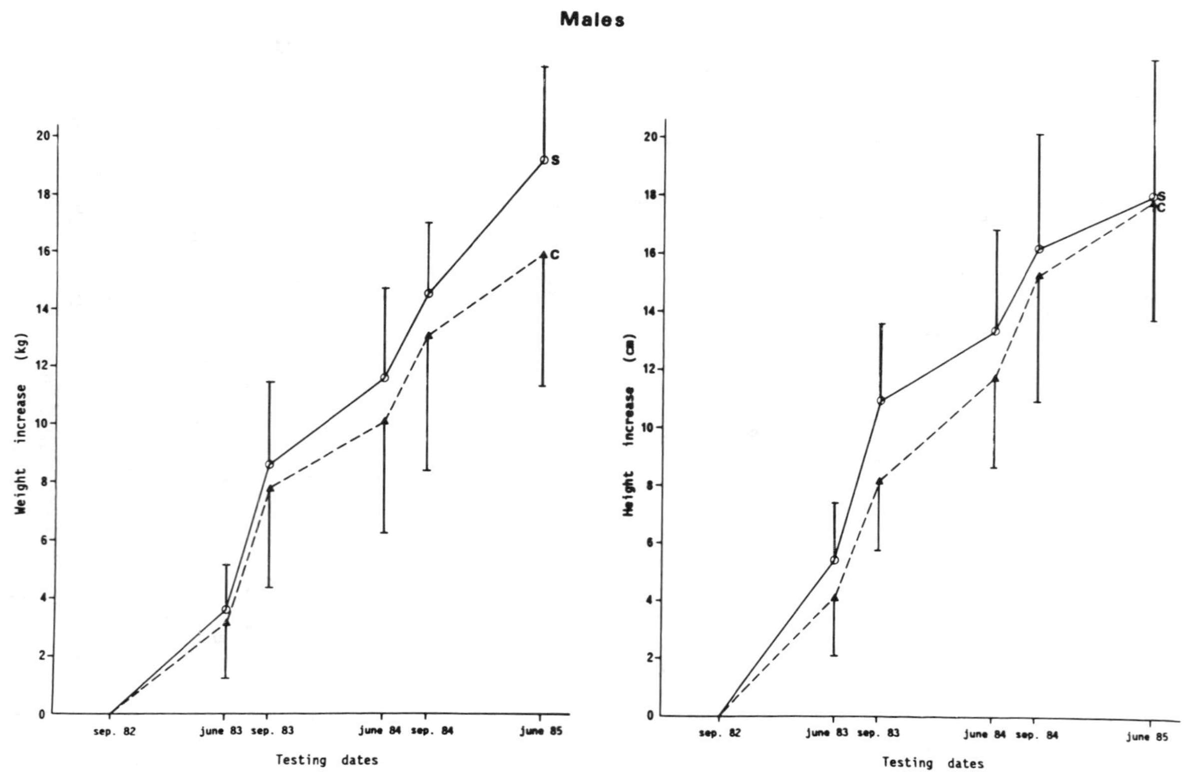

Figure 1. Average height and weight increase in boys of the sports (S) and control (C) classes during the 3-year study period (mean ± 1 *SD*).

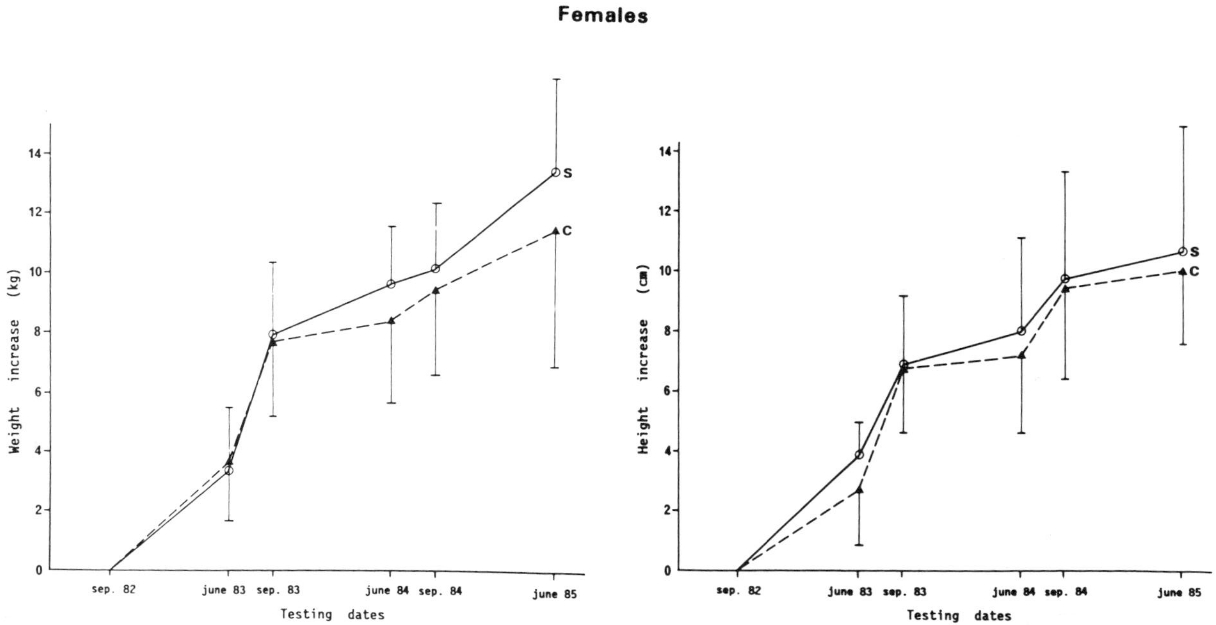

Figure 2. Average height and weight increase in girls of the sports (S) and control (C) classes during the 3-year study period (mean ± 1 *SD*).

Table 1 Height, Weight, Adiposity, and Grip Strength Values for the Sport (S) and Control (C) Classes at the Pre- and Posttest (Mean ± *SD*)

Variable			Group			
			Boys		Girls	
			S n = 13	C n = 9	S n = 16	C n = 11
Height (cm)	Mean ± 1 *SD*	Pre	153.7 9.7	148.0 8.7	152.0 7.4	153.0 4.7
		Post	171.8 [b] 7.4	166.0 [b] 8.1	162.8 [b] 5.3	163.2 [b] 3.6
Weight (kg)	Mean ± 1 *SD*	Pre	42.3 [a] 8.5	36.9 6.8	41.5 7.7	39.1 7.3
		Post	61.5 [ab] 8.9	52.8 [b] 9.9	54.9 [b] 6.4	50.5 [b] 6.3
Sum of 3 skinfolds (mm)	Mean ± 1 *SD*	Pre	35.3 11.9	32.4 14.3	30.8 12.8	33.2 9.8
		Post	33.9 17.3	29.3 8.8	43.3 14.5	47.2 14.2
Grip strength average 2 hands (kg)	Mean ± 1 *SD*	Pre	25.5 [a] 4.8	22.3 3.6	21.9 [a] 3.2	19.2 4.9
		Post	41.3 [ab] 6.9	36.1 [b] 5.1	28.8 [ab] 2.6	24.4 [b] 4.6
Relative grip strength average 2 hands (kg • kg bw^{-1})	Mean ± 1 *SD*	Pre	0.61 0.08	0.61 0.08	0.53 0.06	0.49 0.10
		Post	0.68[b] 0.08	0.69[b] 0.08	0.53 0.06	0.48 0.08

[a]Significant difference between S and C at the .01 level. [b]Significant difference between pre- and posttests at the .01 level.

at the Pre- and Posttest (Mean ± *SD*)

Variable			Group			
			Boys		Girls	
			S $n = 13$	C $n = 9$	S $n = 16$	C $n = 11$
Mean power output (W)	Mean ± 1 *SD*	Pre	296.4[a]	238.7	264.8	220.5
			6.26	54.9	38.0	43.7
		Post	554.8[abc]	438.5[b]	391.4[abc]	314.9[b]
			82.2	105.1	47.3	51.6
Relative mean power output (W • kg^{-1})	Mean ± 1 *SD*	Pre	7.0[a]	6.5	6.5[a]	5.6
			0.6	0.9	0.8	0.7
		Post	9.0[abc]	8.3[b]	7.2[b]	6.3[b]
			0.6	0.8	0.8	0.3
Peak power output (W)	Mean ± 1 *SD*	Pre	400.8[a]	314.5	354.2[a]	289.6
			99.5	69.7	55.6	71.8
		Post	747.2[abc]	571.0[b]	575.0[abc]	450.5[b]
			114.9	106.5	88.3	68.4
Relative peak power output (W • kg^{-1})	Mean ± 1 *SD*	Pre	9.5[a]	8.5	8.5[a]	7.3
			1.2	1.0	1.4	1.4
		Post	12.2[abc]	10.7[b]	10.3[b]	9.0[b]
			0.8	1.1	1.3	0.8
Heart rate at 75 W	Mean ± 1 *SD*	Pre	162.3	169.3	179.1	183.8
			12.1	12.8	14.3	15.0
		Post	113.0[b]	122.8[b]	131.9[b]	149.5[b]
			14.5	18.7	11.8	15.6

[a]Significant difference between S and C at the .01 level. [b]Significant difference between pre- and posttests at the .01 level. [c]Significant interaction effect of groups (S × C).

The exercise HR and anaerobic fitness changes are presented in Table 2. In general, the anaerobic capacity of all subjects increased throughout the 3-year study period. Although the S group initially had higher relative and absolute MP and PP, improvement was significantly greater in both indices among the boys, but in the girls only the absolute MP and PP increased. No differences in the exercise HR response were found between the S and C subjects (Table 2). However, as expected, the actual HR response greatly diminished with age and growth.

DISCUSSION

The degree of children's trainability and the effect of training on their physical development are questions bearing major relevance to both school physical education and young talent cultivation in specialized athletic programs (Bar-Or, 1983; Bar-Or & Zwiren, 1973; Borms, 1986). Introduction of extra physical activity during the growth spurt period is thought to improve physical performance later in life (Bar-or, 1983; Klissouras & Weber, 1973; Malina, 1980). In this study, it was found that the rate of growth in both sexes was not significantly different as a result of 10 additional hr of physical activity per week during a 3-year follow-up. At the end of the 3 years, the height increase was 18.7 and 17.6 cm among the boys and 10.6 and 9.4 cm among the girls of the S and C groups, respectively (Figure 1). However, it should be noted that the S boys were both initially and at the end of the study taller than the C boys by as much as 5.8 cm. There seemed to be a trend of a faster initial growth rate of the S boys, with the C boys gradually catching up, and a greater increase in weight in the S boys and girls (Figures 1 & 2). This trend was probably due to the earlier maturation of the S boys compounded with the training effect resulting in a possible increase in muscle mass.

The height gain observed in this study was similar to the increase reported by Asmussen (1974) and typical of European and other children (Anderson et al., 1984; Bar-Or, 1983; Goslin & Burden, 1986; Wanne & Valimaki, 1983; Watkins, Farrally, & Powely, 1983). The growth rate and height of the two groups of girls did not differ; they were similar throughout. Early maturing boys and girls are generally heavier and taller as compared with their slower maturing peers. Also, young male athletes (9 to 16 years of age) are generally advanced in sexual and skeletal development, heavier, stronger, and more mesomorphic (Bar-Or, 1983; Borms, 1986; Wanne & Valimaki, 1983). The trends observed and the findings of the present study were in agreement with these statements.

The S boys and girls did not undergo specific strength training. However, since the boys played European handball, involving repetitive throws of a ball, it was expected that grip strength would improve. The results of this study showed that all subjects improved their grip strength, whereas the S boys improved somewhat more. Such results have also been reported by others; namely that postpubescent boys showed more strength improvement due to training as compared with prepubescent boys (Bar-Or, 1983; Eriksson & Saltin, 1973; Hamilton & Andrew, 1976). Most studies that included this variable were not longitudinal and lasted only several weeks (Bar-Or, 1983; Rutenfranz, 1986). There is no doubt that all subjects in this study improved their grip strength due to growth and maturation. However, long-term training, although not specific for strength, resulted in grip strength improvement. This improvement was probably due to interaction of the added physical activity in a developmental period of increased male sex-hormone activity (Eriksson & Saltin, 1973).

The only specific training that the S group had was anaerobic; the nature of European handball requires sprints and jumps. Most of the girls also engaged in sprints and jumps in their track training. As expected (Inbar & Bar-Or, 1986; Rotstein, Dotan, Bar-Or, & Tenenbaum, 1986), all subjects improved in their anaerobic performance; however, the improvement of the S group was much greater than that of the C group. Eriksson and Saltin (1973) reported that anaerobic training lasting 6 to 16 weeks resulted in increased muscle ATP, CP, glycogen, and PFK activity. It can safely be assumed that specific training of sufficient dosage will cause an increase in the anaerobic performance at an early age (Fourneir, Ricci, Taylor, Montpetit, & Chaitman, 1982). The question of whether this early training will result in greater improvement as compared with training 2 or 3 years later still remains unanswered (Borms, 1986).

It is well established (Bar-Or, 1983; Borms, 1986) that the training effect is related to the intensity of the training program. HR response to the standardized cycle ergometer load greatly diminished with growth (Bar-Or, 1983; Rowland, 1985). In this study, the decline in HR was similar in the two groups with no observed training effect. It ranged from 37 to 49 bpm and was markedly greater than HR declines reported by others (Bar-Or, 1983). A likely reason for this was the lack of habituation to the testing procedures prior to the first testing session. S boys and girls were very successful in their athletic performance albeit the lack of difference in HR response. Physiological improvement is not the only variable affecting performance. The change in neuromuscular ability (motor skills) has a great effect on it.

It should be noted that the boys were preselected for the sports class using very simple criteria such as ball dribbling and throwing evaluated subjectively by the coach. It is therefore suggested that selection of children for some sports events is possible by identification of specific motor and fitness variables involved and their evaluation using simple field tests. It is further suggested that it may not be necessary to use sophisticated laboratory equipment to identify the potential athlete at this early age. Laboratory testing may be superfluous to the simple and much cheaper field tests and may often prove to be more for the benefit of the investigator than for the coach or the athlete. It is worthwhile emphasizing that these boys, selected on the basis of only very simple tests, won the National Handball Cup and were the Israeli age-group champions for 3 consecutive years.

The results of this study show that maturation is the strongest stimulus for increases in physical performance during the growth-spurt period.

Athletic ability is probably related to early maturation, which brings about better performance when compared with late maturing boys and girls (Asmussen, 1974; Borms, 1986; Malina, 1980). These children were relatively physically fit and engaged in habitual physical activity (Goslin & Burden, 1983; Grodjinovsky et al., 1980). The training effect is not always synonomous with training. In order to have a training effect, training must be specific and the program must be of sufficient intensity, duration, and frequency to bring about the desired changes. It still remains uncertain at which stage of growth training is most effective (Bar-Or, 1983; Borms, 1986).

The extensive physical and physiological changes observed during the growth-spurt period reemphasize the utmost importance of a matching control group. In this study, there was a trend for the controls to improve as much as the experimental subjects in some events and to catch up in other variables. It is, therefore, suggested that such studies be continued at least until children reach the age of 18 (at which time the growth slows down substantially among boys and virtually ceases among girls) in order to arrive at a possible answer as to the effect of early training at a later age.

REFERENCES

Anderson, K.L., Rutenfranz, J., Seliger, V., Ilmarinen, I., Berndt, I., Kylian, H., & Ruppel, M. (1984). The growth of lung volumes affected by physical performance capacity in boys and girls during childhood and adolescence. *European Journal of Applied Physiology*, **52**, 380-384.

Asmussen, E. (1974). Development patterns in physical performance capacity. In L. Larsen (Ed.), *Fitness health and work capacity* (pp. 435-438). New York: Macmillan.

Bar-Or, O. (1983). *Pediatric sports medicine for the practitioner*. New York: Springer-Verlag.

Bar-Or, O., & Zwiren, L.D. (1973). Physiological effects of increased frequency of physical education classes and of endurance conditioning on 9- to 10-year-old girls and boys. In O. Bar-Or (Ed.), *Pediatric Work Physiology Proceedings of the 4th International Symposium* (pp. 183-198). Netanya, Israel: Wingate Institute for Physical Education and Sports.

Borms, J. (1986). The child and exercise: An overview. *Journal of Sports Medicine*, **4**, 3-20.

Dotan, R., & Bar-Or, O. (1983). Load optimization for the Wingate Anaerobic Test. *European Journal of Applied Physiology*, **51**, 409-417.

Eriksson, B.O., & Saltin, B. (1973). Muscle metabolism and anaerobic metabolism in prepubertal boys before and after training. In O. Bar-Or (Ed.), *Pediatric Work Physiology Proceedings of the 4th International Symposium* (pp. 173-181). Netanya, Israel: Wingate Institute for Physical Education and Sports.

Fournier, M., Ricci, J., Taylor, A.W., Montpetit, R.R., & Chaitman, B.R. (1982). Skeletal muscle adaptation in adolescent boys: Sprint and endurance training or detraining. *Medicine and Science in Sports and Exercise*, **14**, 453-456.

Goslin, B.R., & Burden, S.B. (1986). Physical fitness of South African children. *Journal of Sports Medicine and Physical Fitness*, **26**, 128-136.

Grodjinovsky, A., & Bar-Or, O. (1984). Influence of added physical education hours upon anaerobic capacity, adiposity, and grip strength in 12- to 13-year-old children enrolled in a sports class. In J. Ilmarinen & I. Valimaki (Eds.), *Children and sports pediatric work physiology* (pp. 162-169). New York: Springer-Verlag.

Grodjinovsky, A., Inbar, O., Dotan, R., & Bar-Or, O. (1980). Training effect on the anaerobic performance of children as measured by the Wingate Anaerobic Test. In K. Berg & B.O. Eriksson (Eds.), *Children and exercise IX* (pp. 139-145). Baltimore: University Park Press.

Hamilton, P., & Andrew, G.M. (1976). Influence of growth and athletic training on heart and lung functions. *European Journal of Applied Physiology*, **36**, 27-38.

Inbar, O., & Bar-Or, O. (1986). Anaerobic characteristics in male children and adolescents. *Medicine and Science in Sports and Exercise*, **18**, 264-269.

Kemper, H.C.G. (1983). Physiological aspects of endurance sport in young people. *International Journal of Physical Education*, **2**, 22-27.

Klissouras, V., & Weber, G. (1973). Training: Growth and heredity. In O. Bar-Or (Ed.), *Pediatric Work Physiology Proceedings of the 4th International Symposium* (pp. 209-215). Netanya, Israel: Wingate Institute for Physical Education and Sports.

Malina, R.M. (1980). Growth strength and physical performance. In G.A. Stull (Ed.), *Encyclopedia of physical education, fitness and sports: Training, environment, nutrition and fitness* (pp. 443-470). Salt Lake City: Brighton.

Rotstein, A., Dotan, R., Bar-Or, O., & Tenenbaum, G. (1986). Effect of training on anaerobic threshold, maximal aerobic power and anaerobic performance of preadolescent boys. *International Journal of Sports Medicine*, **7**, 281-286.

Rowland, T.W. (1985). Aerobic response to endurance training in prepubescent children: A critical analysis. *Medicine and Science in Sports and Exercise*, **17**, 493-497.

Rutenfranz, J. (1986). Longitudinal approach to assessing maximal aerobic power during growth: The European experience. *Medicine and Science in Sports and Exercise*, **18**, 270-275.

Wanne, O., & Valimaki, I. (1983). The influence of sports training on growth in school children. *Scandinavian Journal of Sports Science*, **5**, 41-44.

Watkins, J., Farrally, M., & Powley, A. (1983). *The anthropometry and physical fitness of secondary school girls in Strathclyde*. The Scottish School of Physical Education, Jordanhill College, Scotland.

Part IV
Health Indicators During Childhood and Adolescence

Hereditary and Environmental Effects on the Metabolism of Some Pharmacons in Young Athletes

Róbert Frenkl
Hungarian University of Physical Education, Budapest, Hungary
Tamás Szabó
Központi Sportiskola, Budapest, Hungary

In the top ranks of competitive sports, the athlete's individual sensitivity to drug administration has become a factor of special significance even in young athletes. Drug administration may be indicated either by the intense preparatory and conditioning training characteristics at this level (e.g., polyvitamins, organic and inorganic electrolyte mixtures, other nondisqualifying preparations, etc.) or else by injuries, conditions, or diseases suffered by the athlete (drug therapy). Attempts approaching or even violating the bans on doping also must be dealt with.

After ingestion, drugs become absorbed, transported, and distributed in the respective fluid spaces and organs, bound to the tissue receptors in the neurons, muscles, heart, lungs, kidneys, and so forth. Then they become metabolized and excreted. In this process, the par excellence individual variations occur mainly during the metabolization phase. The drug molecule is usually rearranged chemically and becomes water soluble. The enzyme systems involved in this complex course of events are under genetic control. Acetylation is one of the individually variable factors of metabolization, and by measuring its rate, individuals can be classified as slow or fast acetylators. The ratio of slow to fast acetylators varies from population to population.

On the other hand, several of the enzymes involved in drug metabolism are capable of responding by developing a higher rate of activity to repeated or regular drug administration. This drug-triggered enzyme induction is one of the theoretically as well as practically important problems in modern pharmacology. It has been shown (Frenkl, Györe, Mészáros, & Szeberényi, 1980; Frenkl, Györe, & Szeberényi, 1980) by both animal experiments and human observations that regular physical exercise can elicit a similar induction of the microsomal enzyme systems of the liver as some drugs undergo biotransformation in the liver. The extent of this kind of induction has been found to be related to the level of physical fitness or training. In humans, the study of antipyrine metabolization has proven the most suitable indicator of enzyme induction among other exogenous inductors such as diet, smoking, and alcohol ingestion (Vestal, 1979).

It was of interest to study whether these changes in metabolism observed previously in adult athletes were demonstrable in an adolescent group of young athletes. Seven weeks of 1.5 hr per week of strength training had no appreciable effect on the rate of antipyrine elimination in schoolchildren of 16 years of age (Frenkl, Szöts, Mészáros, & Szabó, 1986). Another point of interest was whether there was a relationship, on the one hand, between the hereditary and acquired factors of drug metabolism and, on the other hand, between the rate of drug metabolization and the level of endurance fitness in adolescents. The present study dealt with these problems as found in a group of young basketball players participating in intense event-specific training for at least 2 to 3 years.

MATERIAL AND METHODS

The subjects were 12 adolescent male basketball players. In the spiroergometric and acetylator phenotype studies altogether 28 subjects were included. The basketball department of the Központi Sportiskola (Central School of Sports) has since ceased to function, and, owing to loss of contact, only 12 of those studied before could be recruited for the study of antipyrine elimination. The present article refers, therefore, to the results obtained in these 12 subjects only.

The subjects were somatotyped by the anthropometric method of Heath and Carter (1971), and their growth type was assessed by the Conrad method (1963). Body dimensions were taken in accordance with the recommendations of the International Biological Programme (Weiner & Lourie, 1969). Body mass; stature; biacromial, bicondylar (femur and humerus), and chest widths; calf, hand, lower arm, and flexed tensed upper arm circumferences; chest depth; and five skinfolds were measured. As a workable estimate of biological age, the morphological age of Mészáros, Mohácsi, Szabó, and Szmodis (1985), which relies on actual body mass, stature, the plastic index of Conrad, and chronological age, was used.

The spiroergometric data were obtained by using a Mijnhardt Ergo-Analyzer and Universal Ergometer. Lung function parameters were measured by a Medicor Eutest. Serum antipyrine levels were assessed by Brodie's method (1949). Acetylator phenotypes were obtained by using a modified technique of Bratton and Marshall (1939).

RESULTS

The chronological and morphological ages of the subjects are shown in Table 1. There was no significant difference between the two. In some cases, however, the subjects were younger morphologically. Figures 1

Table 1 Chronological (DA) and Morphological (MA) Ages in Decimal Years of the Subjects

	DA	MA
1. V.I.	15.51	14.1
2. B.A.	15.76	15.6
3. L.R.	16.09	15.4
4. R.B.	15.85	14.8
5. D.L.	13.88	14.4
6. H.G.	13.44	12.7
7. B.A.	13.73	13.8
8. D.A.	13.77	13.7
9. P.L.	14.01	13.7
10. M.L.	15.25	15.1
11. V.A.	15.90	15.3
12. F.I.	15.95	15.3

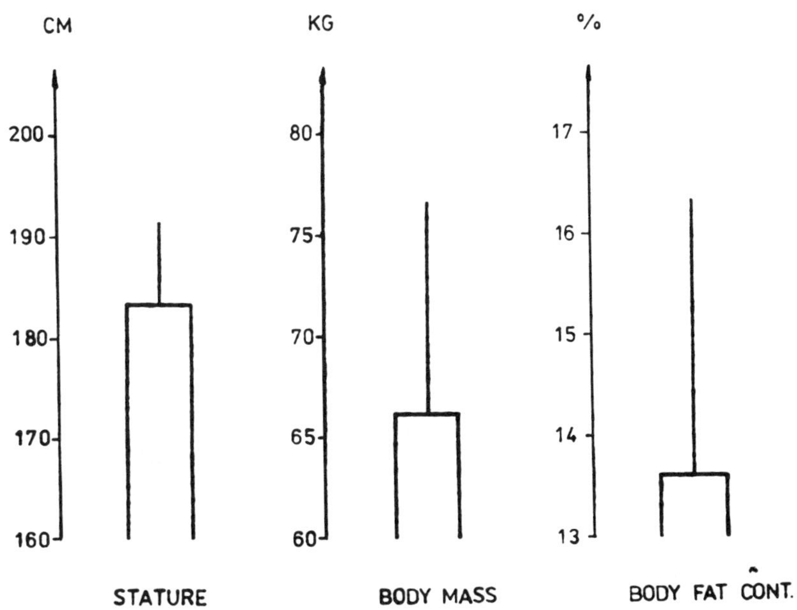

Figure 1. Means and standard deviations for stature, body mass, and percent body fat content (N = 12).

through 3 present some dimensions and the body build of the subjects. Mainly attributable to the coaches' preference in selection, these boys were taller than their peers. In comparison with youngsters of a similar age,

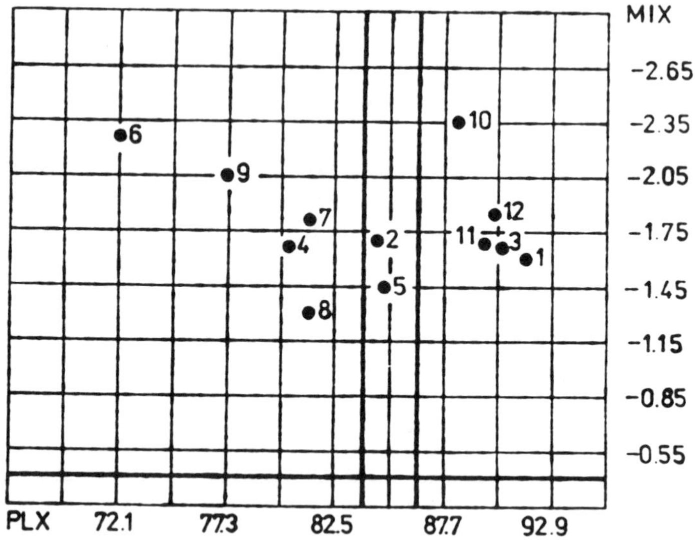

Figure 2. Distribution of the individual growth types in the Conrad grid of growth type. MIX = metric index; PLX = plastic index. Numbers correspond to ordered subject list.

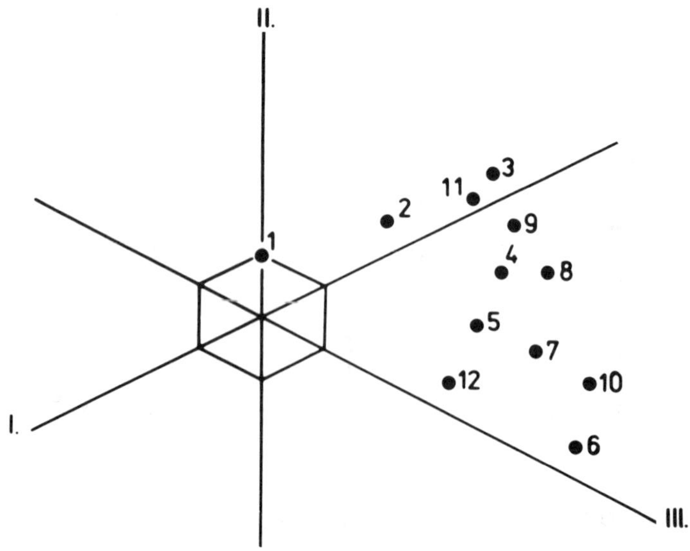

Figure 3. Distribution of the individual anthropometric somatotypes in the schematic somatochart of Heath and Carter (1971).

the appreciably lower body fat content resulted in a lower relative body mass. The majority had somatotypes dominated by ectomorphy along with a hyperplastic leptomorph growth type.

Lung function and ergometric data statistics are shown in Figures 4 and 5. All the obtained parameters speak for a good or high level of physical endurance fitness. Table 2 summarizes the results of the pharmacokinetic

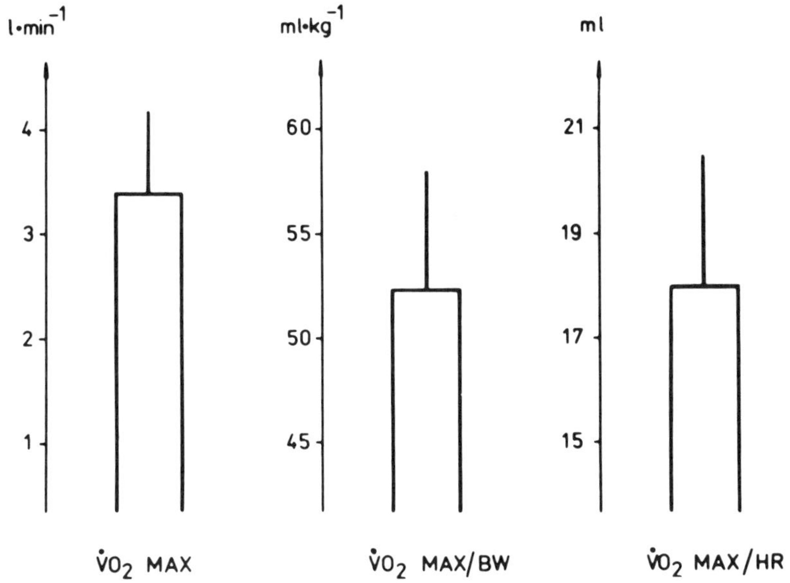

Figure 4. Lung function tests: means and standard deviations for vital capacity, forced 1-s expiratory volume (FEV1) and maximum voluntary breathing capacity (MAX.VENT.) (N = 12).

and pharmacogenetic studies and the individual values of relative aerobic power. Three of the subjects were fast and nine were slow acetylators. It is noted here that this study was carried out in all the 28 original subjects, and this ratio of the phenotype was quite the same for the larger group, too, namely, 7:21.

The rate of antipyrine elimination was indicated by the biological half-times. Table 2 contains the individual values and in Table 3 the group statistics and the correlations of the variables are listed. The relationship between the pharmacokinetic values and the relative aerobic power was close. The two remaining coefficients were moderate and not statistically significant.

DISCUSSION

The study of the young basketball players was used to gain some insight into the problem of whether any relationship exists between endurance

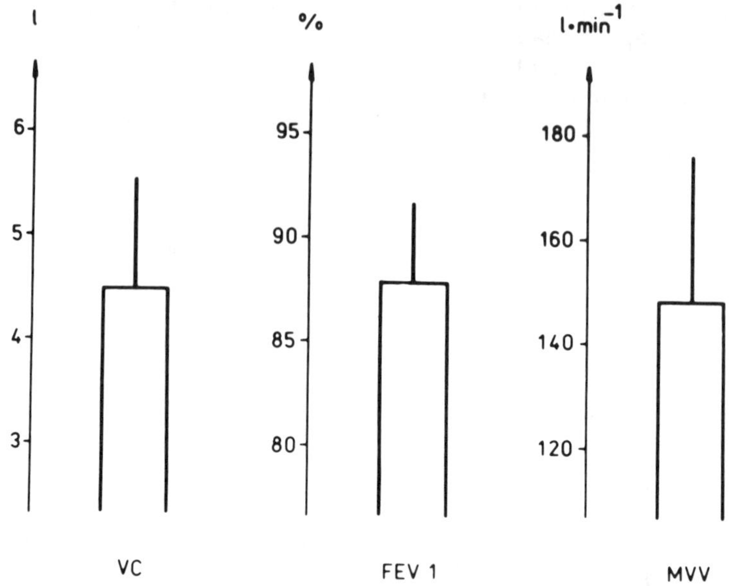

Figure 5. Ergometric tests: means and standard deviations for the absolute ($\dot{V}O_2$) and relative aerobic power ($\dot{V}O_2max \cdot BW$) and for oxygen pulse ($\dot{V}O_2max \cdot HR$ in $ml \cdot bpm^{-1}$).

Table 2 Acetylator Phenotypes (AC%), Rate of Antipyrine Elimination (t/2), and Relative Aerobic Power ($\dot{V}O_2max \cdot kg^{-1}$ BW) of the Subjects. Half-Times in Hours, Aerobic Power in $ml \cdot min^{-1} \cdot kg^{-1}$

	AC %	t/2	$\dot{V}O_2max \cdot kg^{-1}$
V.I.	52 S	16.37	45.80
B.A.	50 S	15.93	52.86
L.R.	52 S	16.37	52.62
R.B.	85 R	14.09	47.87
D.L.	81 R	14.50	50.87
H.G.	54 S	15.94	51.13
B.A.	82 R	17.39	45.86
D.A.	46 S	12.89	54.45
P.L.	50 S	14.75	57.12
M.L.	40 S	16.87	48.44
V.A.	45 S	10.00	63.92
F.I.	46 S	11.83	58.95

Table 3 Means, Standard Deviations, and Correlation Coefficients for the Values of Table 2

	Antipyrine	Potesept	$\dot{V}O_2max/BW$
$\bar{x}$	14.71	56.92	52.49
s	2.21	16.00	5.47
r	Antipyrine–Potesept: 0.45	Potesept–$\dot{V}O_2max/BW$: −0.51	Antipyrine–$\dot{V}O_2max/BW$: 0.83

fitness and either pharmacogenetic or pharmacokinetic parameters. The subjects underwent an estimation of morphological age and body build. These studies evidenced that the sample was suitable for studying this problem, that is, chronological and morphological ages agreed. This fact is worth noting in view of the fact that, on the one hand, stature is the primary criterion of selection for this sport and, on the other hand, tall stature in adolescence is usually related to accelerated growth. In selecting the trainees, the coaches avoided the catch of preferring tall but accelerated boys—an earmark of good work indeed.

The patterns of body build reflect the effects of selection and activity alike. These were tall and slim boys with a small amount of body fat, with moderately or explicitly hyperplastic leptomorph growth type and ectomorphic somatotypes with varying degrees of mesomorphy to age. The several years of physical training resulted in favorable spirometric and ergometric functional indices and in values characteristic of well-trained individuals.

In view of the main point in this study, the results obtained in the pharmacological studies were of greatest importance. The pharmacogenetic pattern observed was a surprise in light of both Szórády's recent findings (personal communication) on a larger group and previous experience (Frenkl et al., 1986) in that the rate of slow acetylator occurrence was higher. Although the reports cited described an occurrence rate of 45% for the slow acetylators, the rate was 75% in the present sample. Naturally, even the sample of 28 is relatively small in this respect and unsuitable for a definitive conclusion. Nevertheless, it should be noted that the previously reported subject groups were recruited from various events; for example, the 134 athletes of Szórády came from soccer, paddling, weight lifting, and track-and-field events. The present findings can be regarded as a need to study acetylator phenotypes in larger and more homogeneously distributed age and activity groups. Of course, this kind of study also retains its practical value in screening individuals.

The pharmacokinetic study revealed that even several years of a suitably intense physical training could bring about the induction of the hepatic microsomal system of enzymes in adolescents, too. In agreement with previous experiments and the work of Boel, Andersen, Rasmussen, Hansen, and Dessing (1984), who also reported on adult athletes, it could be stated that a relationship exists between individual drug metabolizing activity and the level of endurance fitness (relative aerobic power). It seems to be a valid assumption to conclude that the daily repeated physical effort is the factor that eventually results in a higher level of endurance fitness and speeds up drug metabolization. The exact mechanism of this type of enzymatic adaptation has not yet been clarified. It can be hypothesized that one or more of the substances accumulating in the course of the metabolic changes elicited by regular exercise, perhaps the daily repetition of steroidemia associated with the training (Frenkl, Csalay, & Csákváry, 1969), are the prime movers in this phenomenon. This latter aspect should never be neglected in view of the fact that steroid hormones are also metabolized by the same miocrosomal enzyme system.

In this context, it should be noted that there is another unsolved problem that is still a source of concern. The anabolic and catabolic steroids, which even now are used in hormonal doping, are also metabolized by the liver. It has been recognized that the implied dangers are a menace for adolescent and child sports as well. The enzyme-inducing effect of the endogenous steroidemia arising from regular physical training is regarded as a physiological and adaptative phenomenon of a trained liver somewhat analogous to the trained heart. The administration of exogenous steroids, in particular, when long lasting or when employing large doses, must always be associated with a potentially dangerous functional or structural lesion to the liver. This is particularly menacing at young ages because during development the sensitivity of the system to harmful effects is greater than later, after its full stabilization. This greater sensitivity can, on the one hand, ease the adjustment to regular exercise but, on the other hand, it can contribute to the well-known risks of doping. This problem does not lend itself easily to study, particularly using direct means, but experience has already provided several pieces of indirect evidence. In addition, there are few, if any, means to defend or stabilize hepatic functions at this age.

REFERENCES

Boel, J., Andersen, L.B., Rasmussen, B., Hansen, S.H., & Dessing, M. (1984). Hepatic drug metabolism and physical fitness. *Clinical Pharmacological Therapy*, **36**, 121-126.

Bratton, A.C., & Marshall, E.K. (1939). A new coupling component for sulfanilamide determination. *Journal of Biological Chemistry*, **128**, 537-550.

Brodie, B.B., Axelrod, H., Soberman, R., & Levy, B.B. (1949). The estimation of antipyrine in biological materials. *Journal of Biological Chemistry*, **179**, 25-29.

Conrad, K. (1963). *Der Konstitutionstypus. 2.Aufl.* Berlin: Springer.

Frenkl, R., Csalay, L., & Csákváry, G. (1969). A study of the stress reaction elicited by muscular exertion in trained and untrained men and rats. *Acta Physiologica Academiae Scientiarium Hungarica*, **36**, 365-370.

Frenkl, R., Györe, Á., Mészáros, J., & Szeberényi, Sz. (1980). A study of the enzyme inducing effect of physical exercise in man: The "trained liver." *Journal of Sports Medicine*, **20**, 371-376.

Frenkl, R., Györe, Á., & Szeberényi, Sz. (1980). The effect of muscular exercise on the microsomal enzyme system of the rat liver. *European Journal of Applied Physiology*, **44**, 135-140.

Frenkl, R., Szöts, G., Mészáros, J., & Szabó, T. (1986). In J. Rutenfranz, R. Mocellin, & F. Klimt (Eds.), *Children and exercise XII* (pp. 43-50). Champaign, IL: Human Kinetics.

Heath, B.H., & Carter, J.E.L. (1971). Somatotype methodology and kinesiological research. *Kinesiological Reviews*, **1**, 10-19.

Mészáros, J., Mohácsi, J., Szabó, T., & Szmodis, I. (1985). Assessment of biological development by anthropometric variables. In R.A. Binkhorst, H.C.G. Kemper, & W.H.M. Saris (Eds.), *Children and exercise XI* (pp. 341-345). Champaign, IL: Human Kinetics.

Vestal, R.E. (1979). Aging and pharmacokinetics: Impact of altered physiology in the elderly. In A. Cherkin (Ed.), *Physiology and cell biology of aging: Vol. 8. Aging* (pp. 185-201). New York: Raven.

Weiner, J.S., & Lourie, J.A. (Eds.). (1969). *Human biology, a guide to field methods* (IBP handbook No. 9). Oxford: Blackwell.

Tracking of Risk Indicators for Coronary Heart Diseases From Teenager to Adult: The Amsterdam Growth and Health Study

Han C.G. Kemper
Lucienne Storm-van Essen
Robbert Verschuur
Universieit van Amsterdam, Amsterdam, The Netherlands

Coronary heart disease (CHD) is recognized as a serious public health problem in Western industrialized countries. Atherosclerosis, a very important process in the origin of CHD, starts early after birth (Montoye, 1985), and thus preventive pediatric strategies should be developed. The increase in the incidence of morbidity and mortality from CHD is believed to be caused by a number of factors known as risk indicators. Epidemiological studies have resulted in the recognition of coronary risk indicators: hypercholesterolemia, hypertension, fatness, inactivity, and smoking.

The general purpose of the Amsterdam Growth and Health Study was to elicit information on growth, health, and fitness of boys and girls from their early teenage period (12-13 years) to their young adult age (21-22 years). The CHD risk indicators dealt with in this article are serum lipids, total body fat, and blood pressure. The results are an attempt to answer the question of whether these CHD risk indicators in teenagers relate to adulthood. This concept is often referred to as *tracking*, which is defined as (a) the ability to predict future levels from early observations, and/or (b) following the position of a subject in a distribution of values over time (Hofman, 1983).

MATERIAL AND METHODS

Population

The population studied comprised the pupils (n = 307) enrolled in the first and second forms of a secondary school in Amsterdam in 1977. They were measured annually during the years 1977 to 1980. A fifth measurement was made in 1985. During this 9-year longitudinal study, 35% of the subjects dropped out. The results described in this article concern the

200 subjects (93 boys and 107 girls) who remained in the study throughout the 9-year investigation. The mean age in 1977 (the first year of measurement) for both boys and girls was 13.5 ($\pm$0.6) years and in 1985, the last year of measurement, 21.5 ($\pm$0.6) years.

Measurements

To avoid confounding effects, all measurements were performed in a mobile laboratory by the same researchers using the same instruments over the 9-year period. Anthropometric measurements of height, weight, and four skinfolds (biceps, triceps, subscapular, and suprailiac) were made following the guidelines of the International Biological Program (IBP; Weiner & Lourie, 1969). Fat mass (% fat) as a percentage of total body weight was calculated from the sum of the four skinfolds according to the equation of Durnin and Rahaman (1967). Systolic (P_{syst}) and diastolic (P_{diast}) blood pressures were measured with a sphygmomanometer with a standard pressure cuff (23 $\times$ 12 cm). The subjects were measured at the left upper arm while in the sitting position. Two readings were made and the lowest value was recorded. P_{diast} was based on the fifth Korotkoff sound (Phase V).

For the determination of cholesterol in serum, approximately 10 ml of venous blood was taken from the vena antecubitus of each subject with a vacutainer. Blood sampling and serum preparations were done with subjects in a nonfasting state. Analyses met the criteria of the World Health Organization (WHO) reference laboratories: Total serum cholesterol (TC) was analyzed according to the methods of Huang, Chen, Wefler, and Raftery (1961) and Abell, Levy, Brody, and Kendall (1952). The high-density lipoprotein cholesterol fraction (HDL) was analyzed according to Burnstein and Samaille (1960). High-risk values correspond with high values of % fat, P_{syst}, P_{diast}, TC, TC/HDL, and low values of HDL.

Data Analysis

Correlation coefficients were determined between the last measurement in 1985 and each of the annual measurements from 1977 to 1980 to assess the stability of the risk values in the population. The sample was split based on the values of the first year of measurement (1977) into a relatively high-risk group and a normal-risk group for each CHD risk indicator. Data for males and females were analyzed separately. From the subjects in the upper (> P75) quartile of this distribution, the relative probability (RP) was determined of being in the high-risk category of the follow-up 9 years later (1985). Also, the reverse was done: The RP of appearing in the upper quartile in 1985 was determined for subjects with normal levels (P < 75) in 1977. The skewness of the blood pressure distributions did not allow a division of subjects into quartiles; therefore, to assign the males and females to the high-risk group, values of $P_{syst} >$ 130 mmHG (approx 17 kPa) and $P_{diast} >$ 80 mmHG (approx 9 kPa) were used.

To establish the stability of belonging to a relatively high- or low-risk group, each year the sample was split with the median into a high- and a low-risk group. Subjects who were in the upper half (> P50) each year were referred to as at relatively high risk for CHD; those appearing in the lower half (< P50) each year were seen as at relatively low risk for CHD. It was tested whether in the 9th year of measurement these extreme groups were significantly different from each other on the other risk indicators. A search was also made for a possible relation among the CHD risk indicators within subjects by composing a group of males and females who incurred serious risk for future CHD due to a combination of a high-risk value (> P50) each year on more than one CHD risk indicator.

RESULTS

Stability of CHD Risk Indicator Values

Table 1 reveals the correlation coefficients of six CHD risk indicators between the last year of measurement and each of the preceding years of measurement. All correlation coefficients are statistically significant at $p < .05$ in both males and females.

Table 1 Pearson's Product-Moment Correlation Coefficients of Six CHD Risk Indicators Between the Last (5) and Each of the Preceding (4, 3, 2, and 1) Years of Measurement for Males and Females

	Males				Females			
Interperiods	5-4	5-3	5-2	5-1	5-4	5-3	5-2	5-1
TC	0.76	0.71	0.67	0.70	0.66	0.64	0.65	0.65
HDL	0.48	0.35	0.47	0.42	0.57	0.54	0.58	0.52
TC/HDL	0.67	0.57	0.62	0.62	0.62	0.59	0.61	0.68
% fat	0.72	0.69	0.71	0.59	0.71	0.68	0.66	0.62
P_{syst}	0.44	0.49	0.51	0.49	0.46	0.44	0.47	0.35
P_{diast}	0.56	0.49	0.44	0.35	0.45	0.29	0.31	0.32

Probability of Relatively High CHD Risk Values From Early Teenage to Young Adult Age

The estimates of the predictive values of the six CHD risk indicators over a period of 9 years are found in Table 2. Given are (a) the percentage of subjects in the upper quartile of the distribution at the initial

Table 2 The Values of Six CHD Risk Indicators[a]

CDH risk indicators	Male: Initial proportion in 1977 (percentile)	Male: (a) Percentage high in 1985 of high in 1977 (%)	Male: (b) Percentage high in 1985 of not-high in 1977 (%)	Male: (c) RP	Female: Initial proportion in 1977 (percentile)	Female: (a) Percentage high in 1985 of high in 1977 (%)	Female: (b) Percentage high in 1985 of not-high in 1977 (%)	Female: (c) RP
TC	P_{75}	61	13.0	4.7	P_{75}	42	22.0	1.9
HDL	P_{75}	53	12.5	4.2	P_{75}	48	19.5	2.5
TC/HDL	P_{75}	54	16.5	3.3	P_{75}	63	13.0	5.0
% fat	P_{75}	57	14.5	3.9	P_{75}	62	12.5	5.4
P_{syst}	P_{60}	69	23.0	3.0	P_{59}	21	11.0	1.9
P_{diast}	P_{71}	44	22.0	2.0	P_{79}	26	14.0	1.9

[a]These are defined as (a) a percentage of the 4th quartile in the initial measurement period (1977) that were still high after 9 years (1985); (b) the percentage of those who were in the 4th quartile in 1985 but not in the 4th quartile at the first examination in 1977; and (c) the Relative Probability (RP), calculated as (a) divided by (b).

examination (1977) that was also included in the upper quartile after 9 years at the fifth examination (1985) and (b) the percentage of subjects not in the upper quartile of the distribution in 1977 that was in the upper quartile in 1985. The percentage of (a) was in general more than 50% (53-61) for the males and more than 40% (42-63) for the females in TC, HDL, TC/HDL, and % fat.

For P_{syst} these percentages were 69% for boys and 21% for girls and for P_{diast} 44% for boys and 26% for girls. However, the initial proportions were considerably different from the 25% indicated in Table 2. The percentage of (b) for both males and females was lower than 25% in all six CHD indicators.

Table 3 Number (*n*) of Subjects Continuously in the High (> P50) or the Low (< P50) CHD Risk Groups for All 5 Years of Measurement

CHD		Males (risk group)			Females (risk group)		
Risk indicator		low	high	*p*	low	high	*p*
TC (mmol/liter)	*n*	24	30		30	30	
	m	3.7	5.3	*	4.1	5.6	*
	SD	0.4	0.6		0.4	0.3	
	range	2.9-4.3	4.4-6.5		3.2-4.8	5.0-7.1	
HDL (mmol/liter)	*n*	17	15		24	24	
	m	0.96	1.3	*	1.13	1.69	*
	SD	0.13	0.16		0.13	0.28	
	range	0.20	0.49		0.50	1.32	
TC/HDL	*n*	20	26		21	28	
	m	3.0	5.0	*	2.7	4.4	*
	SD	0.4	0.9		0.4	0.8	
	range	2.4-3.7	3.9-7.5		2.2-3.4	3.5-6.7	
% fat (%)	*n*	26	24		29	31	
	m	14.0	24.0	*	24.0	34.0	*
	SD	3.0	9.0		5.0	13.0	
	range	11-18	19-34		21-29	30-40	
P_{syst} (mmHg)	*n*	18	20		17	20	
	m	123.0	146.0	*	116.0	135.0	*
	SD	6.7	6.4		3.9	10.2	
	range	110-130	135-160		110-120	125-155	
P_{diast} (mmHg)	*n*	12	15		15	22	
	m	69.0	90.0	*	68.0	84.0	*
	SD	5.2	4.4		5.2	8.0	
	range	60-75	80-100		60-75	80-110	

Note. For each CHD risk indicator, the mean, standard deviation (*SD*), and range are listed, measured in 1985 for males and females.

*Significant differences ($p < .01$) of the mean values in the high- and low-risk groups.

As the high-risk group from 1985 was composed of subjects coming from a high level at 1977 as well as subjects coming from the normal level, it was relevant to compare the percentage of high in 1977 with the percentage of normal in 1977 that were also high in 1985. This RP is the chance for those at a high level in 1977 to remain at that high level until 1985 in comparison with those at normal levels in 1977 (van Stiphout, 1986). The RP values varied between 3.3 and 4.7 in males and between 5.0 and 1.9 in females. High RPs were found males for TC (4.7), HDL (4.2), and % fat (3.9) and in females for % fat (5.4) and TC/HDL (5.0). In both males and females the P_{syst} and P_{diast} showed the lowest values—in males 3.0 and 2.0 and in females 1.9 and 1.9, respectively.

Stability of CHD Risk Indicators in Groups With Constant Risk Values From Early Teenage to Young Adult Age

Table 3 presents the results of the six CHD risk values in 1985 of those subjects who during the entire longitudinal period were constantly above (high-risk group) or below (low-risk group) the 50th percentile (P50) for all 5 years of measurement. The percentage of males and females in the high- and low-risk groups varied depending on the CHD risk indicator

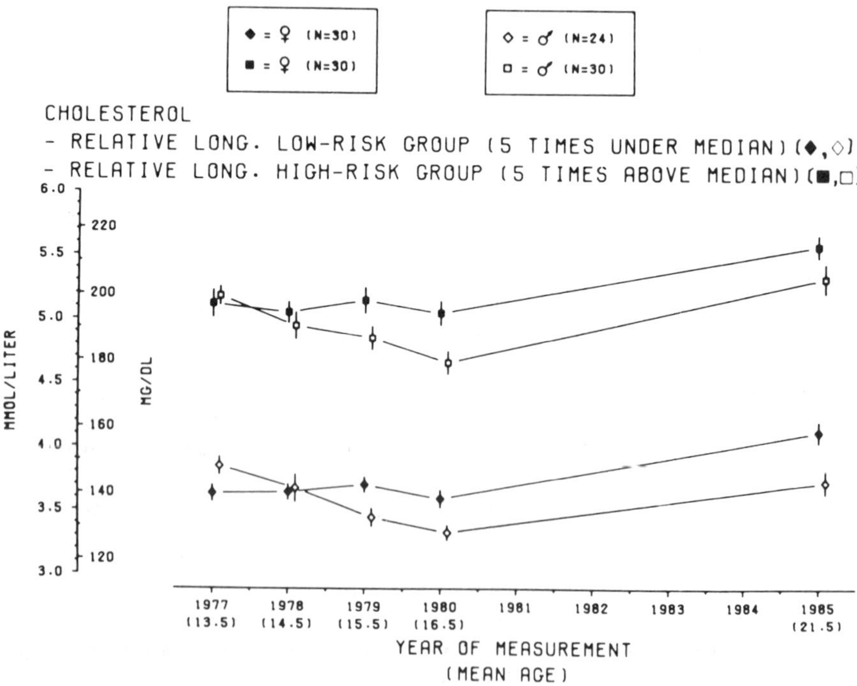

Figure 1. Mean and standard error of total serum cholesterol (TC) in males and females divided into longitudinally "high" (5 times > P50) and "low" (5 times < P50) risk groups.

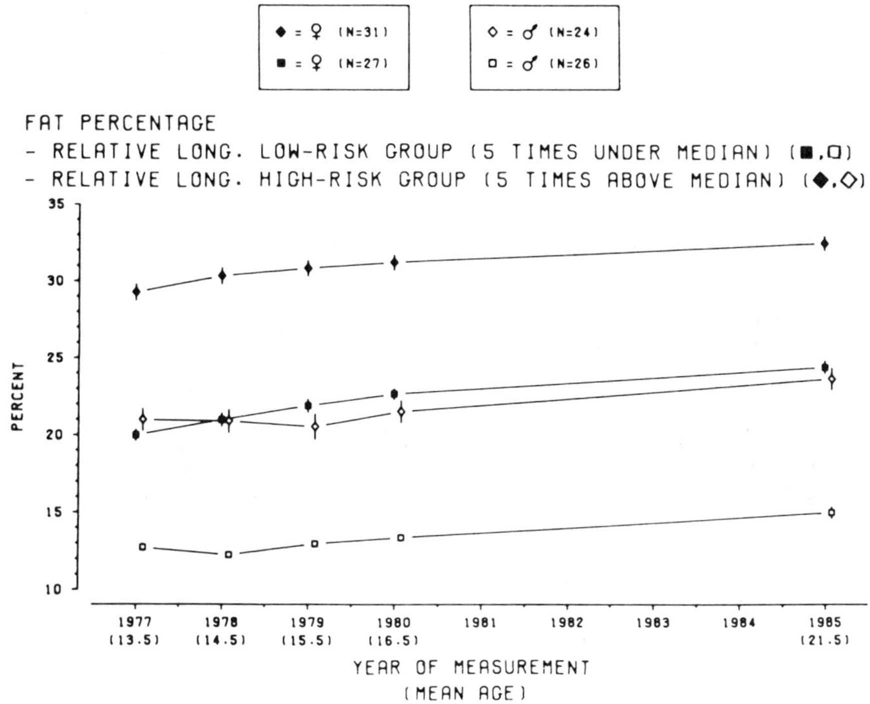

Figure 2. Mean and standard error of fat mass (% fat) in males and females divided into longitudinally "high" (5 times > P50) and "low" (5 times < P50) risk groups.

Table 4 Statistical Differences (*t* test, One-Sided) Between the High- and Low-Risk Groups on the Horizontal (All Years > or < P50) on the Other CHD Risk Indicators Measured in 1985 (Vertical)

		TC	HDL	TC/HDL	% fat	P_{syst}	P_{diast}
TC	Males	—		$p < .01$	$p < .01$		
	Females	—		$p < .01$			
HDL	Males		—				
	Females		—	$p < .05$			
TC/HDL	Males	$p < .01$	$p < .01$	—	$p < .01$		
	Females	$p < .01$	$p < .01$	—	$p < .01$		
% Fat	Males				—		
	Females	$p < .05$			—		
P_{syst}	Males					—	$p < .01$
	Females					—	$p < .01$
P_{diast}	Males					$p < .01$	—
	Females					$p < .05$	—

involved: In TC, HDL, and TC/HDL; % fat between 20% and 30%; and P_{syst} and P_{diast}, between 10% and 20% of the subjects remained in their respective groups through the 5 years of observation (Figures 1 and 2). The differences between the high- and low-risk groups on the six CHD risk values at the fifth measurement are statistically significant at the 1% level of probability ($p < .01$).

CHD Risk Groups and Other Risk Indicators

Besides differences between high- and low-risk groups on the selected CHD risk indicators, the differences between these extreme groups on other CHD risk indicators were also studied. Table 4 summarizes the significance of differences in 1985 between extreme groups (all years > P50) on other CHD risk indicators. Within related risk indicators (the three serum lipids parameters: TC, HDL, and TC/HDL) and the two blood pressure parameters (P_{syst} and P_{diast}), statistical differences appeared. But, in general, differences across risk indicators were not significant. Only extreme groups in % fat also showed high and low TC values in males ($p < .01$) and TC/HDL values in males and females ($p < .01$).

Further attempts to select a group of subjects who had continuous relatively high values on two or more CHD risk indicators have failed. Based on the criteria previously mentioned, none of the combinations revealed a substantially large group of subjects that was above risk levels in two or more CHD risk indicators combined over the entire age range.

DISCUSSION

The interperiod correlation coefficients of the CHD risk indicators (see Table 1) between the last and first year (interval of 8 years) were moderate, explaining 25% to 50% of the total variance, except for P_{diast} in males and females and of P_{syst} in females with an explained variance of less than 10%. The low correlation coefficients of the blood pressure variables were expected from their low test-retest reliabilities estimated from the interperiod correlation matrix of these variables (Kemper & Verschuur, 1985a; Storm-van Essen, Kemper, & Ootjers, 1985). The use of the indirect measurement method for gathering longitudinal data will further be affected by changes of diameter and/or composition of the upper arm (fat mass and muscle mass).

The RP for the subjects to be in the high-risk groups in the first year (upper quartile, P > 75) and also to be in the upper quartile of the distribution in the last year varied from 2 to 5 in TC, HDL, TC/HDL, and % fat (see Table 2). This result indicated a moderate to high predictive value of these risk indicators from early teenage to young adult age in this population. Between males and females there were large differences in the RPs in the same blood lipid indicators: Although females had low values in TC and HDL (1.9 and 2.5) and a high value in TC/HDL (5.0), males showed the opposite results. No explanations for these sex differences seemed logical. The RPs of blood pressure were approximately

3 (P_{syst}) and 2 (P_{diast}) in males and 1.9 (P_{syst} and P_{diast}) in females, showing low predictive values probably caused by the low measurement reliability of these variables.

The high- and low-risk groups, based on a value above or below the 50th percentile of the distribution in each year of measurement, in general, showed mean values that could be considered moderately high and optimal, respectively. For TC the mean values of the high-risk groups were between P75 and P90 of values for their age group (20 to 29 years; Knuiman & Katan, 1985). The TC values of the high-risk group during the teenage period were close to and, at young adult age, above the risk value of 5.2 mmol • l^{-1} (Erkelens, 1987; Wilmore & McNamara, 1974) in both males and females. The low-risk group shows a mean value of 3.7 mmol • l^{-1} in males and 4.1 mmol • l^{-1} in females, which is below or equal to the ideal values of population averages of adults (Blackburn, Berenson, & Christakis, 1979; WHO, 1982).

Bell, Máček, Rutenfranz, and Saris (1986) have recently suggested a checklist of important health-related parameters and values for risk factors during childhood and adolescence. Their adolescent risk values of TC (> 5.9 mmol • l^{-1}), HDL (< 0.8 mmol • l^{-1}), and TC/HDL (> 5.5) were not exceeded by the high-risk groups during the teenage period. Only the female high-risk group surpassed at age 21-22 the TC risk value with a mean of 5.6 mmol • l^{-1}. During the teenage period a risk value for % fat of 20% for boys and 30% for girls was used (Bell et al., 1986; Katch & McArdle, 1977). The high-risk groups approached these risk values with mean values of approximately 20% (boys) and 30% (girls) and at young adult age surpassed these with mean values of 24% (males) and 34% (females).

When P_{syst} of more than 19.0 kPa (140 mmHg) and a P_{diast} of more than 11.4 kPa (90 mmHg) taken from the WHO (1962) were utilized as risk values, the high-risk groups showed only high mean values for males at the end of their teenage period and mean values of P_{syst} of 146 mmHg and P_{diast} of 90 mmHg at adult age. These high values for the males were partially caused by the growth of the muscle mass of the upper arm causing an increase in diameter (Kemper & Verschuur, 1985b). Because a pressure cuff of the same diameter was used for both sets of measurements, the indirect measurement of blood pressure with the sphygmomanometer overestimated the real value. The P_{syst} values in both males and females were on the average 5 to 10 mmHG higher in comparison with other epidemiological studies on teenagers in the Netherlands (Hofman & Valkenburg, 1979; Kromhout, Obermann-de Boer, & de Lerenne-Coulander, 1980; van Beem & Egger, 1979). This could be ascribed to the fact that the measurements in the present study were made prior to a maximal exercise test on the treadmill. The health-related blood pressure profile (Bell et al., 1987) of P_{syst} (100-120 mmHg) and P_{diast} (75-85 mmHg) was present in the low-risk groups of boys and girls, when a 5 to 10 mmHg overestimation of the real values caused by the measurement procedures was taken into account. At young adult age (21-22 years of age), the mean values of the low-risk groups of TC, HDL, and TC/HDL; % fat; and P_{syst} and P_{diast} were considered optimal values for both males and females. In the high-risk groups, % fat and P_{syst} and P_{diast} were taken as seriously high values as read from the risk values indicated in the literature.

As far as the high-risk groups were concerned, the three blood lipid parameters and the two blood pressure parameters were significantly correlated. However, in general there appeared to be no relationship to other risk indicators. Only % fat was related to blood lipids. Attempts to select a group of subjects with relatively high values on more than one CHD risk indicator during the longitudinal study failed.

Acknowledgments

This research project was supported by a grant from the Prevention Fund (No. 28-189A), and from the Dutch Ministry of Wellbeing, Health and Cultural Affairs. We express our thanks to the 200 males and females who were subjects over a period of 9 years.

REFERENCES

Abell, L.L., Levy, B.B., Brody, B.B., & Kendall, F.E. (1952). Simplified method for the estimation of total cholesterol in serum and demonstration of its specificity. *Journal of Biological Chemistry*, **195**, 357-366.

Beem, A. van, & Egger, R.J. (1979). Research on the nutritional status of 15- to 16-year-old schoolchildren (in Dutch). CIVO, Report No. 6564 (TNO, Zeist).

Bell, R.D., Máček, M., Rutenfranz, J., & Saris, W.H.M. (1986). Health indicators and risk factors of cardiovascular diseases during childhood and adolescence. In G.J. Rutenfranz, R. Mocellin, & F. Klimt (Eds.), *Children and exercise XII* (pp. 19-27). Champaign, IL: Human Kinetics.

Blackburn, H., Berenson, G.S., & Christakis, G. (1979). Conference on the health effects of blood lipids: Optimal distributions for populations. Workshop report: Epidemiological section. *Preventive Medicine*, **8**, 612-678.

Burnstein, M., & Samaille, J. (1960). Sur un dosage rapide du cholesterol lie aux alpha- et aux betalipoproteinen du serum [About a rapid cholesterol determination of alpha and beta lipoproteins in serum]. *Clinica Chimica Acta*, **5**, 609-611.

Erkelens, D.W. (Ed). (1987). *Cholesterol Consensus Conference*. (The report of the Dutch consensus meeting, March 20, 1987). Amersfoort: de Flint.

Durnin, J.V.G.A., & Rahaman, M.M. (1967). The assessment of the amount of fat in the human body from measurements of skinfold thickness. *British Journal of Nutrition*, **21**, 681-689.

Hofman, A., & Valkenburg, H.A. (1979). Determinants and tracking of blood pressure in free-living children. *Therapie Woche*, **29**, 45-55.

Hofman, A. (1983). *Blood pressure in childhood—An epidemiological view of early atherogenesis*. Unpublished doctoral dissertation, Erasmus Universiteit, Rotterdam.

Huang, T.C., Chen, C.P., Wefler, A., & Raftery, A. (1961). A stable reagent for the Lieberman-Buchard reaction. *Analytical Chemistry*, **33**, 1405-1407.

Katch, F.I., & McArdle, W.D. (1977). *Nutrition, weight control and exercise*. Boston: Houghton Mifflin.

Kemper, H.C.G., & Verschuur, R. (1985a). Body build and body composition. In H.C.G. Kemper (Ed.), *Growth, health and fitness of teenagers* (pp. 88-95). Basel: Karger.

Kemper, H.C.G., & Verschuur, R. (1985b). Other functions. In H.C.G. Kemper (Ed.), *Growth, health and fitness of teenagers* (pp. 127-136). Basel: Karger.

Knuiman, J.T., & Katan, M.B. (1985). Cholesterol levels in serum in the Netherlands in comparison with the United States. *Nederlands Tijdschrift voor Geneeskunde*, **129**, 2500-2505.

Kromhout, D., Obermann-de Boer, G.L., & de Lerenne-Coulander, C. (1980). Major CHD risk indicators in Dutch schoolchildren, aged 10-14 years. The Zutphen schoolchildren study. *Preventive Medicine*, **10**, 195-200.

Montoye, H.J. (1985). Risk indicators for cardiovascular disease in relation to physical activity in youth. In R.A. Binkhorst, H.C.G. Kemper, & W.H.M. Saris (Eds.), *Children and exercise XI* (pp. 3-25). Champaign, IL: Human Kinetics.

Stiphout, W.A.H.J. van. (1986). Serum lipids in the young, an epidemiological view of early atherogenetics. Unpublished doctoral dissertation, Erasmus Universiteit, Rotterdam.

Storm-van Essen, L., Kemper, H.C.G., & Ootjers, G. (1985). Purpose and design. In H.C.G. Kemper (Ed.), *Growth, health and fitness of teenagers* (pp. 12-25). Basel: Karger.

Weiner, J.S., & Lourie, J.A. (1969). *Human biology, a guide to field methods* (IBP Handbook No. 9). Oxford: Blackwell.

Wilmore, J.H., & McNamara, J.J. (1974). Prevalence of coronary heart disease risk factors in boys 8-12 years of age. *Journal of Pediatrics*, **84**, 527-531.

World Health Organization. (1962). *Arterial hypertension and ischaemic heart disease: Preventive aspects* (Technical Rep. Series No. 23). Geneva: Author.

World Health Organization. (1982). *Prevention of coronary heart disease. Report of a WHO Expert Committee* (Technical Rep. Series No. 678). Geneva: Author.

Integrated Risk Assessment for Cardiovascular Diseases: A Methodological Approach

Miloŝ Máček
Charles University, Prague, Czechoslovakia

Joseph Rutenfranz
Institute Arbeitsphysiologie, Dortmund, West Germany

Richard Bell
University of Saskatchewan, Saskatoon, Canada

It has been demonstrated by genetic-epidemiological studies that patients who have had a myocardial infarction before the age of 55 years are different in at least 19 different independent variables compared with matched pairs (Nora, Lortscher, Spangler, Nora, & Kimberling, 1980). As can be seen in Table 1, the highest risk ratio was associated with a positive family history for ischemic heart disease, the lowest with imprudent diet and relative weight greater than 1.20. Based on such risk probabilities, Nora (1980) introduced a risk formula for an integrated risk assessment of cardiovascular diseases that is partly applicable to children as young as 1 to 2 years, or at least between 5 and 19 years (Table 2). Combining both preconditions, Nora (1980) proposed a risk index for children and adolescents using different weighted scores for 10 risk factors based on risk probabilities. This system should allow an integrated risk assessment using a combination of genetic and environmental risk factors (Table 3). Wilmore et al. (1982) have used a different system for describing the prevalence of risk factors for coronary heart disease in a group of 13- to 15-year-old boys. This latter system is based mainly on special risk factors but does include ECG symptoms. Because neither Nora (1980) nor Wilmore et al. (1982) have included some of the more recently accepted risk factors, an update of the methods would seem appropriate.

A PROPOSAL FOR THE MODIFICATION OF NORA'S (1980) INDEX

Because new parameters must be considered when studying potential CHD in a population of children 6 to 18 years of age, a modification of

Table 1 Independent Variables in Patients With Early-Onset Ischemic Heart Disease Compared With Matched Controls and Presented in the Descending Order of Risk Ratio

	Patients	%	Controls	%	Risk ratio	$p <$
IHD-1° relatives younger than 55	99/207	48	50/621	8	10.4	.001
IHD-1° relatives younger than 65	126/207	61	112/621	18	7.1	.001
J. diabetes-1° relative	9/140	6	2/140	1	4.7	.05
Cholesterol > 270 mg/dl	50/207	24	43/621	7	4.3	.001
Smoking > 1/2 pack/day	141/207	68	217/621	35	4.0	.001
Stroke-1° relatives younger than 55	10/207	5	9/621	1	3.5	.01
Exercise deficiency	199/207	96	546/621	88	3.4	.001
Diabetes (in patient)	12/207	6	14/621	2	2.7	.05
IHD-2° relatives younger than 65	59/140	42	32/140	23	2.4	.001
Cholesterol > 240 mg/dl	77/207	96	130/621	21	2.2	.001
BP ⩾ 160/100 mmHg	44/207	21	81/621	13	1.8	.01
Hypertension-1° relative	41/140	29	26/140	19	1.8	.05
Cholesterol > 220 mg/dl	120/207	58	304/621	49	1.8	.05
Stroke-1° relatives younger than 65	25/207	12	43/621	7	1.8	.05
Type A behavior	56/207	27	124/621	20	1.5	.05
Triglycerides > 200 mg/dl	47/207	23	99/621	16	1.5	.05
BP ⩾ 140/90 mmHg	60/207	27	138/621	22	1.4	.05
Imprudent diet	155/207	75	422/621	68	1.4	NS
Relative weight > 1.20	83/207	40	211/621	34	1.3	NS
Relative weight > 1.20 excluding monogenic cases	80/176	45	174/528	33	1.7	.01

IHD = ischemic heart disease; 1° = first degree; 2° = second degree; J. diabetes = juvenile-onset diabetes; BP = blood pressure.

Note. From "Genetic Epidemiology of Early-Onset Ischemic Heart Disease" by J.J. Nora et al., 1980, *Circulation*, **61**, pp. 503-508. Copyright 1980 by *Circulation*. Adapted by permission.

Table 2 Questionnaire for Children and Adolescents Aged 1-19 Years to Use in Heart Attack Risk Formula

The following information can be obtained when a child is as young as 1 to 2 years.

1. Has a first-degree relative (parent or sibling) had a heart attack or coronary disease with onset before age 55?
2. Has a first-degree relative had a heart attack or cononary disease with onset before age 65?
3. Has a second-degree relative had a heart attack or coronary disease with onset before age 65?
4. Is the cholesterol level greater than 220 mg/dl on two tests?
5. Is the cholesterol level greater than 190 mg/dl on two tests?
6. Are the triglycerides higher than 120 mg/dl on two tests?
7. Does the child or a first-degree relative have juvenile-onset diabetes?
8. Is the relative weight greater than 1.20?

The following information will be obtainable as early as 5 years and as late as 19 years.

1. Is the blood pressure tracking at the 95th percentile, or 140/90 or higher?
2. Does the child show excessive Type A behavior?
3. Does the child get daily, vigorous exercise, some of which is aerobic?
4. Does the child smoke?

Note. From ''Identifying the Child at Risk for Coronary Disease as an Adult: A Strategy for Prevention'' by J.J. Nora, 1980, *Journal of Pediatrics*, **97**, pp. 706-714. Copyright 1980 by *Journal of Pediatrics*. Reprinted by permission.

Nora's risk index has been developed. This index has three separate parts that result in three different scores that can then be used separately or integrated into a single score. The advantage of using the three parts separately can be demonstrated, for example, in a study comparing the risk factors of trained and untrained groups of children. These groups did not differ in the genetic risk factor but were different in the various behavioral and biochemical risk factors that were considered (Máček et al., in press).

The need for changing Nora's formula (1980) was based on experience gained during the data analysis phase of a longitudinal study on children 8 to 20 years old where an attempt was made to follow the development of cardiovascular risk factors during childhood and adolescence. In order to assess the CHD risk potential, first, Nora's method (1980) was used for calculating an integrated risk index. The rationale for using this specific system was to get the most informative and objective data possible in order to recognize the main genetic and environmental factors that might be responsible for increased risk for ischemic heart disease (IHD) in later years.

Because some of the data that were generated in that longitudinal study seemed appropriate for assessing IHD risk (i.e., $\dot{V}O_2max$; percent body

Table 3 Risk Index for Children and Adolescents

Risk factor	Circle and add points
Family history (take the single highest value; maximum score is 3)	
• Coronary disease in 1st-degree relative before age 55	3
• Coronary disease in 1st-degree relative before age 65	2.5
• Coronary disease in 2nd-degree relative before age 65	1
• Stroke in 1st-degree relative before age 55	1
• Stroke in 2nd-degree relative before age 65	.5
Cholesterol and triglycerides (add values to a maximum score of 2)	
• Cholesterol greater than 220 mg/dl	2
• Cholesterol greater than 190 mg/dl	1
• Triglycerides greater than 120 mg/dl	.5
Other risks (add all values)	
• Smoking regularly	1.5
• Diabetes in patient or juvenile diabetes in 1st-degree relative	1
• No regular aerobic exercise	1
• Blood pressure greater than 140/90, or systolic or diastolic pressure greater than 95th percentile	5
• Relative weight greater than 1.20 (20% overweight)	.5
• Type A behavior	.5

See *Note* to Table 2.

fat; biochemical parameters like HDL-C, LDL-C, and apolipoproteins A, A_1, and B) were not included in the original Nora formula, they could not be used for the calculation of the risk index. For this reason a modification of Nora's risk index was developed.

This system divides the risk index into three parts (Table 4). The first part, which represents various genetic factors and emphasizes family history of CHD, was adopted from Nora's original formula. The second part focuses attention on the biochemical data and includes the following parameters: HDL-C; LDL-C; and Apo A, A_1, and B, as well as their ratios HDL:T-Chol, B:A, and B:A_1. The upper and lower limits for all values were arbitrarily defined as ± 2 *SD* from the mean, which corresponds approximately to the 5th and the 95th percentiles, respectively, of the normal distribution in population of central Europe. The mean values and the *SD* were calculated from the sample of randomly selected children of a small Czechoslovakian city used in the longitudinal study. Unfortunately, the upper and lower limits for the lipoproteins presented in

Table 4 Integrated Risk Assessment for Cardiovascular Risk Factors

Family history			Risk points
Coronary disease in 1st-degree relative			
before age 55			3.0
before age 65			2.5
in 2nd-degree relative			
before age 65			1.0
Stroke in 1st-degree relative			
before age 55			1.0
in 2nd-degree relative before age 65			0.5
Hypertension in 1st-degree relative before age 55			0.5
Diabetes in patient or juvenile diabetes in 1st-degree relative			1.0
Maximum I			7.0
Biomechanical risk factors			
Cholesterol	⩾ 5.70 mmol/l		2.0
	⩾ 5.00 mmol/l		1.0
Triglycerides	⩾ 1.35 mmol/l		0.5
HDL-CH	⩽ 1.00 mmol/l		0.5
Apolipoprotein A	⩽ 1.50 mmol/l		1.0
Apolipoprotein A_1	⩽ 0.90 mmol/l		0.5
LDL-CH	⩾ 3.60 mmol/l		0.5
Apolipoprotein B	⩾ 1.20 mmol/l		0.5
HDL-CH/CHOL T	⩽ 0.18		1.0
B/A	⩾ 0.60		1.0
B/A_1	⩾ 1.00		1.0
Maximum II			8.5
Behavioral factors			
Regularly smoking before age 12			1.0
Smoking regularly now			1.0
Blood pressure	⩾ 140/90 Hg		1.0
Fat in boys	⩾ 20%		0.5
in girls	⩾ 30%		0.5
VO_2max in boys	⩽ 35 ml • min^{-1} • kg^{-1}		1.0
in girls	⩽ 30 ml • min^{-1} • kg^{-1}		1.0
Tracking in two measurements in 2 years		⩾ 1 *SD*	0.5
		⩾ 2 *SD*	1.0
Physical activity/sport score	200 points		1.0
Type A behavior			1.0
Maximum III			7.5
S I - III Σ			23.0

Note. From *A Comparison of the Various Coronary Risk Factors in Trained and Untrained Adolescents* by M. Máček et al. Unpublished manuscript.

Nora's formula were not age-dependent and were calculated for the age span of 1 to 19 years. This procedure causes some problems because, for example, there is a general decrease of T-Chol and its subfractions during childhood and adolescence (Kupke, 1983). For general use, a mean value for the age range 8 to 18 years may be acceptable, but, for a more precise analysis, it would be necessary to establish separate limits for the various parameters for each age group. Suggested examples of these limits, which are evaluated with two scores, are given in Table 5.

Table 5 Borderlines for Different Lipoproteins Related to Age and Gender

		Chol ⩾	HDL ⩽	LDL ⩾
12 years	♂	5.7	0.7	3.8
	♀	5.3	0.76	3.9
16 years	♂	5.7	0.94	4.3
	♀	5.0	0.9	3.6
20 years	♂	5.2	0.8	3.5
	♀	5.8	0.8	3.5

The general concept for Nora's formula is based on independent risk factors. The biochemical risk indicators are, however, not totally independent from each other. By using all possible biochemical risk indicators, as in the proposed formula (Table 4), there is the disadvantage of overlapping risk factors, but the introduction of an inherent controlling system for deviations, especially in cases where the upper and lower limits are nearly reached or exceeded, more than offsets this disadvantage. For example, high cholesterol values that do not exceed the risk limits can now be identified as risk values if, for the same child, the HDL-C values exceed the lower limit. The same is true for the apolipoproteins A, A_1, and B and their respective ratios. With the expected future development of newer biochemical indicators, it will probably be necessary to construct further alternative formulas for CHD risk identification.

One of the important new indicators of pediatric CHD risk is the tracking phenomenon. It identifies the fact that some individuals maintain their relative rank near or over the upper or lower limits of the normal distribution for a given population even after several years of repeated measurements.

The third part of the proposed formula (Table 4) includes the environmentally or behaviorally related risk factors. Here the Nora formula seems to be even more inadequate. As is well known from the many surveys on daily physical activity (Lange-Andersen, Shephard, Denolin, Varnauskas, & Masironi, 1971), it is impossible to assess the amount and intensity of activity by answering one simple question about participation in various physical activities. For this reason, the proposed formula includes a method of detailing physical activities by using activity scores calculated from a special questionnaire, but also directly determined $\dot{V}O_2max$ as an objective and integrating measure for monitoring the effects of physical activity.

Similar problems exist in the determination of overweight. By using the original Nora formula, body composition is neglected; a more exact determination of body fat content utilizing the caliper method and with different standards for boys and girls is, in addition to body weight, more appropriate. The proposed system, therefore, includes some additional variables and leads, consequently, to a higher maximal summed score of 23 points compared with the maximal possible score of 10 points in the original Nora formula.

VALIDATION OF THE NEW RISK FORMULA

Unfortunately, Nora did not publish his proposed validation system and cross-validation was therefore not possible. Wilmore et al. (1982) did, however, publish a modification of the Nora formula without using risk scores to determine an integrated risk assessment. Nevertheless, it was possible to calculate the percentage of the population of 308 boys, aged 13 to 15 years, that had either none or several risk factors. As may be seen in Table 6, nearly the same percentages were calculated for the population without risk factors. The validating group was, however, somewhat different in respect to one or more risk factors and quite similar to a study of Gilliam, Katch, Thorland, and Weltman (1977). The further separation based on more risk factors may be a favorable aspect of the proposed modification of Nora's original formula for the development of an integrated risk assessment.

Table 6 Percentages of Risk Factors in Children

Number of factors	Our study (%)	Wilmore et al. (%)	Gilliam et al. (%)
0	33	30	39
1	29	35	25
2	18	22	15
3	11	10	13
4	9	1.9	6
5			2

REFERENCES

Gilliam, T.B., Katch, V.L., Thorland, W., & Weltman, A. (1977). Prevalence of coronary heart disease risk factors in active children, 7 to 12 years of age. *Medicine and Science in Sports*, **9**, 21-25.

Kupke, I.R. (1983). Risikoindikatoren der Atherogenese im frühen Kindesalter. Untersuchungen von kindern in Düsseldorfer Kindergarten [Risk indicators of the atherogenesis in early childhood. Examination of children in kindergarten of the town Düsseldorf]. *Monatschrift für Kinderheilkunde*, **131**, 502-508.

Lange-Andersen, K., Shephard, R.J., Denolin, R., Varnauskas, E., & Masironi, R. (1971). *Fundamentals of exercise testing*. Geneva: World Health Organization.

Máček, M., Bell, D., Rutenfranz, J., Vavra, J., Masopust, J., Neidhart, D., & Schmidt, K.-H. *A comparison of the various coronary risk factors in trained and untrained adolescents*. Unpublished manuscript.

Nora, J.J. (1980). Identifying the child at risk for coronary disease as an adult: A strategy for prevention. *Journal of Pediatrics*, **97**, 706-714.

Nora, J.J., Lortscher, R.M., Spangler, R.D., Nora, A.H., & Kimberling, W.J. (1980). Genetic epidemiology of early-onset ischemic heart disease. *Circulation*, **61**, 503-508.

Wilmore, J.H., Constable, S.H., Stanforth, P.R., Tsao, W.Y., Rotkis, T.C., Paicius, R.M., Mattern, C.M., & Ewy, G.A. (1982). Prevalence of coronary heart disease risk factors in 13- to 15-year-old boys. *Journal of Cardiac Rehabilitation*, **2**, 223-233.

Integrated Assessment of Cardiovascular Risk Factors During a Longitudinal/Cross-Sectional Study of Czech Children

Joseph Rutenfranz
Institute of Occupational Health, Dortmund, Federal Republic of Germany

Miloŝ Máček
Charles University, Prague, Czechoslovakia

Richard Bell
University of Saskatchewan, Saskatoon, Canada

The prevention of cardiovascular diseases may follow different strategies. Low-risk strategies are characterized by motivating whole populations, including low-risk people, to adopt healthier lifestyles and diet and positive daily physical activity and smoking habits. This strategy was responsible for the remarkable decrease in cardiovascular diseases in several countries during previous decades (Nora, Lortscher, Spangler, Nora, & Kimberling, 1980). These preventive strategies are, however, not sufficient for high-risk conditions. High-risk conditions are usually genetically determined and become apparent during adolescence only if the lifestyle of the subject is negatively changed. For this reason, high-risk strategies should try to identify high-risk persons as early as possible to give them a chance to be treated in an optimal manner.

In order to track both low-risk and high-risk strategies and their effectiveness in the prevention of cardiovascular diseases, a combined cross-sectional/longitudinal study of health indicators and risk factors during childhood and adolescence seemed appropriate.

METHODS

Experimental Design

Three groups of about 40 children (20 male and 20 female subjects per group) aged 8, 12, and 16 years, respectively, at the beginning of the study were followed for 4 years. The combined cross-sectional/longitudinal study covered the age span from 8 to 20 years. Of the 129 children involved at the beginning of the study, 12 dropped out as a result of moving or pregnancy or for religious reasons. Furthermore, 18 other subjects could not attend all four test sessions or had some missing values. The results presented, therefore, are based on 99 subjects. The subjects were not paid for participating in the study but received small gifts like oranges, chocolate, or Coca-Cola. All parents gave written consent for the participation of their children in the study, and they were specifically informed about possible risks. The study took place at Nove Mesto, a small village located in South Moravia (ČSSR) at about 400-m altitude. The village is surrounded by hills up to 800-m high that are well suited for cross-country skiing in winter and many other sports activities during summer.

Medical Examination

The medical examination included a standardized family history using a World Health Organization (WHO) questionnaire (Pisa, 1979), anthropometric measures including skinfold measures, blood pressure measures under the prescribed conditions, an activity questionnaire (Lange-Andersen et al., 1984), a questionnaire for smoking habits, and, during the last year, a Type A interview for children.

Lipoprotein Profile

The following lipoproteins were determined by appropriate techniques: total cholesterol, HDL cholesterol, Apolipoprotein A and A_1, LDL cholesterol (calculated by Friedewald equation and, additionally, directly determined during the last 2 years), Apolipoprotein B, and triglycerides, as well as the derived ratios (Ch-T/HDL-C; Apo A/B, etc.).

Aerobic Power

$\dot{V}O_2max$ was determined by the Douglas bag method on a bicycle ergometer using the appropriate criteria (Lange-Andersen, Shephard, Denolin, Varnauskas, & Masironi, 1971). Gas analyses were performed by infrared absorption techniques and paramagnetic measures, both based on regular calibrations by the Scholander technique with calibration gases produced by gas mixture pumps.

RESULTS

Anthropometric measures and general medical examinations revealed the groups to be within the range of the normal pediatric population with appropriate values for growth, size, and fatness. Family history was introduced only in the middle of the study for all children with ages at the time of 10, 14, and 18 years, respectively. Since family history is, in general, dependent on the age of the respondents or their parents, the percentage of children at risk was calculated for each age group separately but no significant differences existed among groups. There were 28 children without risk and 55 with 3 or fewer risk scores. Four or more risk scores represented the 10 subjects at high risk.

Lipoprotein profiles followed, on the average, the trends reported from studies based on larger populations. Cholesterol and its various subfractions showed in general the postpubertal dip; HDL was highest at the age of 12 years for girls, LDL lowest at the age of 20 years for boys (Figure 1). The different ratios remained stable over the years. HDL and LDL on the average never reached the levels indicated for protection or genesis of atherosclerosis.

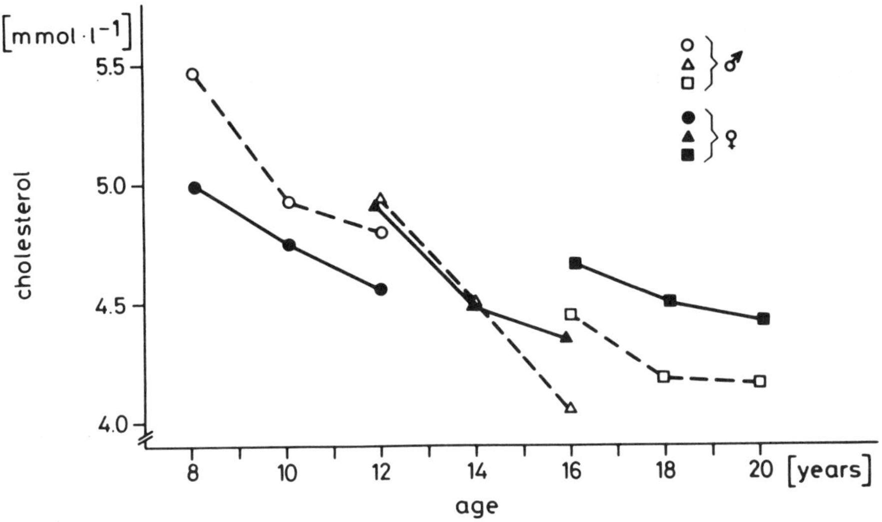

Figure 1. Total cholesterol in relation to age during a combined longitudinal/cross-sectional study (n = 99).

Maximal aerobic power was in the upper limits of the normal range over the years, indicating, in general, an appropriate level of daily physical activity for most of the sample (Figure 2). Only the young female workers had a sudden decrease in their relative maximal aerobic power per body weight as indicated by the comparison conducted at the second cross-sectional point of the longitudinal study (Figure 3).

Children at high risk for CHD were detected by high scores for family history as well as a tracking phenomenon for the biochemical risk factors for a minimum of 2 years. In the group under investigation, there was a total of 10 high-risk children out of the sample of 99 children. This number increased with age as a result of the additional effects of unfavorable lifestyle patterns combined with aging during puberty. All the children were not identified for their special risk by medical examinations

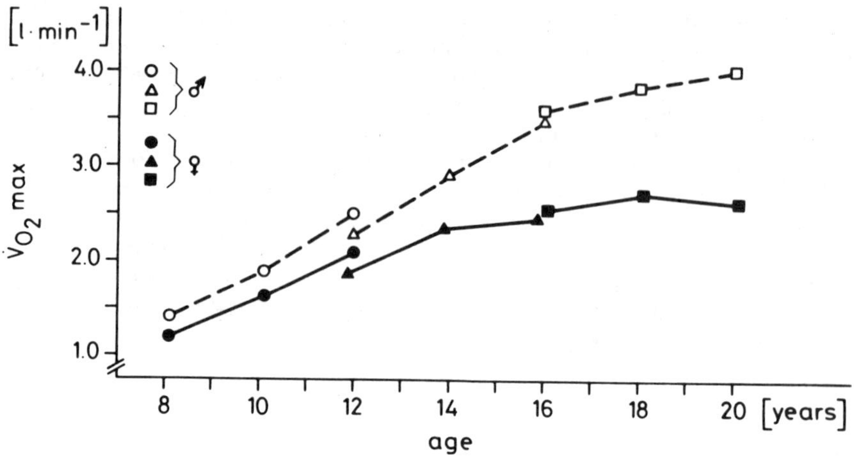

Figure 2. Maximal aerobic power in relation to age during a combined longitudinal/cross-sectional study ($n = 99$).

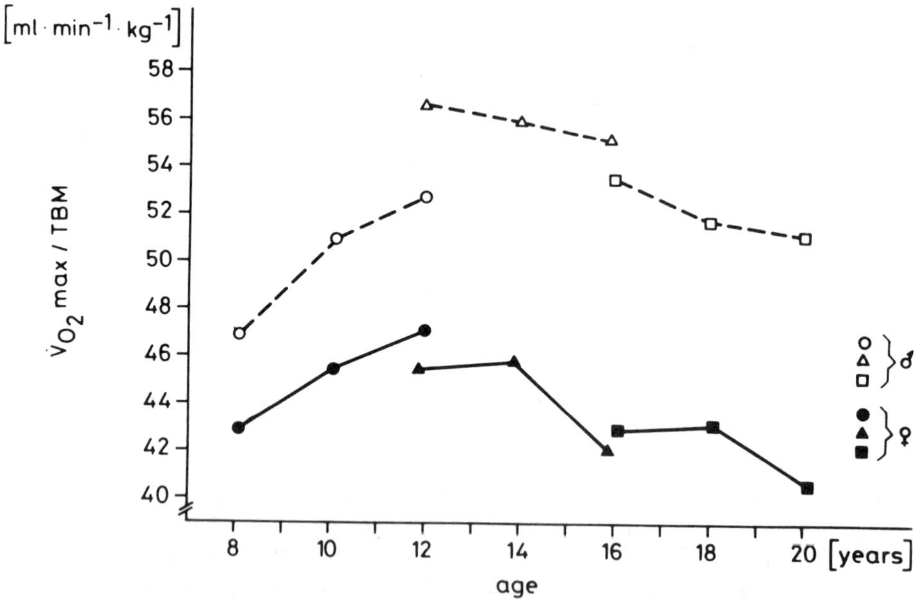

Figure 3. $\dot{V}O_2max$:TBM in relation to age during a combined longitudinal/cross-sectional study ($n = 99$).

and were consequently not included in special preventive health measures. Even if they did come from high-risk families, they had not yet been classified as being under special high risk.

CONCLUSIONS

Even for a population that is traditionally quite open-minded concerning preventive health measures, this study revealed a general lack of information about individuals who might be under high risk for the development of coronary heart disease. The study demonstrated that low-risk strategies should be supplemented by special preventive measures for identified high-risk subjects. Such measures should include a family history taken not later than the age of 12 years, annual blood pressure measures under appropriate conditions, and biannual determinations of cholesterol and, if possible, its subfractions. Smoking habits are, at different ages, difficult to determine but should regularly be checked and their harmful effects should regularly be discussed.

Appropriate daily physical activity is age dependent. Critical periods occur during the postpubertal phase and the time when apprenticeships are usually started. Young female workers appear to be especially susceptible to adopting negative lifestyle habits after having started to work in industry or at vocational schools (Rutenfranz et al., 1981).

REFERENCES

Lange-Andersen, K., Ilmarinen, J., Rutenfranz, J., Ottmann, W., Berndt, I., Kylian, H., & Ruppel, M. (1984). Leisure time sport activities and maximal aerobic power during late adolescence. *European Journal of Applied Physiology*, **52**, 431-436.

Lange-Andersen, K., Shephard, R.J., Denolin, H., Varnauskas, E., & Masironi, R. (1971). *Fundamentals of exercise testing*. Geneva: World Health Organization.

Nora, J.J., Lortscher, R.M., Spangler, R.D., Nora, A.H., & Kimberling, W.J. (1980). Genetic epidemiology of early-onset ischemic heart disease. *Circulation*, **61**, 503-508.

Pisa, Z. (1979). Report of WHO workshop on pilot project for the study and controls of atherosclerosis precursors in childhood and youth. Geneva: World Health Organization Materials.

Rutenfranz, J., Lange-Andersen, K., Seliger, V., Klimmer, F., Berndt, I., & Ruppel, M. (1981). Maximum aerobic power and body composition during the puberty growth period: Similarities and differences between children of two European countries. *European Journal of Pediatrics*, **136**, 123-133.

Is Blood Pressure in Children Related to Physical Fitness?

Stella A. de Man
Willy-Anne H.J. van Stiphout
Diederick E. Grobbee
Albert Hofman
Hans A. Valkenburg
Erasmus University Medical School, Rotterdam, The Netherlands

High blood pressure is one of the main risk factors for cardiovascular disease and appears to be the consequence of a process that starts early in life (Berenson, McMahon, & Voors, 1980; Clarke, Schrott, Leaverton, Connor, & Lauer, 1978; Giovannelli & New, 1981; Hofman, Grobbee, & Schalekamp, 1987; Labarthe, 1983; World Health Organization [WHO], 1985). On the other hand, it has been suggested that physical activity and the level of physical fitness may protect against cardiovascular disease (Echner, 1983; Froelicher & Oberman, 1972; Kannel, Wilson, & Blair, 1985; Paffenbarger & Hyde, 1984).

In order to determine whether physical fitness and physical activity are related to the level or rise of blood pressure early in life, eventually 1,500 children, aged 7 to 11 years, will be examined. In this report preliminary results including 399 (216 girls and 183 boys) children are presented.

SUBJECTS AND METHODS

Between March and July 1987, all pupils from the fourth and fifth group of 12 elementary schools in Zoetermeer, a suburban residential community near The Hague, were invited to participate in the "Run Fast for Your Heart" study. Of 530 children, 487 (92%) participated in the first examination, which took place at school. For the second examination 465 (240 girls and 225 boys) children attended the study center, making the final response of the original group 88%. Nonresponse in girls was somewhat higher than in boys.

As part of the first examination, the parents completed a questionnaire on the medical history of their children. Fifteen children were excluded from participation in the maximal exercise test for the following reasons: asthma and chronic bronchitis (n = 10), congenital heart disease (n = 1), muscular dystrophy (n = 1), epilepsy (n = 1), lung dysplasia (n = 1), and choanal atresia (n = 1).

During the first examination at school, body height and weight were measured with the children wearing indoor clothes and no shoes. Quetelet index, the ratio of body weight and height squared, was used as an index of body mass (Khosla & Lowe, 1967). Thickness of four skinfolds (biceps, triceps, subscapular, and suprailiac) was measured by a Holtain caliper, and the percent fat was calculated according to Durnin and Womersley (1974). At both examinations blood pressure was measured in the sitting position on the left arm with a random-zero sphygmomanometer (Wright & Dore, 1970). Two independent readings were taken, which were separated in time by a count of the pulse rate. In the analysis, the average of these two readings was used. Diastolic blood pressure was based on the fifth Korotkoff sound. The children were familiarized with the procedure of the maximal exercise test by walking on a treadmill for 5 min at different speeds and gradients.

Within 1 week after the first phase, the children visited the study center with their parents for a second examination. Blood pressure was remeasured by the same person. Physical fitness, defined as maximal aerobic power, was determined directly by measuring oxygen uptake during the Bruce treadmill test. According to this protocol, the speed as well as the gradient are increased every 3 min, until further running is impossible despite encouragement of the test leaders (Bruce, Kusumi, & Hosmer, 1973). There is general agreement that the best method for maximal exercise testing in children below 10 years is a treadmill test (WHO, 1968). The Bruce test was chosen because in this workload protocol the speed is variable so that even young children may perform the test without difficulty and because reproducibility among children is high (Cumming, Everatt, & Hastman, 1978; Saris, 1982).

The maximal exercise test on the treadmill (Quinton, Seattle, U.S.A.) was performed during the day in a room at a temperature between 18 and 22 °C. The collected expired air volume was measured with a dry gas meter. Gas analyses were made continuously by a paramagnetic O_2 analyzer and an infrared CO_2 analyzer (Oxycon-4, Mijnhardt, Bunnik, the Netherlands). Heart rate was calculated from a continuous ECG recording. The criteria for reaching maximal exercise were leveling off of oxygen uptake (i.e., no increase or less than 2 ml • kg^{-1} • min^{-1}) and/or leveling off of heart rate despite increased workload. Data of 47 children (10%) were excluded from analysis because they did not follow the protocol correctly (n = 22) or because they did not meet the criteria for reaching maximal oxygen uptake (n = 25). Mean values of weight, height, and systolic and diastolic blood pressure were quite similar between the children who did and who did not reach their maximal aerobic capacity. The parents filled in a questionnaire on their children's daily physical activity and participation in sports, which was cross-checked afterwards by the investigator.

DATA ANALYSIS

To assess the association between blood pressure and physical fitness (as measured by maximal oxygen uptake), multiple linear regression analysis was performed with either systolic or diastolic blood pressure from the second examination as the dependent variable and physical fitness as the independent variable. If a significant relation with both physical fitness and blood pressure was shown by one of the other variables, it was considered to be a confounder and, consequently, it was added to the model of multiple regression analysis.

RESULTS

Average values of blood pressure by age and gender from the children who attended both examinations are presented in Table 1. The age categories of 7 and 11 years included only one boy and one girl and are therefore not shown. Blood pressure at the second examination was slightly lower. By contrast, no decrease in pulse rate at rest was observed. Table 2 shows anthropometric data for boys and girls who completed the maximal exercise test.

Table 1 Mean Values of Systolic and Diastolic Blood Pressure and Pulse Rate at Rest for Boys and Girls by Age at the First Examination (SBP_1, DBP_1, PR_1) and the Second Examination (SBP_2, DBP_2, PR_2)

Age (yrs)	*n*	SBP_1 (mmHg)	DBP_1 (mmHg)	PR_1 (b/min)	SBP_2 (mmHg)	DBP_2 (mmHg)	PR_2 (b/min)
Boys							
8	82	104 (9.5)*	62 (9.4)	84 (10.2)	102 (8.1)	60 (8.6)	84 (10.1)
9	105	104 (8.5)	64 (8.1)	82 (11.2)	102 (9.6)	60 (8.7)	86 (13.8)
10	35	103 (9.4)	63 (8.7)	80 (9.8)	101 (8.5)	59 (7.6)	80 (9.6)
Girls							
8	84	104 (9.3)*	62 (7.5)	88 (12.0)	102 (9.8)	61 (8.4)	90 (12.0)
9	122	108 (9.2)	66 (8.1)	84 (12.8)	105 (9.0)	64 (8.1)	88 (12.4)
10	32	106 (8.2)	63 (8.8)	86 (11.6)	104 (8.4)	61 (9.3)	88 (13.8)

**SD* within parentheses.

Table 2 Mean Values of Anthropometric Variables of Boys and Girls by Age

Age (yrs)	*n*	Height (cm)	Weight (kg)	Sum 4 skin-folds (mm)	Body fat (%)
Boys					
8	65	131.5 (6.5)*	27.7 (4.3)	24.5 (8.0)	10.2 (3.1)
9	92	137.5 (5.7)	30.3 (4.1)	25.9 (9.6)	10.7 (3.7)
10	26	139.8 (7.3)	32.9 (6.0)	30.4 (12.1)	12.6 (3.9)
Girls					
8	79	130.9 (4.7)*	28.1 (3.8)	34.4 (13.8)	20.4 (4.3)
9	108	136.1 (6.0)	30.9 (4.7)	34.4 (14.3)	20.7 (4.7)
10	24	138.2 (7.8)	32.7 (5.9)	41.2 (18.6)	22.3 (5.8)

**SD* within parentheses.

Mean values of maximal oxygen uptake and maximal oxygen uptake per kilogram body weight, measured with the Bruce treadmill test, are presented in Table 3. Maximal oxygen uptake increased with age in both boys and girls. Yet the aerobic power, expressed as $\dot{V}O_2$max per kilogram body weight, remained the same for the different age groups for both boys and girls. Mean aerobic power was higher for boys in all age categories. In order to illustrate the level of maximal exercise, mean values of maximal heart rate, maximal respiratory quotient, and maximal ventilation per minute are also given in Table 3.

Table 4 presents a correlation matrix for variables potentially associated with physical fitness or blood pressure. Age, weight, height, sum of four skinfolds, and pulse rate at rest were related to blood pressure, whether systolic or diastolic, and physical fitness, defined as maximal oxygen uptake in boys and girls. Table 5 shows the results of multiple linear regression analysis for the association between blood pressure and physical fitness. Regression coefficients are presented, both unadjusted and adjusted for weight, height, sum of four skinfolds, pulse rate at rest, and age. The adjusted regression coefficients were positive for systolic blood pressure and negative for diastolic blood pressure in both boys and girls, but only reached statistical significance for diastolic blood pressure in girls.

DISCUSSION

The main finding in this study was that systolic blood pressure and physical fitness in children, aged 8 to 10 years, were not related. In girls, diastolic blood pressure appeared to be inversely related to physical fitness. Average levels of blood pressure in this study were slightly lower than those found earlier in the Dutch EPOZ study by Hofman and Valkenburg (1980). An increase in blood pressure with age, also in contrast to the EPOZ study, was not observed. This could be due to the small

Table 3 For Boys and Girls Mean Values of Maximal Oxygen Uptake ($\dot{V}O_2$max), Maximal Heart Rate (HRmax), Maximal Respiratory Quotient (RQmax), and Maximal Ventilation ($\dot{V}$Emax) by Age as Measured According to the Bruce Treadmill Protocol

Age (yrs)	*n*	$\dot{V}O_2$max (l/min)	$\dot{V}O_2$max (ml/kg/min)	HRmax (b/min)	RQmax	$\dot{V}$Emax (l/min)
Boys						
8	65	1.36 (0.19)*	49.6 (6.0)	204 (8.2)	1.09 (0.09)	52.2 (8.5)
9	92	1.53 (0.20)	50.8 (5.4)	202 (8.0)	1.09 (0.08)	57.7 (7.7)
10	26	1.63 (0.32)	49.8 (6.5)	206 (9.6)	1.10 (0.08)	62.9 (10.9)
Girls						
8	79	1.24 (0.16)*	44.5 (5.6)	207 (8.1)	1.10 (0.09)	50.0 (7.5)
9	108	1.39 (0.19)	45.1 (4.8)	206 (8.4)	1.13 (0.10)	55.2 (8.7)
10	29	1.45 (0.17)	45.5 (6.2)	204 (8.3)	1.13 (0.12)	58.0 (7.0)

**SD* within parentheses.

Table 4 Correlation Coefficients of Maximal Oxygen Uptake and Systolic and Diastolic Blood Pressure at the Second Examination ($n = 399$)

	Boys			Girls		
	$\dot{V}O_2$max	SBP_2	DBP_2	$\dot{V}O_2$max	SBP_2	DBP_2
Age	.36**	.04	.11	.43**	.16*	.18**
Height	.72**	.15*	.08	.69**	.21**	.19**
Weight	.69**	.22**	.14	.67**	.36**	.33**
Quet. index	.36**	.21**	.15	.35**	.33**	.30**
Sum of skinfolds	.16**	.22**	.13	.23**	.26**	.23**
Pulse rate	−.17*	.23**	.13	−.08	.26**	.18**
SBP_2	.14	—	—	.31**	—	—
DBP_2	.04	—	—	.11	—	—
$\dot{V}O_2$max	—	.14	.04	—	.31**	.11
$\dot{V}O_2$max/kg	—	−.10	−.13	—	−.10	−.29**

$^*p < .05$. $^{**}p < .01$.

Table 5 Multiple Linear Regression Coefficients of the Association Between Blood Pressure and Physical Fitness ($n = 399$)

Dependent variable	Independent variable	Regression coefficients	
		Unadjusted	Adjusted
Boys			
Systolic BP	$\dot{V}O_2max$	4.84 (2.82)*	2.83 (4.26)
Diastolic BP	$\dot{V}O_2max$	1.16 (2.76)	−2.54 (4.30)
Girls			
Systolic BP	$\dot{V}O_2max$	15.40 (3.22)***	8.25 (4.59)
Diastolic BP	$\dot{V}O_2max$	5.00 (2.97)	−9.50 (4.23)**

Note. Regression coefficients are presented unadjusted and adjusted for weight, height, sum or four skinfolds, pulse rate at rest, and age.

*Standard error is presented within parentheses. **$p < .05$. ***$p < .01$.

number in the oldest age group or to a small age range. A typical phenomenon is lowering of blood pressure levels when measured twice within a short time (Hofman, Valkenburg, Maas, & Groustra, 1985). The fall in blood pressure was not associated with a decrease in pulse rate. Blood pressure values from the second examination were used for analysis because it has been suggested that repeated measurements are likely to reflect a basal state (Berenson et al., 1980).

Height, weight, and the sum of four skinfolds were similar to Dutch data from van Wieringen, Wafelbakker, Verbrugge, and de Haas (1965) and Saris (1985). Values of maximal oxygen consumption were within the ranges of Dutch reference values measured in the same way by Saris. Their findings of maximal heart rate, maximal respiratory quotient, and maximal ventilation indicated maximal exercise had been achieved. The values of Saris (1985) were higher for boys than found in the present study. The small sample size of Saris's study and the exclusion of those subjects that did not reach a respiratory quotient of 1.1 might explain the difference in these values. Bar-Or (1983) also measured maximal oxygen uptake by an all-out progressive-continuous protocol on a treadmill. These values in boys and girls, aged 8 to 10 years, were quite similar to the values obtained in this study. Irrespective of the general discussion on criteria for reaching maximal aerobic power, maximal exercise was reached by most of the children participating in this study.

The relation between physical fitness and blood pressure in the same age group has been studied by Fraser, Phillips, and Harris (1983) and Hofman, Walter, Connelly, and Vaughan (1987). In the Loma Linda Child-Adolescent Blood Pressure Study ($n = 228$), systolic blood pressure and physical fitness in boys were negatively related (Fraser et al., 1983). In that study, fitness was defined as the physical work capacity at a heart rate of 170 beats per min ($\dot{W}170$), measured with a submaximal treadmill test. The boys and girls were between 7 and 12 years of age. No anthropometric data were provided. In the "Know Your Body" study (n = 2,016), levels of both systolic and diastolic blood pressure in children aged 8 to 10 were positively associated with level of fitness, defined as the post-exercise sum of pulse rates in a modified Harvard Step Test (Hofman et al., 1987). Body height and body weight were the same as in the present study. The larger age range, and thus the greater difference in blood pressure levels, might explain the relation found in the first study. The positive findings of Hofman et al. (1987) may have resulted from the inclusion of more children, although the validity of the method of measuring physical fitness must be considered.

In the present study no relation was found between physical fitness and systolic blood pressure. For girls, diastolic blood pressure appeared to be inversely related to physical fitness. In general, inferences on the association between blood pressure and physical fitness must be made carefully because both physical fitness and blood pressure in children are strongly influenced by growth. Therefore, the trends found in this preliminary analysis await confirmation because the present results are based on less than one-third of the population to be studied.

REFERENCES

Bar-Or, O. (1983). *Pediatric sports medicine for the practitioner. From physiologic principles to clinical application*. New York: Springer.

Berenson, G.S., McMahan, C., & Voors, A.W. (1980). *Cardiovascular risk factors in children*. New York: Oxford University Press.

Bruce, R.A., Kusumi, F., & Hosmer, D. (1973). Maximal oxygen intake and nomographic assessment of functional aerobic impairment in cardiovascular disease. *American Heart Journal*, **85**, 546-562.

Clarke, C.R., Schrott, H.G., Leaverton, P.E., Connor, W.E., & Lauer, R.M. (1978). Tracking of blood lipids and blood pressures in school age children: The Muscatine study. *Circulation*, **58**, 626-634.

Cumming, G.R., Everatt, D., & Hastman, L. (1978). Bruce treadmill test in children: Normal values in a clinic population. *American Journal of Cardiology*, **41**, 69-75.

Durnin, J.V.G.A., & Womersley, J. (1974). Body fat assessed from total body density and its estimation from skinfold thickness. *British Journal of Nutrition*, **37**, 77-97.

Echner, E.R. (1983). Exercise and heart disease. Epidemiology of the exercise hypothesis. *American Journal of Medicine*, **75**, 1008-1023.

Fraser, G.E., Phillips, R.L., & Harris, R. (1983). Physical fitness and blood pressure in children. *Circulation*, **67**, 405-412.

Froelicher, V.F., & Oberman, A. (1972). Analysis of epidemiologic studies of physical inactivity as a risk factor for coronary artery disease. *Progress in Cardiovascular Diseases*, **15**, 41-65.

Giovannelli, G., & New, M.I. (1981). *Hypertension in children and adolescents*. New York: Raven.

Hofman, A., Grobbee, D.E., & Schalekamp, M.A.D.H. (Eds.). (1987). *The early pathogenesis of primary hypertension* (International Congress Series No. 737). Amsterdam: Elsevier Science.

Hofman, A., & Valkenburg, H.A. (1980). The level of blood pressure in childhood. In H. Kesteloot & J.V. Joossens (Eds.), *Epidemiology of arterial blood pressure* (pp. 99-117). The Hague: Nijhoff.

Hofman, A., Valkenburg, H.A., Maas, J., & Groustra, F.N. (1985). The natural history of blood pressure in childhood. *International Journal of Epidemiology*, **14**, 91-96.

Hofman, A., Walter, H.J., Connelly, P.A., & Vaughan, R.D. (1987). Blood pressure and physical fitness in children. *Hypertension*, **9**, 188-191.

Kannel, W.B., Wilson, P., & Blair, S.N. (1985). Epidemiological assessment of the role of physical activity and fitness in development of cardiovascular disease. *American Heart Journal*, **109**, 876-885.

Khosla, T., & Lowe, C.R. (1967). Indices of obesity derived from body height and weight. *British Journal of Preventive Medicine*, **21**, 122-128.

Labarthe, D.R. (1983). Blood pressure studies in children throughout the world. In F. Gross & T. Strasser (Eds.), *Mild hypertension* (pp. 85-96). New York: Raven.

Paffenbarger, R.S.J., & Hyde, R.T. (1984). Exercise in the prevention of coronary heart disease. *Preventive Medicine*, **13**, 3-22.

Saris, W.H.M. (1982). *Aerobic power and daily physical activity in children. With special reference to methods and cardiovascular risk indicators*. Unpublished doctoral dissertation, University of Nijmegen, The Netherlands.

Saris, W.H.M. (1985). Reference values for aerobic power of healthy 4- to 18-year-old Dutch children: Preliminary results. In R.A. Binkhorst, H.C.G. Kemper, & W.H.M. Saris (Eds.), *Children and exercise XI* (pp. 151-160). Champaign, IL: Human Kinetics.

World Health Organization. (1968). *Exercise tests in relation to cardiovascular function* (Technical Rep. Series No. 338). Geneva: Author.

World Health Organization. (1985). *Blood pressure studies in children* (Technical Rep. Series No. 715). Geneva: Author.

Wieringen, J.C. van, Wafelbakker, F., Verbrugge, H.P., & de Haas, J.H. (1965). *Growth diagrams 1965, The Netherlands*. Groningen: Wolters Noordhoff.

Wright, B.M., & Dore, C.F. (1970). A random-zero sphygmomanometer. *Lancet*, **1**, 337-338.

Lipemic Risk Factors in 10-Year-Old Children

Maria L. Zonderland
Wietze B.M. Erich
State University Utrecht, Utrecht, The Netherlands

D. Willem Erkelens
Wouter Kortlandt
University Hospital Utrecht, Utrecht, The Netherlands

Although the clinical symptoms of coronary heart disease (CHD) do not usually occur before the age of 40, the initial stages of atherosclerosis begin in youth (McGill, 1983). Plasma lipid and lipoprotein levels have been identified as predictive of CHD (Kannel, Castelli, & Gordon, 1979), and these risk factors can be measured even at young ages (Berenson, 1980; Rifkind, 1983). Newman et al. (1986) found strong relationships between aortic fatty streaks and antemortem levels of plasma total cholesterol (TC), and low-density lipoprotein cholesterol (LDL-C) in young-deceased persons. These findings support the pediatric approach to the primary prevention of atherosclerotic CHD.

Frequently, the role of the apolipoproteins as indices for CHD risk is emphasized (Maciejko et al., 1983; Sniderman et al., 1985), but data about apolipoproteins in children are still sparse. In the Janus Jongbloed Research Centre in Utrecht, the Netherlands, an investigation is in progress in which intervention with regard to physical activity occurs in a group of schoolchildren (n = 150), with another group as a control. At entry into the study, the participants were 10 years old and they will be followed for 3 years, twice a year. The aim of the investigation is to study the effect of physical activity on lipemic risk factors in relation to growth and biological development. This report describes the baseline levels of plasma lipids and apolipoproteins of the Dutch participants.

METHODS

A total of 73 boys and 95 girls (all Caucasian) living in Utrecht participated in this study after informed consent of the parents had been obtained. The mean age (± SEM) of the boys was 9.9 ± 0.1 years; the girls were 9.8 ± 0.1 years old. The intervention group and control group were studied together because all group variables were similar at entry. Biological development was determined by visual assessment using the photographs of Marshall and Tanner (1969) for girls and Marshall and Tanner (1970) for boys. Only boys in genital development stages (G-stage) 1 or 2 and girls in breast development stages (M-stage) 1 or 2 were selected for this study. Height was recorded to 0.5 cm and weight to 0.5 kg with a standardized anthropometer and balance scale. Skinfold thicknesses were measured in millimeters at the biceps, triceps, subscapular, and suprailiac sites with a Harpenden skinfold caliper according to Durnin and Womersley (1974).

Between 8:30 and 9:30 a.m. and after an overnight fast, blood was sampled from the vena cubiti. The samples were collected in EDTA-coated tubes and centrifuged at low speed for 10 min. The plasma for high-density lipoprotein cholesterol (HDL-C) analysis was incubated immediately in phosphotungstic acid with magnesiumchloride in order to precipitate the apo B containing lipoproteins (Lopes-Virella, Stone, Ellis, & Coldwell, 1977). All plasma was distributed in Eppendorf cups, frozen in liquid nitrogen, and stored at −20 °C until analyzed.

Cholesterol and triglycerides (TG) were determined enzymatically using Boehringer (Mannheim) kit reagents. Apolipoproteins A-I and B (apo A-I and apo B) were measured by immunoturbidimetry on a Multistat centrifugal analyzer. Antisera (Boehringer, Mannheim) were diluted 1:25 in the presence of 6% PEG 4000 (Koch-Light Ltd. Suffolk, England) and samples 1:51 in saline containing 6 M guanidiniumchloride for apo A-I and saline for apo B, respectively. Omega lipid control serum (Hyland) was used for calibration. LDL-C was calculated according to Friedewald, Levy, and Frederickson (1972). No subject had a TG level higher than 3.39 mmol • l^{-1}. The HDL-C to TC, HDL-C to LDL-C, and apo A-I to apo B ratios were also calculated.

Descriptive statistics of all variables included the mean ± SEM. For the plasma lipids and apolipoproteins, the 10th, 50th, 75th, and 90th percentiles were given. Differences in height, weight, and sum of skinfolds between boys and girls were tested with students' t tests. To determine differences in lipid and apolipoprotein levels and to determine possible effects of the body composition on the variance of these levels, a one-way analysis of covariance was used. Gender was used as a nonmetric factor, and body weight and sum of skinfolds as covariates. For all statistical tests a p value of less than .05 was taken to indicate significance.

RESULTS

The boys were taller and heavier than the girls (Table 1). The difference in the sum of skinfolds did not quite reach statistical significance. The mean levels of lipids and apolipoproteins were similar in the two groups (Table 2). The grand means of TC, LDL-C, HDL-C, TG, apo A-I, and apo B were 4.65, 2.87, 1.45, and 0.67 mmol • l^{-1} and 182 and 73 mg • dl^{-1}, respectively. The covariates were processed after the main effects for the nonmetric factor, and then the explained variance of the TG level became statistically significant. Also the covariates showed a substantial effect on TC, LDL-C, and apo B but no effect on HDL-C or apo A-I variances. Therefore, the latter are not shown (Table 3). The distributions of TC and LDL-C in the boys were a little skewed to the left, which resulted in small deviations in percentile values as compared with the girls (Table 2). No differences in the various ratios were found (Table 4).

Table 1 Characteristics of the Groups

	Boys	Girls
n	73	95
Height (cm)	141.7 ± 0.7	139.1 ± 0.7*
Weight (kg)	34.1 ± 0.7	32.3 ± 0.6*
Sum of 4 skinfolds (mm)	35.1 ± 2.7	41.3 ± 2.7
G-stage 1	39 (53.4%)	
2	34 (46.6%)	
M-stage 1		82 (86.3%)
2		13 (13.7%)

*$p < .05$, Students' t test. Mean ± SEM are given.

Table 2 Mean ± SEM and the 10th, 50th, 75th, and 90th Percentiles of the Plasma Lipids and Apolipoproteins

		Percentiles			
	M	10	50	75	90
Boys (n = 73)					
TC (mmol • l^{-1})	4.68 ± 0.12	3.61	4.46	5.20	5.82
LDL-C	2.85 ± 0.09	1.91	2.78	3.31	3.86
HDL-C	1.46 ± 0.04	1.02	1.49	1.68	1.85
TG	0.69 ± 0.03	0.38	0.62	0.88	1.14
apo A-I (mg • dl^{-1})	182 ± 3	151	181	201	212
apo B	73 ± 3	49	70	83	99
Girls (n = 95)					
TC (mmol • l^{-1})	4.63 ± 0.08	3.82	4.56	4.94	5.64
LDL-C	2.89 ± 0.07	2.09	2.87	3.16	3.82
HDL-C	1.44 ± 0.03	1.06	1.41	1.61	1.81
TG	0.66 ± 0.03	0.40	0.61	0.79	0.97
apo A-I (mg • dl^{-1})	182 ± 2	152	182	196	210
apo B	73 ± 2	53	74	82	94

Table 3 One-Way Analysis of Covariance of TG, TC, LDL-C, and apo B

	F	Significance of F		F	Significance of F
TG			*TC*		
Main effect (sex)	.722	NS		.144	NS
Covariates	5.727	< .01		3.134	< .05
body weight	0.972	NS		5.019	< .05
skinfolds	1.207	NS		6.102	< .02
Explained	4.058	< .01		2.137	NS
LDL-C			*apo B*		
Main effect (sex)	.120	NS		.050	NS
Covariates	3.022	< .05		2.724	NS
body weight	4.215	< .05		2.976	NS
skinfolds	6.039	< .05		5.378	< .05
Explained	2.055	NS		1.818	NS

Gender (sex) was used as nonmetric factor, body weight and sum of skinfolds as covariates. The covariates were processed after the main effects of the nonmetric factor.

Degrees of freedom: main effect = 1, covariates = 3, explained = 5.

Table 4 The Lipid and Apolipoprotein Ratios

	Boys	Girls
n	73	95
HDL-C/TC	0.32 ± 0.01	0.32 ± 0.01
HDL-C/LDL-C	0.55 ± 0.02	0.53 ± 0.02
apo A-I/apo B	2.69 ± 0.08	2.60 ± 0.06

$^*p < .05$, ANOVA. Mean ± SEM are given.

DISCUSSION

It has been largely accepted that primary prevention, started as early as possible, may be the best approach to reduce CHD risk. Hypercholesterolemia is only one risk factor among others (e.g., smoking, hypertension, and physical inactivity), but it is a substantial one. According to the estimations of Goldman and Cook (1984), reductions in serum cholesterol levels accounted for 30% of the decline in coronary mortality rates between 1968 and 1976. Recently, in the United States and in the Netherlands, cholesterol consensus development meetings have been organized in order to agree upon strategies for (lipemic) risk factor reduction (National Institutes of Health Consensus Development Conference Statement [NIH-CDCS], 1985; Erkelens, 1987). With regard to the youngest age category (5 to 19 years), the American National Institutes of Health Consensus Development Panel indicated a cholesterol level between 4.5 and 4.9 mmol • l^{-1} to be moderately increased and a level beyond 4.9 mmol • l^{-1} severely increased (NIH-CDCS, 1985). Boys and girls were considered together. The TC levels in the present study were similar to those reported by Knuiman and Katan (1985) and by Stiphout, Hofman, Bruijn, and Valkenburg (1985).

Both are reports of Dutch investigations, and the values are higher than reported in the LRC program (Rifkind, 1983). According to the previously mentioned standards, 50% of the children in the present investigation would be at risk! This finding is in accordance with the overall picture of cholesterol levels in the Netherlands, which shows that the levels in all age categories are 10% to 15% higher than in the United States (CBO, 1987; Knuiman & Katan, 1985), probably indicating a higher prevalence of hypercholesterolemia.

Comparison of the HDL-C levels gave a more optimistic result. HDL-C is generally accepted to be an inverse risk factor (Kannel et al., 1979). For children no standards for HDL-C are available, but the levels found in the present study, like those of Stiphout et al. (1985), were higher than reported in the LRC-program (Rifkind, 1983). Moreover, the HDL-C to TC and the HDL-C to LDL-C ratios were higher than the Framingham data (Castelli, Abbott, & McNamara, 1983). However, methodological and interlaboratory variation in the HDL-C analysis might explain these differences. These ratios are useful expressions for combining cholesterol information and appear to be strong predictors for CHD (Castelli et al., 1983). High values are associated with a low risk. As apo A-I is the major apolipoprotein in HDL and apo B in LDL, the apo A-I to apo B ratio is a reflection of the HDL-C to LDL-C ratio and, similarly, may be a predictor for CHD risk. Sons of fathers with severe atherosclerosis had a lower ratio than sons of fathers free of this disease (Stiphout, Hofman, Kruijssen, Vermeeren, & Groot, 1986). No differences existed among the daughters. In the present study, this ratio was even higher than reported in previous studies, but this may have been due to interlaboratory variation, which is a major problem in apolipoprotein assays (Cooper, Smith, Wiebe, Kuchmak, & Hannon, 1985).

It can be concluded that the TC levels in the present study were rather high as compared to levels in the United States, which may point to an increased risk for CHD. This risk may be decreased when HDL-C and the various ratios are taken into consideration. The relationships of TG and TC to body weight and sum of skinfolds found were in accordance with the fact that in obese children the levels of TG, and to a lesser extent those of TC, are higher than in nonobese peers (Berenson, 1980).

In summary, similar plasma lipid and apolipoprotein profiles were found in 10-year-old boys and girls. The levels of TC (and LDL-C) indicate an increased risk for CHD, but the HDL-C levels and the various ratios may neutralize the possible risk. The further investigation may provide more clarity concerning the natural history of the lipemic risk factors in youth.

REFERENCES

Berenson, G.S. (1980). *Cardiovascular risk factors in children*. New York: Oxford University Press.

Castelli, W.P., Abbott, R.D., & McNamara, P.M. (1983). Summary estimates of cholesterol used to predict coronary heart disease. *Circulation*, **4**, 730-734.

Cooper, G.R., Smith, S.J., Wiebe, D.A., Kuchmak, M., & Hannon, W.H. (1985). International survey of apolipoproteins A_1 and B measurements (1983-1984). *Clinical Chemistry*, **31**, 223-228.

Durnin, J.V.G.A., & Womersley, J. (1974). Body fat assessed from total body density and its estimation from skinfold thickness. *British Journal of Nutrition*, **32**, 77-97.

Erkelens, D.W. (Ed.). (1987). Cholesterol Consensus Conference. *Het resultaat van de Consensus-Bijeenkomst Gehouden op 20 maart 1987 te Amersfoort* [The report of the Dutch Consensus Meeting, March 20, 1987]. Amersfoort: de Flint.

Friedewald, W.T., Levy, R.I., & Frederickson, D.S. (1972). Estimation of the concentration of LDL-C in plasma. *Clinical Chemistry*, **18**, 488-502.

Goldman, L., & Cook, E.F. (1984). The decline in ischemic heart disease mortality rates. *Annals of Internal Medicine*, **101**, 825-836.

Kannel, W.B., Castelli, W.P., & Gordon, T. (1979). Cholesterol in the prediction of atherosclerotic disease. *Annals of Internal Medicine*, **90**, 85-91.

Knuiman, J.T., & Katan, M.B. (1985). Cholesterol niveaus in serum in Nederland in vergelijking met die in de Verenigde Staten [Serum cholesterol levels in the Netherlands as compared with those in the United States]. *Nederlands Tijdschrift voor Geneeskunde*, **129**, 2500-2505.

Lopes-Virella, M.F., Stone, P., Ellis, S., & Coldwell, J.A. (1977). Cholesterol determinations in HDL separated by three different methods. *Clinical Chemistry*, **23**, 882-884.

Maciejko, J.J., Holmes, D.R., Kottke, B.A., Zinsmeister, A.R., Dinh, D.M., & Mao, S.J. (1983). Apolipoprotein A-I as a marker of angiographically assessed coronary heart disease. *New England Journal of Medicine*, **309**, 385-389.

Marshall, W.A., & Tanner, J.M. (1969). Variations in the pattern of pubertal changes in girls. *Archives of Disease in Childhood*, **44**, 291-303.

Marshall, W.A., & Tanner, J.M. (1970). Variations in the pattern of pubertal changes in boys. *Archives of Disease in Childhood*, **45**, 13-23.

McGill, H.C. (1983). Natural history of human atherosclerotic lesions. In M. Sandler & G.H. Bourne (Eds.), *Atherosclerosis and its origin* (pp. 39). New York: Academic Press.

National Institutes of Health Consensus Development Conference Statement (NIH-CDCS). (1985). Lowering blood cholesterol to prevent heart disease. *Journal of the American Medical Association*, **253**, 2080-2088.

Newmann, W.P., III, Freedman, D.S., Voors, A.W., Gard, P.D., Srinivasan, S.R., Cresanta, J.L., Williamson, G.D., Webber, L.S., & Berenson, G.S. (1986). Relation of serum lipoprotein levels and systolic blood pressure to early atherosclerosis. *New England Journal of Medicine*, **314**, 138-144.

Rifkind, B.M. (1983). Lipid research clinics program reference values for hyperlipidemia and hypolipidemia. *Journal of the American Medical Association*, **250**, 1869-1872.

Sniderman, A., Teng, B., Genest, J., Cianflone, K., Wacholder, S., & Kwiterovich, P., Jr. (1985). Familial aggregation and early expression of hyperapobetalipoproteinemia. *American Journal of Cardiology*, **55**, 291-295.

Stiphout, W.A.H.J. van, Hofman, A., Bruijn, A.M. de, & Valkenburg, H.A. (1985). Distributions and determinants of total and high density lipoprotein cholesterol in Dutch children and young adults. *Preventive Medicine*, **14**, 169-180.

Stiphout, W.A.H.J. van, Hofman, A., Kruijssen, H.A.C.M., Vermeeren, R., & Groot, P.H.E. (1986). Is the ratio of apo B/apo A-I an early predictor of coronary atherosclerosis? *Atherosclerosis*, **62**, 179-182.

Blood Lipoprotein Profiles in Trained and Untrained Adolescents

Richard Bell
University of Saskatchewan, Saskatoon, Canada

Miloŝ Máček
Charles University, Czechoslovakia

Joseph Rutenfranz
University of Dortmund, Dortmund, West Germany

It is generally agreed that aerobically trained athletes have higher high-density lipoprotein cholesterol (HDL-C) concentrations than other non-aerobically trained athletes or sedentary subjects of adult age (Haskell, 1984). Other studies, however, have not yielded such consistent results in children and adolescents. Thorland and Gilliam (1981) found a higher HDL-C total cholesterol (T-Chol) ratio and a lower triglyceride (TG) concentration in highly active adolescents but no differences in other measured parameters. By way of contrast, Linder, DuRant, and Mahoney (1983) found nonsignificant decreases in HDL-C in adolescent boys following an 8-week walk-jog exercise program. Other investigators have also reported nonsignificant changes (Heiss, Johnson, Reiland, Davis, & Tyroler, 1980), but some have cited significant decreases associated with exercise (Moore, Pentold, Simpson, Mann, & Turner, 1979). Data are generally lacking for children, and from the few exercise studies available only Gilliam and Burke (1978) have reported an increase in HDL-C as a result of an exercise program, and Wilmore et al. (1982) showed lower T-Chol in more fit subjects. It is possible that these different results were obtained from groups because of different initial fitness levels or because various training intensities and durations were involved.

Accordingly, it seemed to be of interest to compare a group of highly trained endurance adolescent athletes with a group of judokas and wrestlers of the same age, as well as a randomly selected group of boys and girls also of the same age group. All athletes were students at a specialized Czechoslovakian sports school at the time of the study.

METHODS

Table 1 presents the ages of the different groups. The first experimental group consisted of 29 boys (aged 17.3 ± 0.65 years) and 26 girls (aged

17.3 ± 0.95 years) who were elite swimmers and athletes attending a sports school where at least 5 hr a day were devoted to intense physical training (Groups 1.1 and 2.1a). A special group of female endurance athletes who regularly used contraceptives (aged 17.9 ± 0.55 years) was also evaluated (Group 2.1b). The second major experimental group consisted of 22 boys (aged 16.2 ± 0.52 years) trained in wrestling and judo at the same school (Group 1.2). The control group consisted of 20 boys (aged 18.0 ± 0.35 years) and 18 girls (aged 18.1 ± 0.27 years) randomly selected from a general school population (Groups 1.3 and 2.3).

Table 1 Ages ($\overline{X}$ ± *S*) of Different Athletic Students and Controls

		Group 1.1 Endurance athletes	*Group 1.2* Heavy athletes	*Group 1.3* Control
Boys	*n*	29	22	20
	Age (years)	17.3 ± 0.65	16.2 ± 0.52	18.0 ± 0.65
		Group 2.1a Endurance athletes without contraceptives	Group 2.1b Endurance athletes with contraceptives	Group 2.3 Control
Girls	*n*	26	10	18
	Age (years)	17.3 ± 0.95	17.9 ± 0.55	18.1 ± 0.27

The level of sport activity of the control male subjects was lower than that of the trained sports school subjects even though most were, in fact, members of sports clubs that emphasized skiing and ice hockey during the winter months and football (soccer) and tennis in the summer. The training duration of these subjects usually amounted to approximately 10 hr per week. The mean physical activity level of the control female subjects, as assessed by a questionnaire, was also significantly lower than that of the female experimental group. Biochemical data were obtained by standardized methods from fasting venous blood samples and included the determination of T-Chol, HDL-C, LDL-C, and serum triglyceride concentrations, as well as the concentrations of the apolipoproteins A, A_1, and B.

RESULTS

The *t* tests shown in Table 2 indicate no significant differences in T-Chol and HDL-C between the endurance-trained athletes (Group 1.1), the more heavy-intensity trained athletes (Group 1.2), and the control group of male subjects (Group 1.3). Both training groups were characterized by higher levels of the apolipoproteins A and A_1, although only the concentration of APO-A was significantly different. The endurance-trained group also had significantly lower TG concentrations than heavy-intensity trained athletes and the control subjects. Similarly, LDL-C and apolipoprotein B values were significantly lower in the endurance-trained group than in the control group and the heavy-intensity trained athletes. The APO-B/APO-A and APO-B/APO-A_1 ratios also show more favorable values for the endurance-trained male subjects as compared with the control subjects and the heavy-intensity trained athletes.

Table 2 Serum Lipid and Lipoprotein Values ($\overline{X} \pm S$) in Male Athletes and Controls

Variables	Group 1.1 Endurance athletes (n = 29)	p	Group 1.2 Heavy athletes (n = 22)	p	Group 1.3 Control (n = 20)
Age/years	17.3 ± 0.65		16.2 ± 0.52		18.0 ± 0.35
Total cholesterol (mmol/l)	4.17 ± 0.43	NS	4.20 ± 0.80	NS	4.15 ± 0.65
HDL-C (mmol/l)	1.38 ± 0.23	NS	1.36 ± 0.23	NS	1.27 ± 0.20
—APO A_1	1.41 ± 0.15	.05	1.48 ± 0.07	.01	1.34 ± 0.19
—APO A	2.34 ± 0.24	NS	2.38 ± 0.40	NS	2.21 ± 0.33
LDL-C (mmol/l)	1.83 ± 0.21	.001	2.39 ± 0.67	.001	2.48 ± 0.66
APO B	0.76 ± 0.12	.01	0.91 ± 0.20	NS	0.83 ± 0.24
Ratios					
—HDL-C/T-Chol	0.33 ± 0.04	NS	0.33 ± 0.06	NS	0.31 ± 0.06
—APO B/APO A	0.33 ± 0.05	.01	0.39 ± 0.09	NS	0.38 ± 0.12
—APO B/APO A_1	0.54 ± 0.09	.05	0.62 ± 0.14	NS	0.63 ± 0.20
Serum triglyceride (mmol/l)	0.67 ± 0.28	.01	0.91 ± 0.32	NS	1.11 ± 0.43

Note. t tests for independent samples with significant differences at $p \leqslant .05$, $p \leqslant .01$, $p \leqslant .001$; NS = nonsignificant.

The following results refer to the endurance and control groups only (Groups 1.1, 1.3, 2.1a, and 2.3). Using a two-way analysis of variance for both gender and endurance training groups (Table 3), significant effects for training were noted with respect to HDL-C, APO-A_1, APO-A, LDL-C, APO-B, and serum triglyceride concentrations. The only main effect for gender was the higher HDL-C concentration for the female athletes. The single interaction effect between training and gender was related to the serum triglyceride concentration.

Table 3 Serum Lipid and Lipoprotein Values ($X \pm S$) in Athletic Students (Endurance Training) and Controls

Variables	Boys		Girls				
	Group 1.1 (n = 29)	Group 1.3 (n = 20)	Group 2.1a (n = 26)	Group 2.3 (n = 18)	Main effect training	Main effect gender	Interaction training and gender
Total cholesterol (mmol/l)	4.17 ± 0.43	4.15 ± 0.65	4.19 ± 0.55	4.48 ± 0.60	1.27	2.27	1.83
HDL-C (mmol/l)	1.38 ± 0.23	1.27 ± 0.20	1.52 ± 0.30	1.40 ± 0.21	5.75*	6.80**	0.01
—APO A_1	1.41 ± 0.15	1.34 ± 0.19	1.50 ± 0.24	1.36 ± 0.22	6.80**	1.95	0.75
—APO A	2.34 ± 0.24	2.21 ± 0.33	2.50 ± 0.30	2.24 ± 0.35	9.32**	2.06	1.11
LDL-C (mmol/l)	1.83 ± 0.21	2.48 ± 0.66	1.95 ± 0.27	2.63 ± 0.42	59.28***	2.53	0.03
—APO B	0.76 ± 0.12	0.83 ± 0.24	0.72 ± 0.13	0.93 ± 0.30	11.30***	0.70	2.96
Ratios							
—HDL-C/T-Chol	0.33 ± 0.04	0.31 ± 0.06	1.37 ± 0.07	0.31 ± 0.04	9.88**	2.57	2.08
—APO B/APO A	0.33 ± 0.05	0.38 ± 0.12	0.29 ± 0.07	0.42 ± 0.13	21.05***	0.06	3.23
—APO B/APO A_1	0.54 ± 0.09	0.63 ± 0.20	0.49 ± 0.12	0.70 ± 0.24	19.07***	0.15	3.48
Serum triglyceride (mmol/l)	0.67 ± 0.28	1.11 ± 0.43	0.73 ± 0.24	0.86 ± 0.27	18.84***	2.20	5.95*

$^*p \leqslant .05$. $^{**}p \leqslant .01$. $^{***}p \leqslant .001$.

Values for an additional group of 10 girls (endurance athletes) were determined separately (Group 2.1b) because of regular use of oral contraceptives that might influence the various lipoprotein values (Table 4). In some cases, the use of contraceptives was only suspected, but in others it was confirmed. At present, it is difficult to speculate on how the regular use of oral contraceptives might influence the lipoprotein profile and, if indeed it does, what specific mechanisms might be involved. In comparison with the other female endurance athletes (Group 2.1a) and with the control group (Group 2.3), significantly higher values of T-Chol, HDL-C, APO-A_1, and APO-A were noted (Table 4). This could be partially interpreted as the protective effects of contraceptives for atherogenesis. However, for this special group significant increases in LDL-C and APO-B as well as in total cholesterol were found. This had to be interpreted as an increased precondition for atherogenesis, and in this respect this subgroup of endurance athletes did not differ from the controls.

DISCUSSION

An elevated HDL-C concentration should theoretically represent a protective mechanism as far as potential coronary heart disease risk is concerned. Both control groups of subjects appeared to have relatively normal values with somewhat higher concentrations for girls, which is probably the result of hormonal factors. Both groups of endurance-trained male and female athletes had significantly higher HDL-C, APO-A_1, and APO-A concentrations than their respective controls, with the female athletes having higher values than the males (see Table 3).

Elevated LDL-C concentrations have been identified as a major atherogenic factor and as a significant contributor to coronary heart disease. Both male and female endurance-trained athletes (Groups 1.1 and 2.1a) had significantly lower LDL-C, APO-B, and TG concentrations than their respective controls, which reflects the specific effect of the endurance training program. The male athletes also had significantly lower serum triglyceride values than did their female counterparts.

The subjects in the various sport groups in this study were different from most previous studies of selected groups of gifted children. The high level of training intensity combined with a training program of at least 8 to 10 years duration would seem to characterize these individuals as a unique group. The relatively controlled nutritional environment at the sports school also represented a unique situation in that major dietary differences in the athletic subjects were not a significant factor in the various lipoprotein and apolipoprotein concentration changes.

The control group of subjects, especially the boys, also had relatively high sports participation levels up to the age of 18 years, and these elevated levels of activity may represent a minimum threshold level of daily exercise intensity that is necessary to cause positive changes in the various lipoprotein and apolipoprotein profiles. This elevated activity level might also have caused the relatively favorable values of the lipoprotein

Table 4 Serum Lipid and Lipoprotein Values ($X \pm S$) in Female Endurance Athletes Without and With Contraceptives

Variables	Group 2.1a Endurance athletes without contraceptives (n = 26)	p	Group 2.1b Endurance athletes with contraceptives (n = 10)	p	Group 2.3 Controls (n = 18)
Age/years	17.3 ± 0.95		17.9 ± 0.55		18.1 ± 0.27
Total cholesterol (mmol/l)	4.19 ± 0.55	.001	5.40 ± 0.63	.001	4.48 ± 0.60
HDL-C (mmol/l)	1.52 ± 0.30	.001	2.08 ± 0.27	.001	1.40 ± 0.21
—APO A_1	1.50 ± 0.24	.01	1.77 ± 0.17	.001	1.36 ± 0.22
—APO A	2.50 ± 0.30	.05	2.74 ± 0.24	.001	2.24 ± 0.35
LDL-C (mmol/l)	1.95 ± 0.27	.001	2.51 ± 0.27	NS	2.63 ± 0.41
—APO B	0.72 ± 0.13	.01	0.85 ± 0.12	NS	0.93 ± 0.30
Ratios					
HDL-C/T-Chol	0.37 ± 0.07	NS	0.38 ± 0.06	NS	0.31 ± 0.04
APO B/APO A	0.29 ± 0.07	NS	0.31 ± 0.07	.05	0.42 ± 0.13
APO B/APO A_1	0.49 ± 0.12	NS	0.48 ± 0.11	.02	0.70 ± 0.24
Serum triglyceride (mmol/l)	0.73 ± 0.24	NS	0.66 ± 0.11	.05	0.86 ± 0.27

and apolipoprotein profile exhibited by the control group of subjects. For this reason it should be emphasized that the higher training intensity of the endurance-trained group may have further decreased the LDL-C and TG values and elevated the concentrations of the more specific protective risk indicators HDL, APO-A, and APO-A_1 (see Table 3).

CONCLUSION

It may be concluded from this study that participation in very rigorous endurance exercise and/or training programs is generally associated with beneficial changes in the lipoprotein and apolipoprotein profiles even for adolescents. It may also be stated that the nutrition of the control group was at least partially similar to that of the trained group because both got the same governmentally controlled diet at school.

REFERENCES

Gilliam, T.B., & Burke, M.B. (1978). Effects of exercise on serum lipids and lipoproteins in girls aged 8-10 years. *Artery*, **4**, 203-213.

Haskell, W.L. (1984). The influence of exercise on the concentrations of triglyceride and cholesterol in human plasma. *Exercise and Sport Science Reviews*, **12**, 205-244.

Heiss, G., Johnson, N.J., Reiland, S., Davis, C.E., & Tyroler, H.A. (1980). The epidemiology of plasma high-density lipoprotein cholesterol levels. The Lipid Research Clinics Program Prevalence Study [Summary]. *Circulation*, **62**(Suppl. 4), 116-136.

Linder, C.W., DuRant, R.H., & Mahoney, O.M. (1983). The effect of physical conditioning on serum lipids and lipoproteins in white male adolescents. *Medicine and Science in Sports and Exercise*, **15**, 232-236.

Moore, R., Pentold, W., Simpson, R., Mann, J., & Turner, R. (1979). High-density lipoprotein, lipid, and carbohydrate metabolism during increasing fitness. *Annals of Clinical Biochemistry*, **16**, 76-80.

Thorland, W.G., & Gilliam, T.B. (1981). Comparison of serum lipids between habitually high and low active pre-adolescent males. *Medicine and Science in Sports and Exercise*, **13**, 316-321.

Wilmore, J.H., Constable, S.H., Stanforth, P.R., Tsao, W.Y., Rotkis, T.C., Paicius, R.M., Mattern, C.M., & Ewy, G.A. (1982). Prevalence of coronary heart disease risk factors in 13- to 15-year-old boys. *Journal of Cardiac Rehabilitation*, **2**, 223-233.

Relationship Between Habitual Physical Activity and Cardiovascular Responses to Exercise in Young Children

Frank A. Treiber
William B. Strong
Frederick W. Arensman
Mike Gruber
Medical College of Georgia, Augusta, Georgia

Cardiovascular disease (CVD) continues to be the leading cause of morbidity and mortality in the United States and most industrialized societies (Haulek & Feinlieb, 1979). The etiology of CVD is multifactorial and includes environmental, psychosocial, biological, and genetic influences (Dembroski, 1986). Regarding environmental influences, a number of positive lifestyle behaviors have been associated with lower levels of the classic CVD risk factors of blood pressure, cigarette smoking, and serum cholesterol. The lifestyle behaviors most commonly associated with lower levels of CVD risk factors include prudent consummatory behaviors (e.g., with regard to alcohol, tobacco, diet), appropriate physical activity, lack of Type A behavior components of hostility and anger proneness, and effective stress management coping strategies (Dembroski, 1986; Dimsdale, Alpert, & Schneiderman, 1986; Engel, Glasgow, & Gaarder, 1983; Gordon, Fisher, & Ripkinol, 1984).

With regard to physical activity, studies of adults have indicated that increased levels reduce CVD risk via reduction in blood pressure, blood glucose levels, low-density lipoprotein levels, fat weight, triglyceride values, and Type A behaviors and via increases in high-density lipoprotein levels and maximum oxygen consumption (Dimsdale et al., 1986; Pollock, 1973). Because chronic CVD begins in childhood (Newman et al., 1986), efforts have begun to assess the development of various lifestyle behaviors and their relationship to CVD risk factors in children (Berenson, 1980). Some evidence does exist for children that indicates a positive association between their levels of habitual physical activity and aerobic fitness (Saris, Binkhorst, Cramwinckel, Van Waesberghe, & Vander Veen-Hegemans, 1980; Weymans, Reybrouck, Stijns, & Knops, 1986). Given the importance of habitual physical activity to cardiovascular health in adults, further exploration of this relationship in children is warranted. The purpose of this study was to investigate in children the relationship between reported levels of habitual physical activity and cardiovascular responses to exercise.

METHODS

Prepubescent Caucasian (n = 29) 10-year-olds (15 males, 14 females) were recruited from two summer recreational programs in Augusta, Georgia. Parents provided informed written consent for their child's participation in the study. All children had normal findings on a cardiovascular physical examination, and none had any history of cardiac, respiratory, or neurological disorders. There were no trained athletes in the study. Prior to initial exercise, subjects were positioned on an exercise table and their feet were attached to an electronically braked cycle ergometer. Exercise was performed in the supine position. Silver-silver chloride electrodes were attached to the chest for use with a Hewlett-Packard Model 1151B electrocardiograph and a blood pressure cuff for use with a Critikon 6000 automated blood pressure instrument that was placed on the right arm. The electrocardiograph was a direct-writing model with a paper speed of 25 mm • s^{-1} and a standard of 1MV = 10 mm. The electrocardiograph was calibrated for paper speed and frequency response weekly. A Hewlett-Packard Model 7702AC Echo Doppler Machine was used to visualize the ascending aorta. A 2-D derived M-mode echocardiogram was used to measure systolic separation of the aorta valve leaflets immediately prior to and following cessation of exercise. Flow area was calculated as $1/2\ D^2 \times \pi$. Continuous Doppler using a 1.9 M-Hertz Transducer from the suprasternal notch measured the aortic flow velocity. All measurements were made at rest, during the last 30 s of an exercise stage and at 3 and 5 min following exercise. Blood pressure and heart rates were also measured in the same fashion.

After the subjects were prepared for exercise, a 1-min preexercise assessment of their heart rate and blood pressure was conducted. They then began to pedal the cycle at 50 to 60 rotations with at least three continuous workloads of 3 min each using a protocol established in previous studies in the laboratory (e.g., Strong, Spencer, Miller, & Salehbhai, 1978). Initial workloads were 150, 175, or 200 kg • min^{-1} depending on the child's body size. Progression of the workloads is shown in Table 1.

Following completion of the three workloads, additional workloads were included based upon the judgment of the attending physician. Workloads were added to achieve a maximal voluntary effort (MVE) that was defined as a point at which the required pedaling could no longer be maintained.

Computer-assisted analysis of the Doppler tracing was completed to assess cardiac output where $CO = 1/2\ \bar{V} \times (ET \times HR) \times \bar{AA}$, CO = cardiac output (cc • min^{-1}), V = velocity (cm • sec^{-1}) (1/2 V = average velocity), ET = ejection time (sec), HR = heart rate (beats • min^{-1}), and

Table 1 Progression of Workloads (kgM • m^{-1}) Used for the Subjects

	Workload progression (kg • min^{-1})		
Workload 1	150	175	200
2	300	350	400
3	450	525	600
4	525	625	700
N	20	2	7

AA = aortic area (cm^2). The product of ET and HR gives total time of ejection per minute (R–Marx). Cardiac output was adjusted for body surface area (BSA) to yield cardiac index (CI) such that CI = CO/BSA. Systemic vascular resistance was calculated from the relation SVR = mean BP, where mean BP = 1/3 (systolic BP–diastolic BP) + diastolic BP.

The habitual level of physical activity in the children was assessed via two rating scales completed by the child's mother while the child was performing the exercise test. A review of the literature failed to reveal any validated parent-completed scales of young American children's habitual physical activity. One validated measure of general motor activity in American children of this age range is the motor activity subscale of the Swanson, Nolan, and Pelham (1981) checklist (SNAP). The SNAP is a 23-item Likert rating scale in which parents or teachers rate components of children's hyperactivity (DSM 3 criteria) and negative peer interactions. Factor analyses across different studies have consistently yielded four factors: motor activity, inattention, impulsivity, and negative peer interactions. The SNAP has been shown to have adequate test–retest and interrater reliability and concurrent validity (Johnston, Pelham, & Murphy, 1985; Pelham & Bender, 1982).

A recently developed parent rating scale of young children's habitual physical activity was also administered (Treiber, Strong, Carr, & Levy, 1987). The physical activity rating scale (PARS) is an 18-item Likert scale developed from a review of the literature in which rating scale items were selected that correlated with children's physical activity (e.g., motion sensors, direct observation). Initial analyses indicated adequate internal consistency (Alpha = .85) as well as 1-week test–retest reliability (r = .90). Evidence of convergent validity is accumulating with significant positive correlations obtained with the motor activity subscale of the SNAP (r = .59), and number of aerobic sports activities per week (r = .50). Discriminant validity has also been established with no correlations noted with measures of depression (r = .14) or social withdrawal (r = .04) (Treiber et al., 1987).

RESULTS

Children were divided into a less physically active or more physically active (PA) group using a median split by gender of the raw scores from the SNAP motor activity subscale. the SNAP was chosen to categorize children because it has been validated with American children of this age range and a significant positive correlation was noted with this sample on the other measure of physical activity (r = .61 with PARS). It should be noted that the questionnaires were scored after the child had completed the exercise. Therefore, the individuals conducting the exercise test did not know whether the child was categorized as a low- or high-activity individual.

The demographic characteristics of the two groups are presented in Table 2. Initial analyses indicated no differences between these two groups on any of these variables except that the less PA group weighed slightly more. The means and standard deviations of the less and more PA groups on the various cardiovascular responses and measures of aerobic power across preexercise, submaximal exercise (PWC 170), and maximal exercise levels are presented in Tables 3 and 4.

A series of univariate analyses of variance were conducted comparing the two groups across the various cardiovascular responses and measures of aerobic power for preexercise, submaximal exercise (PWC 170), and maximal exercise. Results of the preexercise comparisons indicated that the less PA group showed higher mean heart rate, systolic blood pressure, cardiac output, rate pressure product, and trends toward greater cardiac index and lower systemic vascular resistance. Results of the submaximal exercise (PWC 170) comparisons indicated that the less PA group showed greater mean arterial pressure, systolic blood pressure, and a trend toward greater rate pressure product. On the other hand, the more PA group showed a greater duration of exercise and a trend toward greater power.

Table 2 Demographic Characteristics of the Less and More Physically Active (PA) Groups

	Less PA		More PA	
Variable	*M*	*SD*	*M*	*SD*
Males (n = 15)	9		6	
Females (n = 14)	8		6	
Height (cm)	142.21	4.33	141.17	5.81
Weight (kg)*	39.60	8.81	34.04	3.42
BSA (m^2)	1.24	.14	1.16	.08

*$p < .05$.

Table 3 Cardiovascular Responses to Exercise for the Less and More Physically Active (PA) Groups

	Preexercise				Submaximal exercise (PWC 170)				Maximal exercise			
	Less PA		More PA		Less PA		More PA		Less PA		More PA	
Variable	*M*	*SD*	*M*	*SD*	*M*	*SD*	*M*	*SD*	*M*	*SD*	*M*	*SD*
Heart rate (b • min^{-1})	94.18	14.06***	80.42	12.64	170.00		170.00		184.18	14.40	174.50	16.75
Systolic (mmHg)	105.24	8.48**	98.08	7.63	147.12	17.84**	130.75	19.44	158.20	23.77**	139.70	19.35
Diastolic (mmHg)	65.29	10.25	63.50	10.00	81.59	10.94	73.08	15.60	82.33	9.78	74.70	16.85
MAP (mmHg)	78.61	8.59	75.03	7.43	103.43	10.10***	92.31	11.98	107.62	10.93**	96.37	14.28
RP product	9976.76	2027.05**	7871.42	1235.14	25010.00	3032.66*	22227.50	3304.48	29359.80	4403.69***	23713.90	3677.79
CO (cc/min)	3995.35	935.13**	3201.83	704.21	7047.10	1897.50	5808.30	1393.10	6963.35	1980.42	6100.75	1518.93
CI (cc • min • m^2)	3239.41	674.22*	2763.67	604.15	5729.41	1353.59	5091.67	1262.36	5619.65	1383.62	5266.50	1352.54
SVR (Wood units)	2.05	.48*	2.46	.67	1.55	.47	1.67	.44	1.63	.45	1.64	.47

Note. MAP = mean arterial pressure, RP product = rate pressure product, CO = cardiac output, CI = cardiac index, SVR = systemic vascular resistance.
*$p < .06$ (trend). **$p < .05$. ***$p < .01$.

Table 4 Measure of Aerobic Power for the Less and More Physically Active (PA) Groups

Variable	Submaximal exercise (PWC 170)				Maximal exercise			
	Less PA		More PA		Less PA		More PA	
	M	*SD*	*M*	*SD*	*M*	*SD*	*M*	*SD*
Workload (kgM)	502.06	99.00	497.17	55.91	585.29	59.99	577.08	95.62
Watts	84.36	14.61	82.13	9.93	95.64	9.80	94.29	15.62
Power ($W \cdot kg^{-1}$)	2.17	.33	2.43	.37	2.48	.36*	2.79	.50
Time of exercise (min)					11.06	2.19**	13.04	2.73
Total work $kgM \cdot min^{-1} \times$ time (in minutes)					4272.06	1087.68	4865.63	1596.51

*$p < .06$ (trend). **$p < .05$.

DISCUSSION

Cardiovascular disease (CVD) has its origins in childhood (Berenson, 1980; Newman et al., 1986). Although significant genetic contributions influence the manifestations of CVD, many environmental/lifestyle components may also alter the outcomes. A lifestyle behavior of physical activity has been shown to beneficially influence the largest number of CVD risk factors including the ratio of total cholesterol/high density lipoprotein cholesterol, serum triglyceride, obesity, blood pressure, Type A behavior, and possible cigarette smoking (Dimsdale et al., 1986; Pollock, 1973). Many of these findings have been observed in adults, but both the European and North American pediatric communities are beginning to show beneficial relationships of physical activity with some of these CVD risk factors in children (Hofman, Walter, Connelly, & Vaughan, 1987; Saris et al., 1980; Weymans et al., 1986).

The current findings indicate that physical activity questionnaires can provide a simple means of assessing childhood cardiovascular risk status. Children were categorized into a less or more physically active (PA) group based upon a brief parent-completed rating scale of physical activity. The children who were less PA were heavier but were not taller and did not have greater body surface area. The less-PA children demonstrated higher resting systolic blood pressures and heart rates, and their mean cardiovascular endurance was less. When performing supine submaximal exercise (PWC 170) on a cycle ergometer there were no significant differences in the work performed for at that level, but when encouraged to pedal to exhaustion the more PA group performed for a greater duration and there was a trend toward greater aerobic power.

Cardiovascular measures demonstrated that the children who were more PA had a lower BP response at maximum voluntary effort and a rate pressure product that was lower, indicating less myocardial oxygen consumption and therefore a more efficient cardiovascular system. The less-PA children did not demonstrate an increased systemic vascular resistance during exercise. Although their blood pressures were greater, so were their cardiac indices, hence the normalization of the calculated systemic vascular resistance. This result was consistent with recently reported data (Marx, Hicks, & Allen, 1987). Therefore, children who are less PA have been demonstrated to perform more cardiovascular work to achieve approximately the same work output. This decrease in myocardial efficiency would not likely result in any clinical symptomatology through early and possibly even middle adult life. However, as the coronary arterial circulation becomes compromised by encroaching atherosclerosis, this inefficient myocardium would likely begin to manifest evidence of coronary insufficiency by symptoms of angina.

CONCLUSION

This study has demonstrated a relationship between reported levels of physical activity in childhood and cardiovascular responses to exercise that were suggestive of a coronary-prone pattern in the less physically active individuals.

Acknowledgment

This research was supported by funds from the National Heart, Lung, and Blood Institute (HL 35073-01) and the American Heart Association, Georgia Affiliate.

REFERENCES

Berenson, G.S. (1980). *Cardiovascular risk factors in children*. New York: Oxford University Press.

Dembroski, T.M. (1986). Overview of classic and stress-related risk factors: Relationship to substance effects on reactivity. In K.A. Matthews, S.M. Weiss, T. Detre, T.M. Dembroski, B. Falkner, S.B. Manuck, & R.B. Williams (Eds.), *Handbook of stress reactivity and cardiovascular disease* (pp. 275-290). New York: Wiley & Sons.

Dimsdale, J.E., Alpert, B.S., & Schneiderman, N. (1986). Exercise as a modulator of cardiovascular reactivity. In K.A. Matthews, S.M. Weiss, T. Detre, T.M. Dembroski, B. Falkner, S.B. Manuck, & R.B. Williams (Eds.), *Handbook of stress reactivity and cardiovascular disease* (pp. 365-384). New York: Wiley & Sons.

Engel, B.T., Glasgow, M.S., & Gaarder, K. (1983). Behavioral treatment of high blood pressure: III. Follow-up results and treatment recommendations. *Psychosomatic Medicine*, **45**(1), 23-29.

Gordon, T., Fisher, M., & Ripkinol, B.M. (1984). Some difficulties inherent in the interpretation of dietary data from free-living populations. *American Journal of Clinical Nutrition*, **39**, 152-156.

Haulek, R.J., & Feinlieb, M. (Eds.). (1979). *Proceedings of the Conference on the Decline in Coronary Heart Disease Mortality* (pp. 79-161). Bethesda, MD: National Institutes of Health.

Hofman, A., Walter, H.J., Connelly, P.A., & Vaughan, R.D. (1987). Blood pressure and physical fitness in children. *Hypertension*, **9**, 188-191.

Johnston, C., Pelham, W.E., & Murphy, H.A. (1985). Peer relationships in ADDH and normal children: A developmental analysis of peer and teacher ratings. *Journal of Abnormal Child Psychology*, **13**, 89-100.

Marx, G.R., Hicks, R.W., & Allen, H.D. (1987). Measurement of cardiac output and exercise factor by pulsed Doppler echocardiography during supine bicycle ergometry in normal young adolescent boys. *Journal of American College of Cardiology*, **10**, 430-434.

Newman, W.P., Freedman, D.S., Voors, A.W., Gard, P.D., Sprinivasan, S.R., Cresenta, J.L., Williamson, G.D., Webber, L.S., & Berenson, G.S.

(1986). Relation of serum lipoprotein levels and systolic blood pressure to early atherosclerosis. *New England Journal of Medicine*, **314**, 138-144.

Pelham, W.E., & Bender, M.E. (1982). Peer relationship in hyperactive children: Description and treatment. *Advances in Learning and Behavioral Disabilities*, **1**, 365-436.

Pollock, M.L. (1973). The quantification of endurance training programs. *Exercise and Sports Science Reviews*, 155-188.

Saris, W.H.M., Binkhorst, R.A., Cramwinckel, A.B., Van Waesberghe, F., & Vander Veen-Hegemans, A.M. (1980). The relationship between working performance daily physical activity, fatness, blood lipids, and nutrition in schoolchildren. In K. Berg & B.O. Eriksson (Eds.), *Children and exercise IX*, (pp. 166-174). Baltimore: University Park Press.

Strong, W.B., Spencer, D., Miller, M.D., & Salehbhai, M. (1978). The physical working capacity of normal black children. *American Journal Diseases in Children*, **132**, 2244.

Swanson, J.M., Nolan, W.J., & Pelham, W.E. (1981). *A parent-teacher rating scale for operationalizing DSM III symptoms of attention deficit disorder*. Unpublished manuscript, University of California–Irvine.

Treiber, F.A., Strong, W.B., Carr, T., & Levy, M., (1987). *Development of a parent rating scale of children's habitual physical activity*. Manuscript submitted for publication.

Weymans, M.L., Reybrouck, T.M., Stijns, H.J., & Knops, J. (1986). Influence of habitual levels of physical activity on the cardiorespiratory endurance capacity of children. In J. Rutenfranz, R. Mocellin, & F. Klimt (Eds.), *Children and exercise XII* (pp. 149-156). Champaign, IL: Human Kinetics.

Quantitative and Qualitative Aspects of Nutrition in Young, Talented Athletes

Agnes Marie J. van Erp-Baart
Rob A. Binkhorst
University of Nijmegen, Nijmegen, The Netherlands
Wim H.M. Saris
University of Limburg, Maastricht, The Netherlands

Increasing numbers of young athletes are involved in intensive training programs. The question of whether this is beneficial for the growing body remains unanswered. Saris and Brouns (1986) and Birrer and Levine (1987) have pointed out the concerns in nutrition with respect to athletic performance in young athletes. From the preventive point of view, the quantity and quality of nutrition have to be considered. It is for these reasons that part of a national survey in the Netherlands on nutritional habits of elite athletes dealt with the nutritional intake of young talented athletes.

In this survey, the following groups were investigated: male swimmers (SM), female swimmers (SF), male judokas (JM), female subtop gymnasts (GF), and female top gymnasts (TGF). They all trained at least 7 hr per week and competed in national and/or international competition. The SM, JM, and TGF participated in this study on request of their medical staff and coaches. The GF and SF participated in this study based on the findings of Peltenburg et al. (1984) that, despite the same age, girl swimmers are taller and heavier and have a higher percentage of body fat than female gymnasts. She concluded that nutrition might play a role in this phenomenon.

METHODS

Information on food data was obtained by a 7-day food diary. In advance, personal instructions were given on household measurements and the type of foods. Afterwards, if necessary, a telephone control was made to complete the information on amounts and types of foods.

The following anthropometric data were collected: body height, body mass (BM), body fat, and fat-free mass (FFM). Body fat was assessed by taking four skinfold measurements (biceps, triceps, subscapula, and suprailiaca) according to Durnin and Womersley (1974). FFM was calculated by subtracting fat mass from total BM. Table 1 contains the group means and standard deviations for these anthropometric data. For detailed information about the methods used, see van Erp-Baart, Saris, Binkhorst, Vos, and Elvers (1987).

Table 1 Anthropometric Data (Mean ± *SD*) of Young Athletes

	N	Age (yr)	Height (cm)	Body mass (kg)	Body fat (%)	Fatfree-mass (kg)
SM	20	18 ± 3	182.0 ± 16	72.9 ± 8.1	10.7 ± 3.3	66.0
JM	28	18 ± 1	175.6 ± 6.8	68.7 ± 10.0	9.7 ± 2.5	61.9 ± 8.0
SF	50	12 ± 2	155.0 ± 13.5	43.6 ± 11.1	21.4 ± 5.6	33.0 ± 7.5
GF	40	13 ± 1	150.3 ± 10.2	39.8 ± 11.1	16.0 ± 5.4	32.7 ± 7.6
TGF	11	15 ± 1	158.0 ± 7.0	46.9 ± 6.3	13.9 ± 2.7	40.3 ± 4.8

Note. SM = male swimming, JM = male judo, SF = female swimming, GF = female subtop gymnasts, TGF = female top gymnasts.

RESULTS

Unless otherwise stated, the food intake was without the use of vitamin and mineral supplements. To obtain objective criteria about the quality of the food intake, the Dutch Recommended Daily Allowances (DRDA) for these groups were used (Voedingsraad, 1986). If the intake was less than 80% of the DRDA, then the intakes of at least some individuals within the group were considered insufficient. (Waterlow, 1979).

Energy Intake

In Table 2 the mean total energy intake and the mean energy intake per kilogram BM and in terms of basal metabolic rate (BMR) units are presented. Absolute values show a higher energy intake for boys than for girls. The World Health Organization (WHO)/Food and Agricultural Organization (FAO) standard for young adolescents who are involved in intensive physical work is 2.2 BMR for girls and 2.5 BMR for boys (WHO/FAO/UN, 1985). The DRDA is 200 kJ • kg BM^{-1}. Compared with the recommendations of the WHO/FAO, the energy intake for all the regularly training athletes was low. If comparisons are made with the DRDA energy intake for SM, SF and FG was the same, whereas it was low for the JM and TGF groups.

Table 2 Energy, Protein, and Carbohydrate Intakes (Mean, Mean ± *SD*) of Young Athletes

	SM*	JM	SF	GF	TGF
Energy (MJ**)	16.0 ± 3.1	12.1 ± 3.4	8.7 ± 2.1	7.9 ± 1.4	7.3 ± 1.6
Energy (kJ • kg BM^{-1})	221	177 ± 54	200 ± 49	206 ± 58	158 ± 42
Energy (BMR units)	2.0	1.6	1.6	1.5	1.3
Protein (g • kg BM^{-1})	1.9	1.4	1.5	1.2	1.7
Carbohydrate (En%)	49 ± 9	50 ± 14	51 ± 13	52 ± 10	54 ± 12

*Legends as indicated for Table 1. **1 MJ = 238 kCal.

Protein and Carbohydrate

Mean nutrient intake is also given in Table 2. The DRDA for protein was 1.2 g • kg BM^{-1} for girls and 1.5 g • kg BM^{-1} for boys. Compared with these recommendations, protein intake was low in JM. For carbohydrate (CHO) a daily intake of at least 55 energy percent (En %) is recommended. Only the intake of TGF approximates this recommendation; the other group means were lower.

Minerals and Vitamins

Figures 1 and 2 present the mineral and vitamin intake of all athletes. Figure 1 compares mineral intake (calcium and iron) with the DRDA (for calcium 1,200 mg/day, for iron 15 mg/day). Figure 2 presents vitamin intake including vitamin supplements and makes comparisons with the DRDA (for vitamin A, 0.85 mg/day; for vitamin B_1, 0.4 mg/4.2 MJ/day; for vitamin B_2, 0.025 mg/g protein/day; and for vitamin B_6, 1.6 mg/day for females and 2 mg/day for males, and for vitamin C 70 mg/day).

Mineral intake, calcium as well as iron, was low for all female athletes. Vitamin A intake was low in GF and TGF, and vitamin B_6 was low in GF and TGF. With respect to the vitamin supplementation, it was surprising to see that the only group, SM, whose vitamin intake in general was more than sufficient, took vitamin supplements.

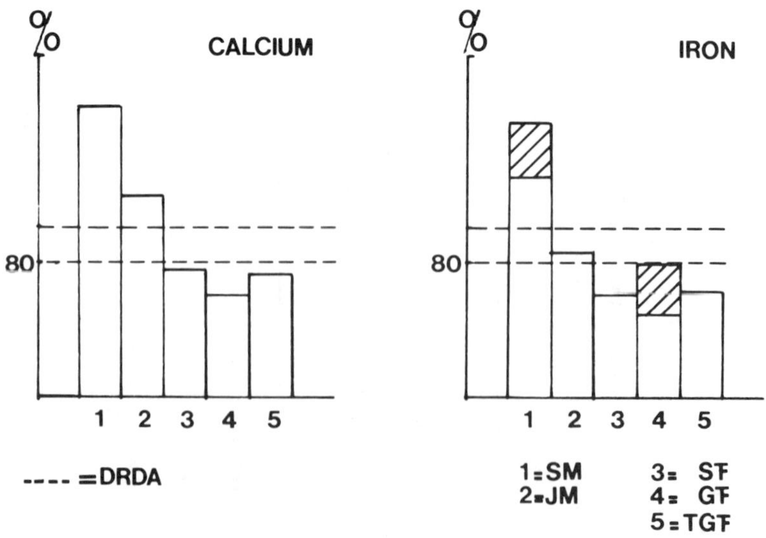

Figure 1. Calcium and iron intake of young athletes (see legend to Table 1).

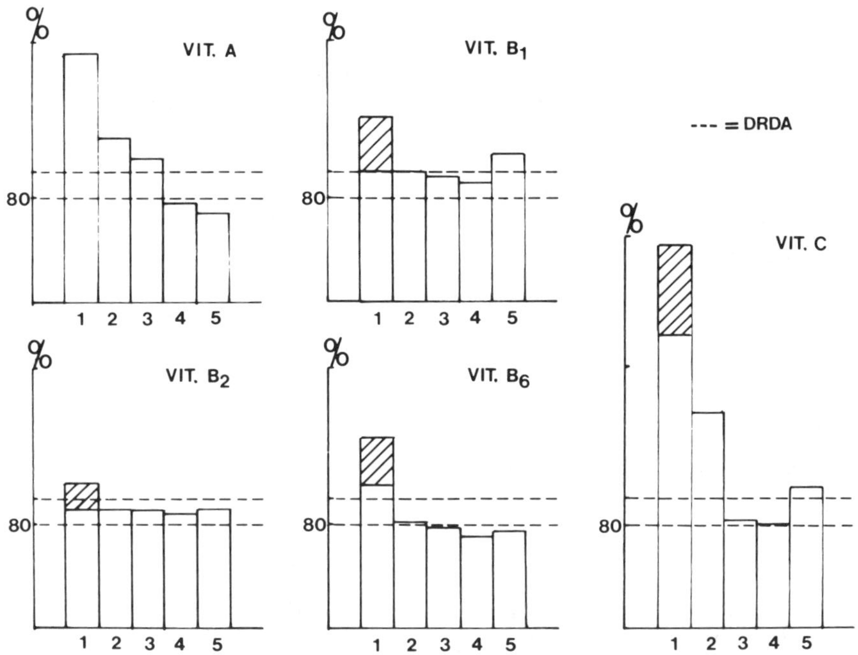

Figure 2. Vitamin intake in young athletes (see legend to Table 1).

Contribution of Foodstuffs to Energy Intake

Table 3 presents the contribution of the most important foods to energy intake. Contributions of less than 2% are not presented. Bread, margarine, and milk are the most important energy sources. It is striking that in general the same foods are chosen by all groups of athletes.

DISCUSSION

Energy Intake

Low energy intake is one of the major nutritional concerns due to weight classes and body shape. Table 1 gives the energy intakes in BMR units. It was surprising to see that no group satisfied the recommendations. The TGF had the lowest energy intake. The energy expenditure for this group was investigated, the results of which were reported elsewhere. It was concluded that although energy intake was low, only a few had inadequate energy intake (van Erp-Baart et al., 1985). Some of the girls were constantly aware of their body image. In the JM group, 10 of the 28 boys reported that they followed a weight-reducing diet to compete in certain weight classes.

Table 3 Contribution (%) of Foods to Energy Intake in Young Athletes

Food	Percent contribution				
	SM	JM	SF	GF	TGF
Bread (white meal)	8.4	7.9	10.4	7.0	12.3
Bread (white, rolls)	2.4	6.7	5.9	7.5	
Margarine, butter	9.9	7.2	6.0	5.4	5.9
Milk, milk products	13.5	9.4	9.6	3.1	6.7
Sugar, soft drinks	4.3	7.1	5.5	7.9	2.9
Cheese	3.6	3.1	2.7	2.7	2.0
Potatoes	2.4	3.8	3.5	3.9	2.9
French fries	2.3	2.1	3.1	4.0	
Apples					2.9

With respect to the female subtop gymnasts (GF), the urge to be concerned about a certain body image seemed to be less present. Furthermore, it was surprising to find that the energy intake for intensive-training athletes did not exceed the recommended energy intake for young adolescents who are not training intensively (1.5 and 1.6 BMR for girls and boys, respectively). Schneider, Zerbes, Götte, Wendelin, and Kühne (1980) found the same situation in their young athletes involved in the biathlon. They concluded that because no problems were found in body weight and body composition, the recommendations are in general too high. Another explanation might be that children not involved in elite sport engage in physical activity and expend the same amount of energy.

Intake of Protein and Carbohydrate

In endurance training, the glycogen content of the muscle is important for the duration of the exercise. At least 70% of the energy intake must be derived from CHO sources to replenish the muscle with glycogen (Costill & Miller, 1980). It also has been reported that glycogen is used in training for explosive sports (Jacobs, Westlin, Karlsson, Rasmusson, & Houghton, 1983). None of the groups met this criterion of a carbohydrate-rich diet. This can be explained partly by the lack of awareness that in these types of sports, glycogen storage before exercise is necessary. On the other hand, the levels found were higher than the CHO intake of a comparative group of adolescents not participating in sport activities (Kemper et al., 1983).

For protein, the recommendations for adolescents are 1.2 to 1.5 g • kg BM^{-1}. From the results of this study it can be concluded that protein intake was in accordance with the recommendations. However, the question often arises whether there exists an increased need for protein in these groups. Only in East Germany (GDR) Schneider et al. (1980) recommended a protein intake of at least 2.0 g per kg body weight. However, a scientific basis for these recommendations was not given. A possible explanation can be the higher level of fat-free mass that is found in this group of intensive-training athletes compared with their peers who are not physically active (Kemper et al., 1983; Peltenburg, 1984). On the other hand, Butterfield and Calloway (1984) have found a better protein utilization in young physically active men than in men who are not active. This might imply that an increase in protein intake in young athletes is not necessary. However, energy intake must be adequate (Todd, Butterfield, & Calloway, 1984).

Calcium and Iron Intake

Calcium intake was found to be lower than the DRDA in the female athletes. Recently the need for calcium has been stressed, especially in athletes who are amenorrheic (Nelson et al., 1986). It is well known that in top gymnasts this is a common condition (Loucks & Horvath, 1985). In the present group of top gymnasts only one girl had just had her first menstruation.

From regression analysis derived from calcium intake in the survey including all sport groups (van Erp-Baart et al., 1987), it was determined that at least 10 MJ per day must be eaten to get an intake of 1,200 mg calcium per day. This energy intake is greater than the intakes of the SF, GF, and TGF groups. Supplementation of calcium for young female athletes with amenorrhea should be considered.

The same results were found for iron intake. Due to the fact that energy intake was low, iron intake was low in all female athletes. From the regression analysis in the national survey (van Erp-Baart et al., 1987) it was reported that an energy intake of at least 10 MJ is needed to have an iron intake of 15 mg daily. Whether a lower intake will lead to iron deficient anemia is questionable. As already mentioned, the young female gymnasts have often a delayed menarche, and therefore, the risk is reduced.

Intake of Vitamins

With respect to vitamin intake, only vitamin A in GF and TGF and vitamin B6 in SF and TGF was low. It is assumed that with proper food choices part of the problem could be solved. A low margarine intake can cause low vitamin A intake. In the Netherlands margarine is enriched with vitamin A. In gymnasts, margarine is often avoided because of the fat content. Van der Beek (1985) has reviewed the need for vitamins in relation to athletic performance. He concluded that the intake must meet the recommendations, but higher intake does not increase athletic performance.

The use of vitamin supplements in SM can be considered as a good example of the difference between facts (low intake) and fiction (belief). In contrast with athletes in the United States (Loosli, Benson, Gilien, & Boudet, 1986; Parr, Porter & Hodgon, 1984), the use of vitamin supplements was not frequent, except in SM.

CONCLUSION

The food intake of young talented athletes is in general better than their nonphysically active peers. In judo and gymnastics weight-reducing diets are often used. If energy intake is lower than 10 MJ per day, mineral intake should be considered. Vitamin supplementation is not needed. Low vitamin intake can be alleviated by proper food choices.

REFERENCES

Beek, E.J. van der (1985). Vitamins and endurance training. Food for running and faddism claims. *Sports Medicine*, **2**, 175-197.

Birrer, R.B., & Levine, R. (1987). Performance parameters in children and adolescent athletes. *Sports Medicine*, **4**, 211-227.

Butterfield, G.E., & Calloway, P. (1984). Physical activity improves protein utilisation in young men. *British Journal of Nutrition*, **51**, 171-184.

Costill, D.L., & Miller, J.M. (1980). Nutrition for endurance sport: Carbohydrate and fluid balance. *International Journal of Sports Medicine*, **1**, 2-14.

Durnin, J.V.G.A., & Womersley, J. (1974). Body fat assessed from total body density and its estimation from skinfold thickness: Measurements of 481 men and women aged 16 to 72 years. *British Journal of Nutrition*, **32**, 77-97.

Erp-Baart, A.M.J. van, Fredrix, L.W.H.M., Binkhorst, R.A., Lavaleye, T.C.L., Vergouwen, P.C.J., & Saris, W.H.M. (1985). Energy intake and energy expenditure in top female gymnasts. In R.A. Binkhorst, H.G.C. Kemper, & W.H.M. Saris (Eds.), *Children and exercise XI* (pp. 218-233). Champaign: IL: Human Kinetics.

Erp-Baart, A.M.J. van, Saris, W.H.M., Binkhorst, R.A., Vos, J.A., & Elvers, J.W.H. (1987). *National survey on nutritional habits in elite athletes: Part 2. Mineral and vitamin intake*. Unpublished manuscript.

Jacobs, I., Westlin, N., Karlsson, J., Rasmusson, M., & Houghton, B. (1982). Muscle glycogen and diet in elite soccer players. *European Journal of Applied Physiology*, **48**, 297-302.

Kemper, H.C.G., Dekker, H., Ootjers, G., Post, B., Ritmeester, J.W., Snel, J., Splinter, P., Storm-van Essen, L., & Verschuur, R. (1983). *Growth and health of teenagers*. Unpublished manuscript, University of Amsterdam, The Netherlands.

Loosli, A.R., Benson, J., Gilien, D.M., & Boudet, S.U. (1986). Nutrition habits and knowledge in competitive adolescent female gymnasts. *The Physician and Sportsmedicine*, **14**(8), 118-130.

Loucks, A.B., & Horvath, S.M. (1985). Athletic amenorrhea: A review. *Medicine and Science in Sports and Exercise*, **17**, 56-72.

Nelson, M.E., Fischer, E., Catsos, P.D., Meredith, C.N., Turksoy, R.N., & Evans, W.J. (1986). Diet and bone status in amenorrheic runners. *American Journal of Clinical Nutrition*, **43**, 910-916.

Parr, R.B., Porter, M.A., & Hodgon, S.C. (1984). Nutrition knowledge and practice of coaches, trainers and athletes. *The Physician and Sportsmedicine*, **12**, 127-138.

Peltenburg, A.L., Erich, W.B.M., Bernink, M.J.E., Zonderland, M.L., & Huisveld, J.A. (1984). Biological maturation, body composition and growth of female gymnasts, and control groups of school girls and girl swimmers, aged 8 to 14 years: A cross-sectional survey of 1,064 girls. *International Journal of Sports Medicine*, **5**, 36-42.

Saris, W.H.M., & Brouns, F. (1986). Nutritional concerns for the young athlete. In J. Rutenfranz, R. Mocellin, & F. Klimt (Eds.), *Children and exercise XII* (pp. 11-19). Champaign, IL: Human Kinetics.

Schneider, F., Zerbes, H., Götte, H-Chr, Wendelin, T., & Kühne, H. (1980). Untersuchungen zur Ernährungssituation jugendlicher Sportler [Dietary situation of young athletes]. *Medizin und Sport*, **20**(7), 213-217.

Todd, K.S., Butterfield, G.A., & Calloway, D.H. (1984). Nitrogen balance in men with adequate and deficient energy intake at three levels of work. *Journal of Nutrition*, **114**(11), 2107-2119.

Voedingsraad. (1986). *Recommended daily allowances for energy and nutrients*. The Hague: Dutch Nutrition Board.

Waterlow, J.C. (1979). Uses of recommended intakes. *Food Policy*, **4**, 107.

World Health Organization/Food and Agricultural Organization/United Nations Expert Consultation. (1985). *Energy and protein requirements* (Technical Rep. Series No. 724). Geneva: WHO.

School Sport as a Motivational Determinant for Lifetime Sport Participation

Inge Berndt
Gudrun Schmidt
Monika Werpup
University of Bielefeld, Bielefeld, West Germany

Sport activities may reduce movement deficits and improve the physical performance capacity of children. Therefore, school sport should stimulate sport activities in order to reduce bad movement patterns, poor performance capacity, and impaired health (Bar-Or, 1983). School sport should be especially centered on children with low physical performance capacity who have limited sport interests.

In reality, however, this does not always seem to happen. Time budget studies reveal that children differing in physical performance capacity also often differ in their patterns of physical activities, especially in sport activities of high intensity (Rutenfranz, Berndt, & Knauth, 1974). Additionally, it has been shown in longitudinal studies that postpubertal boys who regularly engaged in sports did not increase their physical performance capacity during adolescence relatively more than those not engaged in sports, but started at the same age on a higher level than the inactive group (Rutenfranz & Singer, 1980). Children interested and active in sports seem to be a self-selected group, gifted with a high physical performance capacity that may be mainly genetically determined.

Because of their high physical performance capacity, many of these children are attracted by physical exercise and therefore are motivated to participate in sports. The opposite is often true for adolescents with low physical performance capacity. Because motivation for continued participation in sport activities in later life has often been mentioned as a main goal of school sport, and because teachers should motivate children to participate in lessons of physical education and sports, it seems to be of interest to study motivational determinants for sport activities in a group of adolescents. This age may be of special interest because the observed tendency to decrease physical activities in the transition period from school to work may lead to health problems in later life (Ilmarinen & Rutenfranz, 1980). Therefore, teachers should stimulate their pupils not only to learn special sport activities but also to continue their physical activities after they leave school.

The questions then arise, how does motivation occur, and in what manner does an individual develop an incentive to participate in sport activities? According to the attributional theory of achievement motivation (Weiner, 1985), it is assumed that individuals primarily utilize four causal elements to ascribe outcomes in achievement-related situations. These perceived causal determinants of achievement-related outcomes are ability, effort, task difficulty, and luck, which may be classified according to the degree of stability and the locus of control (see Table 1).

Table 1 Classification Scheme for the Perceived Determinants of Achievement Behavior

Stability	Locus of control	
	Internal	External
Stable	Ability	Task difficulty
Unstable	Effort	Luck

Note. From *Perceiving the Causes of Success and Failure* by B. Weiner et al., 1971, Morristown, NJ: General Learning Press. Copyright 1971 by General Learning. Reprinted by permission.

The causal attribution of success and failure on these perceived determinants may later influence an individual's motivation to be active in similar situations. Therefore, such perceived determinants are leading cognitions for achievement motivation needed for all sport activities.

Based on this theoretical model, Meyer (1984) pointed out that individual factors, for example, self-concept of ability and fear of consequences are related to certain patterns of causal attribution and, as a consequence, the causal attributions may influence and stabilize the self-concept of ability. For this reason there may exist a positive or negative self-reinforcement cycle, a self-concept of ability, causal attribution of failure or success, and the tendency to be active or not active in achievement-related situations, as for example, sport activities. These assumptions were tested by an experimental teaching lesson under field conditions.

EXPERIMENTAL DESIGN

Achievement situations in sport lessons can be simulated by team sport activities, and these activities are often considered the most adequate measure to stimulate sport interests and attitudes. Volleyball was therefore selected as the paradigm. The experiment was designed as a field study and took place in an actual school sport situation. Two classes from the upper grades of a grammar school in Bielefeld took part in a volleyball tournament at the end of a teaching unit lasting for several weeks.

METHODS

Before the tournament and during the periods between games, the subjects were asked questions dealing with different motivational items on analog visual scales (Likert scale). The subjects' answers allowed the investigation of the relations between the self-concept of own abilities, fear of consequences, and causal attribution of success and failure on the four perceived determinants previously mentioned. This should be used as an explanatory approach to the subjective decisions of adolescents to be active or not active in school sport situations (Kelley & Michela, 1980).

The contents of the volleyball questionnaire included related items concerning the following factors:

1. Concept of own ability (Meyer, 1984);
2. Attributions related to the individual and the team (Willimczik, Rethorst, & Riebel, 1986), for example, internal factors (ability vs. effort) and external factors (task difficulty vs. luck) in accordance with Weiner et al. (1971) and Kelley and Michela (1980);
3. Fear of consequences.

SUBJECTS

The experimental sample included 16 female and 33 male adolescents, aged 17 to 19 years, belonging to the 12th form of a grammar school (Gymnasium). The students, taught by faculty of the University of Bielefeld, had for several weeks participated in volleyball classes given by experienced teachers and students.

DATA ANALYSIS

The data were analyzed by using appropriate statistical techniques like student *t* tests and analysis of variance (ANOVA).

RESULTS

The study focused on the relationship between the behavior of the teacher and the reactions of the pupils. This article, however, only addresses the motivational determinants reflected by the adolescents.

As can be seen from Table 2, there were clear differences in perceived causes of success or failure between subjects with high or low self-concepts of abilities. In the case of success, students with a self-concept of high ability showed a stronger tendency to attribute their own success to their ability than students with a low self-concept. On the contrary, in the case of failure, students with a low self-concept of ability attributed this outcome more strongly to their own ability than did people with a high self-concept. The effects of the situational outcomes and the self-concept of ability on this attributions could not be detected. Adolescents with a high self-concept ascribed their success during the game to a significantly higher degree ($p \leqslant .05$) to their own abilities than their classmates with a lower self-concept.

Table 2 Differences in the Causal Attribution of Success or Failure in Subjects With Different Self-Concepts

	Attribution on individual abilities							
	Success				Failure			
	$\overline{X}$	*S*	*t* value	*p*	$\overline{X}$	*S*	*t* value	*p*
Concept high	1.33 (10)	0.89			0.27 (12)	0.65		
			−3.09	.05			2.19	.41
Concept low	0.42 (12)	0.52			1.00 (10)	0.89		

The same was principally true for the opposite condition. Failures during the game were more ascribed to a lack of abilities by subjects with a low self-concept than by subjects with a high self-concept, but this tendency was not statistically significant.

These results indicate that both the self-concept of ability as a personal precondition and the result of the sports game as a characteristic of the situation influence important cognitions of an individual and may motivate him or her to be more active in team sports.

This will be more clarified by testing the relationship between the causal attribution of failures during the game to the effort of the team and the different potentials for fear of social consequences (Table 3). Adolescents who fear social consequences tend to ascribe failure in a lower degree to a lack of team effort than their less anxious classmates. This tendency, however, was not statistically significant ($p \geqslant .21$).

Because in both attributions two factors are included, the main effects and interaction effects were tested by a two-way analysis of variance (ANOVA). As can be seen from Table 4, a significant interaction ($p \leqslant .02$) existed between the conditional factors (low vs. high self-concept) and the situational factors (success or failure) on the attribution to individual abilities.

The same was true for the emotional area. Using ANOVA, a significant interaction effect ($p \leqslant .005$) was found between low versus high perceived fear of social consequences and the attribution of failure or success to team effort. After success and failure, people with high versus low fear of social consequences differed with respect to their attributions on the internal factor of team effort (Table 4). Subjects with a high potential for fear of social consequences attributed their failures not to team effort, but ascribed their success to the self-concept factor.

Table 3 Differences in the Causal Attribution of Failures on Team Effort in Subjects With Different Potentials of Fear of Social Consequences

	Attribution on team effort of failure			
	M	*S*	*t* value	*p*
FOSC high	0.50 (11)	0.67		
			2.61	0.21
FOSC low	1.73 (12)	1.42		

Note. FOSC = fear of social consequences.

DISCUSSION

These results demonstrate that subjects have cognitions from lessons in physical education that can be described as perceived causes of achievement results. These perceived causes are related to personal dispositions such as self-concept of abilities, to the individual internal area, and to social aspects of the school sport lessons (the effort of the team).

Taking into account that, according to the theoretical concepts of motivation (Weiner, 1985), certain patterns of causal attribution may stabilize high or low self-concepts of ability and influence, therefore, the motivation to be active in subsequent similar situations. It is assumed that by this way a negative reinforcement of motivation for sport activities for several subjects must be feasible. Therefore, adolescents who believe that failures are mostly caused by a lack of their own abilities will miss the motivation to act again in achievement-related situations like team sports. Therefore, they will become more and more frustrated in such activities and they may avoid this activity for the remainder of their lives. As a consequence, they will never acquire the needed abilities for performing successfully during team sport games, and they will never be able to build up an adequate self-concept in the area of sports that may reinforce the needed positive motivation for lifetime sport participation.

Table 4 Causal Attributions on Individual Abilities and Team Effort in Dependence on Success/Failure Outcomes, the Self-Concept of Ability, and the Fear of Social Consequences

	Self-concept of ability					Fear of social consequences			
	Low		High			Low		High	
Outcomes	Success	Failure	Success	Failure	Outcomes	Success	Failure	Success	Failure
Attributions on individual abilities	0.42	0.90	1.30	0.25	Attributions on team effort	2.45	1.67	3.25	0.45
	(12)	(10)	(10)	(12)		(11)	(12)	(12)	(11)
ANOVA results	self-concept of ability		$p = .608$		ANOVA results	fear of social consequences		$p = .538$	
	outcomes		$p = .216$			outcomes		$p = .000$	
	interaction		$p = .002$			interaction		$p = .005$	

PRACTICAL CONSEQUENCES

The results indicate that team games in school sport lessons with the context of competition and social comparison are not a meaningful approach for stimulating sport interests in adolescents. Especially for subjects with a low self-concept of their abilities, team games such as volleyball seldom present situations in which abilities can be improved, in which self-initiated success can be perceived, and in which a stable positive concept of abilities can be developed.

For those adolescents with low self-concepts of their abilities, it would be better to train in situations that gave them opportunities for individual success. This should help them gather step-by-step positive movement experiences that may lead such persons to be more active in movement and sport.

REFERENCES

Bar-Or, O. (1983). *Pediatric sports medicine for the practitioner. From physiologic principles to clinical applications*. New York: Springer-Verlag.

Ilmarinen, J., & Rutenfranz, J. (1980). Longitudinal studies of the changes in habitual physical activity of schoolchildren and working adolescents. In K. Berg & B.O. Eriksson (Eds.), *Children and exercise IX* (pp. 149-159). Baltimore: University Park Press.

Kelley, H.H., & Michela, J.L. (1980). Attribution theory and research. *Annual Review of Psychology*, **31**, 457-501.

Meyer, W.U. (1984). *Das Konzept von der eigenen Begabung*. Bern: Huber.

Rutenfranz, J., Berndt, I., & Knauth, P. (1974). Daily physical activity investigated by time budget studies and physical performance capacity of school boys. *Acta Paediatrica Belgica*, **28**(Suppl.), 79-86.

Rutenfranz, J., & Singer, R. (1980). The influence of sport activity on the development of physical performance capacities of 15- to 17-year-old boys. In K. Berg & B.O. Eriksson (Eds.), *Children and exercise IX*, (pp. 160-165). Baltimore: University Park Press.

Weiner, B. (1985). An attributional theory of achievement motivation and emotion. *Psychological Reviews*, **92**, 548-573.

Weiner, B., Frieze, I.H., Kukla, A., Reed, L., Rest, S., & Rosenbaum, R.M. (1971). *Perceiving the causes of success and failure*. Morristown, NJ: General Learning.

Willimczik, K., Rethorst, S., & Riebel, H. (1986). Cognitions and emotions in sport games—a cross-cultural comparative analysis. *International Journal of Physical Education*, **23**(1), 10-16, **23**(2), 23-30.

Time Budgets of Working Adolescents Aged 17 to 21 Years

Juhani Ilmarinen
Institute of Occupational Health, Helsinki, Finland

Peter Knauth
University of Karlsruhe, Karlsruhe, Federal Republic of Germany

Joseph Rutenfranz
Institute of Occupational Health, Dortmund, Federal Republic of Germany

Previous studies have indicated that a dramatic decrease in daily physical activity occurred when schoolchildren graduated from school and joined the work force (Ilmarinen & Rutenfranz, 1980). Those adolescents who were serving time as apprentices and who were physically more active (e.g., aerobic sport) in their leisure time had superior health indicators and $\dot{V}O_2max$ when compared with less active apprentices (Ilmarinen et al., 1986). So, daily activities seemed to play an important role with regard to health, especially after the school years had been completed. In order to provide for a healthy lifestyle, it is necessary to know which leisure time activities have the highest priorities among working adolescents. The object of this investigation was to evaluate the time budgets of young workers during both workdays and weekends.

METHODS

A total of 77 male apprentices (aged 17 to 21 years) who worked in the electro-industry (Siemens, Berlin) completed 8-day diaries (see Table 1) that included the duration of working time, time in school, traveling time, sleeping time, homework, household work, voluntary activities, leisure time indoors and outdoors (e.g., taking a walk), sport, and watching television (Rutenfranz, Berndt, & Knauth, 1974). The diary entries for weekdays, Monday to Thursday, were combined and analyzed together (a total of 308 days) and compared with entries for Fridays (77 days), Saturdays (72 days), and Sundays (70 days). School activities, which did not occur every day (e.g., toolmakers had school on different days from electricians), were summed up for Mondays to Thursdays, while holidays, days of sick leave, and imperfect diaries were excluded from the analysis (a total of 12 days out of 616 days, 1.9%).

Table 1 Example of the Diary Used in the Study

Monday, 19.01.87				
1. Waking up	at	______		
2. Traveling time	from	______	to	______
3. Working time	from	______	to	______
4. School	from	______	to	______
5. Homework	from	______	to	______
6. Voluntary lessons	from	______	to	______
7. Household/job	from	______	to	______
8. Leisure time				
indoors	from	______	to	______
	from	______	to	______
outdoors	from	______	to	______
	from	______	to	______
9. Sports	from	______	to	______
	from	______	to	______
10. Walk	from	______	to	______
11. Television	from	______	to	______
	from	______	to	______
	from	______	to	______
12. Bedtime	at	______		

RESULTS

Working days from Monday to Thursday were characterized by waking up early (on 80% of the days the subjects awoke before 6:00 a.m.), traveling to work from 6:00 to 7:00 a.m., and working from 7:00 a.m. to 4:00 p.m. School activities took place between 7:00 a.m. and 2:00 p.m. on the different days and occupied apparently by this mode of data treatment about 20% of the time from 7:00 a.m. to 4:00 p.m. (see Figure 1). The proportions of leisure time indoors and outdoors between 5:00 and 10:00 p.m. were similar (both about 20%), and sport activities, which occurred between 6:00 and 8:00 p.m., occupied about 10% of the time. Much more pronounced were the hours spent watching television, which covered the time span from 8:00 to 10:00 p.m. and occupied about 30% of the leisure time. About 60% of the subjects were in bed by 10:00 p.m.

The time on Fridays was spent differently from that of Monday to Thursday. Outdoor leisure time shifted to the evening, indicating that about 30% of time between 8:00 p.m. and midnight was allocated for outdoor activities. Sport activities were somewhat more prevalent (about 20%) on Fridays than on the other weekdays and took place between 6:00 p.m.

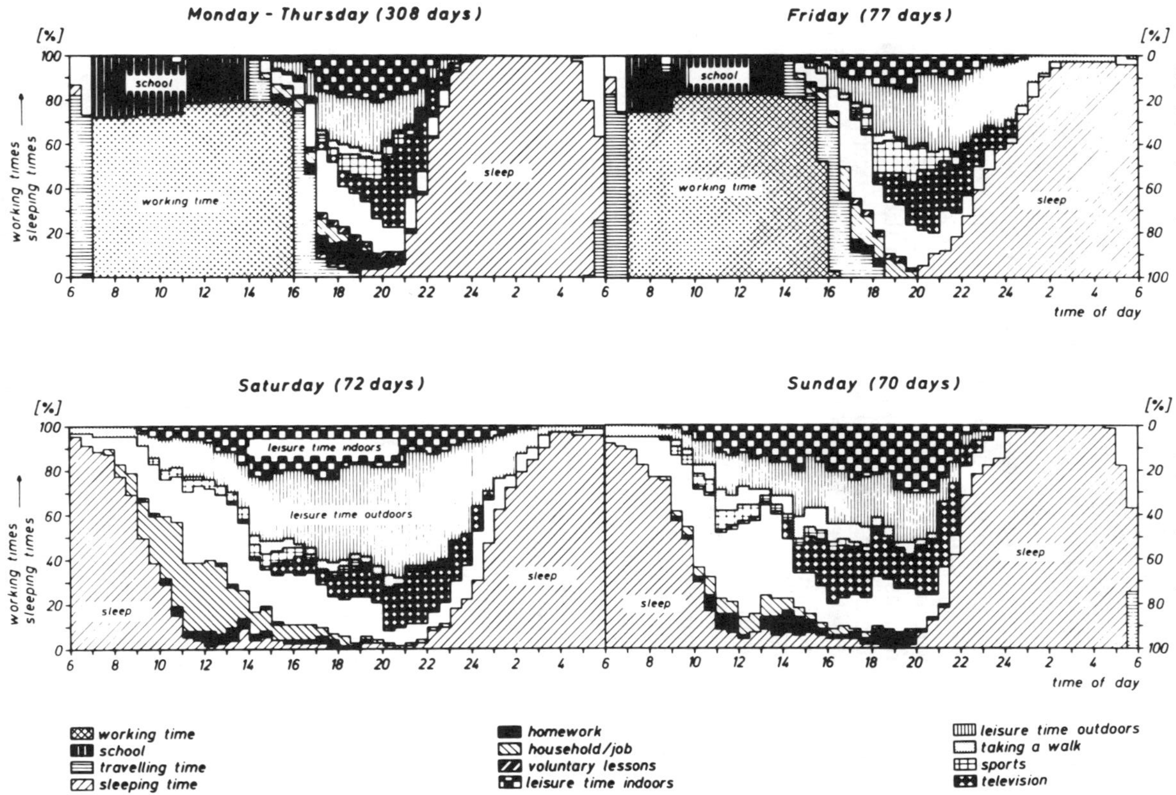

Figure 1. Relative frequency and timing of different activities from Monday to Sunday. Percentage of observation days represented on the ordinate.

and 9:00 p.m. The TV activities shifted to the right on Figure 1 and covered about 10% of the time after 11:00 p.m. About 50% of the subjects were sleeping by midnight, but some did not wake up before noon the next day.

Saturday was therefore characterized by prolonged hours of sleep in the morning (70% were still sleeping at 9:00 a.m.), by household activities, and by a large proportion of leisure time outdoors. About 40% of the time was spent in outdoor activities between 5:00 and 11:00 p.m. Watching television occupied the hours from 6:00 to 8:00 p.m. and represented about 20% of the time during that period and about 30% of the time between 8:00 and 11:00 p.m. About 60% of the subjects were sleeping by 1:00 a.m. Sport activities were prevalent between 10:00 a.m. and 5:00 p.m. and represented a small portion of leisure time available.

Sunday differed from Saturday and was characterized by fewer household activities, more indoor leisure time, and less outdoor leisure time even though there was more walking, more TV in the afternoon, and earlier bedtime in the evening. Indoor leisure time plus TV occupied about 40 to 50% of the time between 3:00 and 10:00 p.m.; outdoor leisure time covered about 20% of the time with walking taking 5 to 10% of the total time between 11:00 a.m. and 9:00 p.m. Television watching took 20 to 30% of the afternoon and evening hours between 2:00 and 10:00 p.m. Over 60% of the subjects were sleeping by 10:00 p.m. (see Figure 1).

The number of minutes spent in different activities indicated that the average sleeping time was longer on Friday (including sleep on Saturday morning: 548 min) than on Monday to Thursday (441 min). The number of minutes spent in homework and in household and voluntary activities were few, and on Saturdays household activities were most prevalent (81 min) (see Table 2).

Table 2 Mean Number of Minutes Spent in Different Activities During Mondays-Thursdays, Fridays, Saturdays, and Sundays

Activity	Mon-Thur (308 days) min	Fri (77 days) min	Sat (72 days) min	Sun (70 days) min
Working time	412	432	—	—
School	101	78	—	—
Traveling time	78	75	—	—
Sleeping time	441	548*	486**	418
Homework	18	3	12	23
Household/job	14	21	81	31
Voluntary lessons	8	5	1	—

*Includes sleep on Saturday morning. **Includes sleep on Sunday morning.

The number of minutes spent in indoor leisure time activities was greater on weekends than on weekdays and, especially, on Sundays (140 min). On the other hand, outdoor activities were mostly carried out on Saturdays (326 min). Taking a walk was more popular on Sundays than on other days. Sport activities did not vary much during the week: On workdays 19 to 30 min and during the weekend 25 to 26 min were spent participating in sports. Television interested the subjects most on Sundays (103 min).

DISCUSSION

These results indicated that work and school days (Monday-Thursday) had a clear impact on the time spent on leisure time activities. After work was completed on Friday, the need for outdoor leisure time was clearly seen: 140 min were spent outdoors on Fridays; the corresponding number was 69 min on Monday to Thursday. Another interesting trend was that Fridays were also the most active in terms of sport activities even though the number of minutes for sports was still lower than minutes occupied by television and indoor activities.

Weekend sport activities seemed to play only a minor role in the time budgets of 17- to 21-year-old apprentices. Indoor and outdoor activities as well as watching television occupied much more time than sports activities. A similar trend has also been reported in the time budgets of 11-year-old schoolboys (Rutenfranz, Berndt, & Knauth, 1974). Therefore, it is difficult to say whether the low level of sport activities after school was merely a continuation of the habits of 11- to 12-year-old individuals or if the main factor was the time spent in various occupational duties. There is some evidence that the change from school to work markedly decreased the time spent in sport activities (Ilmarinen & Rutenfranz, 1980). It seems more plausible to suggest that (a) occupational duties limit the motivation to spend time in sport activities; and (b) the more active a person is in sports during the school years, the larger the decrease in the level of sports activity after school has been completed.

The results reported here are generally supported by the number of minutes spent in sport activities and agree with the calculations from heart rate recordings of a smaller sample of these apprentices (Ilmarinen et al., 1986). The reported daily minutes for sports activities according to the time budget (from 19 to 30 min) and the measured minutes (about 19 min spent in activities higher than 5 METs) indicated, however, that the level of involvement in sport activities was lower than that needed to maintain good health for young workers.

REFERENCES

Ilmarinen, J., & Rutenfranz, J. (1980). Longitudinal studies of the changes in habitual physical activity of school children and working adolescents.

In K. Berg & B.O. Eriksson (Eds.), *Children and exercise IX* (pp. 149-159). Baltimore: University Park Press.

Ilmarinen, J., Rutenfranz, J., Kylian, H., Hussels, C., Klimmer, F., & Knauth, P. (1986). Daily physical activity and some health indicators in young workers. In J. Rutenfranz, R. Mocellin, & F. Klimt (Eds.), *Children and exercise XII* (pp. 131-139). Champaign, IL: Human Kinetics.

Rutenfranz, J., Berndt, I., & Knauth, P. (1974). Daily physical activity investigated by time budget studies and physical performance capacity of schoolboys. *Acta Paediatrica Belgica,* **28**(Suppl.), 79-86.

Part V

Exercise Physiology and Physical Activity After Surgical Correction of Congenital Heart Disease

The Clinical Value of Exercise Testing on Treadmill in Children After Surgical Correction of Congenital Heart Disease

Dirk M. Matthys
Gent State University, Gent, Belgium

The increasing number of children undergoing surgery for congenital heart disease (CHD) creates new problems concerning physical activities (Freed, 1984). Children with severe heart disease must be excluded from strenuous sports, but on the other hand, children with CHD must participate as much as possible in the activities of children of their own age. The aim of this study was to determine the clinical usefulness of exercise testing on the treadmill as a noninvasive test to evaluate the clinical fitness of postoperative children and so advise them on recreational and competitive sports. In addition, there is a lack of objective data concerning exercise testing in young normal children as well as in young heart patients.

METHODS

A total of 210 children (104 boys and 106 girls) aged 5 to 14 years (mean age 9 years) were studied after surgery for CHD. The time interval between the operation and exercise testing was at least 6 months. Normal values were obtained from 132 age-matched schoolchildren (70 boys and 62 girls).

Exercise tests were performed using the Bruce treadmill protocol (Cumming, Everatt, & Hastmann, 1978). This study included only patients undergoing total repair of CHD; palliative and prosthetic valve operations were not considered. The Bruce treadmill test is a continuous graded protocol with stepwise increases in speed and gradient at 3-min intervals from 2.7 to 6.7 km • hr^{-1} and from 10 to 20%. The goal is to reach the level of maximal voluntary effort until the subject is unable to continue. Heart rate, blood pressure, and the electrocardiogram are continuously monitored and recorded at the end of each stage, at the end of maximal exercise, and after 1, 2, 4, and 6 min of recovery.

Maximal endurance time (MET) was used as a criterion of exercise capacity in the present study. Comparisons between children of different ages and of either sex were possible by calculating the relative endurance time (RET), relative heart rate (RHR), and relative systolic blood pressure (RSBP), computed by subtracting the predicted from the observed value for each patient and dividing this difference by the standard deviation for that index in the normal group (Driscoll et al., 1984).

RESULTS

Exercise Performance

One may note in Table 1 that a mildly shorter MET was observed in children after surgical correction for CHD. The mean RET of all the patients was 0.77 *SD* below the predicted norm, significantly lower ($p < .001$) than the control group. The best results were obtained for the ostium secundum atrial septal defects (ASD II), ventricular septal defects (VSD), pulmonary stenosis (PS), and patent ductus arteriosus (PDA), followed by the coarctation of the aorta (COA) and tetralogy of Fallot (TOF). The worst results were from patients with ostium primum atrial septal defects (ASDI) and transposition of the great arteries (TGA). These data are plotted out in Figure 1.

Table 1 The Mean Relative Endurance Time (MRET) in Children After Surgical Correction of Congenital Heart Disease

Defect	Number	MRET	*SD*	*p*
VSD	53	−0.76	0.79	< .001
ASD II	48	−0.45	1.00	< .01
TOF	33	−0.88	0.92	< .001
COA	31	−0.82	0.86	< .001
TGA	16	−1.33	0.92	< .001
ASD I	11	−1.20	1.02	< .01
PDA	10	−0.75	0.59	< .01
PS	8	−0.49	0.54	< .05
All	210	−0.77	0.91	< .001

Note. SD = standard deviation, VSD = ventricular septal defect, ASD II = ostium secundum atrial septal defect, TOF = tetralogy of Fallot, COA = coarctation of the aorta, TGA = transposition of the great arteries, ASD I = ostium primum atrial septal defect, PDA = patent ductus arteriosus, PS = pulmonary stenosis.

Table 2 shows the percentage distribution of the patients according to the range of the standard deviation from the predicted endurance time. Almost half of the patients (46%) had a RET between O and −1 *SD* from the predicted normal value, and in about one quarter (26%) the perfor-

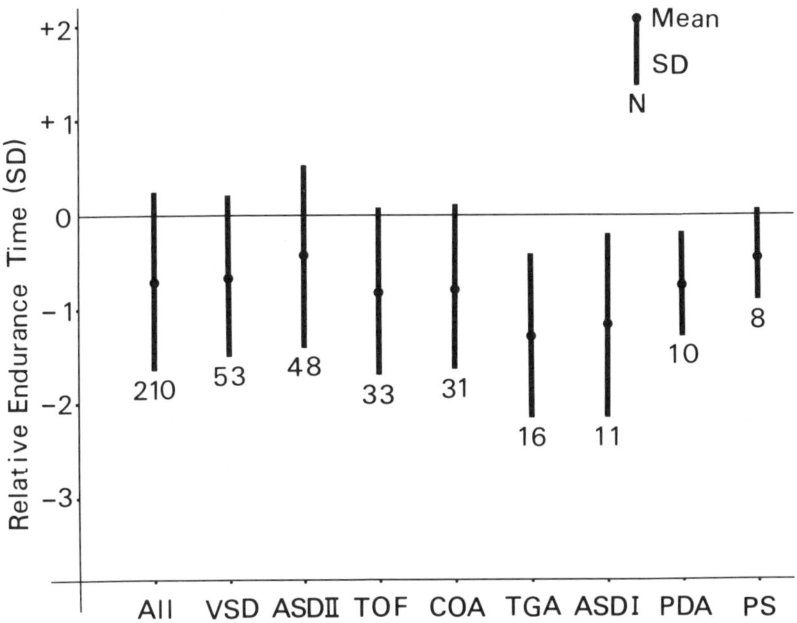

Figure 1. Standard deviations from predicted endurance time (relative endurance time) in all patients and in various subgroups. See footnote to Table 1.

mance was poor (between −1 and −2 *SD*). Almost 1 heart patient out of 10 had a very low exercise capacity (< −1 *SD*), four times more frequent than the 2.5% expected in a normal population. Eighteen percent of the children had a positive RET, that is, their performance was better than the mean of the control group of the same age. Here too, ASD II and VSD showed the best scores, with ASD I and TGA showing the worst. About one out of six patients in the TOF, TGA, and ASD I group had a very low exercise capacity (< −1 *SD*). No correlation was found between RET and patient's age at exercise testing, patient's age at operation, and interval between operation and exercise testing. In TOF group, however, a significant negative correlation ($p < .01$) was present between RET and right ventricular peak systolic and end-diastolic pressures (Figure 2) obtained by postoperative catheterization.

Heart Rate

At rest the mean heart rate of the patients was somewhat slower than the normals (MRHR − 0.31 ± 1.27; $p < .001$). At Stages 2 and 3, the submaximal level, the MRHR of the patients was identical to the heart rate of the normals; however, at maximal output, heart patients did not reach pulse rates as high as the control group. This was probably the result

Table 2 Standard Deviation Range From Predicted Endurance Time (Percent of Patients)

Defect	*N*	−4	−3	−2	−1	0	+1	+2	+3
VSD	53	0	5	24	47	19	4	0	
ASD II	48	2	4	23	48	19	2	2	
TOF	33	0	15	21	45	18	0	0	
COA	31	3	3	38	38	16	0	0	
TGA	16	6	12	37	37	6	0	0	
ASD I	11	0	18	36	36	9	0	0	
PDA	10	0	10	10	70	10	0	0	
PS	8	0	0	12	75	12	0	0	
All	210	1.4	7.6	26	46	16	1.4	0.5	

Note. See footnote to Table 1.

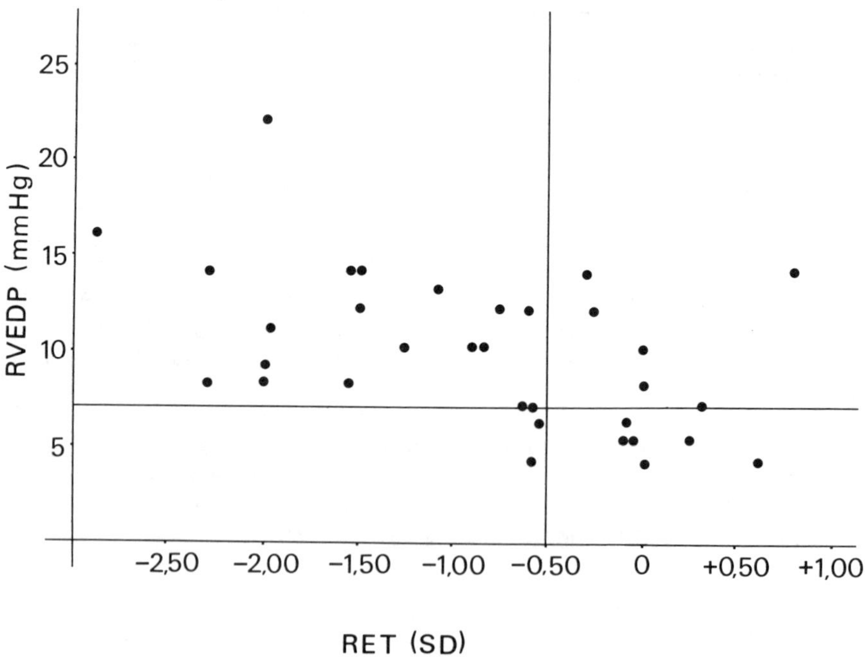

Figure 2. Right ventricular end-diastolic pressure (mmHg) obtained by postoperative catheterization versus relative endurance time (standard deviations from predicted endurance time) in children after surgical correction of tetralogy of Fallot. RVEDP = right ventricular end-diastolic pressure (post-operative catheterization), RET = relative endurance time.

of the shorter MET. It is interesting to note that at the submaximal level, most common in daily life, the mean heart rate of the operated patients was the same as the normals.

Systolic Blood Pressure

There was no difference between heart patients and controls at rest and at submaximal exercise in systolic blood pressure. Somewhat unexpectedly, there was a higher systolic blood pressure at the maximal level in heart patients (0.52 *SD*; $p < .001$). This was particularly the case in children after a correction of a left to right shunt.

Arrhythmia

Exercise-induced arrhythmia occurred mainly in patients with TOF: 36% had ventricular or supraventricular ectopic beats versus only 15% in the entire group of operated patients. The detection of arrhythmias in patients with TOF after surgical correction is extremely important. Ectopic beats at exercise not only may be associated with sudden death, but are also related to abnormal hemodynamic status and are an indication for further invasive investigations. In this study (Table 3) four patients had the combination of premature ventricular or atrial contractions with an increase in J point depression at maximal exercise. All of them showed a very low RET, with cardiomegaly on chest films and elevated right ventricular pressures in postoperative catheterization. One died suddenly and three required re-operation for right ventricular outflow tract obstruction or aneurysmal dilatation of the pericardial patch.

Table 3 Combination of Arrhythmia With J Point Depression at Maximal Exercise in Patients After Surgical Correction of Tetralogy of Fallot

RET (*SD*)	CTR	RVPSP (mmHg)	RVEDP (mmHg)	
1. −2.28	0.68	48	14	Sudden death
2. −2.0	0.56	104	22	Reoperation
3. −1.55	0.63	44	8	Reoperation
4. −1.23	0.60	42	10	Reoperation

Note. RET = Relative endurance time, SD = standard deviations, CTR = cardio-thoracic ratio, RVPSP = right ventricular peak systolic pressure (postoperative catheterization), RVEDP = right ventricular end diastolic pressure (postoperative catheterization).

DISCUSSION

This article describes the application of the Bruce treadmill protocol for exercise testing in children after surgical correction of congenital heart disease and confirms its suitability for the examination of children aged 5 years and older (Cumming et al., 1978). There is a lack of information concerning noninvasive exercise testing in young operated heart patients. The majority of studies have dealt with older patients (James, 1981) or with subgroups such as TOF (James et al., 1977; Mocellin, Bastanier, Hofacker, & Bühlmeyer, 1976; Wessel et al., 1980) and coarctation of the aorta (Freed, Rocchini, Rosenthal, Nadas, & Casteneda, 1979), where specific topics (arrhythmia, blood pressure profile) are considered.

In some studies, the patients operated on were only a minority (Cumming, 1978). The present data demonstrate that exercise testing provides important information regarding desirability of different degrees of physical activity in children after surgical correction of CHD (James, 1982). If the performance is poor, other investigations are necessary to rule out residual pathology. In this way it is possible to distinguish a poor performance due to a bad hemodynamic condition that requires medical treatment from a lack of exercise that, on the contrary, requires encouragement to participate in more physical activities.

In conclusion, from these results one can recommend no restrictions in recreational or competitive sports in children operated upon for VSD, ASD, PS, PDA, and COA with normal blood pressure profile and without associated lesions if the exercise test is normal. Only recreational activities should be advised for children with TGA, TOF, and COA with severe residual hypertension or associated lesions. Children operated upon for CHD must be encouraged to participate in athletic activities, competitive or recreational, according to the authorized level.

REFERENCES

Cumming, G. (1978). Maximal exercise capacity of children with heart defects. *American Journal of Cardiology*, **42**, 613-619.

Cumming, G., Everatt, D., & Hastmann, L. (1978). Normal values in a clinic population. *American Journal of Cardiology*, **41**, 69-75.

Driscoll, D., Staats, B., Heise, C., Rice, M., Puga, F., Danielson, K., & Ritter, D. (1984). Functional single ventricle: Cardiorespiratory response to exercise. *Journal of the American College of Cardiology*, **4**, 337-342.

Freed, M. (1984). Recreational and sports recommendations for the child with heart disease. *Pediatric Clinics of North America*, **31**, 1307-1320.

Freed, M., Rocchini, A., Rosenthal, A., Nadas, A., & Castaneda, A. (1979). Exercise induced hypertension after surgical repair of coarctation of the aorta. *American Journal of Cardiology*, **43**, 253-258.

James, F. (1981). Exercise testing in normal individuals and patients with cardiovascular disease. In M.A. Engle (Ed.), *Pediatric cardiovascular disease* (pp. 227-231). Philadelphia: Davis.

James, F. (1982). Standards for exercise testing in the pediatric age group. *Circulation*, **66**, 1377A-1397A.

James, F., Kaplan, S., Schwartz, D., Chou, T., Sandker, M., & Nayler, V. (1977). Response to exercise in patients after total surgical correction of tetralogy of Fallot. *Circulation*, **54**, 671-679.

Mocellin, R., Bastanier, G., Hofacker, W., & Bühlmeyer, K. (1976). Exercise performance in children and adolescents after surgical repair of tetralogy of Fallot. *European Journal of Cardiology*, **4**, 367-374.

Wessel, H., Cunningham, W., Paul, M., Bastanier, C., Huster, A., & Indriss, F. (1980). Exercise performance in tetralogy of Fallot after intracardiac repair. *Journal of Cardiovascular Surgery*, **80**, 582-593.

Respiratory Gas Exchange During Exercise After a Venous Switch Operation in Boys With Transposition of the Great Arteries

Tony M. Reybrouck
Lucas G. Van der Hauwaert
University of Leuven, Leuven, Belgium

In patients with transposition of the great arteries (TGA) the right ventricle has to cope with systemic pressures at rest and during exercise (Murphy et al., 1983; Ramsay, Venables, Kelly, & Kalff, 1984). As right ventricular dysfunction has frequently been documented in these patients (Benson et al., 1982; Parrisch et al., 1983), it may be questioned whether they have the same exercise capacity as their healthy peers. In children operated on for TGA, only limited information is available on maximal exercise performance, but to these writers' knowledge no data are available on gas exchange and ventilatory threshold during submaximal exercise in this patient group. The purpose of the present study was to measure respiratory gas exchange during graded submaximal exercise to assess cardiorespiratory endurance capacity.

METHODS

Patients

Nine boys with TGA were selected from a larger group of TGA patients to perform graded exercise on a treadmill after a venous switch operation. Children younger than 4 years and patients with overt sinoatrial dysfunction, hemodynamically important associated lesions, gross cardiomegaly, or mental retardation were excluded. Age at the time of correction varied from 11 months to 4.2 years. A Mustard operation was performed in six patients and a Senning procedure in three. The interval between the operation and the exercise testing varied from 3 to 15 years. The average age at exercise testing was 9.8 years (range: 4 to 18.5 years).

Testing Procedures

The methods used have already been described elsewhere (Reybrouck, Weymans, Stijns, & Van der Hauwaert, 1986a). In summary, exercise tests were performed on a treadmill. Oxygen uptake ($\dot{V}O_2$) and carbon dioxide output ($\dot{V}CO_2$) were measured by the Douglas bag method. Exercise performance was assessed by determination of the ventilatory threshold, expressed as $mlO_2 \cdot min^{-1} \cdot kg^{-1}$ or in units of time. The ventilatory threshold was determined as the highest $\dot{V}O_2$ at which a continuous increase was found for the ventilatory equivalent for O_2 ($\dot{V}_E/\dot{V}O_2$) without a concomitant increase in the ventilatory equivalent for CO_2 ($\dot{V}_E/\dot{V}CO_2$) (Caiozzo et al., 1982).

RESULTS

Exercise Performance Capacity

In eight of the nine patients with TGA, the ventilatory threshold could be determined. Individual data are presented in Figure 1. In all patients the value for the ventilatory threshold was below the 95% confidence limit obtained in normal children of comparable age (Reybrouck, Weymans, Stijns, Knops, & Van der Hauwaert, 1985). The mean value for the ventilatory threshold was significantly ($p < .01$) lower than the normal mean value obtained in children of the same sex and comparable age. It averaged 64.3 ± 11.3 (*SD*) %.

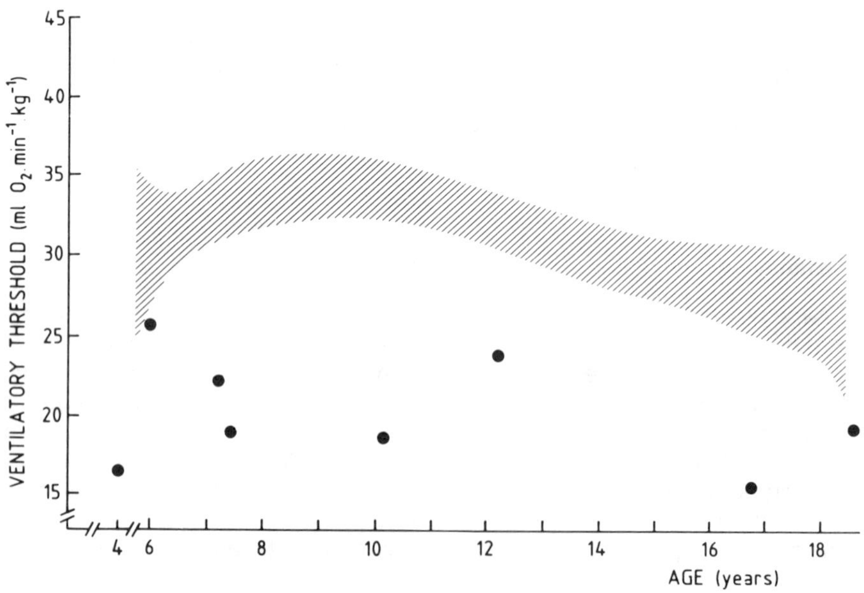

Figure 1. Individual values for ventilatory threshold in eight boys operated on for transposition of the great arteries. The 95% confidence limits of the normal value are shown by the shaded area.

When expressed in units of time, the ventilatory threshold was attained sooner in all patients than in normal children. The ventilatory threshold was reached after 1.9 ± 1.4 min in the patients compared with 4.5 ± 1 min in normal controls. This difference was also statistically significant.

DISCUSSION

When cardiorespiratory endurance capacity was assessed by respiratory gas exchange, using the ventilatory threshold method, a subnormal exercise capacity was found in all patients studied in this series. Poor exercise capacity has also previously been reported in a considerable number of patients who underwent a Mustard or Senning operation for TGA, using maximal exercise testing (Benson et al., 1982; Hesslein, Gutgesell, Gilette, & McNamarra, 1982). However, when using the ventilatory threshold method a larger fraction of patients had a subnormal value for exercise performance than noted in previous studies. This may be attributed to the sensitivity of the method elected for the present study. Also, in previous investigations on cardiorespiratory endurance capacity in children with congenital heart disease and a left-to-right shunt (Reybrouck et al., 1986a) and in children operated on for tetralogy of Fallot (Reybrouck, Weymans, Stijns, & Van der Hauwaert, 1986b), it was found that the ventilatory threshold method is more sensitive for detection of subnormal exercise capacity than other indices of cardiorespiratory endurance capacity such as $\dot{V}O_2max$ (Mocellin, Bastanier, Hofacker, & Bühlmeyer, 1976) or the maximal endurance time on a treadmill (Cumming, 1978).

Subnormal exercise performance capacity in patients after a venous switch operation for TGA has generally been attributed to right (systemic) ventricular dysfunction, as demonstrated by hemodynamic (Parrisch et al., 1983) or echocardiographic indices (Alpert et al., 1979). Observations in the present study indicated that the ventilatory threshold was subnormal and also was attained sooner in TGA patients compared with normal controls, which was in agreement with these findings.

CONCLUSION

These observations showed that exercise capacity assessed by determination of the ventilatory threshold method was subnormal in all patients studied in this limited series after a venous switch operation for TGA, although they were clinically well and the result of surgery was considered to be excellent.

REFERENCES

Alpert, B.S., Bloom, K.R., Olley, P., Trusler, G.A., Williams, C.M., & Rowe, R.D. (1979). Echocardiographic evaluation of right ventricular function in complete transposition of the great arteries. *American Journal of Cardiology*, **44**, 270-275.

Benson, L.N., Bonet, J., McLaughlin, P., Olley, P.M., Feighlin, D., Druck, M., Trusler, G., Rowe, R.D., & Morch, J. (1982). Assessment of right ventricular function during supine exercise after Mustard's operation. *Circulation*, **65**, 1052-1059.

Caiozzo, V., Davis, J.A., Ellis, J.F., Azus, J.L., Vandagriff, R., Prietto, C.A., & McMaster, W.C. (1982). A comparison of gas exchange indices to detect the anaerobic threshold. *Journal of Applied Physiology*, **53**, 1184-1189.

Cumming, G.R. (1978). Maximal exercise capacity of children with heart defects. *American Journal of Cardiology*, **42**, 613-619.

Hesslein, P.S., Gutgesell, H.P., Gilette, P.C., & McNamarra, D.G. (1982). Exercise assessment of sinoatrial node function following the Mustard operation. *American Heart Journal*, **102**, 351-357.

Mocellin, R., Bastanier, C., Hofacker, W., & Bühlmeyer, K. (1976). Exercise performance in children and adolescents after surgical repair of tetralogy of Fallot. *European Journal of Cardiology*, **4**, 367-374.

Murphy, J.H., Barlai Kovatch, M.M., Mathews, R.A., Beerman, L.B., Park, S.C., Neches, W.H., & Zuberbuhler, J.R. (1983). Rest and exercise right and left ventricular function after the Mustard operation: Assessment by radionuclide ventriculography. *American Journal of Cardiology*, **51**, 1520-1526.

Parrisch, M.D., Graham, T.P., Bender, H.W., Jones, J.P., Patton, J., & Partain, L.C. (1983). Radionuclide angiographic evaluation of right and left ventricular function during exercise after repair of transposition of the great arteries. Comparison with normal subjects and patients with congenital corrected transposition. *Circulation*, **67**, 178-183.

Ramsay, J.M., Venables, A.W., Kelly, M.J., & Kalff, V. (1984). Right and left ventricular function at rest and with exercise after the Mustard operation for transposition of the great arteries. *British Heart Journal*, **51**, 364-370.

Reybrouck, T., Weymans, M., Stijns, H., Knops, J., & Van der Hauwaert, L. (1985). Ventilatory anaerobic threshold in children: Age and sex differences. *European Journal of Applied Physiology*, **54**, 278-284.

Reybrouck, T., Weymans, M., Stijns, H., & Van der Hauwaert, L. (1986a). Ventilatory anaerobic threshold for evaluating exercise performance in children with congenital left-to-right intracardiac shunt. *Pediatric Cardiology*, **7**, 19-24.

Reybrouck, T., Weymans, M., Stijns, H., & Van der Hauwaert, L. (1986b). Exercise testing after correction of tetralogy of Fallot: The fallacy of a reduced heart rate. *American Heart Journal*, **112**, 998-1003.

Exercise Tests of a Group of 52 Patients After Total Correction of Tetralogy of Fallot

Jiří Radvanský
Jan Vávra
Jaroslav Hruda
Václav Sazima
Charles University, Prague, Czechoslovakia

Poor exercise capacity in patients with tetralogy of Fallot before correction is well known as well as the great subjective improvement in exercise tolerance after a total correction (TOFtc). Despite this improvement many investigators have demonstrated persistent intolerance for exercise of TOFtc patients as expressed by $\dot{V}O_2max$ below the range of a healthy population. The explanation was the low cardiac output during exercise. Moreover, in the literature there was a lack of information concerning submaximal exercise test data and its interpretation in TOFtc patients, despite better reproducibility and lower risk of exercise test complications.

The present study focused on cardiorespiratory variables in TOFtc patients at an exercise level low enough to be tolerated even in the case of serious exercise intolerance (below 60% of $\dot{V}O_2max$). In such situations, the cardiac output should not be the limiting factor for the cardiorespiratory variables. Late residuals of preoperative hypoxemic adaptation thus could be revealed.

METHODS

Subjects

A total of 52 TOFtc patients of the Department of Cardiosurgery, Motol, with a mean age of 13.9 ± 3.8 years, mean time after total correction 3.2 ± 1.1 years, were studied. A total of 26 patients underwent paliative correction for TOFtc. At least 16 patients had significant postoperative residuals (R$\dot{V}$OT transanular patch, pulmonary and/or tricuspidal valvular insufficiency). Three patients of the group died later from cardiac problems.

Exercise Protocol

An ergometric all-out stepwise test was performed with the first step at the constant relative load of 1 W • kg^{-1} body weight of 6-min duration. After the second submaximal step, a symptoms-limited maximal exercise test was done. Heart rate (HR), ECG, oxygen consumption (expressed in milliliters of O_2 per kilogram of body weight [$\dot{V}O_2$]) and utilization, carbon dioxide production, and RQ were recorded at sampling intervals of 30 s (Oxycon Mijnhardt). Normal values at the workload of 1 W • kg^{-1} BW were obtained from an unpublished study of a normal healthy population (n = 300) of the respective age.

RESULTS

In Table 1 the main results are given: $\dot{V}O_2max$ in terms of standard deviations of the normal values. Forty-six percent of the patients were within the normal range (i.e., $\dot{V}O_2max$ > [mean −2 *SD*]). At least three children were limited more phychically than by fatigue, and four children were excluded (arrythmia, tracheal stridor—postoperative tracheal stenosis). Sixty-six percent of patients had $\dot{V}O_2max$ over 30 ml • kg^{-1} • min^{-1} (Figure 1).

Table 1 $\dot{V}O_2max$ in Terms of Standard Deviations of the Normal Values

Parameter	Unit	*M*	*SD*
$\dot{V}O_2max$	ml • kg • min^{-1}	34.5	7.4
HRmax	beats • min^{-1}	178.6	16.7
Rmax		0.995	0.105
$\dot{V}O_2$ 1 W • kg^{-1}	*SD* of norm.	−1.24	1.92
HR 1 W • kg^{-1}	beats • min^{-1}	120.6	15.3
RQ 1 W • kg^{-1}		0.827	0.1

$\dot{V}O_2$ at 1 W • kg^{-1} BW ($\dot{V}O_2sub$) results showed that (a) mean $\dot{V}O_2sub$ of the total group was −1.24 *SD* below normal values; (b) 30% of the patients in the group had $\dot{V}O_2sub$ below −2 *SD* of normal values, ranging from −5.4 to −2 *SD* (Figure 2; these are referred to in this article as *low submaximal $\dot{V}O_2$ group* [$L\dot{V}O_2$]); and (c) dividing the total group into subgroups, Normal and $L\dot{V}O_2$, the subgroups did not differ in $\dot{V}O_2max$, HRmax, R, and RQ on both maximal and submaximal levels, in age and age of correction of cardiac defect. The only significant difference was found in HR at 1 W • kg^{-1} exercise level. The $L\dot{V}O_2$ subgroup had relative bradycardia (114 vs. 124 beats • min^{-1}).

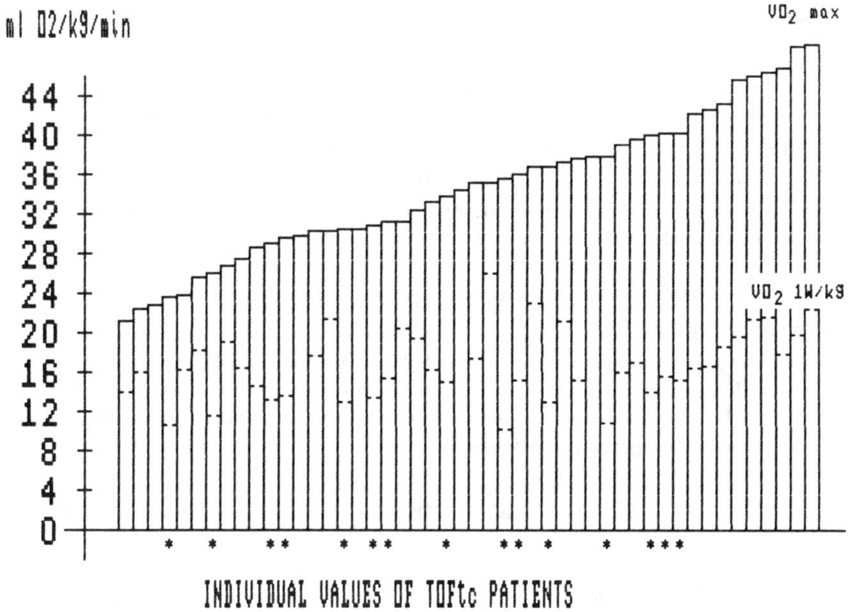

Figure 1. $\dot{V}O_2$max, $\dot{V}O_2$ at the level of 1 W • kg^{-1} × L$\dot{V}O_2$ patients.

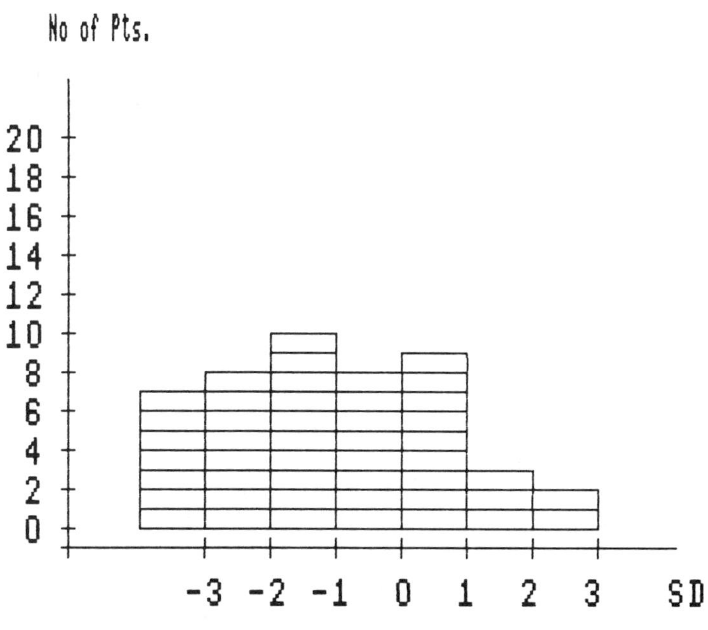

Figure 2. Distribution of $\dot{V}O_2$ at the level of exercise 1 W • kg^{-1} in *SD* of normals.

DISCUSSION

Due to relatively constant work efficiency (22% to 24%), it is generally known that oxygen consumption in healthy subjects varies minimally during the same mild work loads (e.g., 1 W • kg^{-1} BW), regardless of the subject's working capacity, sex, and body weight. From this point of view, it is difficult to explain the low $\dot{V}O_2$ at 1 W • kg^{-1} in 33% of the TOFtc group. However, one can offer the following hypotheses:

1. Work efficiency of the $L\dot{V}O_2$ subgroup is higher.
2. Exercise level 1 W • kg^{-1} BW is over the lactate threshold in $L\dot{V}O_2$ patients, and thus a part of energy cost was covered anaerobically.
3. Measurement was in error (improbable because patients were measured by the same team, in the same place, and with the same equipment as the normal subgroup).

The following points should be stressed with regard to hypotheses 1 and 2:

1. In all cases of the $L\dot{V}O_2$ subgroup, when the subject worked at higher work loads the $\dot{V}O_2max$ achieved was at least twice as high as the $\dot{V}O_2$ measured at the 1 W • kg^{-1} BW exercise level (Figure 1). This means that the subjects were able to increase their oxygen uptake, but at the lower workload they did not reach the normal value found in a healthy population.

2. Both RQ and heart rates were not high enough to indicate that, for the $L\dot{V}O_2$ subgroup, the exercise level of 1 W • kg^{-1} BW was above their lactate threshold.

3. Repeated tests in 6 of 15 subjects of $L\dot{V}O_2$ subgroup 3 years later showed significant increases in $\dot{V}O_2sub$. All these retested patients reached the $\dot{V}O_2sub$ about −1 *SD* below the mean normal value. Lactacidemia in these patients was low with the exception of one boy

Table 2 Test Results of 6 of 15 Subjects of $L\dot{V}O_2$ Subgroup, 3 Years Later

Patient	$\dot{V}O_2$ at 1 W • kg^{-1} 3 yr ago	$\dot{V}O_2$ at 1 W • kg^{-1} now	Lactate at rest [mmol • kg^{-1}]	Lactate at 1 W • kg^{-1}
1	12.7	15.7	1.2	2.0
2	15.2	16.5	4.7	8.5
3	15.2	16.4	1.8	1.8
4	11.7	18.3	1.9	1.7
5	13.8	16.3	2.0	3.3
6	13.3	16.7	2.4	1.7

whose left ventricle contractility even at rest was worsened shortly before retesting (Table 2).

CONCLUSION

Standard relative submaximal tests in TOFtc patients revealed an abnormal cardiorespiratory reaction to mild exercise in 33% of subjects, but this reaction seemed to disappear 3 to 6 years after correction. Whether it is a higher work efficiency or some regulation abnormality will be the focus of further studies.

REFERENCES

Máček, M., & Vávra, J. (1988). Fyziologie a patofyziologie tělesné zátěže (2nd ed.). Prague: Avicenum.

A Survey of the Physical Activity of 926 Norwegian Schoolchildren With Congenital Heart Diseases

Nina Kahrs
The Norwegian College of Physical Education and Sport, Oslo, Norway

The Norwegian Parent's Organization of Children with Congenital Heart Diseases was founded in 1976. The organization is primarily concerned with the children's interests and rights, but its aim is also to distribute information on children with heart disease. The members of the parent's organization have anticipated the problems their children encounter in relation to school physical education and sport. Consequently, the chairman of the organization in 1983 requested that the Norwegian College of Physical Education and Sport conduct research in this field. The Norwegian College of Physical Education and Sport accepted the challenge and developed a project consisting of the following three phases:

1. A screening of problems Norwegian children with manifest congenital heart diseases encountered in physical activities.
2. A personal interview with children who encountered problems in relation to physical activities.
3. Testing and physical training of children with congenital heart diseases.

The results of this investigation will be used to educate teachers, parents, and health personnel in an attempt to improve the conditions in school physical education and sport for children with congenital heart diseases. The purpose of this article is to present some results from the screening process. The children's involvement in sport in relation to sex, diagnosis, and medical surgery is emphasized.

METHOD AND PROCEDURES

The method used in the screening process was a postinquiry. The questionnaire was based on information from the parent's organization, older youth with congenital heart diseases, and medical experts. It consisted of questions on the following subjects: (a) sex and age; (b) medical diagnosis, operations, and other disabilities; (c) involvement in physical education and sport; (d) exposure to adapted physical activity and physiotherapy; and (e) problems encountered in physical education.

The results of a pilot study, an empirical study of children with heart diseases in the Norwegian city of Drammen, and a survey of the present literature on children with congenital heart diseases revealed that no previous research had been conducted, particularly with regard to physical education in Norwegian schools (Kvikstad, 1986). Also, to the best of my knowledge, no similar investigations have been conducted in Europe or in North America. Lack of knowledge, therefore, made it necessary to present the questions about problems encountered in physical activity as open ended. The information gathered thus far will be used in the construction of an interview guide for Phase II.

SAMPLING

According to the General Plan for Cardiac Children in Norway, dated 1985, Rikshospitalet and Ullevål Hospital in Oslo and Haukeland Hospital in Bergen carried out 96.3% of the special cardiac examinations in Norway in 1983 (Norsk Cardiologisk Selskap, 1985). Therefore, this survey was conducted in cooperation with medical experts at these three university hospitals. To maintain confidentiality, the questionnaire was mailed to the children directly by the hospitals involved. The sample consisted of the children born between 1967 and 1978 with a manifest congenital cardiac disease. Children with light types of ductus arteriosus spontaneously healed at an early age as well as those with pathological heart murmurs (without any manifest problems) were excluded from the study. The total number of children sampled in the appropriate age group was 1,314. In all, 961 children responded, which represented a response rate of 85.1%.

Preliminary inspection of the returned questionnaires revealed that 35 children had declared themselves healthy after surgery, had died from their diseases, or were given another diagnosis (e.g., hydrocephalus, hemophilia, apoplexy) and, therefore, these children were excluded from the sample. Consequently, the data presented were based on the responses from 926 children with manifest congenital heart diseases. No sex differences were expected as far as congenital heart diseases were concerned. Table 1 shows that the proportions of boys and girls in the sample were about the same. Since there was no direct contact with the children, it was not possible to determine their functional levels.

As a first step in the treatment of the data, therefore, the children were divided into four groups according to the diagnoses and the possible consequences for the children with the corresponding diseases if they were exposed to sufficiently strenuous physical activity. The four groups can briefly be described as follows:

Group 1. Simple defects: arterial septal defects, ventricular septal defects, and patient ductus arteriosus.

Table 1 Distribution of Cardiac Children From the Three Hospitals

	Rikshospitalet		Haukeland sykehus		Ullevål sykehus		Total	
Sex	*N*	%	*N*	%	*N*	%	*N*	%
Female	357	38.6	74	8.0	39	4.2	470	50.8
Male	340	36.7	86	9.3	30	3.2	456	49.2
Total	697	75.3	160	17.3	69	7.4	926	100

Group 2. Obstructions: pulmonary stenosis, aortic stenosis, and coarctation of the aorta.

Group 3. Complex defects: Tetralogy of Fallot, transposition of the large arteries, and truncus arteriosus.

Group 4. Other complex defects: cardiomyopatia, anomalia in the heart construction, and other insufficiences of the heart (Hordvik, Rosland, & Falck, 1985).

Table 2 shows the distribution of the 926 subjects according to sex and diagnosis. There was a tendency for a higher percentage of boys than girls to have complex defects. This was in agreement with general expectations (Kvikstad, 1986). Since the sample was drawn from 96.3% of the total population of children with congenital heart diseases in Norway, the sample was representative of the group of cardiac children in the age group of 10 to 20 years, particularly since the percentage of questionnaires returned exceeded 80% (Fowler, 1985).

Table 2 Distribution of the 926 Subjects According to Sex and Diagnosis

	Female (n = 470)		Male (n = 456)		Total (n = 926)		X^2	*p*
Diagnosis	*N*	%	*N*	%	*N*	%		
Simple defects	338	72	252	55	590	64	27.04	.001
Obstructions	124	26	187	41	311	34	21.54	.001
Complex defects	50	11	87	19	137	15	12.42	.001
Other defects	32	7	42	9	74	8	1.50	.217
Totals[a]	544	116	568	124	1,112	121		

[a]Some of the children had more than one diagnosis, and therefore the total percentages exceeded 100%.

RESULTS AND DISCUSSION

The Participation of Subjects in Leisure Time Sport

A total of 58% (N = 537) of the children with congenital heart diseases participated in leisure time sports as indicated in Table 3. Research on Norwegian children less than 17 years of age has claimed that between 50 and 60% of the normal children participate in out-of-school sport. Therefore, the children with congenital heart disease did not deviate from the normal group of Norwegian children as far as participation in leisure time sport was concerned. Stensaasen (1976) reported that about 54% of the girls and 58% of the boys involved participated in sport. The corresponding figures for the sample of children with congenital heart diseases were 53% (N = 249) for the girls and 63% (N = 288) for the boys.

Table 3 Participation in Out-of-School Sport in Relation to Sex

Participation	Female		Male		Total	
	N	%	*N*	%	*N*	%
Participants	249	53	288	63	537	58
Nonparticipants	221	40	168	37	385	42
Total	470	100	456	100	926	100

χ^2 = 9.919. p = .007. F = 2.

The percentages of boys and girls with congenital heart diseases who participated in out-of-school sport seemed to be higher than in the ordinary group of children. Tested with chi-square, the percentage difference between boys and girls with congenital heart diseases concerning participation in leisure time sport was statistically significant (see Table 3). This percentage of participation was similar in the three different hospitals, as is shown in Table 4 by the nonsignificant chi-square value of 5.83 with a probability level of .21.

The Participation in Sport of Children Relative to Diagnosis

The relationship between the degree of participation and the complexity of the cardiac defects can be seen in Table 5. The lowest degree of participation occurred in the groups with complex defects, which would be expected from a medical point of view. The distribution of boys and girls relative to diagnosis groups and participation level in sport was a bit alarming. Relative to diagnosis groups, the boys had more complex diseases than girls. Therefore, one might expect a greater percentage of girls than

Table 4 The Participation of Children With Congenital Heart Diseases and Hospital Relationship

Participation in sport	Rikshospitalet		Ullevål		Haukeland		Total	
	N	%	*N*	%	*N*	%	*N*	%
Participants	401	57.5	47	68.1	89	55.6	537	58
Nonparticipants	296	42.5	22	31.8	71	44.4	389	42
Total	697	100	69	99.9	160	100	926	100

$\chi^2 = 5.83$. $p = .21$. $F = 4$.

Table 5 Participation of Children With Congenital Heart Diseases in Sport in Relation to Diagnosis

Participation in sport	Female		Male		Total	
	N	%	*N*	%	*N*	%
Simple defects	189	56	166	66	355	61
Obstructions	61	49	121	65	182	59
Complex defects	21	42	47	54	68	50
Other complex defects	9	28	22	52	31	42

boys to take part in sport, but that was not the case in this survey. More research concerning the girls with congenital cardiac diseases seems to be needed to determine the reasons for their lack of participation in sport.

Open-Heart Surgery and Participation of Children in Leisure Time Sport

Table 6 indicates that there was a larger number of children engaged in sport in the group of children that had received open-heart surgery, age 0 to 8 years, than in the group operated on at 9 years of age or later. This might have been due to the fact that the children did not change their activity habits after the operation, although they were reasonably healthy. The problems most frequently mentioned by the children with congenital heart diseases in relation to physical activity were related to endurance. Such statements as "I can't keep up with my mates," "I get tired easily," and so forth, were expressed by 36.8% (N = 341) of the children in this survey. There was no significant difference between boys

Table 6 Engagement in Out-of-School Sport in Relation to Time of Open-Heart Surgery

Time of open-heart surgery	Out-of-School Sport Yes		No		Total	
	N	%	*N*	%	*N*	%
0-1 year	90	60	61	40	151	100
2-5 years	199	56	159	44	358	100
6-8 years	135	58	98	42	233	100
9-12 years	38	40	58	60	96	100
over 13 years	22	49	23	51	45	100

(36.2%) and girls (37.4%) in the total number of problems reported (Kahrs, 1987). However, further analysis showed that there was a significant difference between boys and girls with reported problems and participation in sport after medical surgery, as shown in Table 7. This is in agreement with data presented earlier in this article where a significant difference was found between boys' and girls' involvement in out-of-school sport.

Table 7 Endurance Problems in Relation to Sex and Participation in Out-of-School Sport in the Group of Children Who Have Been Exposed to Open-Heart Surgery

Sex	Participate in sport					
	Yes		No			
	N	%	*N*	%	χ^2	*p*
Female	75	43	101	57	13.93	.001
Male	92	56	72	45	6.12	.047

$F = 1$.

Most Common Choices of Sport Activities

The five most common activities for the children with congenital heart diseases as well as for the normal children less than 17 years old who were members of Norwegian Confederation of Sport (NIF), according to the 1985 statistics, are shown in Table 8. Slight differences in the sport activities chosen by the children with congenital heart diseases and the NIF members can be noted. The children with congenital heart diseases probably had to base their choice of activities on their functional levels. Therefore, more often than other children, they chose sports with relatively less demand on aerobic capacity. The percentage distribution of involvement of cardiac children in the different sport activities was as follows: (a) skiing (37%), (b) soccer (34%), (c) swimming (16%), (d) gymnastics (15%), and (e) bicycling (11%). Both skiing and swimming were as popular among girls as among boys in the group of children with congenital heart diseases.

One may note that nearly 40% of the children with congenital heart diseases engaged in Alpine skiing. As can be seen from Table 8, there was a difference in the activity program for boys and girls. The girls' reports of activities were dominated by gymnastics (i.e., rhythmical activities, dance, and gymnastics), and the boys' program was dominated by soccer. This may not be surprising because it corresponded to cultural tradition. There were no significant differences in choice of activities

Table 8 Most Common Sport Activities for the Groups of Cardiac Children and the Norwegian Sport Confederation Less Than 17 Years of Age

Order of choices	Female		Male	
	Cardiac children	NIF members	Cardiac children	NIF members
1	Gymnastics	Gymnastics	Football	Football
2	Skiing	Handball	Skiing	Skiing
3	Handball	Football	Swimming	Track & field
4	Football	Track & field	Cycling	Handball
5	Swimming	Skiing	Track & field	Gymnastics

among diagnosis groups. These preliminary results must be analyzed more thoroughly and more research may be needed to confirm this finding.

DISCUSSION

Perhaps one might expect to find that congenital heart diseases severely affect physical activities and children's possible involvement in sport, if not completely exclude such participation. Surprisingly, this survey indicated the same rate of involvement in sport among cardiac children as among a normal group of children in Norway (Kahrs, 1986). This does not mean that the children with congenital heart diseases participate in sport without problems. Some of the problems the children have may quite obviously be related to the diseases. A cardiac disease does not necessarily prevent a child from developing physical skill, but his or her reduced aerobic capacity may influence the choice of activity (Cumming, 1978; Goldberg et al., 1966).

One may also wonder if open-heart surgery can result in a more or less incomplete solution to the problem of aerobic capacity. Furthermore, it is not known if the child's age at the time when surgery was undertaken was of any importance. There might be reasons to believe that the earlier open-heart surgery is performed, the greater the likelihood that the child will take part in leisure time sport. Perhaps the reason why children exposed to open-heart surgery later in life did not become involved in sport to the same extent was the fact that they did alter their way of living after the operation was performed. This would be one of the long-term benefits of postoperative training (Longmuir & Goode, 1987).

The results of sex differences in sport participation in this survey were in agreement with cultural expectations. Looking at the activity distribution for boys and girls in relation to diagnosis groups, however, revealed somewhat surprising results. The boys seemed to have more complex diseases than girls, and therefore one would expect the girls to be more active than the boys. But the opposite was found in this case. More research concerning girls with congenital cardiac diseases is needed to determine what barriers exist that keep them from engaging in physical activity.

Acknowledgment

This survey has been conducted in cooperation with Dr. Per G. Bjørnstad and Dr. Svein J. Sørland at Rikshospitalet, Dr. Asbjørn Langslet at Ullevål Hospital, and Dr. Gunnar A. Rosland at Haukeland Hospital, Norway.

REFERENCES

Cumming, G.R. (1978). Maximal capacity of children with heart defects. *The American Journal of Cardiology*, **42**, 613-619.

Fowler, F.J. (1985). *Survey of research methods* (2nd ed.). Beverly Hills, CA: Sage.

Goldberg, B., et al. (1966). Effect of physical training on exercise performance of children following surgical repair of congenital heart disease. *Pediatrics*, **68**, 691-699.

Hordvik, E., Rosland, Alm G., & Falck, V.E. (1985). Barn med medfødte hjertefeil [Children with congenital cardiac diseases]. In D. Nilsson (Ed.), *Barn og unge med spesielle behov* [Children and youth with special needs] (pp. 126-136). Oslo: Universitetsforlaget.

Kahrs, N. (1986). *Cardiac children and physical education. The cardiac children's involvement in different types of sport*. Paper presented at the Norwegian Society of Sport Research Conference, "Sport, Sex and Gender," Lillehammer.

Kahrs, N. (1987). *Cardiac children and physical education. A screening of children's problems in physical education in Norwegian Public Schools*. Paper presented at the 6th International Symposium on Adapted Physical Activity, IFAPA, Brisbane, Australia.

Kvikstad, I. (1986). *Hjertesyke barn—Deres fysiske funksjonsevne og deltagelse i kroppsøvingsfaget* [Children with cardiac diseases—Their functional level and involvement in school physical education]. Oslo: Hovedfagsoppgave Norges idrettshøgskole.

Longmuir, P., & Goode, R.C. (1987). *Postoperative exercise training provides long-term benefits for children with congenital heart diseases*. Paper presented at the 6th International Symposium on Adapted Physical Activity, IFAPA, Brisbane, Australia.

Norsk Cardiologisk Selskap. (1985). *Generalplan for medfødte hjertefeil i Norge* [The general plan for children with congenital heart diseases in Norway]. Oslo.

Stensaasen, S. (1976). Project leisure and sport. *Idrettspedagogiske problem, Notater og rapporter fra Norges idrettshøgskole, Nr.* 42 [Notes and reports from the Norwegian College of Physical Education and Sport, NORA, Nr. 42]. Oslo.

Part VI
Exercise and Asthmatic Children

The Response of Children With and Without Bronchial Asthma to Heavy Swimming Exercise

Kai-Håkon Carlsen
Svein Oseid
Hilde Odden
Children's Asthma and Allergy Institute Voksentoppen, Oslo, Norway
Elisabeth B. Mellbye
The Norwegian College of Physical Education and Sport, Oslo, Norway

Exercise-induced asthma (EIA) occurs among 70% to 80% of children and adults with bronchial asthma (Lee & Anderson, 1985). EIA may be prevented by inhaling warm, humid air during exercise (Chen & Horton, 1977), and swimming is therefore considered to be a beneficial exercise for asthmatic children. To further explore the responses to swimming, the metabolic, respiratory, and cardiovascular responses to heavy swimming exercise were examined in 19 elite child swimmers, 12 to 15 years of age. The responses of 6 of the children with bronchial asthma were compared with the responses of those without bronchial asthma. The pulmonary responses to the swimming exercise were compared with the responses to treadmill running with submaximal workload.

METHODS

The 19 children included in the study, 12 girls and 7 boys, all regularly practiced extensive swim training and had been doing so for at least 1 year before the study. They were at a high competitive level according to their age (12 to 15 years) and used to swim for 2 to 3 hr daily. All employed the same training model, which consisted of calculating their anaerobic threshold during swimming with the heart rate as a measure, in the same manner as described in running by Conconi, Ferrari, Ziglio, Droghetti, and Codeca (1982). The children then repeatedly swam intervals at this threshold to improve the threshold. Six of the children suffered from severe to moderate bronchial asthma, requiring regular antiasthmatic medication.

Lung function was measured during all tests by a bellow spirometer (Vitalograph) connected to a computer (Apple). The heart rate was recorded electronically and stored on tape (Sport Tester PE 3000 with a memory function). Metabolic responses were measured during the swim tests by blood gas analyses (pO_2, pCO_2, pH, base excess [BE]) and blood lactate analyses. Bronchial responsiveness was measured by inhalation of nebulized histamine diphosphate in doubling concentrations from 0.03 to 32 mg/ml histamine, determining the concentration at which the forced expiratory volume in first second (FEV_1) fell 20% from the starting value (PC_{20}). PC_{20} was first measured on a separate day, and then before and after the interval swim as described later. The children underwent a submaximal exercise test by treadmill running at constant speed for 6 min with a steady state heart rate of at least 170 beats/min. The measurement of PC_{20} and of the treadmill running have been described in detail previously (Carlsen, Bech, Oseid, & Schrøder, 1986).

The children underwent two swim tests. The first test involved an interval swim of 200 m with a rest of 1 min between each interval. They swam 1,000 m at 200-m intervals at a rate 5% below the calculated anaerobic threshold, rested for 5 min, then swam 1,000 m at 200-m intervals at the calculated anaerobic threshold, and finally, after 5-min rest, swam 1,000 m at 200-m intervals at a rate 5% above the calculated anaerobic threshold. Lung function was measured before swimming, between each main interval of 1,000 m, and after the complete swimming procedure. Blood gases and blood lactate were measured simultaneously. The heart rate was recorded continuously during and in between the swimming intervals. PC_{20} was measured before the swimming procedure and 15 min after completing the swimming procedure.

Before starting swimming and before measuring PC_{20} after the swimming, lung function had to be at baseline values. The children had a swimming warm-up for 15 min before the interval swims.

In the second test the children swam in a counter-current swimmill with variable speed of the water flow at their maximal capacity measuring their maximal oxygen uptake ($\dot{V}O_2max$) by the Douglas bag method. Lung function was measured before and after this procedure, as were blood gases and blood lactate. The heart rate was recorded electronically during the swimming.

The results were evaluated by Pearson's product-moment correlation coefficients (r), the chi-square test, the Wilcoxon rank test for paired differences (W), the Mann-Whitney U-test for two independent samples (M-W), and the student's t test. All tests were two-tailed. Differences were considered to be significant at a level of 5% ($p \leqslant .05$).

RESULTS

Baseline lung function did not differ significantly between children with and children without asthma for FEV_1, forced expiratory flow at 25% of vital capacity (FEF_{25}) and forced expiratory flow between 25% and 75% of vital capacity (FEF_{25-75}; M-W $p > .10$). After the submaximal treadmill test, the asthmatic children had a greater reduction in lung function (FEV_1: Mean [M] + standard error of the mean [SEM]: 19.1 + 4.4) than the nonasthmatic children (FEV_1: M ± SEM: 2.2 ± 0.9) (M-W $p < .01$). The reduction in FEV_1 after treadmill running correlated significantly to the bronchial responsiveness (PC_{20}) ($r = .83$, $p < .001$) (Figure 1). The asthmatic children had lower PC_{20} than the nonasthmatic children (M-W: $p < .01$). PC_{20} measured on the separate day did not differ from that measured before the interval swim (W: $p > .10$).

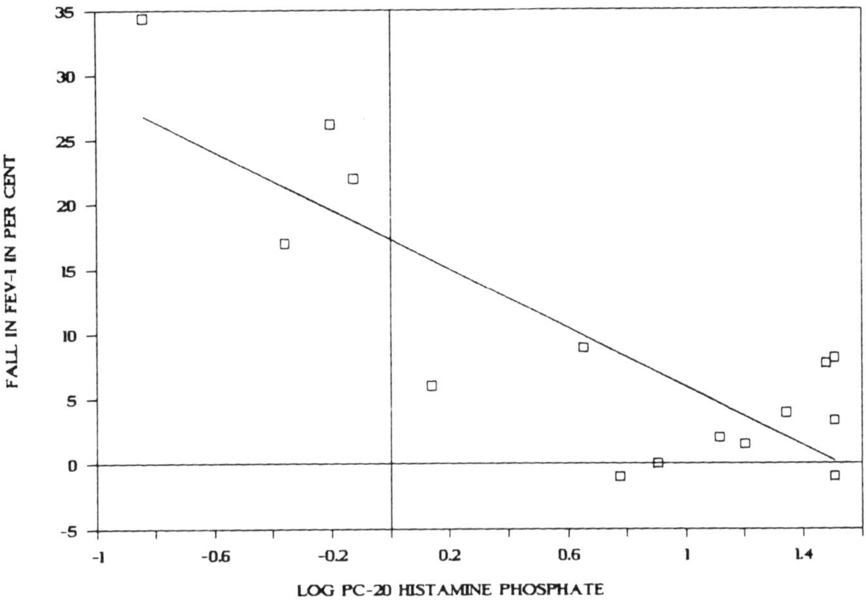

Figure 1. Correlation between maximal change in FEV_1 after running on a treadmill at submaximal load and log PC_{20} measured by histamine inhalation tests ($r = -.83$, $p < .001$, regression equation: $y = 17.29 - 11.35x$).

The changes in lung function during the interval swim and swimming during maximal O_2 uptake in the swimmill are shown in Table 1. One can note that lung function increased for FEV_1, FEF_{25}, and FEF_{25-75} during the interval swim in the nonasthmatic children but not in the asthmatic children. However, the asthmatic children had mostly unchanged lung function during the interval swim, and change in FEV_1 after the interval swim did not correlate significantly to PC_{20} ($r = .20$, $p > .05$). The change in lung function after swimming in the swimmill did not differ between the two groups (M-W: $p > .10$).

Bronchial responsiveness increased significantly from before to after the interval swim (W: $p < .001$), as seen from Figure 2. The change in PC_{20} during swimming did not differ significantly between the children with and the children without asthma (M-W: $p > .3$). The change in log PC_{20}

Table 1 Change in Lung Function During and After Interval Swim and After Swimming for Maximal Oxygen Uptake in the Swimmill

Parameter	After interval 1	After interval 2	After interval 3	After max. swim
FEV_1				
Nonasthma	1.07 ± 0.02	1.06 ± 0.02	1.10 ± 0.02	0.97 ± 0.02
Asthma	0.98 ± 0.04	0.97 ± 0.04	1.00 ± 0.05	0.93 ± 0.03
	$p < .05$	NS	$p < .05$	NS
$FEF_{25\text{-}75}$				
Nonasthma	1.15 ± 0.04	1.20 ± 0.04	1.27 ± 0.04	0.98 ± 0.04
Asthma	0.92 ± 0.08	0.96 ± 0.10	1.05 ± 0.11	0.91 ± 0.06
	$p < .01$	$p < .05$	NS	NS
FEF_{25}				
Nonasthma	1.25 ± 0.06	1.29 ± 0.06	1.36 ± 0.06	1.10 ± 0.11
Asthma	0.95 ± 0.13	0.97 ± 0.06	1.09 ± 0.12	0.82 ± 0.14
	$p < .05$	$p < .001$	$p < .05$	NS

Note. Starting value is set to 1.00. Values are given as mean values ± SEM.

during swimming correlated significantly to maximum BE during the interval swim ($r = -.70, p < .01$; Figure 3) and to maximal increase in blood lactate ($r = .82, p < .001$), (Figure 4).

Blood lactate and BE increased and pH decreased gradually during each interval in the interval swim, and the greatest change was found after the maximal swim in swimmill. The change in blood lactate, pH, and BE during the interval swim did not differ significantly between children with and without asthma (Table 2).

The heart rate increased gradually during the interval swim and most during the swim in the swimmill. The asthmatic children had the greatest increase in heart rate (Table 2). Maximal oxygen uptake during swimming in the swimmill did not differ significantly between children with asthma (M ± SEM: 47.83 ml/kg • min ± 3.60) and children without asthma (M ± SEM: 48.47 ml/kg • min ± 1.40), (W-M-W: $p > .10$).

DISCUSSION

The anaerobic threshold calculated as the basis of training in these elite child swimmers was found to be fairly accurate when evaluated by blood gas and lactate determinations during swimming (Table 2). This corresponded to what was found by Conconi et al. (1982) in runners and to the lactate threshold of 4 mmol • l as suggested by Heck et al. (1985).

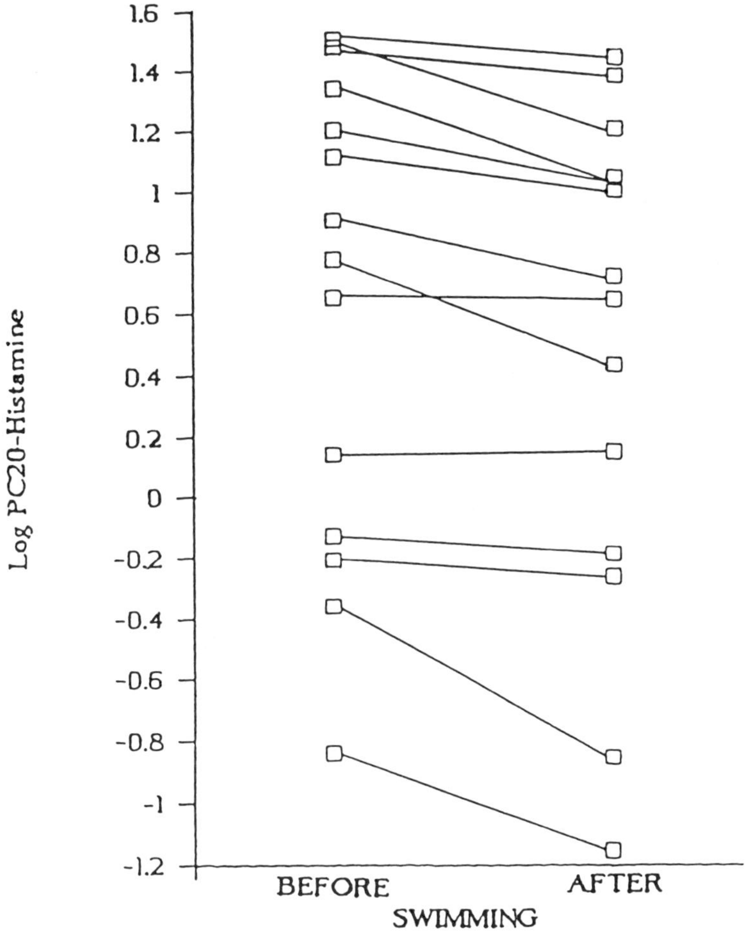

Figure 2. Log PC_{20} as measured by histamine inhalation tests before and after the interval swim. Only the results from children in which blood lactate increased at least 1 mmol/l during the swimming are included. The difference in log PC_{20} from before and after swimming are statistically significant (W: $p < .001$).

This way of calculating the anaerobic threshold during swimming may be a valuable tool in improving swimming skills. It is generally accepted that interval training improves fitness, and interval training has been found to be especially useful in asthmatic children (Oseid, 1982). Of the different types of physical activity, swimming has been said to be the least asthmogenic (Inbar, Dotan, Dlin, Neuman, & Bar-Or, 1980), and Szentágthai, Gyene, Szócska, and Osváth (1987) recently published favorable results of a physical exercise program in children with asthma, employing swimming as a major activity.

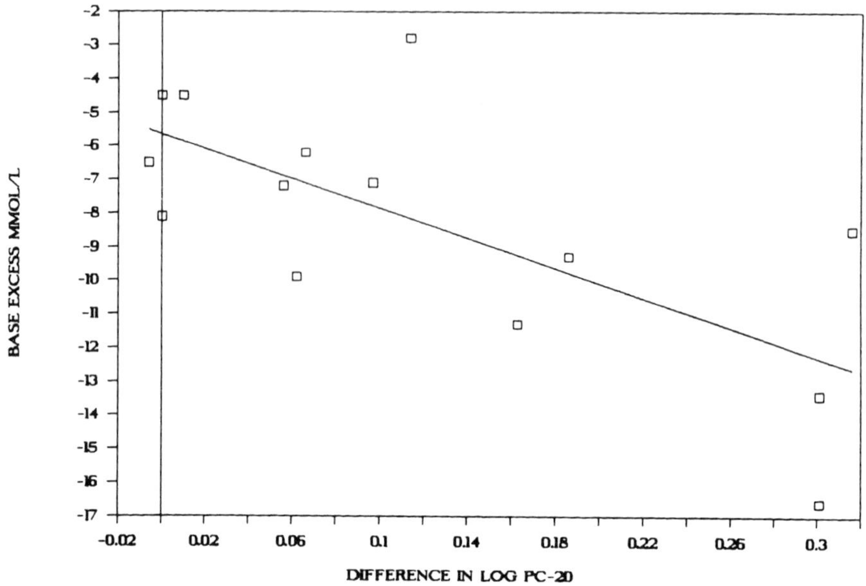

Figure 3. Correlation between change in bronchial responsiveness (log PC_{20}) and base excess after the interval swim ($r = -.70$, $p < .01$, regression equation: $y = -5.6 - 22.1x$).

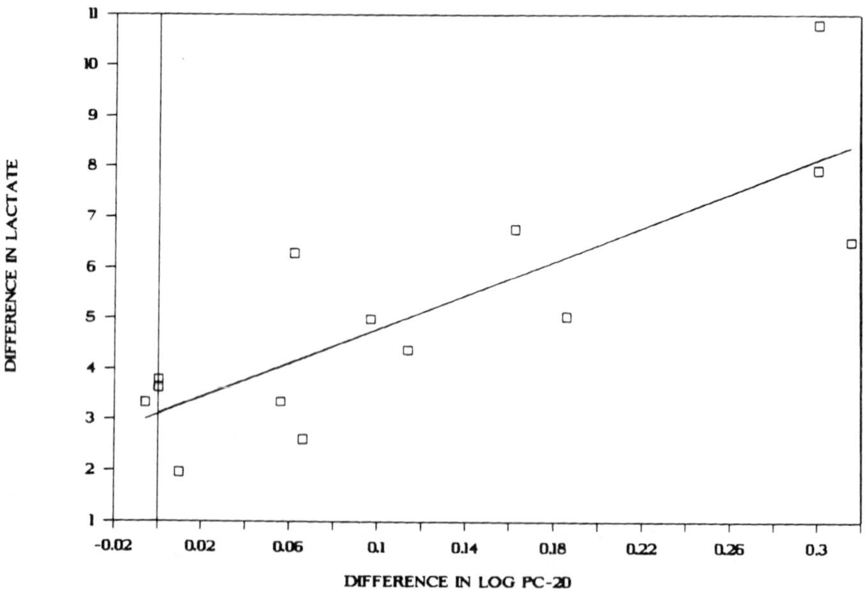

Figure 4. Correlation between change in bronchial responsiveness (log PC_{20}) and change in blood lactate during the interval swim ($r = .82$, $p < .001$, regression equation: $y = 3.11 + 16.7x$).

Table 2 Base Excess (mmol/l), Blood Lactate (mmol/l), pH, and Heart Rate (beats • min⁻¹) During Interval Swim and After Swim in Swimmill for Maximal Oxygen Uptake

Parameter	Start	After interval 1	After interval 2	After interval 3	After max. swim
Heart rate					
Nonathsma		163 ± 4	172 ± 4	183 ± 3	184 ± 2
Asthma		173 ± 2	180 ± 2	191 ± 3	193 ± 4
		$p < .05$		$p < .05$	$p < .05$
Base excess					
Nonasthma	−0.4 ± 0.4	−2.8 ± 0.7	−4.2 ± 1.0	−6.5 ± 1.3	−10.4 ± 0.9
Asthma	−0.8 ± 0.8	−4.1 ± 0.8	−4.6 ± 1.0	−6.7 ± 0.9	− 8.2 ± 1.7
Blood lactate					
Nonasthma	1.5 ± 0.1	2.9 ± 0.4	3.8 ± 0.6	5.5 ± 0.9	7.4 ± 0.6
Asthma	1.4 ± 0.2	3.2 ± 0.6	3.7 ± 0.8	5.3 ± 0.7	7.3 ± 1.0
pH					
Nonasthma	7.40 ± 0.01	7.38 ± 0.01	7.37 ± 0.01	7.33 ± 0.02	7.27 ± 0.02
Asthma	7.40 ± 0.01	7.37 ± 0.02	7.37 ± 0.02	7.33 ± 0.02	7.30 ± 0.02

Note. Values are given as mean values ± SEM. Differences are not statistically significant where p values are not given.

In the present study, significant differences in metabolic responses were absent after the interval and the maximal swims between the nonasthmatic and the asthmatic children (Table 2). The lung function increased during the interval swim in the nonasthmatic children, but remained greatly unchanged in the asthmatic children who did not use premedication before the interval swim. Lung function after swimming in the swimmill, when the asthmatic children employed premedication, did not differ significantly between the two groups (Table 1), and neither did the maximal oxygen uptake, thus confirming the ability of asthmatic children to compete in swimming when trained and treated properly. During the Olympic championships in 1972, an asthmatic individual won the 400-m freestyle swimming competition but was later disqualified when it was detected that he had used ephedrine-containing bronchodilators (Weiler, Metzger, Donnelly, Crowley, & Sharath, 1986).

Of 19 child swimmers included in the study, 6 suffered from bronchial asthma. Two more children from the same group of active elite swimmers were not included due to bronchial obstruction at the time of the study. Thus, altogether 8 of 21 children (38%) suffered from bronchial asthma. This represents an increased prevalence of asthma, which in this area of Norway has been found to affect between 6% and 9% of schoolchildren (Skarpaas & Gulsvik, 1985). This increased prevalence of asthma may suggest that a higher proportion of children with asthma have chosen swimming as their competitive physical activity or, on the other hand, it may suggest that heavy physical exercises may provoke bronchial asthma. However, the number of children in the present study was too few to draw firm conclusions. Still, these findings agree with the findings of Weiler et al. (1986) in their study of the prevalence of asthma and bronchial hyperresponsiveness in highly trained competetive football players.

The pulmonary responses to swimming intervals when compared with the pulmonary responses to treadmill running confirmed that interval training and swimming activities are preferable for asthmatic children. Because clinical improvement has been reported in asthmatic children participating in physical exercise programs (Szentágothai et al., 1987), we wanted to study whether bronchial responsiveness also improved during interval swimming training after first having shown the PC_{20} to be reproducible on two different days. Magnussen, Reuss, and Jörres (1986) found no significant change in airway response to metacholine 30 min after two exercise tests 45 min apart on a bicycle ergometer, combined with cold air inhalation. However, in the present study we found increased bronchial responsiveness as measured by histamine inhalation 15 min after completing the interval swim. This corresponds to the findings of Suzuki, Chonan, Sasaki, and Takishima (1985), who found an increased response to metacholine after bicycle ergometry in 9 out of 10 asthmatics.

Furthermore, these findings suggest that the increase in bronchial responsiveness (reduction in PC_{20}) correlated to the load of physical activity as measured by change in blood lactate and BE (Figure 3 and 4). This may explain the increased prevalence of asthma and bronchial hyperresponsiveness in highly trained competitive athletes in the present study and in the investigation of Weiler et al. (1986). Although we measured the short-term effects upon the bronchial responsiveness, repeated daily or sometimes twice daily, heavy training sessions may induce permanently increased bronchial responsiveness, thus provoking asthmatic symptoms in susceptible individuals. These suggestions do not contradict the findings of clinical improvement and improved mastering of illness in asthmatic children involved in more moderately and more balanced physical training programs. The clinical improvement is a measure not only of the activity of the illness, but also of the improved social relations of the children participating in such programs (Backman, 1983).

Asthmatic individuals competing in other sports such as cross-country skiing may be at a further disadvantage when other unhappy conditions such as inhalation of cold air are combined with the effect of the heavy physical activity itself. Further studies are needed in this field to evaluate the most favorable training models for asthmatic individuals that also improve physical fitness.

Acknowledgments

We thank Robert Stallman and Jan Roger Nygaard for skilled technical help during the study and for their enthusiastic training of the children participating in the study. Financial support has been received from the Norwegian Red Cross Research Fund for asthmatic children.

REFERENCES

Backman, A. (1983). Physiological and psychological aspects of the training of asthmatic children. In S. Oseid & A.M. Edwards (Eds.), *The asthmatic child in play and sport* (pp. 277-282). London: Pitman Books.

Carlsen, K.H., Bech, R., Oseid, S., & Schroder, E. (1986). Bronchial reactivity measured by EIA-test and PC_{20}-histamine: A comparison of two methods. In J. Rutenfranz, R. Mocellin, & F. Klimt (Eds.), *Children and exercise XII* (pp. 295-300). Champaign, IL: Human Kinetics.

Chen, W.Y., & Hortin, D.J. (1977). Heat and water loss from the airways and exercise-induced asthma. *Respiration*, **34**, 305-313.

Conconi, F., Ferrari, M., Ziglio, P.G., Droghetti, P., & Codeca, L. (1982). Determination of the anaerobic threshold by a noninvasive field test in runners. *Journal of Applied Physiology*, **52**, 869-873.

Heck, H., Mader, A., Hess, G., Mucke, S., Muller, R., & Hollman, W. (1985). Justification of the 4 mmol • l lactate threshold. *Journal of Sports Medicine*, **6**, 117-130.

Inbar, O., Dotan, R., Dlin, R.A., Neuman, I., & Bar-Or, O. (1980). Breathing dry or humid air and exercise-induced asthma during swimming. *European Journal of Applied Physiology*, **44**, 43-50.

Lee, T.H., & Anderson, S.D. (1985). Heterogeneity of mechanisms in exercise induced asthma. *Thorax*, **40**, 481-487.

Magnussen, H., Reuss, G., & Jörres, R. (1986). Airway response to metacholine during exercise induced refractoriness in asthma. *Thorax*, **41**, 667-670.

Oseid, S. (1982). Asthma and physical activity. *Scandinavian Journal of Social Medicine*, **29** (Suppl.), 227-234.

Skarpaas, I.J.K., & Gulsvik, A. (1985). Prevalence of asthma and respiratory symptoms in schoolchildren in Oslo. *Allergy*, **40**, 295-299.

Suzuki, S., Chonan, T., Sasaki, H., & Takishima, T. (1985). Bronchial hyperresponsiveness to metacholine after exercise in asthmatics. *Annals of Allergy*, **54**, 136-141.

Szentágothai, K., Gyene, I., Szócska, M., & Osváth, P. (1987). Physical exercise program for children with bronchial asthma. *Pediatric Pulmonology*, **3**, 166-172.

Weiler, J.M., Metzger, W.J., Donnelly, A.L., Crowley, E.D., & Sharath, M.D. (1986). Prevalence of bronchial hyperresponsiveness in highly trained athletes. *Chest*, **90**, 23-28.

Lung Function and Exercise Testing in Asthmatic Children at a Special School for Children With Severe Asthma

Vasiliki Gemou Engesæth
Kai-Håkon Carlsen
Kjell Aas
Children's Institute of Asthma and Allergy Voksentoppen, Oslo, Norway

The Voksentoppen School is associated with the Voksentoppen Institute and Hospital (the Norwegian national center for children with asthma and allergy). Children from all over Norway are admitted to the hospital and attend the school during their stay. In addition, approximately 30 children from the Oslo area attend the school during daytime but live at home. The latter outpatient pupils have not been able to attend ordinary schools due to difficulties caused by their illness. In the Voksentoppen School special care is taken toward factors provoking illness. The education program, including sports and gymnastics, is individually adjusted to the child and his or her illness. The children are under medical supervision at school, and they are admitted to the hospital whenever needed. In the present study the outpatient children attending the Voksentoppen School were studied via lung function tests, exercise tests, and allergological examination.

PATIENTS AND METHODS

Patients

Eighteen children (11 boys and 7 girls), aged 8 to 15 years, with asthma were included in the study. Their asthma was graded as Grade 4 in 14 children, Grade 3 in 3 children, and Grade 2 in 1 child (Aas, 1981). Three children did not use antiasthmatic drugs daily; 6 children used beta-2-agonists, theophylline, and/or inhalation of disodium cromoglycate, and 9 children used beclomethasone by aerosol on a regular basis.

Of the remaining 12 outpatient pupils, 4 were not included due to other chronic disease. Two children did not suffer from asthma, but from other severe atopic diseases. One was below 8 years of age. The remaining 5 children did not return the informed consent or refused to participate. The children were studied in periods free from respiratory infections and other concurrent illnesses. Sustained-release theophylline, sustained-release terbutaline, and antihistamines were stopped 72 hr before the tests. Beta-2-agonists, usual theophylline, and disodium cromoglycate were stopped 8 hr before the tests. Corticosteroid treatment remained unchanged. Astemizole, used by one patient, was stopped 10 weeks before the study.

Methods

Lung function was measured by maximal expiratory flow volume curves (MEFVC) (Vitalograph compact spirometer) and total airways resistance (RT) according to the shutter method (AW-screen, Erich Jaeger GMBH & Co. KG) (Klein, Urbanek, Kohler, & Matthys, 1983; Plas & Vooren, 1982). Reversibility tests were performed by measuring lung function before and after inhalation of Salbutamol in saline 0.9% in the dose of 0.05 mg/kg body weight, nebulized by the PARI standard nebulizer (Paul Ritzau Pari Werk KG). Forced expiratory volume in first second (FEV_1), forced expiratory flow at 25% (FEF_{25}), 50% (FEF_{50}), 75% (FEF_{75}), and between 25% and 75% (FEF_{25-75}) of the forced vital capacity (FVC) were measured. RT was measured during tidal ventilation and throughout a forced expiratory maneuver in steps of 0.2 s. The latter was recorded by a X-Y plotter. During the forced expiration, RT at 50% (RT_{50}) and 75% (RT_{75}) of FVC were estimated from the plot and compared to the corresponding values of the flow volume curves, FEF_{50} and FEF_{75}.

Exercise tests were performed by running for 6 min on a motor driven treadmill with an inclination of 4° at a steady state heart rate of at least 170 beats per min (submaximal workload) (Anderson & Schoeffel, 1985; Oseid & Haaland, 1978). Running was performed in stable environmental conditions (relative humidity of the air: 55% to 65%; temperature: 20 to 22 °C). Lung function (MEFVC) was measured before running, immediately after, and 3, 6, 10, 15, and 20 min thereafter. A fall in FEV_1 of more than 15% was considered to be diagnostic for exercise-induced asthma (EIA). Transcutaneous pO_2 ($tcpO_2$) and transcutaneous pCO_2 ($tcpCO_2$) (Roche Microgass 7140, Kontron Instruments) were recorded continuously during and for 20 min after the exercise tests. One child participating in the study was not tested on the treadmill due to chronic bronchial obstruction.

All patients were evaluated by routine allergological examination consisting of case histories, skin prick tests (SPT) (Aas & Belin, 1972), radioimmunosorbent test (Phadebas-PRIST), and radioallergosorbent tests (Phadebas RAST). Allergen preparations were selected according to the case history. The patients were considered to be atopic by fulfilling any two of the following three criteria: (a) raised total IgE (above the normal values according to age), as reported by the manufacturer; (b) positive SPT; and (c) positive RAST (at least Class 2).

Statistical Methods

Statistical analyses were performed using the Spearman's rank correlation coefficient (*rs*), the Pearson's correlation coefficient (*r*), Wilcoxon Rank test for pair differences (WRT), and the chi-square test. All tests performed were two-tailed. Differences were considered to be statistically significant at a 5% level ($p < .05$).

RESULTS

Of the 18 children, 14 were found to be atopic. Absenteeism from school during the last year before admission to the Voksentoppen School was 26.7 days (mean value), range 3 to 70 days of a total of 185 school days per year, compared with the 3.3 days per year (mean value), range 0 to 9, after beginning at the Voksentoppen School (WRT: $p < .01$). A positive correlation was found between absence from school the last year before admittance to Voksentoppen and baseline FEV_1 (percent of predicted value; $rs = .51$, $p < .5$).

The results of lung function and reversibility tests are shown in Table 1. Baseline lung function (mean values) were lower than predicted values based upon height, age, and sex (Knudson, Lebowitz, Holberg, &

Table 1 Lung Function (Maximal Expiratory Flow Volume Curves and Total Airways Resistance) in 18 Asthmatic Children and Percent Increase After Inhalation of Nebulized Salbutamol[a]

	Mean value ± SEM	
% (of predicted)	Starting lung function	Percent increase after salbutamol inhalation
FEV_1	79.8 ± 1.93	10.48 ± 1.43
FEF_{25-75}	63.83 ± 4.33	37.19 ± 5.55
FEF_{75}	56.5 ± 4.75	47.85 ± 7.07
FEF_{50}	66.44 ± 4.5	40 ± 6.93
FEF_{25}	73.11 ± 4.78	19.85 ± 4.62
RT (Kpascal • L • s)	0.66 ± 0.06	28.11 ± 4.36
RT_{50}	0.59 ± 0.08	39.44 ± 5.68
RT_{75}	1.55 ± 0.15	34.07 ± 5.94

[a]The results are given as mean values and standard error of the mean (SEM).

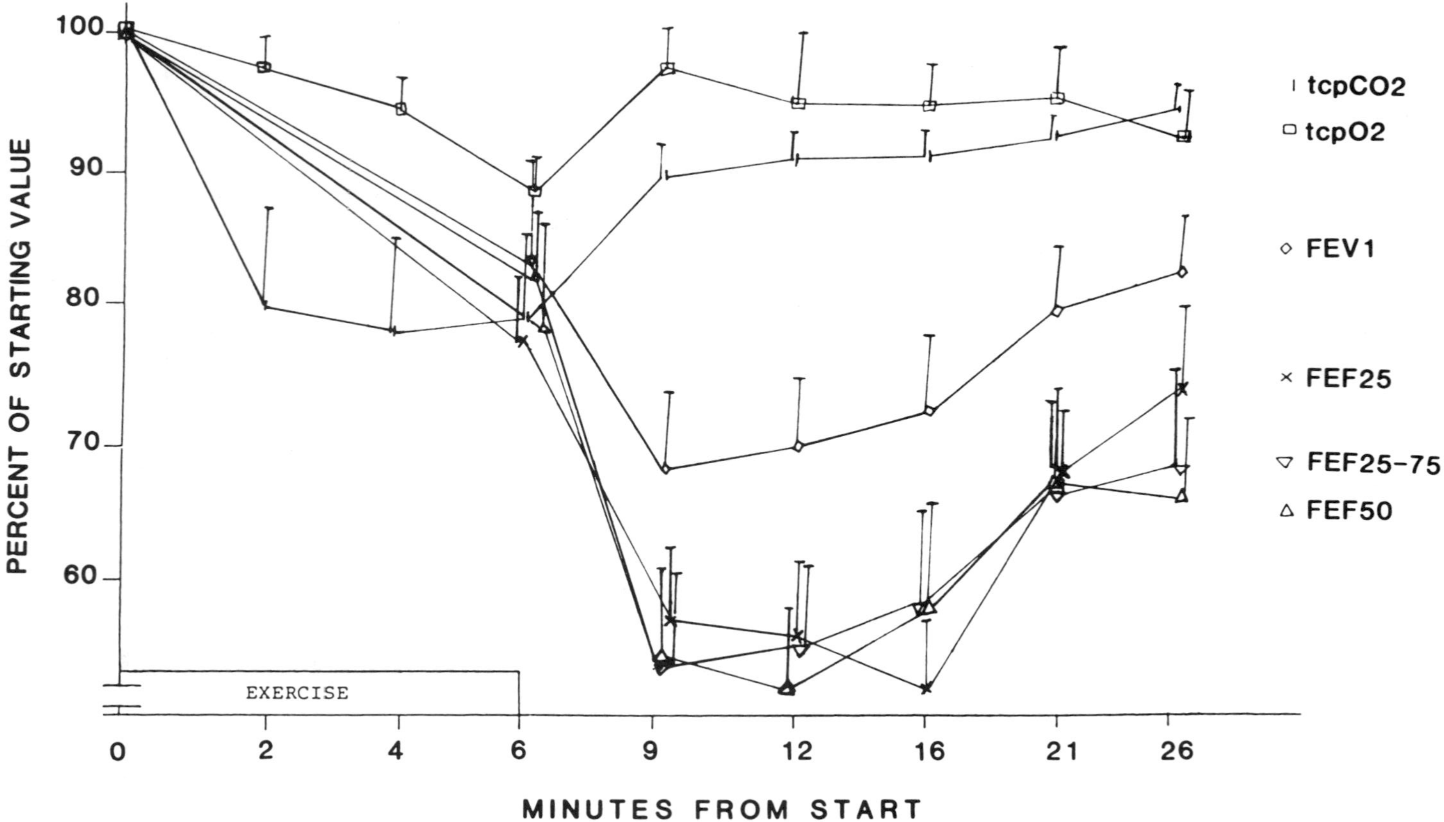

Figure 1. Change in lung function, transcutaneous pO_2, and transcutaneous pCO_2 during and after 6 minutes of treadmill running at submaximal work load in 17 asthmatic children. The results are given as mean values and standard error of the mean.

Burrows, 1983; Polgar & Promadhat, 1971), and increased after inhalation of salbutamol. A significant correlation was found between FEV_1 in percent of predicted value and increase of FEV_1 after salbutamol inhalation ($r = .46$, $p < .05$). RT decreased after salbutamol inhalation. RT_{75} and RT_{50} showed a negative correlation to FEF_{75} and FEF_{50} after salbutamol inhalation ($r = .44$, $.01 < p < .05$ and $r = .43$, $.01 < p < .05$, respectively).

The results of the exercise tests are given in Figure 1. MEFV values fell after exercise to a maximum reduction of FEV_1, FEF_{75}, and FEF_{50} after 3 to 6 min. FEF_{25} and FEF_{25-75} reached their minimum 10 min after exercise. FEV_1 fell more than 15% in 13 of 17 children, whereas FEF_{25-75} fell more than 35% in 14 children (the same 13 and 1 more).

Mean values of $tcpO_2$ and $tcpCO_2$ also decreased during exercise. After some increase in $tcpO_2$ immediately after termination of exercise, a reduction again occurred 3 min after the exercise. Positive correlations between $tcpO_2$ and FEF_{75} ($r = .51$, $p < .05$), FEF_{50} ($r = .51$, $p < .05$), and FEF_{25-75} ($r = .49$, $p < .05$) after exercise were found. Mean $tcpCO_2$ gradually increased after exercise but did not reach the preexercise levels within the observation time. No significant correlation was found between $tcpCO_2$ and FEF_{50}, FEF_{75}, and FEF_{25-75}. No significant correlation was found between baseline lung function and improvement of lung function after salbutamol inhalation, decrease of lung function after exercise, and the daily antiasthmatic medication used by the children.

DISCUSSION

Bronchial asthma, a common chronic disease of childhood, is often associated with absenteeism from school and reduced participation in school activities and games (Chai, Purcell, Brady, & Falliers, 1968; Hill, Britton, & Tattersfield, 1987). For the asthmatic child the approach to the illness at school is important for the child's capability of learning in school and his or her social adaptation, as well as for the disease activity.

The children of the present study were not able to attend ordinary schools due to exacerbations of their asthma during school attendance. School absenteeism was associated with the severity of their asthma, as illustrated by the positive correlation between number of days absent from the previous school and their baseline lung function. Despite their severe asthma, the children's school attendance significantly improved after they began at Voksentoppen School. Properly educated teachers with knowledge about the illness play an important role in the supervision of children with asthma, and close cooperation with medical personnel gives optimum results for mastering the disease and for the child's general well-being. The reversibility of lung function (see Table 1) may represent a slight persistent airflow obstruction. The improvement of both RT and MEFV curves after salbutamol inhalation confirms the need of bronchodilator therapy and/or local steroid inhalation in these children.

EIA occurs in 70% to 80% of the asthmatic population (Andersson, 1983; Bungaard, 1986) and depends upon the mode of exercise (Oseid & Haaland, 1978). This corresponds to the finding of EIA in 76% of our patients. The reduction in lung function after exercise reflects the bronchial hyperreactivity of these patients (Carlsen, Bech, Oseid, & Schroder, 1986). West (1987) underlined pO_2 as a measure of gas exchange. A close relationship of $tcpO_2$ and arterial pO_2 has been reported by several investigators (Hansen & Tooley, 1979; Rooth, Huch, & Huch, 1987). Wennergren, Engstroem, and Bjure (1986) found good agreement between changes in $tcpO_2$ and $tcpCO_2$ and the clinical features of the acute asthmatic child. The reduction found in $tcpCO_2$ (see Figure 1) may be due to hyperventilation. Reduction of lung function after exercise corresponded to $tcpO_2$ values but not to $tcpCO_2$ values. The reduced $tcpO_2$ during and after exercise together with the correlation to the reduction in FEF_{25}, FEF_{50}, and FEF_{25-75} demonstrate that increased demands of oxygen during exercise are not met fully by hyperventilation in these asthmatic children.

To sum up, we have demonstrated reduced lung function and increased bronchial hyperreactivity in asthmatic children who were unable to attend ordinary schools. Despite the severity of illness, they were able to attend school and master their illness when proper precautions were taken in a special school with the supervision of trained teachers and medical personnel.

REFERENCES

Aas, K. (1981). Heterogeneity of bronchial asthma. *Allergy*, **36**, 3-14.

Aas, K., & Belin, L. (1972). Standardization of diagnostic work in allergy. *Acta Allergol.*, **27**, 439-468.

Anderson, S.D. (1983). Current concepts of exercise induced asthma. *Allergy*, **38**, 289-302.

Anderson, S.D., & Schoeffel, R.E. (1985). Standardization of exercise testing in the asthmatic patient, a challenge in itself. In F.E. Hargeave & A.J. Woolcock (Eds.), *Airway responsiveness measurement and interpretation* (pp. 51-59). Canada: Astra Pharmaceuticals.

Bungaard, A. (1986). Exercise-induced asthma. *European Journal of Respiratory Diseases*, **68** (Suppl. 143), 51-56.

Carlsen, K.-H., Bech, R., Oseid, S., & Schrφder, E. (1986). Bronchial reactivity measured by EIA-test and PC_{20}-histamine: A comparison of two methods. In J. Rutenfranz, R. Mocellin, & F. Klimt (Eds.), *Children and exercise XII* (pp. 295-300). Champaign, IL: Human Kinetics.

Chai, H., Purcell, K., Brady, K., & Falliers, C.J. (1968). Therapeutic and investigational evaluation of asthmatic children. *Allergy*, **41**, 23-36.

Hansen, T., & Tooley, W. (1979). Skin surface carbon dioxide tension in sick infants. *Pediatrics*, **64**, 942-945.

Hill, R.A., Britton, J.R., & Tattersfield, A.E. (1987). Management of asthma in schools. *Archives of Disease in Childhood*, **62**, 414-415.

Klein, G., Urbanek, K., Kohler, D., & Matthys, H. (1983). Inhalative bronchiale provokationstests bei kinder: Vergleichende messungen der oszilations-, verschlussdruck-und plethysomographicschen resistance. *Klin. Paediat.*, **195**, 33-37.

Knudson, R.J., Lebowitz, M.D., Holberg, C.J., & Burrows, B. (1983). Changes in the normal maximal expiratory flow volume curve with growth and aging. *American Review of Respiratory Diseases*, **127**, 725-734.

Oseid, S., & Haaland, K. (1978). Exercise studies on asthmatic children before and after regular physical training. In B. Eriksson & B. Furberg (Eds.), *Swimming medicine, IV* (pp. 32-41). Baltimore: University Park Press.

Plas, K., & Vooren, P. (1982). The opening interrupter. *European Journal of Respiratory Diseases*, **63**, 449-458.

Polgar, G., & Promadhat, U. (1971). *Pulmonary function testing in children*. Philadelphia: W.B. Saunders.

Rooth, G., Huch, A., & Huch, R. (1987). Transcutaneous oxygen monitors are reliable indicators of arterial oxygen tention (if used correctly). *Pediatrics*, **76**, 283-286.

Wennergren, G., Engstroem, I., & Bjure, J. (1986). Transcutaneous oxygen and carbon dioxide levels and a clinical symptom scale for monitoring the acute asthmatic state in infants and young children. *Acta Paediatrica Scandinavica*, **75**, 465-469.

West, J.B. (1987). Assessing pulmonary gas exchange. *New England Journal of Medicine*, **316**, 1336-1338.

Physical Education for Asthmatic Children: The Relationship Between Changes in Heart Rate, Perceived Exertion, and Motivation for Participation

Wenche Nystad
Svein Oseid
Elisabeth B. Mellbye
Voksentoppen School, Oslo, Norway

It is well known that asthmatic children need physical training as part of their rehabilitation programs. Numerous studies have shown the importance of this (Oseid & Edwards, 1983). Children with severe asthma are often delayed in various motor skills and have poor working capacities compared with their peers (Strunk, Kelly, & Rubin, 1983). Psychosocial factors such as low self-esteem, emotional problems, and poor body awareness also characterize these children (Andrasch, 1982).

At Voksentoppen, a special school for asthmatic children, physical activity is an important part of the school program. In fact, the children enrolled in this school have more time devoted to physical education classes than the normal children in the public schools in Norway. The school is part of and works in close cooperation with the Voksentoppen Asthma and Allergy Institute. At the institute, play and sport activities are part of the total approach to the rehabilitation of the asthmatic child (Aas, 1983).

BACKGROUND OF THE STUDY

The purpose of this study was to determine how the asthmatic children responded to the physical education programs conducted at Voksentoppen School. The physical education programs were developed in order to enhance both physical fitness and psychosocial factors. Play and sport activities, in addition to problem solving, teaching of theory, and group discussions, are part of each lesson. This teaching method was developed following the pedagogical principles underlying the concept of confluent education (Brown, 1971), educational involvement (Glasser, 1981; Nissen, 1983), and development through play and sport (Åhs, 1987).

Data are needed concerning children's exercise intensity levels in different play and sport activities. First, through different ways of organizing teaching and the choice of activities, it is possible to increase and decrease the children's activity levels. Asthmatic children may work below their submaximal exercise intensity levels because of their apparent difficulty in differentiating between wheeziness and natural dyspnea. Second, it was important to ascertain how asthmatic children perceived their exertion compared with their actual heart rate. This relationship was ascertained by use of the Borg Scale.

Normal children aged 10 to 12 years are generally highly motivated to take part in physical education (Kjϕrmo & Knutsen, 1986). Asthmatic children may have a totally different attitude toward physical activity and exercise intensity because of their chronic disease. Because of fear of difficulty in breathing, the children may lower their motivation for participating in play and sport activities when the heart rate increases. Studying the relationship between heart rate and motivation for participation was the third purpose of the study.

METHODS

The study took place during one 60-min physical education class once a week during 1 school year (September to May) in 1985. A group of 10 prepubertal asthmatic children, aged 10 to 12 years (4 girls and 6 boys), from Voksentoppen special school for asthmatic children in Oslo were chosen for the study.

Table 1 Descriptive Data of the Subjects (N = 10)

Subject (no)	Age (yr)	Sex	HR maxs (beats.min^{-1})	Asthma grade
1	10	girl	205	IV
2	11	girl	218	III
3	11	boy	216	II
4	11	boy	215	IV
5	11	boy	216	IV
6	12	boy	217	III
7	12	girl	210	II
8	12	girl	215	III
9	12	boy	205	II
10	12	boy	214	III

(M= 214 beats.min^{-1})

This school group was one of the four permanent classes at Voksentoppen School, which has approximately 50 pupils ranging in age from 7 to 16 years (Table 1). The children's severity of asthma varied from lighter to severe asthma, Grades III to IV. The grade of obstruction and daily asthmatic problems formed the basis for this clinical classification of I to V developed by the Voksentoppen Asthma and Allergy Institute (Aas, 1987).

Maximum heart rate was measured by treadmill running to exhaustion after premedication and a warm-up period of 10 min. PEF, FVC, and FEV_1 were measured by a Pocket Spirometer before and after premedication and immediately after each physical education lesson. In order to measure heart rate, each subject wore a Sport Tester PE 2000 System (receiver, microcomputer, pulstransmitter, and an electrode belt) with a memory function that stored values every 30 s. Perceived exertion was estimated by each child's using the Borg Scale (6-20 categories) three to five times during each physical education lesson. Stick figures were used to help the children utilize the scale (Figure 1). Motivation for participation in

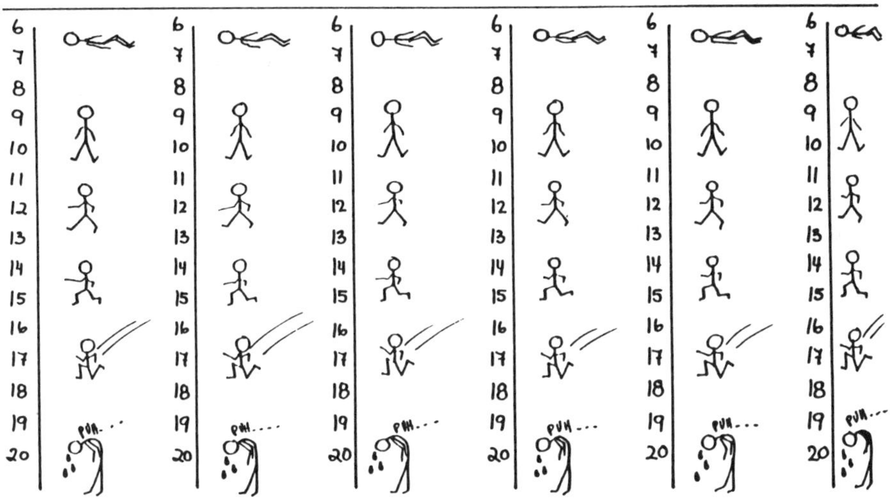

Figure 1. Borg scale with stick figures.

different play and sport activities was evaluated by every child indicating on a 5-point scale (Figure 2) three to five times during each physical education lesson. Each physical education lesson was accurately described by an observer and the physical education teacher.

RESULTS

The mean maximum heart rate measured by treadmill running (Table 1) was 214 beats • min^{-1}, and HRmax ranged from 205 to 218 beats • min^{-1}.

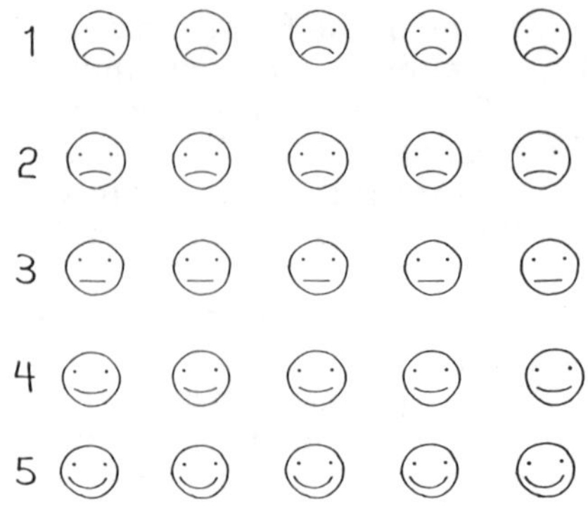

Figure 2. A scale of motivation for participation.

The exercise intensity levels of these asthmatic children were mostly below HR 150 beats • min^{-1} during physical education lessons. On the average the heart rate exceeded 150 beats • min^{-1} only 20% of the time during the physical education lesson (Table 2). The principle of interval training functioned well as shown by a typical example (Figure 3). Interval training in this connection means that the activities were organized in a way that gave the children natural changes in exercise intensity levels.

The children had difficulties in using the Borg 6-20 category scale to accurately assess their exercise intensity levels (Figure 4). They had a ten-

Table 2 Percentages of Time for Various Heart Rates (beats • min^{-1}) During Physical Education Lessons

No of p.e.lesson	percent of the p.e. lesson		
	HR 134 and <	HR 135-149	HR 150 and >
1	55	19	26
2	80	12	8
3	68	18	14
4	55	18	37
5	59	17	29
6	43	26	31
7	67	14	19
8	64	18	18
9	74	15	11
10	82	10	7
M	64	16	20

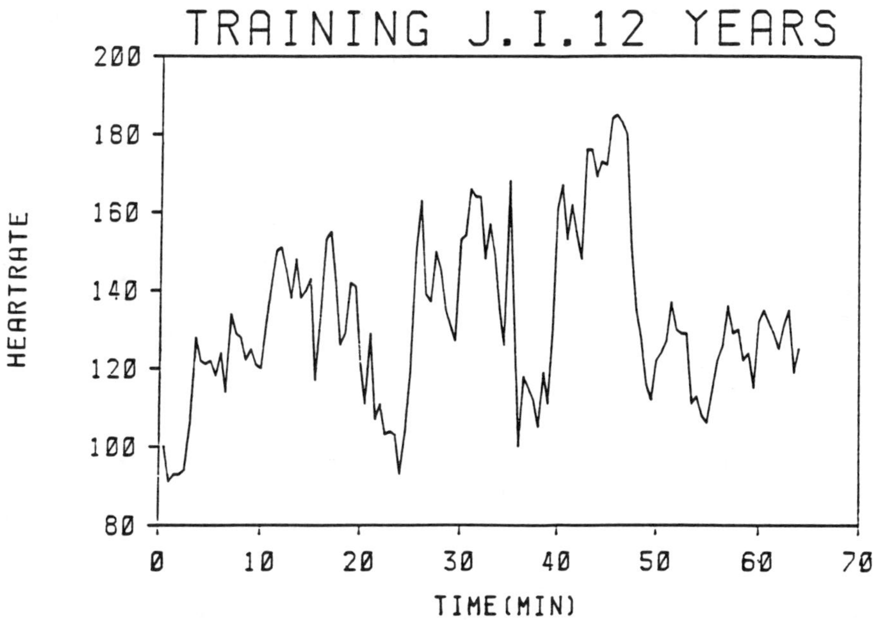

Figure 3. A typical example of short natural exercise periods during a physical education lesson of 60-min duration.

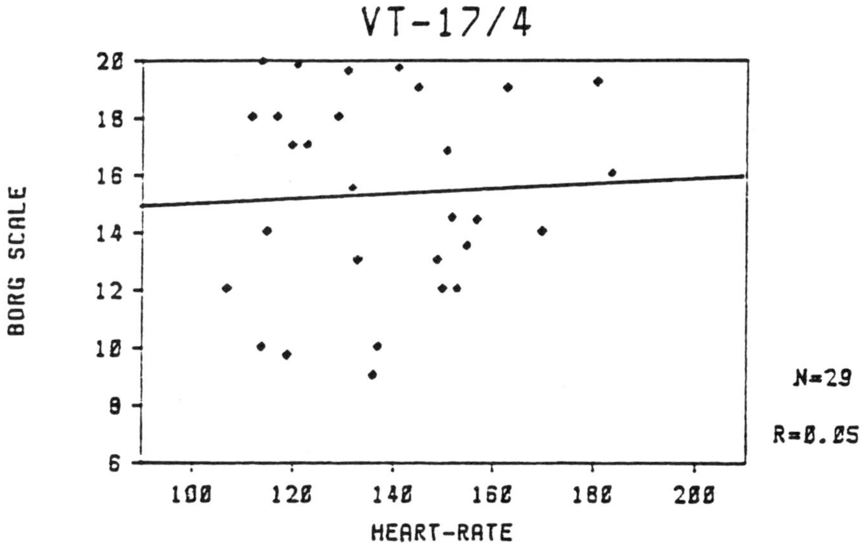

Figure 4. The children's perceived exertions.

dency to perceive their exertion as being more strenuous than the actual heart rate indicated. On the average 55% of the ratings on the Borg scale

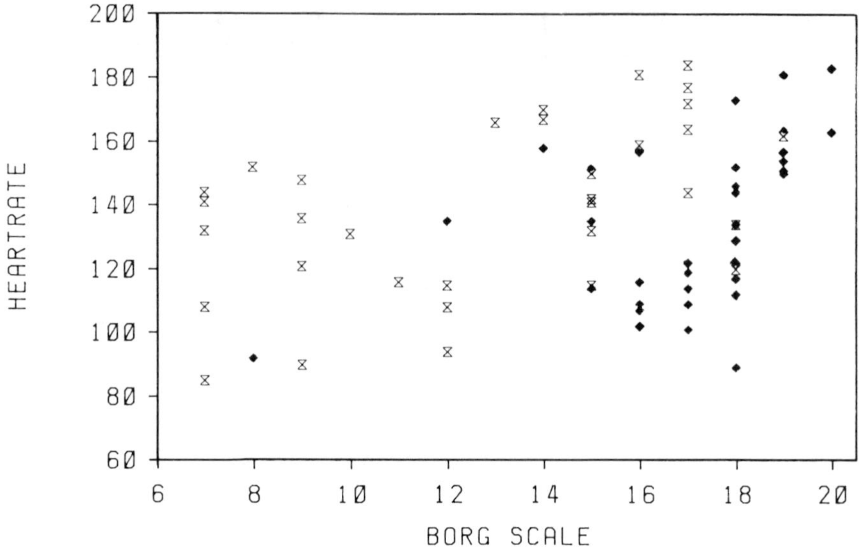

Figure 5. Comparison of the relationships between HR (beats • min^{-1}) and perceived exertion for a child with severe asthma Grade IV (closed symbols) and a child with asthma Grade II (open symbols).

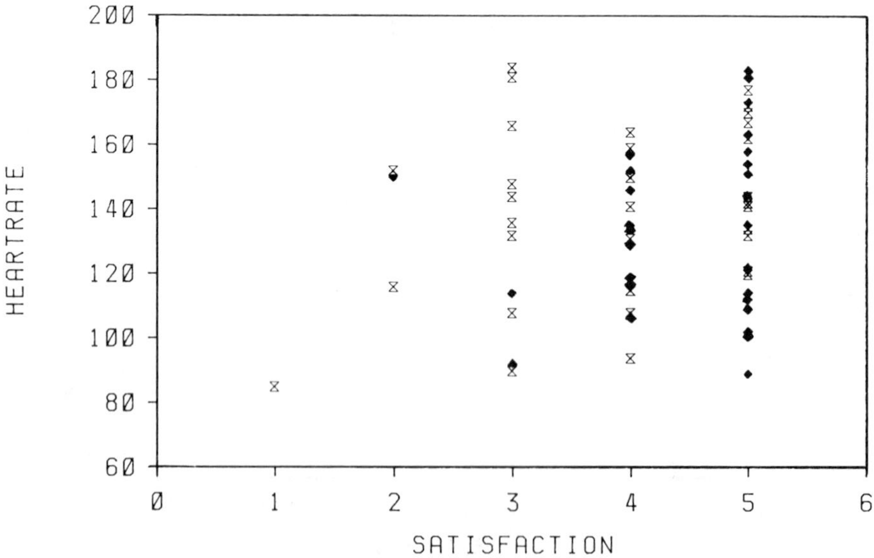

Figure 6. Comparison of the relationships between HR (beats • min^{-1}) and the motivation for participation (satisfaction) of a child with severe asthma Grade IV (closed symbols) and a child with mild asthma Grade II (open symbols).

were 15 or greater although the mean heart rates during 80% of the time were less than 150 beats • min^{-1}.

There was a tendency for a child with severe asthma, Grades III to IV, to perceive his or her exertion as being more strenuous than a child with mild asthma, Grades I to II (Figure 5). This tendency did not affect the motivation for participation (Figure 6).

The asthmatic children's motivations for participation in different play and sport activities were high (Table 3). On the average 77% of the children's evaluations on the 5-point scale were positive. Children marking the smiling faces (4-5) (Figure 2) on the scale were pleased (satisfied) with their participation in the different play and sport activities. Their motivations to participate in activities were independent of their heart rates and perceived exertion. The asthmatic children did not develop any severe bronchial obstruction during the physical education lessons. There were only three extra medications given to three of the children during or after the physical education lessons.

Table 3 Children's Motivation for Participation

No of p.e.lesson	Percent of motivation per lesson.		
	positive	indifferent	negative
1	87	4	9
2	80	10	10
3	59	14	27
4	50	32	18
5	90	3	7
6	82	7	11
7	81	19	-
8	76	10	14
9	100	-	-
10	68	22	10
M	77	12	11

DISCUSSION

It is impossible to generalize from the results of this study because of the small number of subjects and because the responses of asthmatic children to exercise are quite individualistic. Little has been done to quantify the responses of asthmatic children to different play and sport activities. The children's exercise intensity levels tended to be lower than submaximal heart rate (150-170 beats • min^{-1}). This tendency may be due to the school situation. Children tend to have low exercise intensity levels during physical education lessons in school. Asthmatic children taking part in special training groups as a leisure activity may have higher exercise intensity levels in their activities.

Asthmatic children have difficulties in using the Borg category 6-20 scale. This scale may require more experience with and consciousness of different exercise intensity levels during physical training, play, and sport than is usual for asthmatic children. They also may not have understood perceived exertion when explained theoretically to them with examples and tried out during a preproject period of 3 months.

The tendency to perceive their exertion as more strenuous than their actual heart rates may have been caused by the lack of experience with hard exercise intensity levels through natural play activities in early childhood. The high motivation for participation in play and sport activities may be the result of the special educational models used at Voksentoppen School. Each child's need for adapted physical education is given preference in the development of the physical education programs.

The routines for premedication were arranged by the school nurse and doctor in cooperation with the physical education teacher. To premedicate was an important part of the learning process for the children. As a consequence of administration of the medications and the exercise intensity levels, no child developed severe obstruction during the physical education lessons. They were well protected by their individual premedication.

CONCLUSION

Asthmatic children's exercise intensity levels may be below submaximal heart rate 150 to 170 (beats • min^{-1}) in different play and sport activities. They have difficulties in using the Borg scale in estimating their exercise intensity levels. Children with severe asthma may have a tendency to perceive their exertion as being more strenuous than children with less severe asthma. These children derived satisfaction from their participation in all kinds of play and sport activities both outdoors and indoors.

REFERENCES

Aas, K. (1987). *Eczema and asthma among children*. Oslo: Voksentoppen Asthma and Allergy Institute.

Aas, K. (1983). The place of physical activity in the life of children and adolescents with asthma. In S. Oseid & A.M. Edwards (Eds.), *The asthmatic child in play and sport* (pp. 3-9). London: Pitman.

Åhs, O. (1987). *Development through play and sport*. Stockholm: Nature and Culture Publishers.

Andrasch, R.H. (1983). The use of training programmes in the rehabilitation of asthmatic children. In S. Oseid & A.M. Edwards (Eds.), *The asthmatic child in play and sport* (pp. 283-292). London: Pitman.

Brown, George (1971). *Human teaching for human learning*. New York: Viking Press.

Glasser, W. (1981). *Reality therapy*. Copenhagen: Gyldendal.

Kjφrmo, O., & Knudsen, O. (1986). *Attitudes towards physical education and limits for teaching physical education in schools in Oslo*. Oslo: Norwegian College of Physical Education.

Nissen, P. (1983). *Pedagogical involvement—growth in school through classroom meetings with children and adults*. Copenhagen: Gyldendal.

Oseid, S., & Edwards, A.M. (1983). *The asthmatic child in play and sport*. London: Pitman.

Strunk, R.C., Kelly, L.J., & Rubin, D.L. (1983). Recreation therapy in the rehabilitation of asthmatic children. In S. Oseid & A.M. Edwards (Eds.), *The asthmatic child in play and sport* (pp. 283-292). London: Pitman.

Cold Air Inhalation Test in Broncho-Hyperreactive Individuals

Magnus Wickman
Children's Asthma and Allergy Institute, Oslo, Norway

Bronchial hyperreactivity (BHR) is considered to be the basic prerequisite of bronchial asthma and may be measured quantitatively by several different methods. Inhalation of nebulized histamine or methacholine with measurement of the change in lung function are the most commonly used methods (Hargreave et al., 1981). The response in lung function to submaximal exercise (EIA-test) may also be used as a measure of BHR as shown by Silverman and Anderson (1972). Recently, inhalation of cold, dry air has been introduced by O'Byrne et al. (1982) as another method for estimating BHR.

The correlation between bronchial responsiveness to hyperventilation with cold air and inhalation of methacholine in asthma has been demonstrated by O'Byrne et al. (1982); Weis, Rossing, McFadden, and Ingram (1983); and Nair, Hoop, Alper, Bewtra, and Townley (1986). These cold-air tests have been performed with the subjects at rest and with different frequencies of ventilation. Another approach has been to perform a provocation with cold air −18 °C plus or minus 5 °C at rest and during submaximal exercise. With this as a background an attempt was made to develop a simple method for a cold-air inhalation test with or without a simultaneous standardized exercise test.

METHODS

Cold-Air Test Apparatus

Figure 1 shows the construction of the cold-air test apparatus. A two-stage single-housing diving regulator device (Poseidon Jetstream, V. Frolunda, Sweden) was designed for connection to a conventional diving apparatus that can supply pressures up to 3,000 psi (200 bar). The volume of the tank with compressed air may vary from 5 + 5 to 12 + 12 l. This allows the production of an adequate volume of dry air. The first stage reduced the pressure to 145 psi (10 bar). The second-stage valve functions as an on-demand inhalation system. Voluntary inhalation triggers a diaphragm-operated valve system as long as the inhalation phase continues.

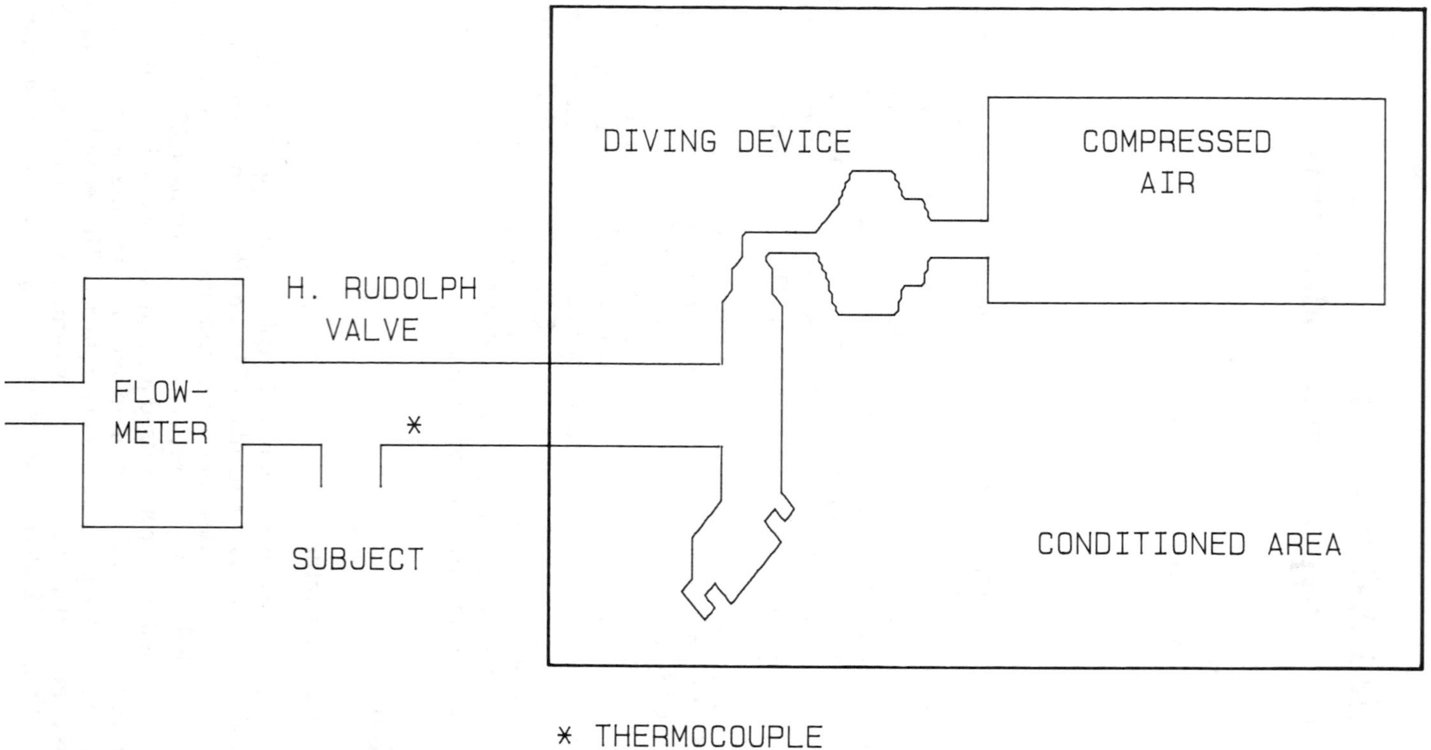

Figure 1. Construction of the cold air test apparatus.

The system provides air with a nearly constant intermediate pressure and maximum flow independent of the pressure in the tank. The tanked air has a humidity of maximum 20 ppm H_2O. The tanks with compressed air are conditioned in a conventional deep freeze down to a temperature of -19 °C $\pm$ 2 °C. Cold air is supplied to the subject through a Hans Rudolph Valve No. 2700 (Hans Rudolph, Kansas City, MO, U.S.A.).

A probe, positioned at a distance of 0.5 to 2 cm from the inspiratory outlet of the valve, measures the temperature of the inspired air. A rapidly responding thermocouple allows the assessment of the temperature of the inspired air. The probe is connected to a high-speed digital thermometer (Jumotherm, TDAt-30/kb., M.K. Juchheim GMBH & Co., Fulda, West Germany). The inspiratory part of the apparatus outside the deep freeze, including the Hans Rudolf Valve, should not exceed a length of 13 to 15 cm. The cost of this apparatus is approximately U.S. $2,000. With this on-demand method, the tests are performed at a standarized inhalation temperature and humidity.

Subjects

To evaluate this method, 10 subjects with moderate to severe bronchial asthma participated in this study. They were 12 to 14 years of age and with a forced expiratory volume during 1 s (FEV_1) greater than 65% of predicted volume after medication on a nebulizer with a beta-2 adrenergic agent (terbutaline) based on Polgar and Promdhat's (1971) reference values. They continued their basic medication during the study except for sustained-release theophyllamine and beta-2 adrenergic preparations, which were not given the morning of the test day. No subject was taking oral steroids. All were in a clinical steady state. They did not report respiratory tract infections and had no relevant antigen exposure in the previous 2 months. The subjects were asked to avoid strenuous exercise on each test day and were at rest in the laboratory 15 min before each test. Baseline FEV_1 was required to stay within $\pm$ 10% from one visit to another.

Performance

The protocol started with a prestudy day with the subject's breathing cold air (-18 °C $\pm$ 5 °C) at rest and with measurement of his or her tidal volume. Respiratory frequency was not controlled and a nose clip was used. Lung function was measured immediately following and at 5, 10, 15, and 20 min after the test. If a decrease in FEV_1 of less than 20% occurred within 20 min after the cold-air breathing at rest, the subject was regarded as being unsuitable for testing with the combination of cold air and submaximal bicycle ergometer exercise for 6 min.

While breathing at rest, the subjects faced a risk of hyperventilation during testing. The use of soft music in the testing room in combination with occupying the subject by having him or her read something of interest prevented this hyperventilation. If the decrease if FEV_1 was 20%

or less within 20 min after the inhalation of cold air, the subject underwent a standardized submaximal bicycle ergometer test at ordinary indoor ambient temperature conditions. A decrease in FEV_1 of more than 20% within 20 min after the exercise test was not allowed for further commitment in the study.

On Day 1, an exercise test on the bicycle ergometer at a submaximal load was performed while breathing cold air. The cold-air tests were conducted on two different days to prevent cumulative effects, as shown by Malo, Cartier, L'Archeveque, Ghezzo, and Martin (1986). Heart rate was electronically recorded (Sport Tester, PE 30000, Polar Electro, Finland). On Day 2, not more than 5 days after Day 1, a metacholine inhalation test (PC_{20}) was performed according to a standardized procedure described by Cockroft, Killian, Mellon, and Hargreave (1977).

Statistical Methods

The results were evaluated by Pearson's product-moment correlation coefficient (r), the chi-square test, and the student's t test. All tests were two-tailed. Differences were considered to be significant at a level of 5% ($p < .05$).

RESULTS

To evaluate the method more effectively, the subjects performed a cold-air exercise test without premedication or their morning medication. Of the 10 subjects, 2 were severe-cold-air hyperactive and showed a significant decrease (> 20%) in FEV_1 during tidal breathing of cold air at rest and were excluded from further challenges. The remaining subjects, 2 girls and 6 boys, fulfilled the criteria to be included in the cold-air exercise test. The mean age of these subjects was 12.89 years (Table 1). They all had a history of BHR, especially to cold air. Informed consent was given by the parents of the children.

Table 1 Subject Characteristics (IB = inhaled beta-2-agonist, OB = oral beta-2-agonist, DT = depot theophylline, SG = sodium cromoglycate, IS = inhaled steroids)

SUBJECT NO	SEX	AGE (YR)	HEIGHT (CM)	REGULAR MEDICATIONS
1	M	12	150	IB, OB, DT, IS
2	F	14	164	IB
3	F	12	157	IB, SG, IS
4	M	12	158	IB, IS
5	M	14	162	IB, OB.DT, SG, IS
6	M	12	145	IB, DT, IS
7	M	13	161	IB, SG
8	M	13	150	IB, DT, SG, IS

Table 2 Functional Results (Subjects Are Arranged According to Their Sensitivity to Methacholine)

SUBJECT NO	TEMP INSP AIR	HEART R STEADY STATE	FEV_1 % PRED	FEV_1 MAX DECREASE AFTER CAC	pc20 MG/ML
1	-18.2	169	75	-69	.0035
2	-17.8	170	75	-24	.26
3	-19.0	167	74	-28	.32
4	-17.9	174	70	-18	.50
5	-16.8	170	66	-22	.76
6	-18.0	178	69	-27	1.05
7	-20.3	166	86	-3	1.80
8	-18.3	172	91	0	3.00

The mean temperature during the test was −18.3 °C (Table 2) with a steady state heart rate during the last minute of exercise of 170 bpm. Of the eight subjects, five had a decrease in FEV_1 of more than 20% with a mean decrease of 34% and a decrease in forced expiratory flow of 25% of the remaining vital capacity (FEF_{25}) of 48.2% (Figures 2 and 3). One subject became obstructive during the last minute of the test. Every lung function measurement was performed twice and the best value selected. All paired recordings were within a variation of ±5%.

Bronchial responsiveness to cold air was correlated with bronchial responsiveness to methacholine (Table 2 and Figures 4 and 5). There was a highly significant positive correlation between PC_{20} methacholine and the cold-air exercise test ($r = .94$, $p < .001$). In regard to the change in FEF_{25} a positive correlation was found between change after methacholine and the cold-air exercise test ($r = .77$, $p < .025$).

Every subject undertook at least 5 cold-air tests except one. Including pretests, there was a total of more than 50 tests administered. No one withdrew from the study, and there were no reports of late reactions. This indicated that the cold-air exercise test was well accepted by all subjects.

DISCUSSION

Different methods of cold-air tests in asthmatic subjects have been described in the literature. The most common systems are based on an air jet stream with continuous flow passing into a modified heat exchanger and rapidly cooled by circulating isopropyl alcohol. Another method was described by Straus, McFadden, Ingram, and Jaegar (1977) using a cooled

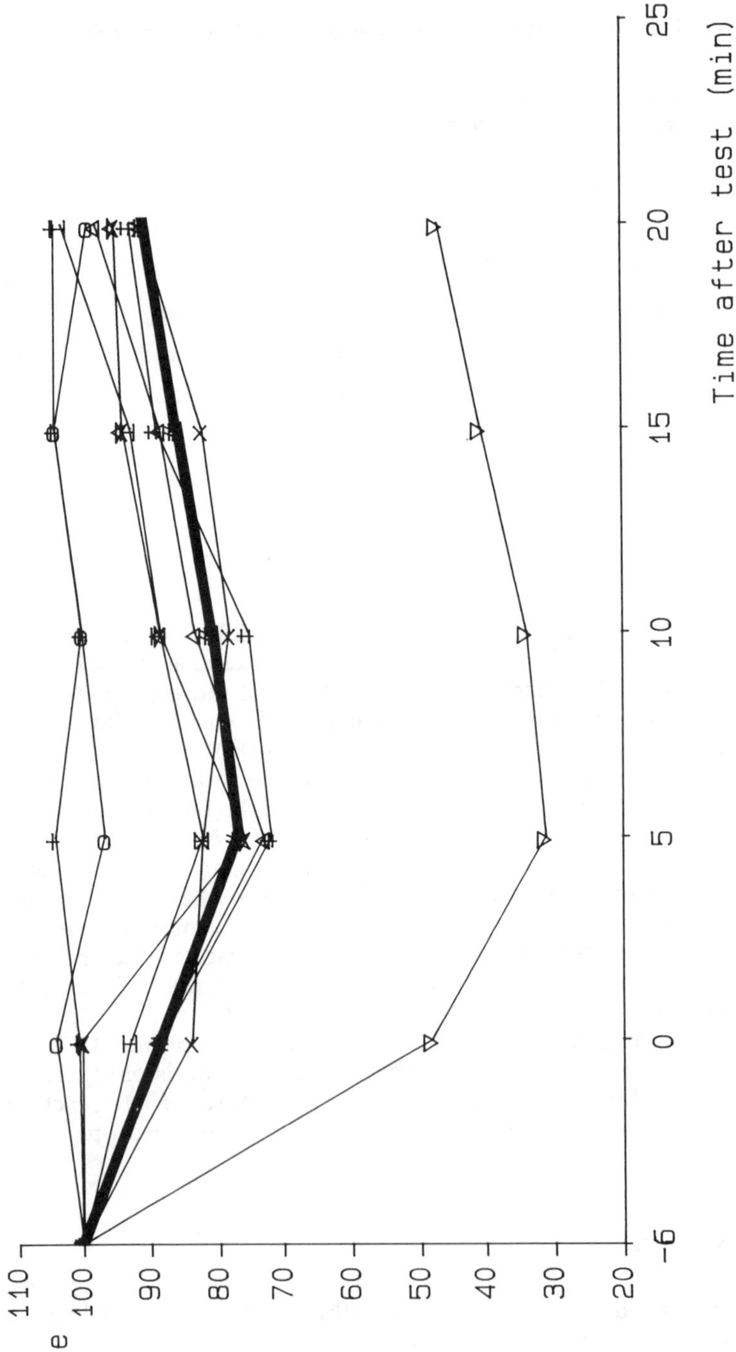

Figure 2. Change in lung function (FEV_1) after cold-air exercise test. Starting value before test is set to 100% (mean value is bold line).

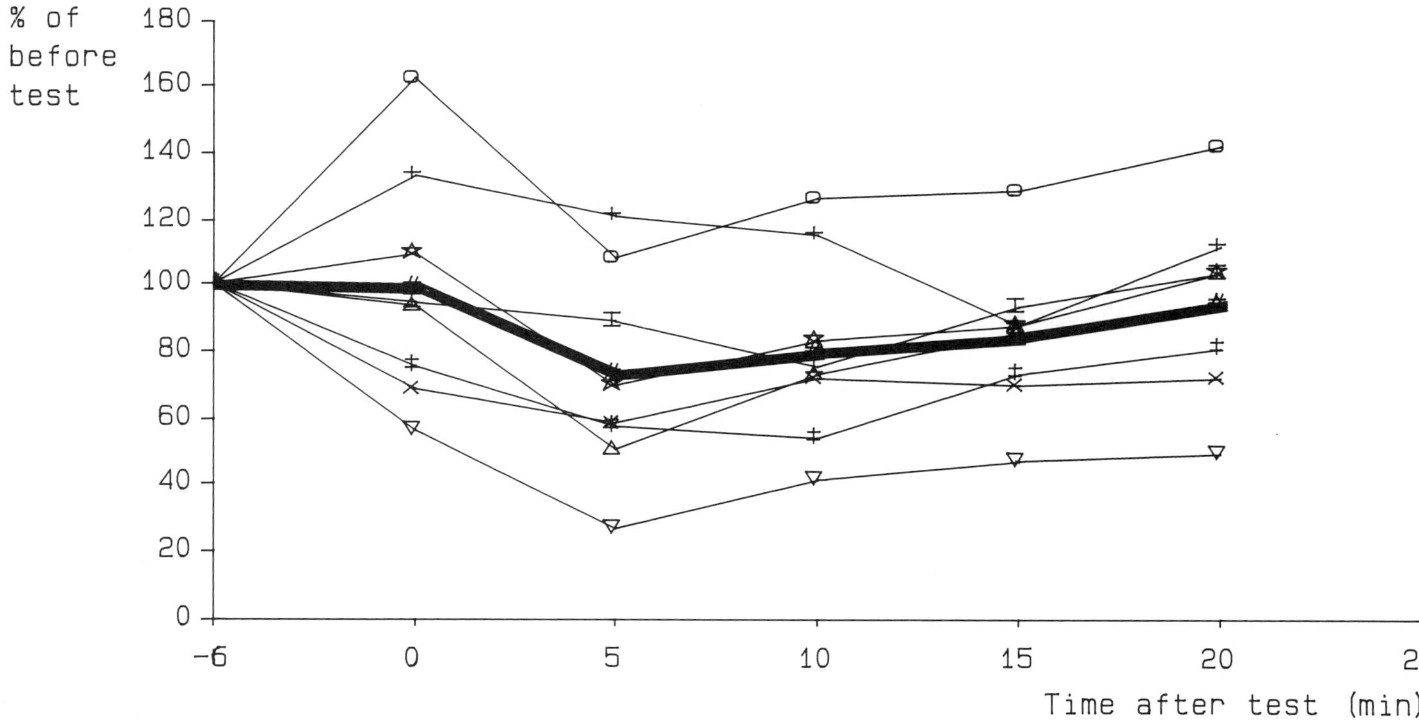

Figure 3. Change in lung function (FEF_{25}) after cold-air exercise test. Starting value before test is set to 100% (mean value is bold line).

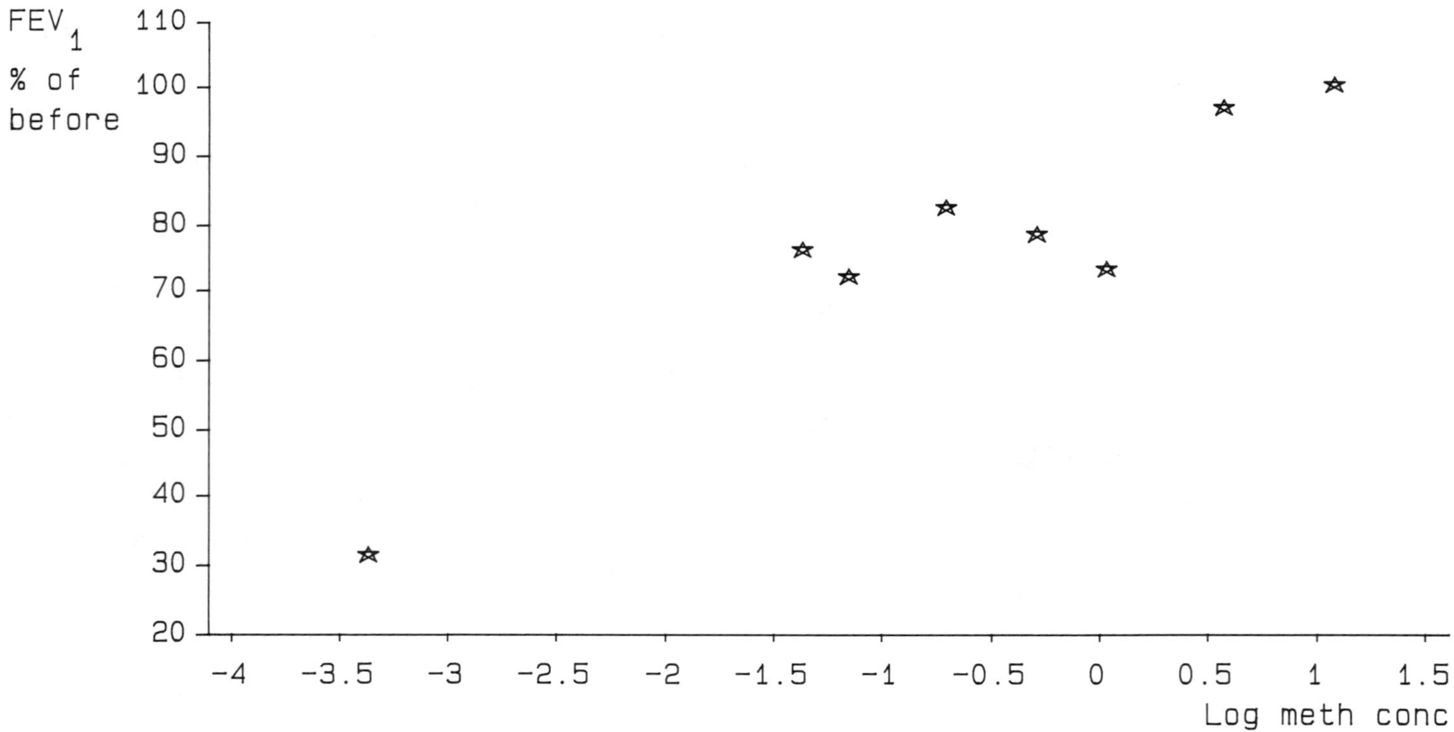

Figure 4. Correlation between maximal fall in FEV_1 after cold-air and submaximal ergometer bicycle exercise test for 6 min and PC_{20} measured by methacholine inhalation test ($r = .94$, $p < .001$).

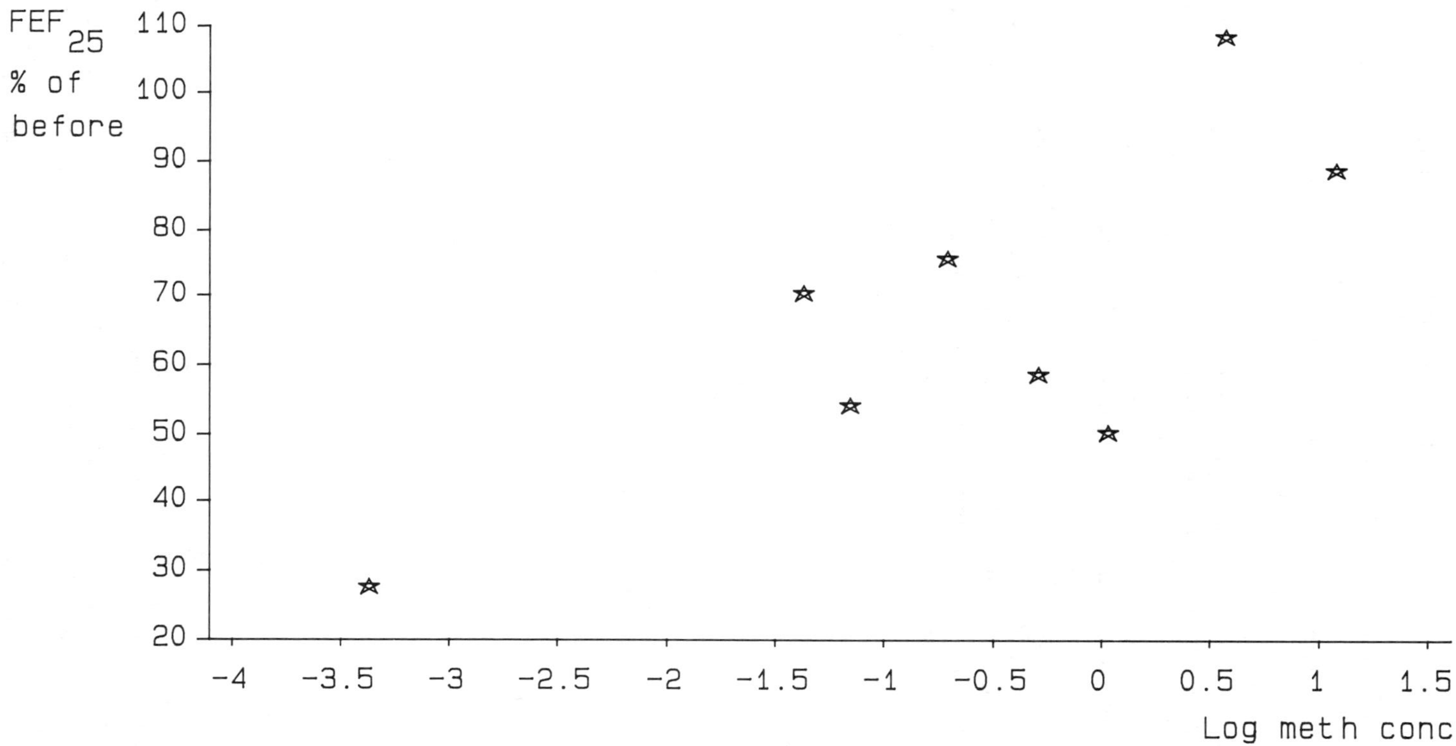

Figure 5. Correlation between maximal fall in FEF_{25} after cold-air and submaximal ergometer bicycle exercise test for 6 min and PC_{20} measured by methacholine inhalation test (r = .77, $p < .025$).

reservoir of air. The cold-air inhalation tests conducted with these different devices were performed with the subject's inhaling cold air at rest for 3 to 5 min at different, but established, frequencies utilizing tidal volumes up to maximal voluntary volume (MVV). The maximal air flow of these systems was mainly between 100 and 120 l • min^{-1}, which limited the air supply needed by the subject when performing a cold-air exercise test for 6 min.

Due to the costs of such apparatus in combination with the disadvantage in practical limitations and especially in gas flow, an attempt was made to develop a simplified *on-demand inhalation method*. The present study shows this method was safe and simple. It may be operated by one to two persons and can easily be performed by subjects above the age of 12 years.

The highly significant correlation of decrease in FEV_1 to PC_{20} methacholine demonstrates that this method is a good measure of BHR. It shows a higher correlation to PC_{20} than an exercise test alone, as shown by Carlsen, Oseid, Odden, and Mellbye (1989), and makes the results of an exercise test more specific. The method should also be of interest for use with athletes who have difficulties in breathing during cold weather, especially individuals participating in winter sports.

Acknowledgments

The author wishes to express his gratitude to all the subjects who participated in this study and to Erlend Hem, Thyra Nylen, and Anngunn Feet for their skillful technical assistance in the preparation of this manuscript. Financial support has been received from the Norwegian Red Cross Research Fund for Asthmatic Children.

REFERENCES

Carlsen, K.-H., Oseid, S., Odden, H., & Mellbye, E. (1989). The response to heavy swimming exercise in children with or without bronchial asthma. In S. Oseid & K.-H. Carlsen (Eds.), *Children and Exercise XIII* (this volume). Champaign, IL: Human Kinetics.

Cockroft, D.W., Killian, D.N., Mellon, J.J.A., & Hargreave, F.E. (1977). Bronchial reactivity to inhaled histamine: A method and a clinical survey. *Clinical Allergy*, **7**, 235-243.

Hargreave, F.E., Ryan, G., Thompson, N.C., O'Byrne, P.M., Latimer, K., Juniper, E.F., & Dolovich, J. (1981). Bronchial responsiveness to histamine or metacholine in asthma: Measurement and clinical significance. *Journal of Allergy and Clinical Immunology*, **68**, 347-355.

Malo, J.L., Cartier, A., L'Archeveque, J., Ghezzo, H., & Martin, R.R. (1986). Cold air inhalation has a cumulative bronchospastisc effect when inhaled in consecutive doses for progressively increasing degree of ventilation. *American Review of Respiratory Disease*, **134**, 990-993.

Nair, N., Hoop, R.J., Alper, B.I., Bewtra, A.K., & Townley, R.G. (1986). Correlation of methacholine-induced nonspecific bronchial reactivity and cold air hyperventilation challenge. *Annuals of Allergy*, **56**, 226-228.

O'Bryne, P.M., Gerard, R., Morris, M., McCormack, D., Jones, N.L., Morse, J.L.C., & Hargreave, F.E. (1982). Asthma induced cold air and its relation to nonspecific bronchial responsiveness to methacholine. *American Review of Respiratory Disease*, **125**, 281-285.

Polgar, G., & Promdhat, V. (1971). *Pulmonary function testing in children—Techniques and standards*. Philadelphia: W.B. Saunders.

Silverman, S., & Anderson, S.D. (1972). Standardization of exercise tests in asthmatic children. *Archives of Disease in Childhood*, **47**, 882-889.

Strauss, R.H., McFadden, E.R., Jr., Ingram, R.H., Jr., & Jaegar, J.J. (1977). Enhancement of exercise-induced asthma by cold air. *New England Journal of Medicine*, **297**, 743-747.

Weis, J.W., Rossing, T.H., McFadden, E.R., & Ingram, R.H. (1983). Relationship between bronchial responsiveness to hyperventilation with cold air and metacholine in asthma. *Journal of Allergy and Clinical Immunology*, **72**, 140-144.

The Effect of Negative Air Ions on Exercise-Induced Asthma

Omri Inbar
Ronald Dlin
Raffy Dotan
Ittai Neuman
Wingate Institute for Physical Education and Sport, Netanya, Israel

Although not unanimously agreed upon, there is ample evidence that air ions of either charge are biologically active (Kreuger & Reed, 1976; Sigel, 1979). The basic effect on biological systems in general and on the respiratory systems in particular is rather poorly understood. However, several theories concerning the mechanisms underlying the negative ion effects on asthma have been proposed:

1. Negative air ions have been shown to reduce blood serotonin levels and, consequently, to alleviate bronchoconstriction (Kreuger & Reed, 1976; Kreuger & Smith, 1960; Kreuger, Smith, & Miller, 1959).
2. An exposure to a negatively ionized environment could result in an increased conversion of succinate to fumarate and in an enhancement of reoxidation of reduced cytochrome (Inbar, Rotstein, Dlin, Dotan, & Sulman, 1982; Kreuger & Reed, 1976; Kreuger & Smith, 1960). Such a reaction will promote oxidative metabolism, thus allowing for less reliance on anaerobic metabolism during exercise stress and reduced lactate buildup, and thereby smaller respiratory heat loss (McFadden & Ingram, 1979; Rebuck & Read, 1968; Seaton, Davis, Gaziano, & Highes, 1969; Vassalo, Gee, & Domm, 1972).
3. It has been suggested that an exposure to negative air ions brings about a lesser increase of afferent activity of vagal bronchopulmonary receptors, thereby preventing an exaggerated ventilatory response, and a reduction of respiratory heat exchange (RHE), and hence a lesser constrictive response following exercise challenge (Bar-Or, Neuman, & Dotan, 1977; Inbar, Alvarez, & Lyons, 1981; McFadden & Ingram, 1979).
4. A favorable action of negative air ions on the ciliated epithilium of the respiratory tract may also occur with a consequent reduction of the airway sensitivity to various stimuli (Priimagi, Krenerman, & Vismapuu, 1979).

Several investigators (Boulatov 1968; Kronbleuh & Griggin, 1955; Kronbleuh, Piersol, & Speicher, 1958; Palti, DeNoun, & Abrahamov, 1966) have reported minor temporary relief of symptoms in patients with bronchial asthma following an exposure to a negatively ionized atmosphere. Others, however, have failed to detect such positive effects (Zylberberg & Loveless, 1960).

The inconsistency found in the relevant literature is probably due in part to the lack of standardization of exposure duration, the measurement used to evaluate bronchial response, the concentration of ions in the test atmosphere, the type of asthma in the sampled patients, and a typical lack of adequate experimental control (Østerballe, Weeke & Albrechtsen, 1979).

Furthermore, to the best of our knowledge, only one attempt has been made to examine the effect of a negatively ionized atmosphere on acute bronchoconstriction in general and exercise-induced asthma (EIA) in particular (Ben-Dov et al., 1983). Because negative ions have been claimed to cause desirable effects, the purpose of the present investigation was to study the influence on EIA of negatively ionized air under controlled and standardized conditions.

PATIENTS AND METHODS

A total of nine males and six females, whose age, weight, and height were (mean ± SE) 16.1 ± 6.6 years, 52.2 ± 19.7 kg, and 158.3 + 14.3 cm, respectively, and whose symptoms met the American Thoracic Society's definition of asthma, took part in this study. Initially they all had clinical symptoms and laboratory findings consistent with perennial asthma and allergic rhinitis of at least 5 years duration. They were all on hyposensitization and had taken medications including bronchodilators, antihistamines, disodiumcromoglycate (DSCG), and beclomethasone aerosol. All patients were symptom free for 1 week or more prior to testing and were instructed to refrain from taking their regular medication at least 12 hr prior to the first session.

Each patient underwent two standardized exercise tests 5 hr apart. The exercise and climatic conditions (Hot Pack, U.S.A., environmental room) of the two sessions were identical except for the ambient negative ion concentration. One session was held under neutral conditions ($1.5 - 2.5 \times 10^2$ of positive and negative ions per milliliter of air—neutral). The other session (ionized) was held in a concentration of $2 - 7 \times 10^4$ negative ions per milliliter of air (including the exercise challenge). This ionic environment was produced by Modalion "Add-On" multipurpose air ionizer (Amcor, Israel) and measured by Kathrein MGK 01 Ionometer (West Germany). Air temperature and humidity in both sessions were 25 ± 1 °C and 50 ± 5%, respectively. Air temperature and humidity were continuously measured and recorded three times during each session. Negative and positive air ion concentrations were measured four times during each session at various locations in the climatic chamber by the same technician, who had no connection with this study.

The exercise consisted of 6 to 8 min of treadmill running that was imposed following 3 hr of rest under the respective atmospheric conditions.

Treadmill slope was set at 5%, and its speed was adjusted to elicit a heart rate (HR) of about 85% of each subject's age-predicted maximum. HR was continuously monitored and recorded every minute, and the mean of the last 3 min of exercise was used for the final analysis. Target HR was reached within 2 min, after which treadmill speed was left unchanged throughout the remainder of the run. Rating perceived shortness of breath (RSB) was determined during the last minute of exercise by asking the patients to rate their breathing difficulties on the Grimby's scale, spanning from 1 through 16 (Grimby, 1976). Session order was randomly assigned with the subjects and the investigators unaware of the type of exposure used or the study's objective (subjects only) (double-blind procedure).

Table 1 Heart Rate (HR) and Rating of Perceived Shortness of Breath (RSB) Measured During the Final Stage of Exercise Under the Two Environments

	HR[a], b • min^{-1}		RSB, units	
Patient	Neutral	Ionized	Neutral	Ionized
Z.S.	160	160	8	6
Z.A.	192	192	9	7
M.O.	210	205	10	7
V.R.	192	192	9	7
S.I.	203	201	7	7
D.M.	145	135	9	7
V.O.	204	206	13	12
G.B.	192	192	5	4
S.N.	204	198	11	11
S.H.	160	158	9	9
H.T.	194	190	12	11
L.D.	187	188	8	7
S.R.	204	204	12	9
A.Y.	185	188	10	10
L.S.	186	189	10	9
$\overline{X}$	187.9	186.5	9.4	8.2
SD	18.9	20.1	2.1	2.2
SE	4.9	5.2	0.5	0.6
p	NS		< .01	

[a]Values are means of data recorded during the last 3 min of exercise.

Following a rest period of approximately 20 min a baseline of pulmonary function was performed using a Hewlett-Packard 47804A pulmonary calculator system. It included forced vital capacity (FVC), forced expiratory volume in one second (FEV_1), midmaximal expiratory flow rate (MMEFR), and peak expiratory flow rate (PF), after which the subjects entered the climatic chamber. Following a rest period of 3 hr within the assigned ionic environment the subjects were retested. They then were given the 6- to 8-min exercise challenge (with or without exposure to negative ions), which was in turn followed by additional pulmonary testing 5 min postexercise. Following the first session, the patients were given a 2-hour lunch break (outside the chamber), after which the second session was commenced. Statistical analysis of the data included descriptive analysis and student *t* tests for paired observations (with vs. without air ions).

RESULTS

The HR and RSB data obtained during the final stage of the treadmill exercise are summarized in Table 1. Despite the similar cardiovascular stress (as indicated by heart rate response) the RSB was significantly lower under the negatively ionized conditions than under the neutral ones.

Depicted in Table 2 are the absolute values of the four pulmonary functions measured prior to exercise (baseline), during recovery, and 5 min postexercise. No significant difference ($p > .05$) between the two environments either prior to or following exercise was evident in any of the pulmonary functions measured. To evaluate the magnitude of postexercise

Table 2 Pulmonary Function in Absolute Terms as Determined Prior to and Following Exercise Under the Two Experimental Conditions[a]

Variable	Condition	Preexercise		Postexercise	
		Neutral	Ionized	Neutral	Ionized
FVC	$\overline{X}$	3.36	3.27	2.50	2.57
(L)	*SEM*	0.28	0.30	0.28	0.29
FEV_1	$\overline{X}$	2.23	2.17	1.40	1.45
(L)	*SEM*	0.23	0.22	0.20	0.20
MMEFR	$\overline{X}$	1.58	1.56	0.83	0.91
($L \cdot sec^{-1}$)	*SEM*	0.24	0.22	0.14	0.19
Peak flow	$\overline{X}$	4.78	4.45	3.02	3.12
($L \cdot sec^{-1}$)	*SEM*	0.57	0.45	0.40	0.43

[a]No significant differences were found in any of the comparisons made ($p < .05$) between the two atmospheric conditions.

Table 3 Postexercise Reduction in Pulmonary Functions Following Exposure to Neutral or Ionized Environment of the Whole Group and its Two Subdivisions

Group	Variable	FVC		FEV_1		MMEFR		Peak flow	
		Neutral	Ionized	Neutral	Ionized	Neutral	Ionized	Neutral	Ionized
Total	$\overline{X}$	74.4	79.0	62.4	66.1	53.7	57.9	64.5	69.8
group									
(*N* = 15)	*SEM*	5.1	4.6	5.2	5.6	5.1	5.9	6.9	5.6
Protected	$\overline{X}$	73.2	81.4	57.9	70.2	45.7	65.0	57.3	68.4
group			*		**		**		**
(*n* = 8)	*SEM*	7.2	5.9	8.1	8.7	6.5	9.3	10.8	9.2
Aggravated	$\overline{X}$	75.7	76.3	67.6	61.3	62.7	49.7	74.6	71.8
group					*		*		
(*n* = 7)	*SEM*	7.9	7.5	6.4	6.9	7.0	6.0	5.2	5.2

Note. Data are presented as percentage of respective preexercise values (100%). * and ** denote *p* values smaller than .05 and .01, respectively, between neutral and ionized conditions.

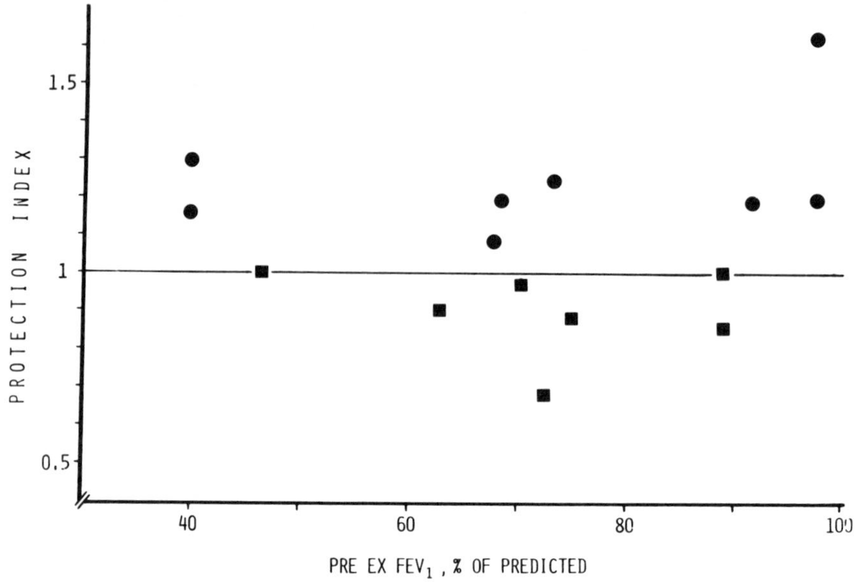

Figure 1. Relationship between the ion-protection index values (PI) and preexercise FEV_1 (% of Pred) in the "protected" (●) and "aggravated" (■) subgroups.

bronchoconstriction in the two environments, a value of 100% was assigned to the preexercise measurement as shown in Table 3. Although all four pulmonary functions were less reduced in the ionized atmosphere compared with the neutral conditions, those differences were not statistically significant.

Retrospective analysis of the individual responses to the ion exposure revealed two distinct subgroups: one whose pulmonary functions deteriorated less following exposure to the ionized atmosphere than under neutral conditions (protected; $n = 8$), and another group with patients who suffered a greater functional reduction or else were unaffected by the same conditions (aggravated; $n = 7$). (Table 3). To quantify the protective effect of the ionized atmosphere, the following protection index (PI) was used:

$$PI = \frac{(FEV_1 \text{ post}/FEV_1 \text{ pre}) \text{ ionized}}{(FEV_1 \text{ post}/FEV_1 \text{ pre}) \text{ neutral}}$$

Figure 1 provides a graphical demonstration of the difference between the two groups expressed in terms of the individual PI values. It also demonstrates the independence of the negative ion's protective effect from the magnitude of the preexercise FEV_1 (% of predicted). However, when individual ratios of post/pre FEV_1 values in the neutral conditions were plotted against the corresponding ones in the ionized atmosphere, a

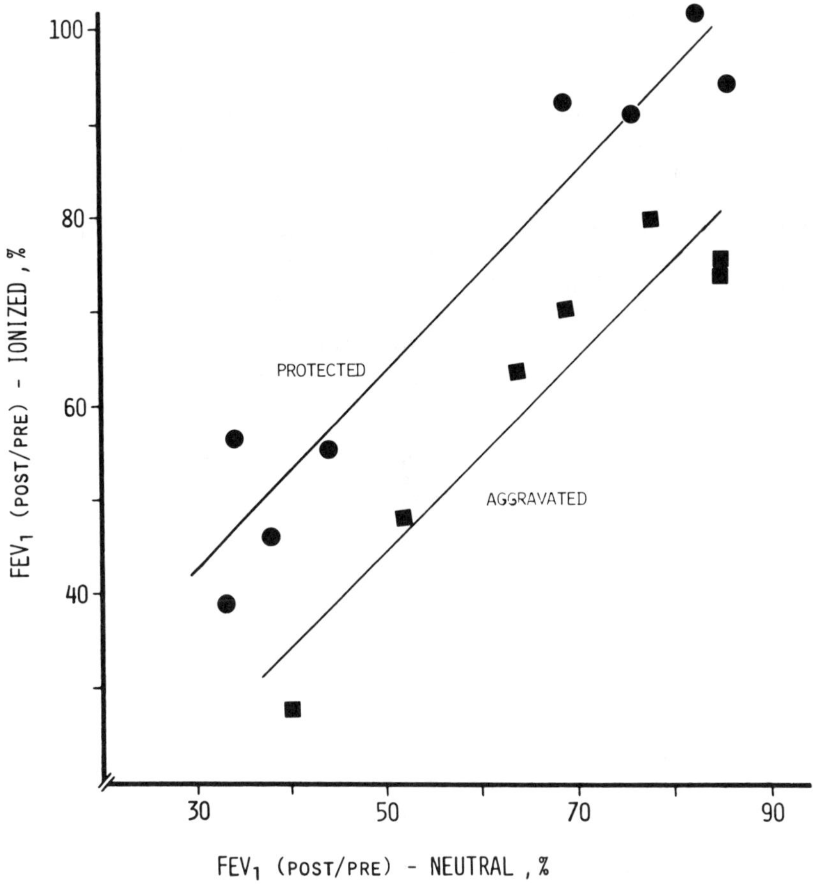

Figure 2. Relationship between FEV_1 post/preexercise under neutral conditions and FEV_1 post/preexercise under ionized conditions in the two samples' subgroups.

highly significant relationship emerged for each of the two groups (Figure 2). The regression lines representing these relationships appear parallel to each other, with that of the protected group being higher than that of the aggravated one.

DISCUSSION

The present investigation demonstrated that in a heterogenous asthmatic group such as used in this study, a 3-hr preexercise exposure to a negatively ionized atmosphere does not have a significant effect on postexercise bronchoconstriction. It did, however, positively affect the patient's perceived breathing difficulty.

This study also suggested that such an exposure may have different effects on different asthmatic patients. In light of the fact that all patients were tested on the same day under carefully controlled air ionization, temperature, and humidity, as well as work loads, it is proposed that negative air ions protect some patients and aggravate or have no effect on others (Figure 1).

Although minute ventilation ($\dot{V}_E$) was not measured, the observed similarity of cardiovascular strain during exercise in the two experimental sessions (Table 1) suggested similar $\dot{V}_E$ in both sessions. Furthermore, even if one assumes unequal $\dot{V}_E$ during the two sessions, thus pointing to a possible differential respiratory heat loss (RHE), which could affect pulmonary function (Bar-Or et al., 1977; Inbar et al., 1981; McFadden & Ingram, 1979), such an unequal $\dot{V}_E$ response would probably be the result

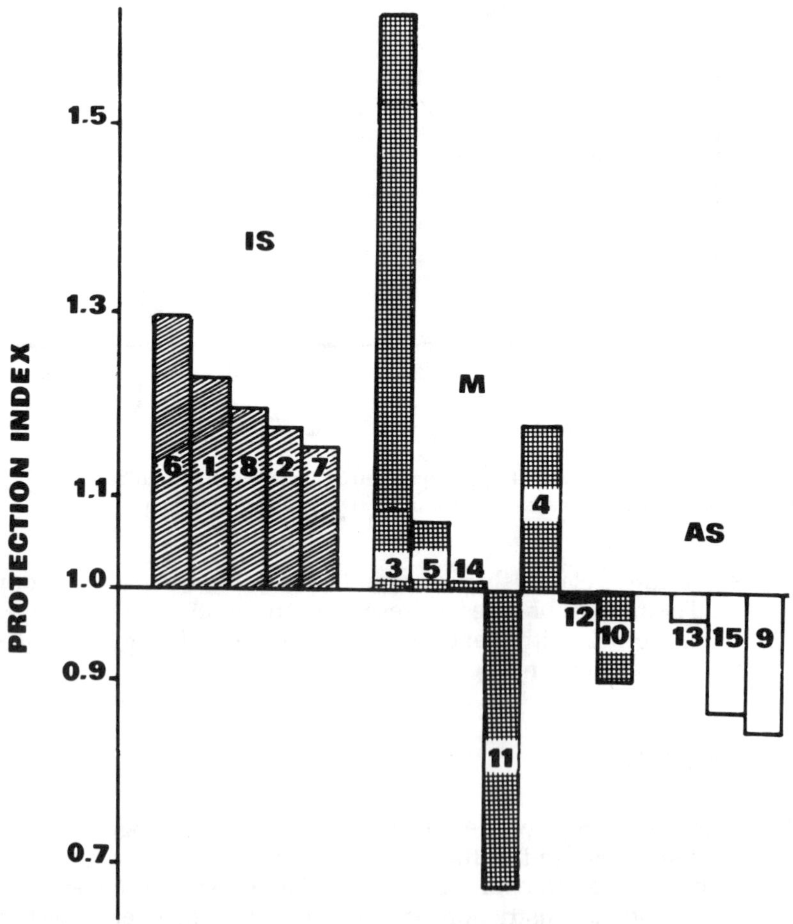

Figure 3. Individual ion-protection index values grouped according to clinical type (see text for symbols).

of the ionization treatment and thus offer a possible mechanism by which the observed response occurred.

The seemingly conflicting results of a study recently reported by Ben-Dov et al. (1983) may be explained by a more clinically homogeneous sample and/or the different mode of ion application imposed in the two studies (mouthpiece vs. free breathing). The heterogeneity in the response of asthmatic patients to various stimuli is well documented (McFadden & Ingram, 1979; Silverman, Konig, & Godfrey, 1973).

The effect of preexercise exposure to negative air ions on postexercise FEV_1, in terms of the PI, was 1.24 ± 0.17 for the protected and 0.89 ± 0.12 for the aggravated group ($p < .01$). It should be pointed out that the exposure had no effect on resting pulmonary functions in either the group as a whole or its subdivisions (Table 2). It appears, therefore, that the negative ions' effect, whether beneficial or detrimental, is brought about by exercise stress and not by the exposure as such.

When the ion effect was evaluated in light of the patients' clinical picture, a relationship became apparent (Figure 3). It appears that in those individuals diagnosed as antigen-sensitive (AS) (symptoms related to elevated blood and nasal eosinophil counts or to seasonal variations), pulmonary functions were aggravated by such a treatment. On the other hand, those diagnosed as irritant-sensitive (IS) (no seasonal variations and no eosinophil response) were protected by it. The mixed group (M), comprised of patients in both categories, demonstrated accordingly a mixed pattern response.

If the differential ion effect shown on the various asthmatic patients can be further corroborated, it may become possible to safely prescribe or proscribe ion treatment for a given patient. However, before a clinical application becomes practical, questions about the optimal exposure duration, ion concentration, type of administration, and the durability of the ion effect must be answered.

Acknowledgments

This research was supported in part by the Sports and Physical Education Authority, Ministry of Education and Culture, Israel. We are most grateful to M. Shinovitz, O. Shimoni, H. Dubrony, M. Bar-Netz, and D. Figenbaum for their technical assistance. We particularly wish to thank all the children and their parents who so enthusiastically took part in the study.

REFERENCES

Bar-Or, O., Neuman, I., & Dotan, R. (1977). Effects of dry and humid climates on exercise-induced asthma in children and preadolescents. *Journal of Allergy and Clinical Immunology*, **60**(3), 163-168.

Ben-Dov, I., Amirav, I., Shochina, M., Amitai I., Bar-Yishay, E., Godfrey, S. (1983). Effect of negative ionization of inspired air on the response of asthmatic children to exercise and inhaled histamine. *Thorax*, **38**, 584-588.

Boulatov, P.C. (1968). Traitement de l'asthme bronchique par l'aerionisation negative [Treatment of bronchial asthma with negative air ions]. In R. Gaultierotti et al. (Eds.), *Bioclimatology, biometerology and aerionotherapy* (p. 104). Milan: Carlo Erba.

Grimby, G. (1976). Respiration as a limiting factor for working capacity. *Pneumonologie Supplement* (pp. 11-16). Springer-Verlag.

Inbar, O., Alvarez, D.X., & Lyons, H.A. (1981). Exercise-induced asthma—A comparison between two modes of exercise stress. *European Journal of Respiratory Diseases*, **62**, 160-167.

Inbar, O., Rotstein, A., Dlin, R., Dotan, R. & Sulman, F.G. (1982). The effects of negative air ions on various physiological functions during work in a hot environment. *International Journal of Biometeorology*, **16**(2), 152-163.

Kreuger, A.P., & Reed, E.J. (1976). Biological impact of small air ions. *Science*, **193**, 1209-1213.

Kreuger, A.P., & Smith, R.F. (1960). The biological mechanisms of air ion action: 2. Negative air ion effects on the concentration and metabolism of 5-hydroxytryptamine in the mammalian respiratory tract. *Journal of General Physiology*, **44**, 269-276.

Kreuger, A.P., Smith, R.F., & Miller, J.W. (1959). Effects of air ions on the trachea of primates. *Procedures of Sociological and Experimental Biological Medicine*, **101**, 506-507.

Kronbleuh, I.H., & Griggin, J.E. (1955). Artificial air ionization in physical medicine. *American Journal of Physical Medicine*, **34**, 618-626.

Kronbleuth, I.H., Piersol, G.M., & Speicher, F.P. (1958). Relief from pollonosis in negatively ionized rooms. *American Journal of Physical Medicine*, **37**, 18-25.

McFadden, E.R., & Ingram, R.H., Jr. (1979). Exercise-induced asthma—observations on the initiating stimulus. *New England Journal of Medicine*, **301**, 763-769.

Østerballe, C., Weeke, B., & Albrechtsen, O. (1979). Influence of small atmospheric ions on the airways in patients with bronchial asthma. *Journal of Allergy*, **34**, 187-194.

Palti, Y., DeNour, E., & Abrahamov, A. (1966). The effect of atmospheric ions on the respiratory system of infants. *Pediatrics*, **38**(30), 405-411.

Priimagi, L., Kremerman, I., & Visnapuu, L. (1979). Application of negatively charged aerosols of leucocytic interferon for the prevention and treatment of acute respiratory infections in children [Abstract]. *Proceedings of the 8th International Congress of Biometeorology*, Israel, p. 194.

Rebuck, A.S., & Read, J. (1968). Exercise-induced asthma. *Lancet*, **1**, 429-431.

Seaton, A., Davis, G., Gaziano, D., & Highes, R.O. (1969). Exercise-induced asthma. *British Medical Journal*, **3**, 556-558.

Sigel, S. (1979). Bio-phychological influences of air ions in man: Effects on 5-Hydroxytryptamine and mood. [abstract]. *Proceedings of the 8th Congress of Biometeorology*, Israel, p. 200.

Silverman, M., Konig, P., & Godfrey, S. (1973). Use of serial exercise tests to assess the efficacy and duration of action of drugs for asthma. *Thorax*, **28**, 574-578.

Vassalo, C.L., Gee, J.B.L., & Domm, B.M. (1972). Exercise-induced asthma—observations regarding hypocapnia and acidosis. *American Reviews of Respiration*, **105**, 42-49.

Zylberberg, B., & Loveless, M.H. (1960). Preliminary experiments with ionized air in asthma. *Journal of Allergy*, **31**, 370-376.

Part VII
Exercise in Muscular and Skeletal Disorders

Metabolic Cost of Walking in Boys With Muscular Dystrophy

Roger G. Eston
David A. Brodie
Janice Burnie
Maria Stokes
Richard D. Griffiths
Richard H.T. Edwards
University of Liverpool, Liverpool, United Kingdom

The muscular dystrophies comprise a group of inherited progressive muscle wasting diseases (Gardner-Medwin, 1980). The most severe form is Duchenne muscular dystrophy (DMD), first described over 120 years ago. In all these disorders the underlying cause of the pathological process remains unknown.

A dystrophic muscle is characterized by progressive loss of muscle fibers with replacement by fat and fibrous tissue. Although minor abnormalities are histologically evident soon after birth, it is not until the child is a toddler or later still that the disease becomes manifest clinically. By this time there are marked histological abnormalities with considerable loss of muscle, particularly from the major proximal muscle groups in the arms and legs. Although eventually the disease confines the child to a wheelchair, the quality of life is understandably enhanced and possibly lengthened by maintaining ambulation. During this period striking physiological adaptations take place to optimize performance. It is important for clinicians managing these patients to appreciate and understand what are features of the pathological process and what are features of adaptation to the disease. The shortening (contractures) of the muscle groups in the major dystrophies is well recognized as a preventable complication of the weakened muscles (Dubowitz & Heckmatt, 1980). That this results in further functional impairment is also recognized, but the timing of physical or surgical intervention is far from straightforward. Indeed, generally decisions are made on anatomical grounds rather than for physiological reasons.

There is a shortage of sound advice for parents and patients with muscular dystrophies about whether exercise or activity is harmful. Cardiac muscle is involved in the dystrophic process, but it is only in the milder, and hence more active, muscular dystrophies that cardiac disease becomes clinically evident. As children with Duchenne muscular dystrophy live longer, or ambulation is prolonged, cardiomyopathies may become more of a problem. The energy costs of working muscle must be met by increased respiratory muscle activity along with increased cardiac output to deliver more oxygen.

There is very little quantitative information on the changes in gait parameters in children with muscular dystrophy compared with normal children. Furthermore, the energy cost of walking in patients with muscular dystrophy has received little attention, largely due to the limited number of subjects who are old enough to be cooperative yet young enough to be mobile. Walking speed is a combination of stride length and frequency. Both parameters may increase with increasing velocity, but in normal walking it is more economical to increase stride length.

This article addresses how patients with muscular dystrophy adapt to walking and whether there is an excessive energy burden for this important activity. Specifically, the purpose of this study was to establish the effect of walking speed on frequency and length of strides in boys with muscular dystrophy and to compare this and the metabolic cost with normal controls when walking at 60%, 80%, 100%, and 120% of their preferred walking speeds (PWS).

METHODS

Subjects

Boys (n = 5), aged 9 to 17 years, with muscular dystrophy (three Duchenne [DMD], and two Becker [BMD]) were matched for age, sex, height, and weight with a group of normal controls. Details of age, height, and weight are shown in Table 1. Informed parental consent was given for each child, who also consented to cooperate in this study.

Procedures

Each subject rested supine for 10 min and resting metabolic rate was then assessed. The expirate was analyzed using the Oxycon 4 ergoanalyzer (Mijnhardt), which measured minute ventilation ($\dot{V}_E$), the fractions of expired air (F_{EO_2} and F_{ECO_2}), and calculated oxygen uptake ($\dot{V}O_2$). The expirate was directed through a low-resistance face mask (Vacumed) that allowed verbal communication during testing—an asset during the exercise stage of the procedure.

In an overground test, the preferred walking speed was established for each subject as an average of three trials. Test speeds of 60%, 80%, 100%, and 120% of the subjects' preferred walking speeds were calculated for use in the experiment. The subjects then walked on an electrically driven treadmill (Woodway ESI) at each test speed at zero inclination for a maximum of 4 min, that is, until steady state (defined as two consecutive readings of oxygen uptake within a range of 150 ml) had been reached. All

Table 1 Descriptive Statistics

Subjects	Age (yrs)	Height (cm)	Weight (kg)
DMD 1	13	158	47.6
DMD 2	9	126	24.1
DMD 3	10	130	26.5
BMD 1	13	169	48.4
BMD 2	17	170	59.0
MD (combined)	12.4 ± 3.1	150.6 ± 21.2	41.2 ± 15.2
Control (n = 6)	12.5 ± 4.0	147.9 ± 10.6	40.6 ± 11.6
t	0.04	0.27	0.74
p	NS	NS	NS

subjects were dressed in shorts and vest, and all were provided with standardized athletic shoes. A safety harness secured to an overhead fixing point was used to prevent any accidents caused by tripping or falling during exercise.

Stride length and frequency were measured by video analysis. Selected anatomical landmarks were identified with adhesive markers. A video camera (Panasonic WV399OE) and recorder (Panasonic VO58OOPS), located perpendicular to the walkway, were used to record a lateral view of several gait cycles at each test speed. A sonic digitizer (Graf Bar) interfaced to the microcomputer (Commodore 4032) was used to record the X–Y coordinates of the required anatomical landmarks.

Heart rates were measured using a direct-wire Lifetrace 12 cardiometer (Albury Instruments). The three lower test speeds were randomly assigned, but the highest speed (120% of preferred walking speed) was always given last to reduce the possibility of fatigue and to assist in the acceptable collection of blood for lactate analysis. Venous blood was collected 5 min after the cessation of exercise and analyzed for lactic acid by the lactate dehydrogenase method.

RESULTS AND DISCUSSION

Preferred Walking Speed (PWS)

Preferred walking speed in the control group (1.40 ± 0.32 m • s^{-1}) was significantly faster ($p < .01$) than the combined MD group (0.94 ± 0.15 m • s^{-1}). This concurs with the work of Khodadedeh et al. (1985).

Stride Length and Cadence

A comparison of stride length, standardized for stature by dividing stride lengths (L) by height (h) (L • h^{-1}) at the preferred walking speed revealed a significantly lower value ($p < .05$) in the combined MD group (0.69 ± .16 m vs. 0.92 ± .06 m) compared with the normals when a Mann-Whitney U test was applied. The values for stride length for the BMD group and DMD group were 0.70, 0.86 m and 0.42, 0.69, 0.78 m, respectively. Cadence at the preferred walking speed was also significantly lower ($p < .01$) in the MD group (0.88 ± 0.08 str • s^{-1} vs. 1.03 ± 0.06 str • s^{-1}) compared with the normals when an independent t test was applied. The values for cadence for the BMD group and DMD group were 0.94, 0.76 str • s^{-1} and 0.82, 0.93, 0.93 str • s^{-1}, respectively.

Figure 1 shows the relationship between stride length (L • h^{-1}) and absolute velocity in the two groups. Although the stride length increased in both groups, there was a consistently shorter stride length in the MD groups at all percentages of preferred walking speed, but the overall trend of increasing stride length with increasing velocity was similar in all groups. Thus, at velocities that were common to all groups, stride lengths were similar.

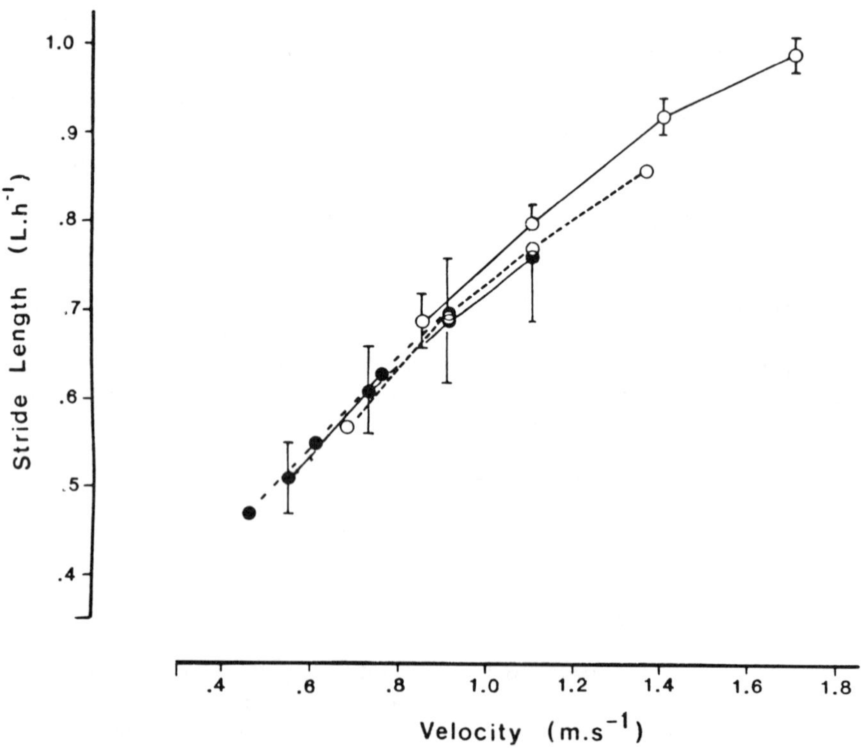

Figure 1. Stride length and absolute velocity in DMD (--•--), BMD (--o--), combined MD (—•—), and control (—o—) groups.

The maximum speeds in the present study were limited by the protocol (120%), but Khodadedeh et al. (1985) showed that at maximum speed DMD boys were significantly slower and had shorter stride lengths than normal controls. This would be anticipated from the pathology that restricts normal range of motion in the pelvis, knee, and ankle. Any equinus deformity at the ankle prevents the full stride length from being realized because the heel-toe rotation along the length of the foot is not available. The continuous loss and gain of equilibrium during the gait cycle in children with muscular dystrophy provides greatest stability by increasing the proportion of time that the feet are in contact with the ground. This is analogous to a novice ice skater's keeping skates in contact with the ice as long as possible. Thus the shortened stride length is not simply imposed by muscular contracture but by the changed kinematics involved in maintaining dynamic equilibrium. These children with DMD could not run. The action of running permits an increase in velocity while increasing stride length because both feet are lifted clear of the ground simultaneously in nonsupport, which is a more advanced example of continuous loss and gain of equilibrium.

Figure 2 shows the mean $L \cdot h^{-1}$ values plotted against a standardized velocity formula ($u \cdot \sqrt{g}h^{-1}$) suggested by Alexander (1984). In this

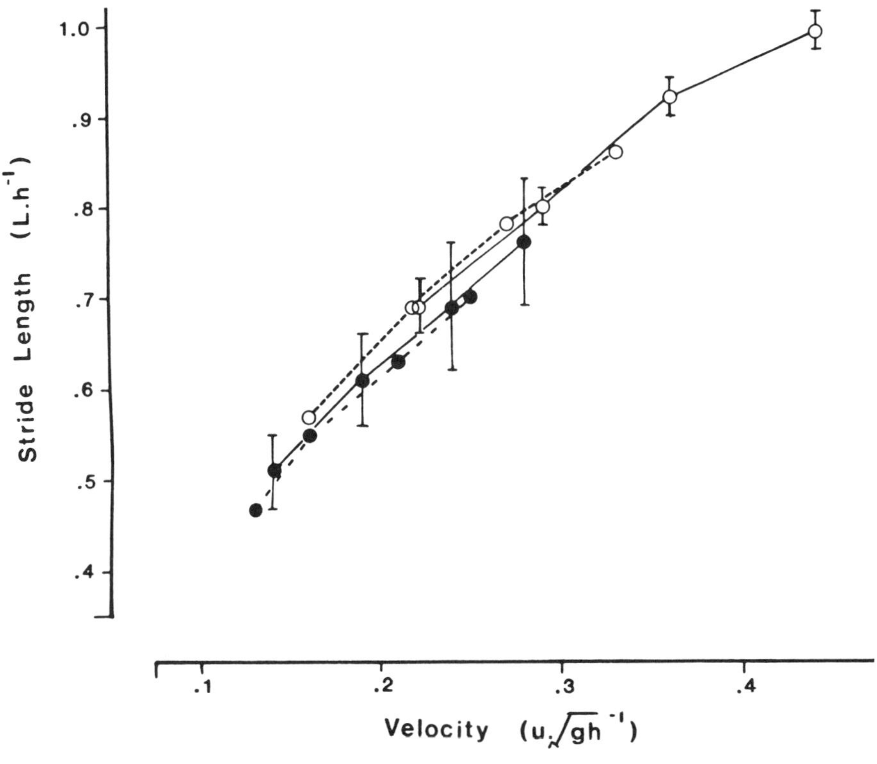

Figure 2. Stride length and velocity standardized for height.

formula, velocity is divided by the square root of the product, g (acceleration due to gravity) and h (stature of the individual). The relative increase in stride length for all groups followed a similar pattern. However, unlike Figure 1, the small BMD group showed a change in position shown in Figure 2 lying above the line for the controls. This was a function of the much greater height of the BMD group, which decreased the magnitude of the standardized velocity formula proposed by Alexander (1984). This demonstrated the importance of matching groups for height when any velocity transformations are applied. The present results agreed with those of Khodadedeh et al. (1985), even though the range of velocities had been extended to include slower speeds.

Energy Expenditures

Figure 3 shows the relationship between heart rate and absolute velocity. Two distinct groups were apparent, with the MD group having a higher heart rate response for a given velocity. Within the MD group, the DMD group had the highest heart rates throughout. The distinction between MD and control also emerged when the relationship between

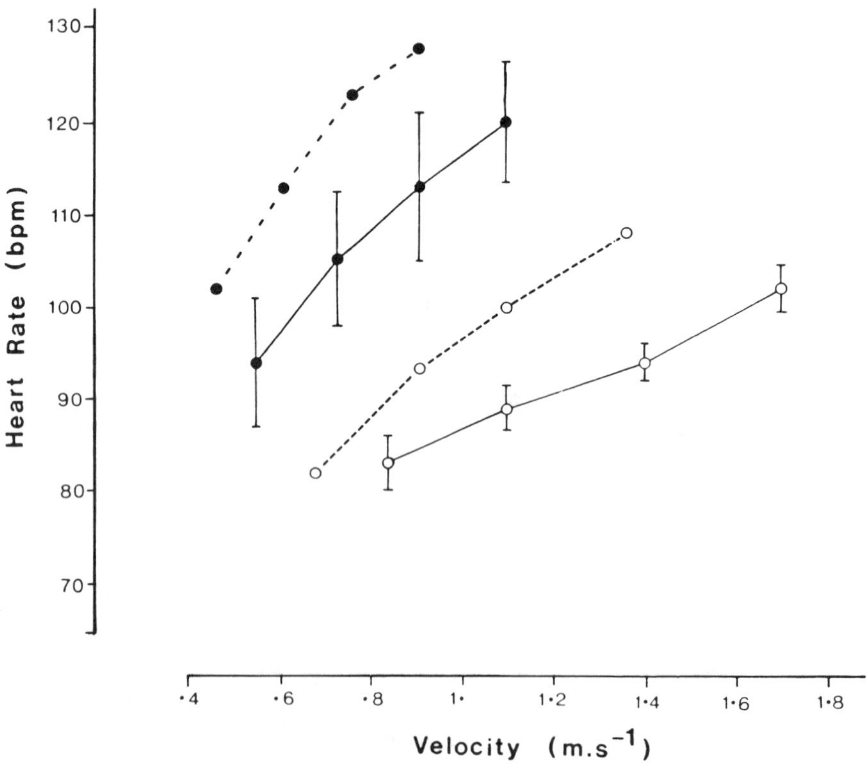

Figure 3. Heart rate and absolute velocity.

oxygen consumption (ml • kg^{-1} • min^{-1}) and walking velocity was examined (Figure 4), although unlike heart rate, the relative oxygen consumption of the BMD group did not differentiate them from the normals.

The relationship between heart rate and oxygen consumption for the two groups is shown in Figure 5. This depicts a steeper slope for the MD group, particularly the DMD group, which would suggest a greater cardiovascular response for a given metabolic requirement. Highly significant correlations (*r*) were computed for heart rate to velocity relationships for the DMD group and BMD group ($r = .94$, $p < .01$ and $r = .93$, $p < .01$), respectively. Evidence to suggest that the two groups were distinct is the nonsignificant correlation ($r = .40$) computed for the combined MD group. The normal controls showed an expected heart rate to velocity relationship ($r = .74$, $p < .01$).

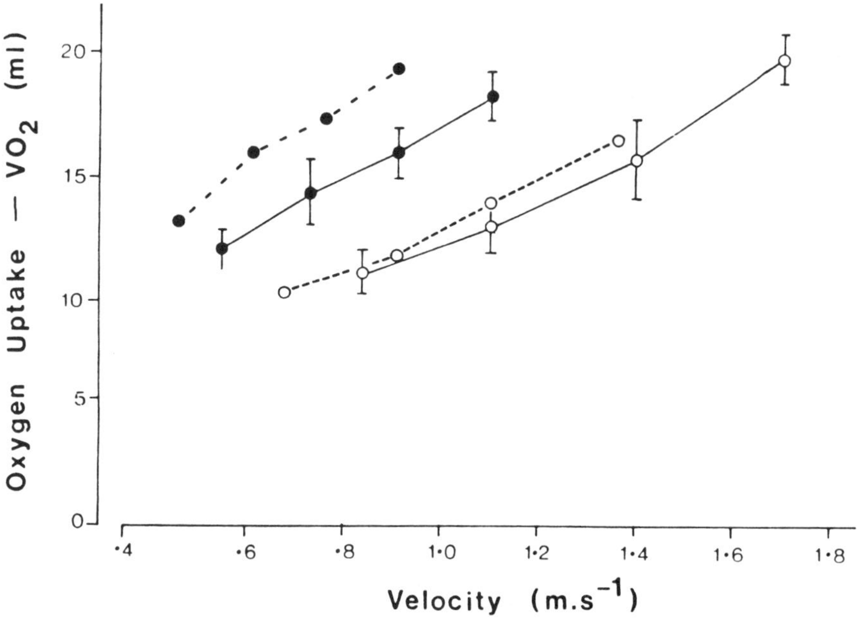

Figure 4. Oxygen uptake and absolute velocity.

Thus all distinct groups, although showing significant heart rate to velocity relationships, produced different adjustments of the cardiovascular system to increased metabolic demand. This was confirmed by comparing heart rate and oxygen uptake (ml • kg^{-1} • min^{-1}) at equivalent proportions of PWS. There were no differences in HR at the lower speeds (−40%, −20%), but at PWS and 20% the heart rate response of the combined MD group was 18 to 20 beats higher ($p < .05$). However, the higher heart rate did not reflect a higher metabolic cost. There was no difference in $\dot{V}O_2$ at each proportion of PWS, indicating that PWS was selected

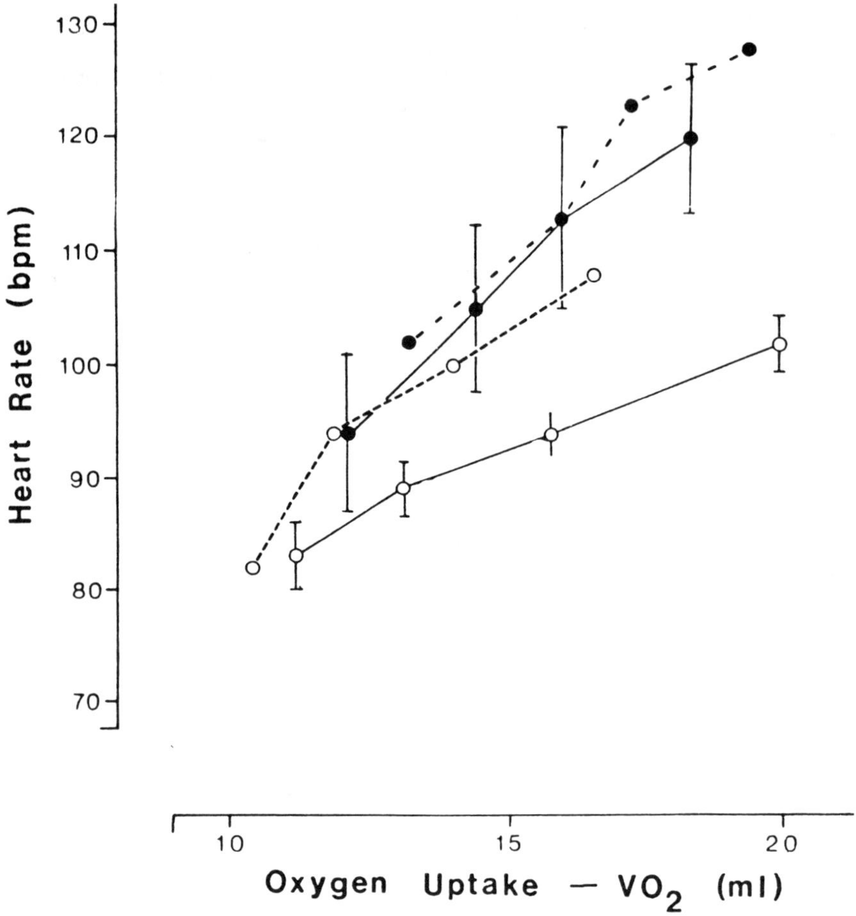

Figure 5. Heart rate and oxygen consumption.

on the basis of a similar metabolic demand. Speculation as to the reasons for a higher heart rate response in the MD group may include several possibilities—for example, dystrophic cardiomyopathy, a compensatory mechanism in response to a lower venous return caused by a less effective muscle pump in the MD group.

Analysis of lactates taken from venous blood after walking at 120% of PWS revealed no significant difference between the two groups. This could partially be attributed to the large range of values for the combined MD group (0.73 mmol • l^{-1} – 3.16 mmol • l^{-1}). Nevertheless, lactate values for both groups indicated that the intensity was well within aerobic capacity, all values being below the suggested 4 mmol • l^{-1} anaerobic threshold level (Heck et al., 1985). It should be noted, however, that the DMD group had a higher ($p < .05$) mean postexercise lactate than the normal controls (2.58 ± 0.50 mmol • l^{-1}, vs. 1.67 ± 0.48 mmol • l^{-1}). This difference was also reflected in a greater respiratory exchange ratio (0.94 ± 0.05 vs. 0.81 ± 0.09) for the DMD group and a greater ventilatory equivalent (30.8 ± 2.4 l • min^{-1} vs. 24.0 ± 4.0 l • min^{-1}), although the small number in these subgroups makes statistical inference tenuous.

These results have important implications for assessing and managing patients with muscular dystrophy. There is a higher metabolic cost for a particular velocity of walking in the patients. This is an expected observation where weakened muscles and joint contractures combine to reduce performance. Of greater interest is that the metabolic costs are the same when the patients walk at their own preferred walking speed. This is an important physiological adaptation linking in some way the selection of pace with a particular metabolic cost. This is clinically reassuring as it demonstrates the ability of these patients, despite their severe muscle disease, to optimize and regulate performance. It is also suggested that surgical or orthotic interventions aimed to improve ambulation must be shown to improve the preferred walking speed, as any slowing is likely to imply an increased metabolic cost.

To increase cardiac output with exercise, the patients with muscular dystrophy make a greater change in heart rate, implying a reduced ability to increase cardiac stroke volume. This is consistent with the known cardiomyopathy (Hunter, 1980) and demonstrates that exercise expectations may be limited for reasons due to cardiac function as well as skeletal muscles. This should have increasing importance as new methods are discovered to preserve skeletal muscles and improve performance.

CONCLUSIONS

1. At PWS the velocity was slower and stride length and frequency were lower in boys with MD compared to normal control subjects.
2. Changes in velocity were attained by a similar proportionate change in stride length and frequency in both groups.
3. The disadvantageous mechanics inherent in the MD group were reflected in the higher metabolic cost for a given absolute velocity.
4. Within the MD group, the DMD group was characterized by higher metabolic costs, slow walking velocities, and shorter stride lengths.
5. All groups selected a pace appropriate to their physiological status; that is, there were no differences in the metabolic cost of the selected, preferred walking speed.

REFERENCES

Alexander, R.M.C.N. (1984). Stride length and speed for adults, children and fossil hominids. *American Journal of Physical Anthropology*, **63**, 23-27.

Dubowitz, V., & Heckmatt, J. (1980). Management of muscular dystrophy. *British Medical Bulletin*, **36**, 139-144.

Gardner-Medwin, D. (1980). Clinical features and classification of the muscular dystrophies. *British Medical Bulletin*, **36**, 109-115.

Heck, H., Mader, A., Hess, G., Mucke, S., Muller, R., & Hollman, W. (1985). Justification of the 4 mmol • L lactate threshold. *International Journal of Sports Medicine*, **6**, 117-130.

Hunter, S. (1980). The heart in muscular dystrophy. *British Medical Bulletin*, **36**, 133-134.

Khodadedeh, S., McClelland, M., Edwards, R.H.T., Stokes, M., Patrick, J., & Evans, G.A. (1985). Gait analysis in Duchenne muscular dystrophy. *Clinical Science*, **69**(Suppl. 12), 27p.

Neurological Signs and Neurophysiological Findings in the Lower Extremities of Young Cross-Country Skiers and Control Children

Seppo T. Mahlamäki
Heikki A. Pekkarinen
University of Kuopio, Kuopio, Finland

Juhani V. Partanen
Kuopio University Central Hospital, Kuopio, Finland

Jarl-Erik Michelsson
Helsinki University Central Hospital, Helsinki, Finland

Neurological signs may indicate neurological illness and/or sciatica (Bannister, 1973). However, Hult (1954a) found neurological signs in the lower extremities of subjects who had never experienced sciatica. The total incidence of neurological signs in the lower extremities of randomly selected adults was about 10% in Hult's (1954b) study. The incidence of neurological deficits in children is not known.

As a routine, the subject's reaction to light touch and pin prick are tested during clinical examinations. Additional tests of sensibility are used in cases of suspicion of neurological disorders. Normally the knee and ankle jerks and the plantar reflexes are also examined during a medical examination. Ordinarily when a subject has no neurological symptoms, little emphasis is put on neurological examination and signs.

Clinical examination has been shown to be a rather nonspecific method in the evaluation of sensory disturbances in the lower extremities (Weise, Garfin, Gelberman, Katz, & Thorne, 1985). Comparative studies on the correlation of clinical testing and neurophysiological measurements of the sensory and motor functions in lower extremities in children have note been published.

The aim of this study was to determine the incidence of neurological signs in the lower extremities of Finnish skiers and control children. The correlation of neurological signs and neurophysiological findings was also estimated among some of the subjects.

SUBJECTS AND METHODS

This was a follow-up study for 3 successive years (1982–84). At the beginning of the survey the subjects were 10 to 14 years of age and were divided into two groups: 233 were cross-country skiers (133 males and 100 females) and 208 were control children (104 males and 104 females). The total number of the subjects was 441 in 1982. During the follow-up there was a drop-out rate of 9%. Neurophysiological measurements were performed on 13 children with one or more clinical neurological signs in 1982.

All subjects underwent a routine medical examination in the spring of each follow-up year. The neurological examination of the lower extremities was done as follows. Sensibility was tested over the skin areas supplied by the fourth and fifth lumbar and first sacral nerve roots. Light-touch sensibility was evaluated by the examiner's drawing his fingertips along the surfaces of the skin on both the right and the left sides at the same time. An abnormal response was recorded if there was a difference in the intensity of the perceived stimulus reported between the two sides. Superficial pain sensibility was evaluated by pinching simultaneously on the two sides. A clear difference in perceived sharpness between the two sides was considered abnormal.

The extensor plantar reflex was tested by drawing the grip of the percussion hammer along the outer border of the sole of the foot. The knee and ankle and thigh adductor jerks were tested with the subject lying supine and relaxed. The examiner lifted the relaxed lower extremity with his hand, and the tendon in question was struck with a percussion hammer. If the reflex was not elicited, the subject also was examined in the sitting position on the edge of the plinth, the legs hanging freely over the edge (knee jerk) or in the kneeling position, the feet over the edge of the plinth (ankle jerk). The Jendrassik's maneuver was used to elicit the jerks if they were lost. Loss or diminution in tendon reflexes was considered abnormal. The possible paresis in the extensor of the great toe was tested against manual resistance of the examiner. Also, a straight-leg-raising test (Lasegue sign) was performed by all of the subjects.

Table 1 Neurophysiological Measurements Performed on Children With Neurological Sign(s)

Root level	Late response	Muscle recorded	Nerve stimulated (site)
L4 - L5	F	M. tibialis anterior	N. peroneus communis (knee)
L5 - S1	F	M. extensor digitorum brevis	N. peroneus profundus (ankle)
L5 - S1	F	M. abductor digiti minimi	N. tibialis (ankle)
S1	H	M. soleus	N. tibialis (knee)

Noninvasive late response measurements of the peroneal and tibial nerves were made to investigate different lumbosacral root levels (Table 1). DISA emg-equipment and surface electrodes were used. An asymmetry of the latency of the late response of more than 1.5 msec or an absence of the late response was considered pathological.

RESULTS

Neurological signs were equally common in skiers and in controls, and they were found most often in the third clinical checkup (Table 2). The most common abnormality was a loss or a diminution of the knee jerk.

Table 2 Neurological Signs in the Lower Extremities in Young Cross-Country Skiers and Control Children (Aged 10 to 16 Years)

Neurological sign	Year of checkup		
	1982 (*N* = 436) *n*	1983 (*N* = 396) *n*	1984[a] (*N* = 374) *n*
Loss or diminution of the jerk			
Thigh adductor jerk	3/3	—	—
Knee jerk	8/8	19/19	28/28
Ankle jerk	3/3	3/2	7/6
Impaired sensibility			
L4 dermatome	—/1	—	—/6
L5 dermatome	1/3	—	2/15
S1 dermatome	2/2	—	6/14
Impaired muscle strength			
Paresis of the great toe	2/2	—	4/5
Positive straight-leg raising test	—/1	—	1/—
Number of subjects with some neurological sign	18	22	49

[a]In 1984 minimal differences in neurological findings between the sides were recorded as abnormal. *N* = number of subjects. *n* = number of the subjects having neurological sign(s) (right/left side).

Sensory impairment was more common in the left lower extremity. One of the control girls had a peripheral peroneal paresis. Two of the control boys had an abnormal Lasegue sign. One had signs of Scheuermann's disease in the lumbar spine, and the other had radicular symptoms and signs, which disappeared after autotraction treatment of the lumbar spine.

Often the clinical estimation and neurophysiological findings of the effected root level were not in agreement (Table 3). There were no differences in the neurophysiological measurements between skiers and control subjects. About half of the subjects with clinical neurological sign(s) also proved to have abnormalities in neurophysiological late response values.

Table 3 Neurological Signs and Neurophysiological Findings According to the Root Level in Cross-Country Skiers (S) and Controls (C)

Subject	Neurological sign		Neurophysiological finding	
	Estimated root level	Side	Root level	Side
S	L4	Right	L5 + S1	Right
S	L4	Bilateral	L5	Left
S	L4	Left	Normal	
S	L5	Left	L5 + S1	Left
S	L5	Left	Normal	
C	L4	Left	Normal	
C	L4	Right	Normal	
C	L4	Bilateral	Normal	
C	L4 + S1	Bilateral	S1	Bilateral
C	L4	Bilateral	L4	Bilateral
C	L4	Bilateral	L5	Left
C	L4	Right	Normal	
C	L4	Bilateral	L4	Right

DISCUSSION

No difference was present in the neurological signs in the lower extremities between the skiers and the control children. In general, however, neurological signs were astonishingly common in these schoolchildren. The incidence was about the same (10%) as in the adult population (Hult, 1954b). It must be remembered that this kind of sensibility testing is very nonspecific and may even be misleading (Weise et al., 1985). Loss of some or all tendon reflexes may be either congenital or due to the subject's lack of relaxation (Bannister, 1973). However, the clinical examination proved to be a sensitive screening method for selecting subjects for neurophysiological measurements.

Great physiological variation in sensibility (Weise et al., 1985) is possibly responsible for the large number of abnormal findings. Further studies on the normal pattern in sensibility are needed. About 2% of the original subjects had neurophysiological abnormalities in the lower extremities. Only some of these reported low back pain or neurological symptoms in the lower extremities. It would be of interest to make neurophysiological studies of children with neurological symptoms but without neurological signs. The etiology of the neurological signs and symptoms as well as of the neurophysiological findings in the present subjects was not known. The majority of the neurophysiological findings were considered to reflect lumbosacral root dysfunction.

Reflex or late response measurements can distinguish a chronic dysfunction (sequelae or chronic compression of the root). However, systematic measurements of different root levels (Aiello, Rosati, Serra, & Manca, 1981; Baylan, Yu, & Grant, 1981; Schuchmann, 1978) are required because the clinical and neurophysiological findings are not always in agreement (Young et al., 1981). If suspicion of acute affection is present, needle EMG could also be performed to find out whether there is axonal destruction (Tonzola, Ackil, Shahani, & Young, 1981).

CONCLUSION

Because of the high incidence of neurological signs in normal children, neurological examinations should be included in routine medical examinations so that the possible changes in sensibility and motor functions would be identified at an early stage. The clinical estimation of neurological functions is subjective. Additionally, there seems to be a great overlap of nerve roots in the lower extremities. Therefore, the application of valid neurophysiological measurement techniques for different nerve roots is necessary.

REFERENCES

Aiello, I., Rosati, G., & Manca, M. (1981). The diagnostic value of H-index is SI root compression. *Journal of Neurology, Neurosurgery and Psychiatry*, **44**, 171-172.

Bannister, R. (1973). *Brain's clinical neurology* (4th ed.). London: Oxford University Press.

Baylan, S.P., Yu, J., & Grant, A.E. (1981). H reflex latency in relation to ankle jerk, electromyographic, myelographic and surgical findings in back pain patients. *Electromyography and Clinical Neurophysiology*, **21**, 201-206.

Hult, L. (1954a). Cervical, dorsal and lumbar spinal syndromes. *Acta Orthopaedica Scandinavica*, (Suppl. 17), 62-64.

Hult, L. (1954b). The Munkfors investigation. *Acta Orthopaedica Scandinavica,* (Suppl. 16), 49-50.

Schuchmann, J.A. (1978). H reflex latency in radiculopathy. *Archives of Physical Medicine and Rehabilitation,* **59**, 185-187.

Tonzola, R.F., Ackil, A.A., Shanani, B.T., & Young, R.R. (1981). Usefulness of electrophysiological studies in the diagnosis of lumbosacral root disease. *Annals of Neurology,* **9**, 305-308.

Weise, M.D., Garfin, S.R., Gelberman, R.H., Katz, M.M., & Thorne, R.P. (1985). Lower-extremity sensibility testing in patients with herniated lumbar intervertebral discs. *Journal of Bone and Joint Surgery,* **67-A**, 1219-1224.

Young, A., Getty, J., Jackson, A., Kirvan, E., Sullivan, M., & Wynn, C. (1983). Variations in the patterns of muscle innervation by the L5 and S1 nerve roots. *Spine,* **8**, 616-624.

Radiological Evaluation of Young Cross-Country Skiers and Control Children With Suspected Skeletal Abnormalities

Seppo T. Mahlamäki
Heikki A. Pekkarinen
University of Kuopio, Kuopio, Finland

Seppo Soimakallio
Olavi Suomalainen
Kuopio University Central Hospital, Kuopio, Finland

Jarl-Erik Michelsson
Helsinki University Central Hospital, Helsinki, Finland

Back pain problems are common even in children and adolescents (Fairbank, Pynsenth, Van Poortvliet, & Phillips, 1984). Though the possible structural causes of low back pain (LPB) are numerous (Jayson, 1983), the exact etiology remains obscure in most cases.

Wedge-shaped lumbar vertebral bodies (Witt, Vestergaard, & Rosenklint, 1984), spondylolysis (Micheli, 1985), and signs of degeneration (Blazek, Streda, Germak, & Skallova, 1985) have been found in radiological studies of young LBP patients. The radiological findings in the lumbar spine in LBP patients and control subjects may, however, be similar (Splinthoff, 1953). On the other hand, the diagnosis of LBP in the athlete by radiological examination has been said to be essential (Spencer & Jackson, 1983). Radiological studies are also often made of children and adolescents suffering from musculoskeletal symptoms. In this study the radiological findings in children with suspected skeletal abnormality were evaluated in order to clarify their value in treating these subjects.

SUBJECTS AND METHODS

In the spring of 1982, 10- to 14-year-old voluntary cross-country skiers from eastern Finland were chosen as participants for this study. The total number of skiers was 233, 133 males and 100 females. In the control groups, there were 208 age- and sex-matched control children. The total number of subjects was 441. The subjects were examined physically once a year in 3 successive years (1982 to 1984). Those who had severe LBP

Table 1 Radiological Findings in the Lumbar and Thoracic Spines of Young Cross-Country Skiers and Control Children

Indication for radiological examination	Radiological findings						
	Scoliosis	Abnormal lordosis	Anomaly	Spondylolysis	Scheuermann's disease	Normal	Additional findings
	n	*n*	*n*	*n*	*n*	*n*	
Low back pain (n = 14)	6	5	2	1	5	4	LV - SI-disc unstable[b] Unfused apophyses of all lumbar vertebral bodies
Abnormal posture (n = 10)	9[a]	2	1	1	3	—	
Neurological sign(s) in lower extremities (n = 2)	1	1	—	1	—	—	Unfused apophyses of vertebral bodies[b]
Impaired lumbar mobility (n = 1)	—	1	—	—	—	—	
Total N = 27	16	9	3	3	8	4	

[a]Three of the subjects had a thoracic scoliosis; the rest of the scolioses were in the lumbar spine. [b]This finding was noticed in 1 subject. n = number of subjects having the radiological sign in question.

symptoms or a suspected skeletal abnormality were X-rayed. A total of 29 children was studied radiologically.

Plain radiographs in lateral and anteroposterior views were taken by a new method described by Soimakallio, Manninen, and Mahlamäki (1985). A recently developed large field image-intensifier photofluorography (Siemens Optilux 57) combined with a 100-mm magazine camera (Sircam 100 L, Siemens) was selected for imaging the entire lower vertebral column. Kodak X-Omat GR film was used and the maximum image size providing an input-screen diameter of 57 cm was selected. The equipment had an X-ray tube with a normal focal spot of 0.6 mm. Focus-to-input screen diameter was 100 cm and high voltage of 77 kVP was chosen. The spinal curves, anomalies, and possible degenerative changes were investigated. The degrees of scoliosis were measured according to the method of Cobb (1948).

RESULTS

Minimal scoliosis of the lower vertebral column (range, 2 to 9 degrees) was a common finding in this study (Table 1). In most cases the apex of the scoliosis was at the level of L2 to L4. Three female subjects had a structural scoliosis in the thoracic spine (range, 15 to 35 degrees). One control girl having a structural scoliosis of 35 degrees was sent for surgical consultation and a follow-up was arranged.

Abnormal lumbar lordosis and signs of Scheuermann's disease were common findings. One male skier had a spondylolysis both at L3 and L4 levels. As a whole, spondylolysis was found in three subjects. One male control subject with severely restricted mobility in his left hip joint proved to have a slipped femoral head (epiphyseolysis capitis femoris). Additionally, one female control subject had hypoplastic fourth and fifth metacarpals. The two control children identified were treated operatively.

DISCUSSION

Radiological studies were performed on 6.5% of the subjects. Only in three of the subjects studied radiologically ($N = 29$) did the radiological findings lead to further studies or to surgical treatment. However, radiological studies were important in excluding progressive diseases of the spinal structures.

Special projections for imaging the sacroiliac joints were not used because neither clinical nor radiological signs of ankylosing spondylitis (Felts, 1982) were found. The radiological method used in this study proved promising. Its main advantages are low radiation dose (one-fifth to one-third of the ordinary) and low film and chemical costs (Soimakallio et al., 1985).

There was no difference in the radiological findings between the skiers and controls. In one skier an unstable disc space (L5 – S1) was noticed.

It has been suggested that intensive cross-country skiing for many years may cause spinal trauma (Frymoyer, Pope, & Kristiansen, 1982). The follow-up of 2 years in this study was too short a time to evaluate the possible long-term effects of skiing on spinal structures. Most of the scolioses registered were judged as functional in clinical examinations. It is not clear if functional scoliosis has any role in the pathogenesis of LBP (Friberg, 1983; Giles & Taylor, 1981, 1982; Papaioannou, Stokes, & Kenwright, 1982).

Abnormal lumbar lordosis was found in one-third of the subjects X-rayed because of LBP symptoms. However, the number of the subjects X-rayed was too small for statistical analysis. Hypolordosis was connected with signs of lumbar Scheuermann's disease in most of the cases. The occurrence of spondylolysis and different anomalies was lower or the same as had been found in LBP patients and control subjects elsewhere (Fredrickson, Baker, McHolik, Yuan, & Lubicky, 1984; Magora & Schwartz, 1978; Splinthoff, 1953).

The role of the above-mentioned radiological findings as a cause of LBP is not clear (Andersson, 1979; Fredrickson et al., 1984; Magora & Schwartz, 1978). Comparative follow-up studies of their connection with LBP should be performed.

Lumbar myelography was performed on one control boy who had sciatica of long duration and a lumbar scoliosis. The finding in myelography was normal. Later, signs of Scheuermann's disease were noticed. Fisk, Baigent, and Hill (1984) found Scheuermann's disease to be connected with LBP symptoms of long duration.

CONCLUSION

No radiological differences in the spine were found between the cross-country skiers and the control subjects. Plain radiographs seldom provide valuable information regarding the actual therapy of LBP in children, but they are necessary in excluding progressive diseases of the spine. When radiological examination of the lumbar spine is indicated, methods with a low radiation dose should be selected.

REFERENCES

Andersson, G. (1979). Low back pain in industry: Epidemiological aspects. *Scandinavian Journal of Rehabilitation Medicine*, **11**, 163-168.

Blazek, O., Streda, A., Germak, V., & Skallova, O. (1985, March). Morphological changes in the spine of sportsmen. *Abstracts for the 4th European Congress of Sports Medicine*. Prague.

Cobb, J.R. (1948). Outline for the study of scoliosis. *American Academy of Orthopaedic Surgeons: Institutional Course Lectures*, **5**, 261-275.

Fairbank, J.C., Pynsent, P.B., Van Poortvliet, J.A., & Phillips, H. (1984). Influence of anthropometric factors and joint laxity in the incidence of adolescent back pain. *Spine*, **9**, 461-464.

Felts, W.R. (1982). Ankylosing spondylitis. The challenge of early diagnosis. *Postgraduate Medicine*, **72**, 184-195.

Fisk, J.W., Baigent, M.L., & Hill, P.D. (1984). Scheuermann's disease. Clinical and radiological survey of 17- and 18-year-olds. *American Journal of Physical Medicine*, **63**, 18-30.

Fredrickson, B.E., Baker, D., McHolik, W.K., Yuan, H.A., & Lubicky, J.P. (1984). The natural history of spondylolysis and spondylolisthesis. *Journal of Bone and Joint Surgery*, **66-A**, 699-707.

Friberg, O. (1983). Clinical symptoms and biomechanics of lumbar spine and hip joint in leg length inequality. *Spine*, **8**, 643-651.

Frymoyer, J.W., Pope, M.H., & Kristiansen, T. (1982). Skiing and spinal trauma. *Clinics in Sports Medicine*, **1**, 309-318.

Giles, L.G.F., & Taylor, J.R. (1981). Low back pain associated with leg length inequality. *Spine*, **6**, 510-521.

Giles, L.G.F., & Taylor, J.R. (1982). Lumbar spine structural changes associated with leg length inequality. *Spine*, **7**, 159-162.

Jayson, M.I.V. (1983). Discussion: Osteoarthritis in the spine and back pain. *Journal of Rheumatology*, (Suppl. 9), 105-107.

Magora, A., & Schwartz, A. (1978). Relation between the low back pain syndrome and X-ray findings: 2. Transitional vertebra (mainly sacralization). *Scandinavian Journal of Rehabilitation Medicine*, **10**, 135-145.

Micheli, L.J. (1985). Back injuries in gymnastics. *Clinics in Sports Medicine*, **4**, 85-93.

Papaioannou, T., Stokes, I., & Kenwright, J. (1982). Scoliosis associated with limb-length inequality. *Journal of Bone and Joint Surgery*, **64-A**, 59-62.

Soimakallio, S., Manninen, H., & Mahlamäki, S. (1985). Examination of the lumbar spine with large-field image intensifier photofluorography. *Electromedica*, **53**, 162-164.

Spencer, C.W., & Jackson, D.D. (1983). Back injuries in the athlete. *Clinics in Sports Medicine*, **2**, 191-215.

Splinthoff, C.A. (1953). Lumbosacral junction. Roentgenographic comparison of patients with and without backaches. *Journal of the American Medical Association*, **152**, 1610-1613.

Witt, I., Vestergaard, A., & Rosenklint, A. (1984). A comparative analysis of X-ray findings of the lumbar spine in patients with and without lumbar pain. *Spine*, **9**, 298-300.

Longitudinal Evaluation of the Development of the Spinal Column and the Possibilities of Influencing It by Specialized Training During Ontogeny

Miroslav Kučera
P. Korbelář
J. Vališ
V. Sazima
Charles University, Prague, Czechoslovakia

The dynamics of spinal development during ontogeny are influenced by a number of factors. The unilateral load plays an important role in this development, especially in some static postures such as sitting at school or during unilateral hard physical work. It is of concern nowadays for the prepubertal age group and even in earlier childhood. The changes affect the spinal system, and the adaptation to these nonphysiological stimuli is usually diagnosed too late, that is, when the changes can no longer be remedied. Therefore, the purpose of this study was to determine the physiological deviations of the spinal axis and to evaluate the influence of physical training on the development of the spine during the ages from 12 to 14 years.

In this study the necessity for a systematic and long-term observation of spinal development is emphasized in order to avoid an acquired and fixed poor posture. Furthermore, the point is stressed that especially during ontogeny, a specific unilateral load should be compensated for by exercises aimed at harmonious development of the whole organism.

METHODS

The device (Kučera, 1986) that was used for evaluation permitted deviations of the axis of vertebral column to be expressed in degrees as well as in centimeters (see Figure 1). The standardization of posture was obtained by having the subject touch the device with the tuber calcanei and the musculus gluteus maximus and also having the subject touch two moving bars with the tuber os occipitale and with the point of the maximum curvature of the thoracic area of the spine. This posture was held with the feet parallel and the body height was measured by a rod. When

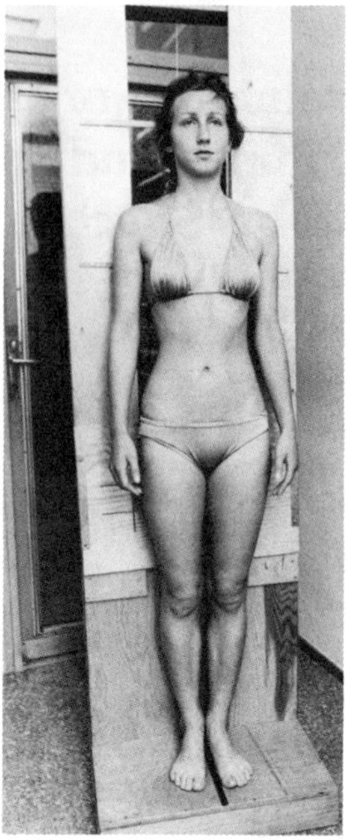

Figure 1. A measurement device permitted deviations of the axis of vertebral column to be expressed in degrees as well as in centimeters.

the proper position was achieved, the deviation of the frontal axis was measured at the thoracic kyphosis by a measuring device (Figure 1). The difference between these values was used for the evaluation of axis deviation. The following values were recorded: (a) body height, (b) amount of the measured deviation, (c) the degree of the cervical and lumbal lordoses, and (d) the lateral deviation at the level of anteroposterior lordosis. In a situation where high values of lateral deviation were obtained, the maximal value of this deviation was also compared with the

Table 1 Experimental Groups

	Athletes		Controls	
	Age (yrs)	*N*	Age (yrs)	*N*
Boys	12	14	12	32
	14	7	14	19
Girls	12	16	12	33
	14	14	14	13

contralateral maximal value. With scapulae alatae greater than 1 cm, the subject's height was also evaluated. The data were statistically evaluated by student *t* tests.

TESTED GROUPS

The experimental subjects consisted of two randomly chosen groups of primary schoolchildren. The tested groups were children attending a special sport school for athletics with 2-hr training sessions held twice a day. The sport school was situated in the same town and district as the primary school. The numbers of measured subjects is given in Table 1. The children in the sport school were trained from the age of 11 years, mainly in running. The children of the control group were not specially trained.

RESULTS AND DISCUSSION

The developmental changes of adolescence resulted in the increase of body height. Therefore, the evaluation of the distance of the cervical lordosis (usually C 3-4) from the thoracic kyphosis (Th 6-7) and lumbar lordosis (L 2-3) is an important variable of the dynamics of development (Table 2). The results indicated that children from the sport school were

Table 2 Distance of the Maximum Cervical and Lumbar Lordosis From the Maximum Thoracic Kyphosis (cm)

	Athletes			Controls		
	Age (yrs)	*M*	*SD*	Age (yrs)	*M*	*SD*
Boys	12	38.0	1.2	12	35.8	2.5
	14	43.5	2.0	14	41.5	3.8
Girls	12	37.8	3.4	12	37.4	2.9
	14	41.6	2.7	14	41.0	2.0

slightly taller. However, their growth was not accelerated compared with the controls (see Figure 2). This difference was probably the result of the selection of taller children for the sport school (Table 3). Table 4 shows the deviations from the frontal axis.

The comparisons of athletes and nonathletes showed the differences in lumbar lordosis of 12-year-old boys and girls and the cervical lordosis at 14 years of age (Table 4). The lateral deviation in the cervical part of

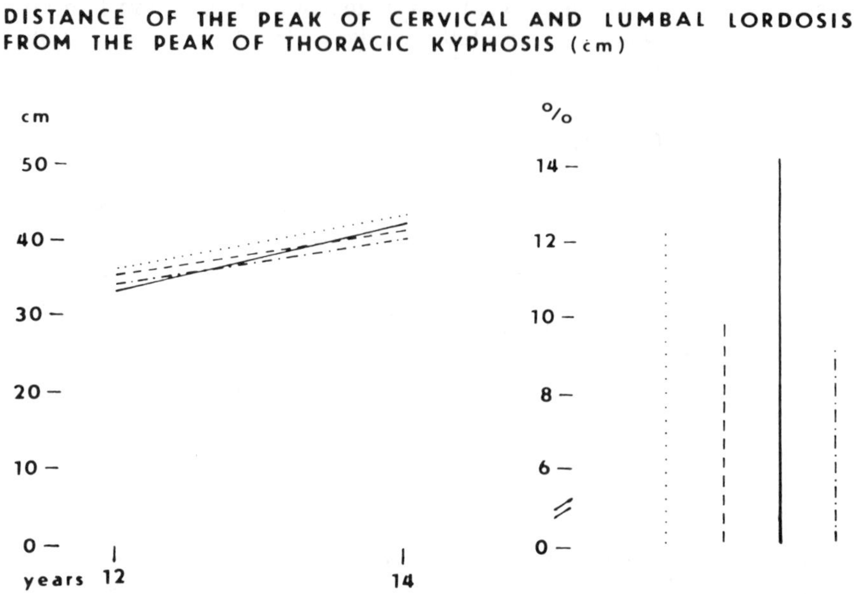

Figure 2. Distance of the peak of cervical and lumbar lordosis from the peak of thoracic kyphosis (cm).

Table 3 Changes in the Distance of the Maximum of Cervical and Lumbar Lordosis From the Maximum of Thoracic Kyphosis After 2 Years (%)

	Athletes	Controls
Boys	12.2	13.7
Girls	9.6	8.8

the vertebral column was greater in the control boys at 12 years of age and in the lumbar region of the control girls at 14 years of age (Table 5). The percentages of individuals with deviations of more than 1 *SD* are given in Table 6. The large decrease in the numbers of deviations in the lumbar lordosis for the 14-year-old sports subjects might be explained by the small numbers of subjects. Nevertheless, this finding suggests the importance of individual measurement for every child training for sports. It also supports the importance of follow-up measurements of the development of the vertebral column as indicated in Figures 3 and 4.

Table 4 Cervical and Lumbar Lordosis (Degrees of the Deviation From Thoracic Kyphosis)

		Athletes				Controls			
		Cervical		Lumbar		Cervical		Lumbar	
	Age (yrs)	*M*	*SD*	*M*	*SD*	*M*	*SD*	*M*	*SD*
Boys	12	12.6	2.88	7.61	2.74	12.5	4.0	11.37	3.36
	14	7.49	2.72	7.26	2.85	12.92	3.95	9.98	3.98
Girls	12	11.3	3.08	6.82	3.11	9.7	3.85	11.12	3.64
	14	7.19	1.66	8.34	2.62	10.2	3.0	10.54	3.62

Table 5 Lateral Deviation in Cervical and Lumbar Spine (Degrees)

		Athletes				Controls			
		Cervical		Lumbar		Cervical		Lumbar	
	Age (yrs)	*M*	*SD*	*M*	*SD*	*M*	*SD*	*M*	*SD*
Boys	12	1.49	1.47	1.47	1.11	0.77	0.76	1.18	0.78
	14	1.11	0.69	0.87	0.67	0.66	0.65	1.01	0.70

Statistical significance

5% Athletes/Controls, girls 14 years — Lat. deviation in cervical spine

1% Athletes/Controls, boys 12 years — Lat. deviation in cervical spine

1% Athletes/Controls, girls 14 years — Lat. deviation in lumbar spine

CONCLUSION

Measurement of the deviations of the axis of the vertebral column is a basic investigation of ontogenesis. It is especially important during adolescence and chronic diseases and in children who are subjected to repeated overloading of particular parts of their bodies. Significant changes may also result from insufficient physical stimulation.

Evaluation of the lateral deviation is relatively common, but antero-posterior curvatures are not usually measured. The relatively high values

Table 6 The Percentage of Subjects With More Than 1 *SD*

		Athletes		Controls	
		Cervical Lordosis	Lumbar Lordosis	Cervical Lordosis	Lumbar Lordosis
	Age (yrs)	%	%	%	%
Boys	12	35.7	28.5	34.3	25.0
	14	28.5 (−7.2%)	57.1 (+28.6%)	28.5 (−5.8%)	31.5 (+6.5%)
Girls	12	18.7	31.2	36.3	30.3
	14	28.5 (+9.8%)	28.5 (−2.7%)	30.7 (−5.6%)	38.4 (+8.1%)

Note. Values in parentheses represent the change in 2-year interval in percentage.

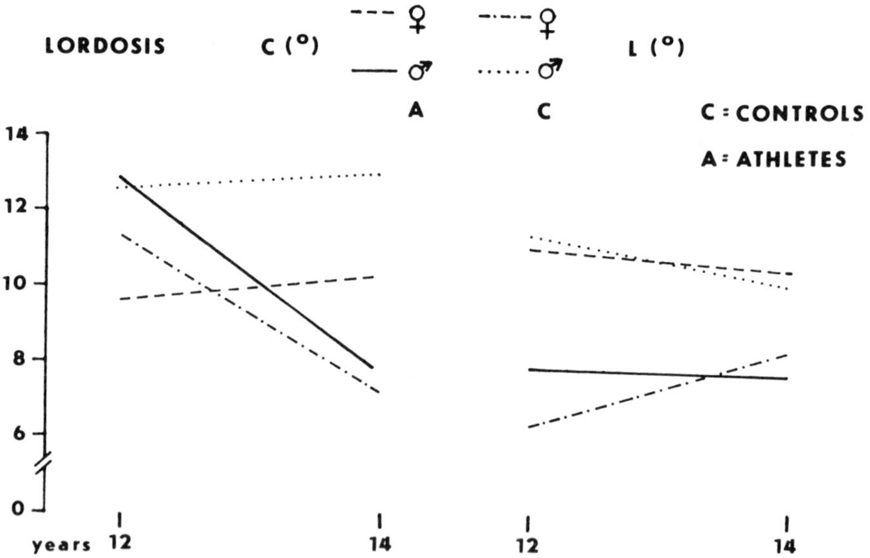

Figure 3. The changes of the spine axis—lateral.

of this variable (approx 10°) should be noted. The local overload during inadequate physical activity may result in clinically important changes of the locomotor system. The measurement of the dynamics of ontogenesis of the vertebral column should, therefore, be one of the basic factors included in the clinical examination during childhood, particularly in children engaged in sport training.

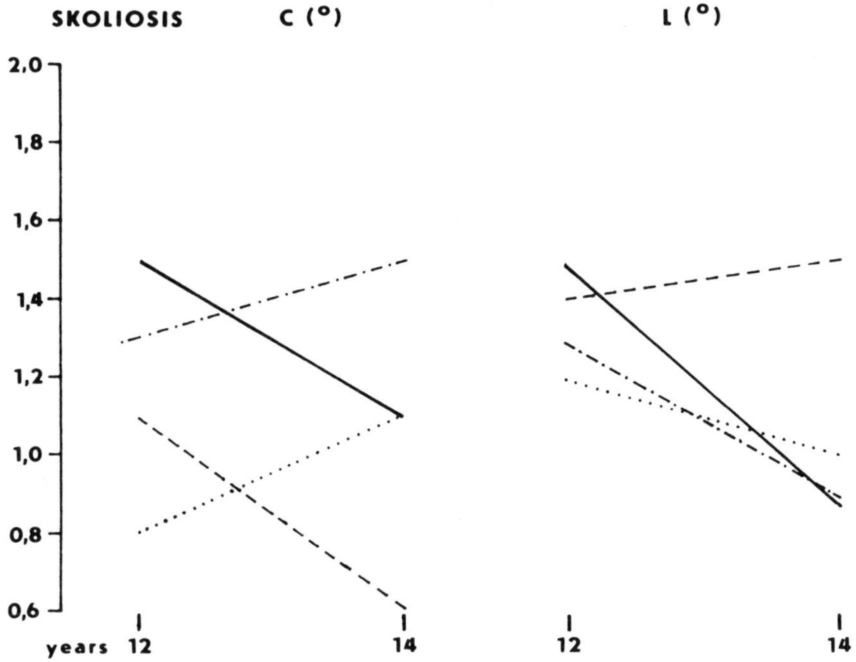

Figure 4. The changes of the spine axis—anteroposterior.

REFERENCES

Kučera, M. (1986). Back pain and skeletal conditions during intensive training in children and adolescents. In J. Rutenfranz,, R. Mocellin, & F. Klimt (Eds.), *Children and exercise XII* (pp. 329-336). Champaign, IL: Human Kinetics.

Pediatric Work Physiology XIII

List of Participants

Bævre, Halvor
2850 Lena
Norway

Barabás, Anikó
Hungarian University of Physical Education
Alkotás U.44
H 1123 Budapest
Hungary

Bar-Or, Oded
Children's Exercise and Nutrition Centre Pediatrics
McMaster University
1200 Main Street West
Hamilton, Ontario L8N 3Z5
Canada

Bell, Richard
College of Physical Education
University of Saskatoon
Saskatoon S7N 0W0
Canada

Berndt, Inge
Abt. Sportwissenschaft
Fakultät für Psychologie und Sportwissenschaft
Universität Bielefeld
Universitätsstrasse
Postfach 8640
Bielefeld 1
West Germany

Beunen, Gaston
Institute of Physical Education
K.U. Leuven
Tervuurse Vest 101
B-3030 Leuven (Heverlee)
Belgium

Bjørholt, Per Gunnar
Beitostølen Health Sport Centre
2953 Beitostølen
Norway

Blimkie, Cameron (Joe)
School of Physical Education and Athletics
McMaster University
Hamilton, Ontario L8N 3Z5
Canada

Blom, Per
National Institute of Occupational Health
P.O.B. 8149 Dep.
0033 Oslo 1
Norway

Borgen, Jorunn Sundgot
The Norwegian College of Physical Education and Sport
Box 40 Kringsjaa
0807 Oslo 8
Norway

Bratteby, Lars-Erik
Unit of Pediatric Physiology
Akademiska Sjukhuset
S 751 85 Uppsala
Sweden

Brodie, David A.
University of Liverpool
P.O.B. 147
Liverpool L69 3BX
England

Calzolari, Armando
Ospedale Bambino Gesu
Piazza S. Onofrio 4
00165 Roma
Italy

Carlsen, Kai-Håkon
Children's Asthma and Allergy Institute Voksentoppen
P.O.B. 50 Voksenkollen
N-0326 Oslo 3
Norway

Coudert, Jean
Laboratoire de Physiologie
Faculté de Medecine
B.P. 38, 63001 Clermont-Ferrand
France

Ellingsen, Finn
The Norwegian College of Physical Education and Sport
P.O.B. 40 Kringsjaa
0807 Oslo 8
Norway

Engesæth, Vasiliki Gemou
Children's Asthma and Allergy Institute Voksentoppen
P.O.B. 50 Voksenkollen
N-0326 Oslo 3
Norway

Erp-Baart, Agnes Marie, van
Department of Physiology
University of Nijmegen
Geert Grotteplein Neord 21A
6525 E2 Nijmegen
The Netherlands

Vanden Eynde, Bavo
Instituut Lichamelijke Opleiding
K.U. Leuven
Tervuurse Vest 101
B-3030 Leuven (Heverlee)
Belgium

Falgairette, Guy
Universite de Clermont-Ferrand II
U.F.R.
Sciences et Techniques des Activites Physiques et Sportives
Complexe Universitaire des Cezeaux
B.P. 66, 63170 Aubiere
France

Farkas, Anna
Department of Medicine
Hungarian University of Physical Education
Alkotás 44
H-1123 Budapest
Hungary

Frenkl, Róbert
Department of Medicine
Hungarian University of Physical Education
Alkotás 44
H-1123 Budapest
Hungary

Froberg, Karsten
Institute of Physical Education
Odense University
Campusvej 55
5230 Odense M
Denmark

Gaisl, Georgine
Institut für Sportwissenschaften
Mozartstrasse 14
8010 Graz
Austria

Galioto, Frank M., Jr.
Georgetown University
Children's Hospital
National Medical Center
111 Michigan Avenue N.W.
Washington, DC 20010
USA

Grodjinovsky, Amos
Zinman College of Physical Education
Wingate Institute
Netanya
Israel

Hamar, Dusan
Research Institute of Sports Science
Comenius University
Svobodovo nabr. 9
814 69 Bratislava
Czechoslovakia

Ilmarinen, Juhani
Institute of Occupational Health
Department of Physiology
Laajanityntie 1
01620 Vantaa
Finland

Inbar, Omri
Wingate Institute
Natanya
Israel

Kahrs, Nina
The Norwegian College of Physical Education and Sport
P.O.B. 40 Kringsjaa
0807 Oslo 8
Norway

Kasch, Fred
San Diego State University
4882 Edgeware Road
San Diego, CA 92116
USA

Kemper, Han C.G.
Department of Exercise Physiology and Health
Free University and University of Amsterdam
Meibergdreef 15
1105 AZ Amsterdam
The Netherlands

Klausen, Klaus
Gymnastikteoretisk Lab
August Krogh Institute
Universitetsparken 13
DK 2100 Köbenhavn
Denmark

Koch, Günter
Department of Physiology
Free University
Arnimallee 22
D-1000 Berlin 33
West Germany

Kučera, Miroslav
Department of Sports Medicine
Charles University
V úvalu 84
CS 15006 Praha 5
Czechoslovakia

Lund Petersen, Inger
Oslo Health Council
St. Olavsplass 5
0165 Oslo 1
Norway

Máček, Miloŝ
Charles University Prague
V úvalu 84
CS 15006 Praha 5
Czechoslovakia

Mälamäki, Seppo
Kalevalankatu 58
70300 Kuopio
Finland

de Man, Stella A.
Department of Epidemiology
Erasmus University Medical School
P.B. 173
3000 Rotterdam
The Netherlands

Matthys, Dirk
U2-Pediatric Cardiology
De Pintelaan 185
B-9000 Gent
Belgium

Meen, Helge Dyre
The Norwegian College of Physical Education and Sport
P.O.B. 40 Kringsjaa
0807 Oslo 8
Norway

Mellbye, Elisabeth
The Norwegian College of Physical Education and Sport
P.O.B. 40 Kringsjaa
0807 Oslo 8
Norway

Melsom, Reidar
The Pediatric Department
Sentralsykehuset in Akershus
1474 Norbyhagen
Norway

Mészáros, János
Department of Medicine

Hungarian University of Physical Education
Alkotás 44
H-1123 Budapest
Hungary

Morehouse, Chauncey
109 Sport Research Building
Pennsylvania State University
University Park, PA 16802
USA

Nakken, Karl Otto
RING Medical Centre
Oslo
Norway

Nemoto, Isamu
Laboratory for Exercise Physiology and Biomechanics
Toho University School for Medicine
5-21-16, Ota-ku
Tokyo 143
Japan

Nystad, Wenche
Voksentoppen School
Children's Asthma and Allergy Institute
P.O.B. 50-51 Voksenkollen
0326 Oslo 3
Norway

Oseid, Svein
The Norwegian College of Physical Education and Sport
P.O.B. 40 Kringsjaa
0807 Oslo 8
Norway

Oyen, Eva-Maria
Johanniter Kinderklinik
Arnold-Jansen Str.
D-5205 St. Augustin
Germany

Peltenburg, Adelheid
H.v.d. Berghln 216
3571 PH Utrecht
The Netherlands

Pluim, Babette
Department of Physiology
State University of Utrecht
van Heutsz Laan 23f Utrecht
6711 KK EDE
The Netherlands

Praagh van, Emmanuel
University of Clermont-Ferrand II
Campus Universitaire des Cezeaux
P.B. 66, 63170 Aubiere
France

Radvanský, Jiří
Department of Sports Medicine
University Hospital
Motol V úvalu 84
CS 15006 Praha 5
Czechoslovakia

Rasmussen, Birger
Gymnastikteoretisk Laboratorium
August Krogh Institute
Universitetsparken 13
2100 Köbenhavn Ø
Denmark

Reseland, Odd Einar
The Norwegian College of Physical Education and Sport
P.O.B. 40 Kringsjaa
0807 Oslo 8
Norway

Reybrouck, Tony
University Hospital Pellenberg
Cardiovascular Rehabilitation
Weligerveld 1
3041 Pellenberg
Belgium

de Ridder, Christine M.
Department of Physiology
State University of Utrecht
Vondellaan 24, 3541 GG Utrecht
The Netherlands

Roaldsen, Kirsti
Sunnaas Hospital
1450 Nesoddtangen
Norway

Rød, Tore
Strømsvn. 82
2010 Strømmen
Norway

Røksund, Ola Drange
Geilomo Children's Hospital
3580 Geilo
Norway

Rutenfranz, Joseph
Institut für Arbeits-physiologie
University of Dortmund, Ardeystr. 67
D-4600 Dortmund
Germany

Schibye, Bente
School of Physiotherapy
Lersø Parkalle 38
DK Copenhagen Ø 2100
Denmark

Stanghelle, Johan Kvalvik
MFI
P.O.B. 8149 Dep.
0033 Oslo 1
Norway

Stoboy, Hans
Clayallee 229
Orthop. Univ. Klinik
1 Berlin 33
Germany

Strong, William B.
Section of Pediatric Cardiology
Medical College of Georgia
Augusta, GA 30912
USA

Sunnegårdh, Jan
Department of Pediatrics
University Hospital
75185 Uppsala
Sweden

Szabó Tamás
Køzponti Sportiskola
Istvanmezei U.1
H-1146, Budapest
Hungary

Szögy, Adalbert
Sportsmedicine Institute
Otto-Fleck-Schneise 10
6000 Frankfurt/Main 71
FRG

Ward, Dianne S.
University of South Carolina
Department of Physical Education
Columbia, SC 29208
USA

Washington, Reginald L.
Department of Pediatric Cardiology
The Children's Hospital
1056 East 19th Avenue
Denver, CO 80218
USA

Wessel, Hans U.
Children's Memorial Hospital
2300 Children's Plaza
Chicago, IL 60614
USA

Weymans, Maria
Institute Physical Education
Department Physical Rehabilitation
U.Z. Gasthuisberg
Herestraat 49
3000 Leuven
Belgium

Wickman, Magnus
Children's Asthma and Allergy Institute Voksentoppen
P.O.B. 50-51 Voksenkollen
0326 Oslo 3
Norway

Wønne, Roland
Universitäts-Kinderklinik
Theodor-Stern-Kai 7
D-6000 Frankfurt 70
BRD

Yoshizawa, Shigehiro
Utsunomiya University
350 Mine Utsunomiya 320
Japan

Zonderland, Maria L.
Department of Physiology
State University Utrecht
Vondellaan 24
3521 GG Utrecht
The Netherlands